"With five little words, Robin opens our eyes, and yes, our hearts, too. See. Set. Seek. Speak. Celebrate. Five simple principles to heal the wounds that hide the warrior in you...Robin holds nothing back in her latest book. She gets our sorrows and fears. This is a book you won't want to miss."

— CATHY KRAFVE, author, speaker, host of *Fireside Talk Radio*

"Infused with hard-won wisdom, *Uncover Your Divine Design: Who did God create you to be?* will inspire you to see yourself made in God's image, with infinite and intrinsic value. I held this profound and courageous book close to my heart as I turned each page. It's a must-read!"

— JOAN ONWILER, mentor, award-winning educator, and women's ministry leader

"Robin leads the spiritually estranged back to a relationship with God the Father and offers assurance of who we are in Christ. I highly recommend *Uncover Your Divine Design* to any woman who doubts her value in the eyes of God."

— PATTI SHENE, host of *Step Into the Light* podcast

"Robin shares personal memories that will inspire you to heal and grow in your relationship with God and yourself. My heart and soul were touched as this former child of an alcoholic speaks the truth of God's power and grace. I highly recommend this book to be part of every woman's personal library!"

— CATHY POWELL, ministry leader for Celebrate Recovery

"Robin invites you to join her on a journey to see how she found God in the midst of trials, uncertainty, and pain. Discover God's grace and be transformed as you reveal your God given identity."

— TRACY BELL, licensed clinical professional counselor

"Grab your Bible and a journal and get ready to uncover your divine design in Robin Melvin's debut masterpiece. Her words spring off the page in authentic glory, stirring your senses, enlightening your mind, and freeing your soul. I recommend this book to anyone longing to meet their Savior beside still waters."

—Christy Brunke, bestselling author of
When Losses Become Legacies

UNCOVER YOUR DIVINE DESIGN

Who did God create you to be?

Peace & Grace,
Robin

2 Tim. 1:7

ROBIN MELVIN

ST. JOSEPH, MISSOURI USA

DIVINE DESIGN: Who did God create you to be?
Copyright © 2022 Robin Melvin
ISBN: 978-1-936501-67-0

All rights reserved No part of this publication may be reproduced or transmitted in any form or by any means, electronic, mechanical, photocopying, recording, or otherwise, without written permission of the publisher. Published by CrossRiver Media Group, 4810 Gene Field Rd. #2, St. Joseph, MO 64506.

Unless otherwise indicated, all Scripture quotations are taken from the Holy Bible, New Living Translation, copyright © 1996, 2004, 2007, 2013 by Tyndale House Foundation. Used by permission of Tyndale House Publishers, Inc., Carol Stream, Illinois 60188. All rights reserved.

Scripture quotations marked (NIV) are taken from the Holy Bible, New International Version®, NIV®. Copyright © 1973, 1978, 1984, 2011 by Biblica, Inc.™ Used by permission of Zondervan. All rights reserved worldwide. www.zondervan.com The "NIV" and "New International Version" are trademarks registered in the United States Patent and Trademark Office by Biblica, Inc.™

Scripture quotations marked (TLB) are taken from The Living Bible copyright © 1971. Used by permission of Tyndale House Publishers, Carol Stream, Illinois 60188. All rights reserved.

Scripture quotations marked MSG are taken from THE MESSAGE, copyright © 1993, 2002, 2018 by Eugene H. Peterson. Used by permission of NavPress, represented by Tyndale House Publishers. All rights reserved.

Scripture quotations marked (AMP) are taken from the Amplified Bible, Copyright © 1954, 1958, 1962, 1964, 1965, 1987 by The Lockman Foundation. Used by permission.

Scripture quotations marked CSB have been taken from the Christian Standard Bible®, Copyright © 2017 by Holman Bible Publishers. Used by permission. Christian Standard Bible® and CSB® are federally registered trademarks of Holman Bible Publishers.

All Scripture marked with the designation "GW" is taken from GOD'S WORD®. © 1995, 2003, 2013, 2014, 2019, 2020 by God's Word to the Nations Mission Society. Used by permission.

DISCLAIMER: This book is not intended as a substitute for the professional advice of counselors or therapists. The reader should consult a professional in matters relating to his/her mental health and particularly with respect to any symptoms that may require diagnosis or medical attention.

For more information on Robin Melvin visit RobinMelvin.com

Editor: Debra L. Butterfield
Proofreader: Deb Allard
Cover Design: Tamara Clymer
Cover art: 115690026 © Panya Kuanun and 139583840 © Hildeanna | Dreamstime.com
Printed in the United States of America

*My dear reader, you are a marvelous creation.
Own it, seek it, and live it. I pray you sense God's measureless grace and peace as you uncover more of who and Whose you are.*

Contents

	Acknowledgments	9
	Introduction	11
1.	Identity Lost: No Worries, It's Just Hiding	13
2.	When Grief Calls: Voiceless Pain and Toxic Escape	25
3.	When Mercy Pursues: Yes, even then.	43
4.	When Holiness Calls: A Holy Pursuit	55
5.	When Mercy Calls: We Have the Same Enemy	73
6.	When Mercy Follows: New Every Morning	87
7.	Life Interrupted: A Holistic Meltdown	105
8.	Rise Strong: Reclaim Your Power	121
9.	Victim Mindset: Reclaim Your Victory	139
10.	Scarcity: Reclaim Your Value & Voice	153
11.	Chameleon: Reclaim Your Place	173
12.	Identity Found: Coming Home to the Father's Heart	191
	Endnotes	199
	About the author	203

Acknowledgments

"To God be the glory, great things He has done."

Jesus, my Savior and Redeemer. Thank You, thank You, thank You—for pursuing me way before I knew it was You. I still marvel at our ashes-to-beauty story. There will never be enough words to tell it, but I'll keep trying. May all I do and become bring You honor and glory.

Thank you, Jeff. Your support and enthusiasm give me courage. Your ninja computer skills calmed my meltdowns and made this book possible. Though your loud and shiny personality often clashes with my introvert, God knew what He was doing when He put us together. We've made it forty years because Jesus loves to heal messy people.

Thank you, Ramona Mae and Edward John. Like all parents, your human struggle made it difficult to be the parents you wanted to be. You nurtured my love for nature and an obsessive friendship with words. Together, they led me to my Healer and my healing. Your gifts are priceless and I am forever grateful.

To my babes—Justin, Preston, and Hannah. Thank you for your grace in forgiving my major parenting fails. We are truly growing up together. May you find hope and healing in my words.

Thank you to my prayer hotline: My mother-in-law Edna Arnold, and friends Joan Onwiler and Nancy Mohr. Your words through texts and chats kept me sane and focused through life's interruptions, deadlines, and the days when I questioned my calling.

Thank you to my MIL Edna, Jessica Karuchit, Carol Remrey, Kim

Gibson, Dee Snyder, Wendy Carver, Elizabeth Hespel, and Nicole Hanson. Since day one, you saw the potential in me and in this book. Your encouragement kept me going when I wanted to quit.

To my launch team of pre-readers and reviewers. You gave me the gift of your time. Ya'll rock.

And to Tami, Debra, and DeeDee at CrossRiver Media Group. Thank you for believing in this book and for your patience with my newbie questions. I'm excited to see what God does with our hard work.

Introduction

We live in a wonky world, don't we? It's easy to get a bit lost—to forget who and Whose we are. But at our created core, we have an inkling we're made for more. So we ask, "God, who am I and what do You want me to do?" And often, answers allude us.

Because somewhere on this zig-zaggy journey, we let our pain and our people define us. We formed unhealthy mindsets that hide us and hold us back from knowing our power and enjoying the abundant life Jesus gives.

But while our history reshaped us, our Creator restores us to the women He already sees—our divine design. So, perhaps a better question is, "God, who are *You* and who am I created to *be*?"

And thus our healing begins.

"Don't copy the behavior and customs of this world, but let God transform you into a new person by changing the way you think" (Romans 12:2a).

True transformation happens by *changing the way we think* about God and ourselves. How many times do we set our hearts on good intentions and then lose the battle in our minds? For me, at least a kajillion.

At about mid-life, I found myself hiding under unhealthy mindsets and protective habits. I realized how seven years of my adolescence—life with a dad who numbed his pain with alcohol—shaped and defined me for decades. Determined to find the real me, to live whole and free, I did the work to transform unhealthy thought patterns. In these pages, you'll find raw honesty. Written as I connected dots and untangled thoughts—fleshed out, cried out, and screamed out. I kid you not.

Uncover Your Divine Design: Who did God create you to be? is my transparent story to find and free the woman God designed. There are no villains in it, only perfectly imperfect humans like all of us. As we journey together, I hope you see transformation is truly possible. I pray you believe that, in Christ, you are already a new creation and you have the power to live it.

At the end of each chapter, you'll find a study guide to dig deeper into Scripture and answer questions. Since we are designed for God's nature to live in us, we will train ourselves to uncover it.

See. Set. Seek. Speak. Celebrate.

The study guides will help us *See* mindsets that define us. As we consider our thinking, we will learn to discern what's true and what's not. As we *Set* our mind on what is "true…authentic…the best, not the worst; the beautiful, not the ugly," we will transform toxic thought patterns (Philippians 4:8b MSG).

When we see and set our trust in what God says, we will find who He created us to be and whom He resurrected when we asked Jesus to save us and to lead us. In Christ, we have all we need to live healed, whole, and free.

Empowered by Scripture and the Holy Spirit, we will *Seek* God and *Speak* what is true about who and Whose we are. We are loved, accepted, redeemed daughters of a good Father. Defined by Him, we will *Celebrate* this relationship that empowers us to live an abundant life in our divine design.

Are you ready to heal the wounds that hide the warrior in you?

As you reflect on your own transparent story to find the woman God designed you to be, you might need a separate notebook. Maybe even grab some crayons or colored pencils. The uninterrupted words, prayers, and/or doodles might surprise you. Process your thoughts however it works for you. This is your space. Your time. Your transformation.

Peace to you on your journey to uncover who God created you to be.

CHAPTER 1

Identity Lost: No Worries, It's Just Hiding

"It takes courage to grow up and become who you really are." ~ E.E. Cummings

So, if you woke up tomorrow and could do the one thing you've always wanted—no limits on time or money or resources—what would you do?"

I sat there, unmoving. Un*thinking* really. If I was in a comic strip instead of a counseling room, this is where you sketch a question mark over my head or pencil in chirping crickets. Beyond growing my faith and helping people, I couldn't articulate one personal goal or dream.

What was the hang up? Life was falling into place. My youngest child had just graduated high school, so my husband and I were almost empty-nesters. I hear this distresses some women. Not me, sister. For the first time in my adult life, my time was *my time.*

For thirty years, I raised kids and grandkids. I was a homemaker, a home-schooler, and a volunteer for Sunday school, PTA, and Vacation Bible School. I led women's ministries, volunteered in youth groups, and counseled girls in pregnancy resource centers. I was the soccer mom who drove a mini-van and the neighbor who cooked casseroles and carpooled kids.

Alongside this, I was an Army wife. My husband's military and civilian careers included countless separations, two deployments, and thirteen household moves. Wow, I get a little breathless just thinking about it.

I love that season of my life. And for the most part, I rocked it. But after decades of pouring into others, I was so ready to pursue something brand new. To feed and grow me.

In the weeks before I met with the counselor who asked me that baffling question, my brain buzzed with ideas. But I worried about spending money and wasted time fretting about wasting time. I waited for the perfect decision to appear on the wall like a neon sign framed with flashing arrows. The internal pressure to decide *now* and the fear of making a wrong choice paralyzed me.

Twisted up in this cycle, I finally asked for help. That's how I ended up in the counseling room. I don't even remember our conversation before the question:

"So, if you woke up tomorrow and could do the one thing you've always wanted—no limits on time or money or resources—what would you do?"

Why, in those cricket moments, could I not voice one concrete goal or dream waiting for me at the end of my forties?

Because it exposed my lost identity, bare-naked.

And so started the journey to unravel me.

We peeked back into my childhood to uncover why I was wrapped tight in my roles and responsibilities—in what I did and who I did it for. We discovered a little girl shaped by culture, authoritarian parenting, and a depressed, alcoholic father who suffered from PTSD. She had low self-worth, and her fear of conflict often made her timid and voiceless. I was surprised to see how her fears, hurts, and habits still influenced me.

We uncovered messages like "Children will be seen, not heard" that make it difficult to speak up and make decisions. We talked about the tension in my childhood home and its hard-set rules. How I wasn't allowed to disagree, voice an opinion, or even talk about grief.

This common authoritarian approach to parenting produces shame and underscores a message that children are inferior. These formed unhealthy thought patterns that skewed my sense of self and stunted

CHAPTER ONE: IDENTITY LOST

my autonomy. I went into adulthood hiding.

I walked out of my counselor's office thinking, *Wow. I'm more messed up than I thought.* But I was excited and determined to dig deeper, to uncover the real me. I wanted to see how I got there so I could get out of there. After twenty-three years of knowing Jesus as Savior and Healer, there was more to see and more to restore. This required a closer look at my childhood, especially my formative adolescent years.

Research shows that when we were little girls, between three and six years old, we adapted to our environments. Without adult resources and reasoning, we created coping skills to feel protected, loved, and valued. Which is brilliant. But if those childish habits don't change, we remain bound by them in adulthood. That scared little girl still lives in us. While she's resourceful and capable, her protective layers no longer serve her. And they don't allow us to grow up all the way.

That's why we get stuck in an emotional loop. Especially when we want to move forward. After my appointment with the counselor, I wanted to see how toxic mindsets dictate our internal dialogue and life choices. Not to whine, point blame, or wallow in self-pity, but to understand our self-defining moments—those turning points in life that formed our sense of self. Harsh words, bad decisions, and difficult experiences hid us, the *real* us.

Ready to transform thoughts and habits to live a freer, more abundant life, we ask God, "How do You see me and define me? Under all this stuff, who did You create me to be?"

Our truest identity is our God-given design. Made in His image, our value is intrinsic and infinite. In seeking this healthy sense of self, we find our voices and our unique personalities. We shamelessly let the world see us—the real and wonderful us.

But since we live in a messed-up world with messy people, our thoughts and opinions of who we are get distorted. Shame and self-protective habits hide our divine design. And traumatic experiences—especially in childhood—wire these deeper.

Even adults get overwhelmed by emotional pain. And we were just kids. We didn't know what to do with our parents' problems or a hush-

and-stuff, male dominant culture. We weren't supposed to. Our brains weren't wired for that yet, so we formed coping skills.

To keep the peace and please people, I kept quiet. I conformed to their opinions and performed to their expectations. These habits kept me safe. But deep down, the real me was a fighter and a rebel. So eventually, I found a place to belong and be loud. I became the party girl and the family black sheep. It was my escape and pressure release.

Many of us learned to conform and perform early in life. People's applause, or lack thereof, might still determine our worth. But here's our hope—our confident assurance—we aren't created to be copies. We are originals. The finest details of you and me were birthed in God's heart and mind. Our worth is not determined by what we did, what we do, or who we do it for. Our Creator isn't a critic or a controlling parent. He wants to free us, the real us. In Him, we are safe to be seen, heard, and known.

Going into teen marriage and parenting, I see how it was easy to lose myself further. I loved my jobs. Being a wife and mom gave me beautiful purpose. But I didn't dream about what would come next when my kids left the nest and those roles and responsibilities changed. I didn't plan past diapers and dinners, soccer games and school dances.

Maybe, as you read this, something stirs in you. Truth is, life's dramas and traumas usher us into adulthood—and our Christian journey—with common needs and struggles.

We wear hand-me-down habits and think conditioned thoughts. Some good, some not so much. But God gives us a new heredity that's stronger than what our parents passed on to us. He empowers us to shed cultural labels and generational sin. He teaches us to put on His genetics by transforming our minds.

Outside-in thinking, expecting anything or anyone besides God to fill our need and fix our struggle, won't free us to be who we *are*. It defines us by what we *do* and who we do it for. The good news—the God news— is that losing our real selves doesn't change our divine design. It's just hiding. Right there under all those darn protective layers. And like slivers of glass that cut deep and take time to surface, so do subtle unhealthy thoughts and habits. So, we are patient in knowing and

CHAPTER ONE: IDENTITY LOST

growing into who God made us to be.

Veiling Our True Self

Alexandra Headrick, in her article "Remembering Original Glory," writes: "We've been taught by life that being ourselves is dangerous, risky, wrong. We've been hurt, scarred, disappointed, and wounded… so like a turtle retreating to its shell, we've retreated behind our walls. But in the process, we've lost something precious, and we know it. It's embedded into our souls; before original sin there was original glory."

Our original glory is our divine design. Genesis 1:26–27 confirms we are created in God's image with His spiritual nature and qualities. So, our God ID has always been there, woven into our souls by our Father's hands.

As for our unhealthy mindsets, we don't always know how or when they got there and that's okay. More important than their origins is that we replace them with what is true.

In Romans 12:2a, Paul tells us, "Don't copy the behavior and customs of this world, but let God transform you into a new person by changing the way you think." Aren't you glad we can renew our minds from the inside-out?

God transforms us into who He intended us to be before we slipped into this world, new and wrinkly pink. Before we were born into imperfect homes with imperfect parents who struggled with their own pain and self-worth. Before we grew up in a society riddled with less-than messages. Way before we believed the lie, *You will never measure up.*

Let the Unveiling Begin

"For the Lord is Spirit, and wherever the Spirit of the Lord is, there is freedom. So all of us who have had that veil removed can see and reflect the glory of the Lord. And the Lord—who is the Spirit—makes us more and more like him as we are changed into his glorious image" (2 Cor. 3:17–18).

My friend, this transforming journey may feel a bit like a seek and destroy mission. But it's always a mission of mercy. When we invite Jesus to save us and teach us, we step into His Spirit and a whole new inner wardrobe. We are pure, set apart, and made right with God. We are empowered to unveil the naked truth of our identity in Christ.

In 2 Peter, we see God's promise, "His divine power has given us *everything we need for a godly life* through our knowledge of him who called us by his own glory and goodness. Through these he has given us his very great and precious promises, so that through them you may participate in the divine nature, having escaped the corruption in the world caused by evil desires" (2 Peter 1:3-4 NIV, author's emphasis).

We "participate in the divine nature" by putting on God's character.

He wants to free us—heart and soul. He wants to liberate our mind, our will, and our emotions. Empowered by His Spirit, we peel off remnants of our old grave clothes. Believing His promises, we are covered and clothed by God's grace.

In this grave to grace transformation, we look back without shame and see what hides us—the real us. Transparency is raw and risky, but we are done hiding. We have to go there so we can get out of there.

Join the Journey

I didn't know this identity search to become God's woman would be a journey to see myself as God's beloved child. I'm still learning and healing habits and mindsets from the drama and trauma of life experiences. By God's grace, I am growing out of childish responses by learning childlike trust.

Child of God, as I let you in on my deepest hurts, I hope you uncover unhealthy mindsets and see you truly are the Father's beloved child. As you let go of old habits, others' opinions, and society's stereotypes, I pray you see yourself as He does: holy, righteous, redeemed for a purpose. Free from guilt, right with Him, and valuable beyond human measure.

John Eldredge, in his book *Waking the Dead*, encourages us, "Think of it: your original glory was greater than anything that's ever taken

CHAPTER ONE: IDENTITY LOST

your breath away in nature."

Yes, let's think about that a minute.

You are more beautiful than pink sunsets and emerald oceans and snow-blanketed mountains. You're more powerful than hurricane-driven winds, raging wildfires, and swirling white rapids. Does that surprise you? Remember, you are created in God's image. So own it.

When we try to find peace and purpose in things or people, we war against ourselves. Only God can restore our true identity.

On this baring-all journey, we find why it's hard to dream past empty nests, board meetings, soccer games, and science projects. We trust that God wastes nothing and our past—especially the pain—prepared us for our present. We step into our power and thrive in our own unique story.

The study guides at the end of each chapter will help you reveal unhealthy mindsets and self-defining moments. I pray you're inspired to *See* your thoughts, *Set* your mind, *Seek* the Father, and *Speak* what's true. Then, as you uncover your divine design, I hope you *Celebrate* the power and promises of who you are in Christ.

Your story—its uniqueness, even its unique *mess*—has hurts and hang-ups that are common to all of us. So, you are not alone. And remember, our heavenly Father's definition of you is the only one that matters. You are created in *His* image, to wear *His* identity. It's time to express it through your unique personality. Quirks and all.

Again, in *Waking the Dead*, I love how Eldredge describes our journey: "We are in the process of being unveiled. We are created to reflect God's glory, born to bear His image, and He ransomed us to reflect that glory again."

Our glory, our born identity, is rescued and being restored so we can reflect Jesus' nature. All things redeemed, to be used for His glory.

Can you hear Him whisper?

You were made for more.

Let's rephrase the question that stumped me in the counseling room: If you woke up tomorrow and could *be* the person you're created to be, who would *you* be?

STUDY QUESTIONS

> *"We desire to possess a beauty that is worth pursuing, worth fighting for, a beauty that is core to who we truly are. We want beauty that can be seen; beauty that can be felt; beauty that affects others; a beauty all our own to unveil."*
>
> ~ Stasi Eldredge, Captivating Revised and Updated:
> Unveiling the Mystery of a Woman's Soul

See Your Thoughts

What are the roles and responsibilities you fill each day?

Take a moment to pray. Ask God to clear your mind and help you not to over-think these next questions. And remember, there are no right or wrong answers here. Just enjoy this time of reflection.

Imagine you are alone on a deserted island and your roles and responsibilities do not exist. Who are you? What are your dreams, passions, interests—apart from what you do and who you do it for?

CHAPTER ONE: IDENTITY LOST

Maybe you hear crickets. Or maybe you have a whole list of ideas.

Do you sense some of the best parts of you are hidden—waiting to be unveiled and expressed? If so, what hinders you from knowing and experiencing more of who God made you to be?

Our history shapes us, in healthy and not-so-healthy ways. A seven-year span in my adolescence molded and defined me for decades.

Have you ever peeked back into your history to see what people, events, or cultural messages shaped your thought processes?

Ask God to show you: Whose words or actions still define me? What parts of my story still influence me?

The healthy messages:

The not-so-healthy messages:

Set Your Mind

God, I'm determined to find who You say I am. I seek to live in the wholeness and freedom I have in Christ. How do You define me? Help me recognize lies and replace them with truth.

See who you are in Christ and renew your mind. Read and reflect on the following Scripture:

UNCOVER YOUR DIVINE DESIGN

Inside-out transformation: Romans 12:1–2
Think on these: Philippians 4:8
Old life to new life: 2 Corinthians 5:17
Take off old, put on new: Ephesians 4:22–24

"For the Lord is the Spirit, and wherever the Spirit of the Lord is, there is freedom. So all of us who have had that veil removed can see and reflect the glory of the Lord. And the Lord—who is the Spirit—makes us more and more like him as we are changed into his glorious image." 2 Cor. 3:17–18

"By his divine power, God has given us everything we need for living a godly life. We have received all of this by coming to know him, the one who called us to himself by means of his marvelous glory and excellence. And because of his glory and excellence, he has given us great and precious promises. These are the promises that enable you to share his divine nature and escape the world's corruption caused by human desires." 2 Peter 1:3–4

Seek & Speak What's True

I am defined by I AM. God is my Redeemer. I am rescued and being restored to who I am in Christ—my divine design.

Because God, _____

_____, I am _____

_____.

Celebrate

Father God, because Your love is unrelenting, we are never truly lost. Thank You for calling us out to more peace, power, and freedom in our divine design. Our full potential is beyond what we can even imagine. But You already see us clothed in Christ. Thank you for giving us Jesus as a role model. We are grateful for this lifelong privilege to know and grow more like Him. — Your redeemed Daughter

A Gentle Reminder

If anything in my story brings up something you're not sure you can handle right now, please stop and pray. After a chat with Jesus, maybe consider calling a friend or a counselor. I am not a professional and can only tell you what worked for me. Your beautiful, unfolding story may be similar to mine, but we are uniquely wired and on our own timelines.

CHAPTER 2

When Grief Calls: Voiceless Pain and Toxic Escape

"Don't ever discount the wonder of your tears. They can be healing waters and a stream of joy. Sometimes they are the best words the heart can speak." ~ *William Paul Young,* The Shack

Grief rumbled in on what was supposed to be a kite and picnic July day. I was babysitting my niece at my sister's house when the phone rang.

"Robin, your parents aren't answering their phone." It was my oldest brother's wife. Her calm, medicated words spun my already-teetering world. "Craig was killed in a car crash."

My big brother...dead? How am I going to get to the theater to tell my sister?

God's mercy was already at work. Two friends stopped by on a bike ride to the park. They'd never stopped before that day. They stayed with my niece as their mom drove me to my sister.

In the back seat, I stared out the car window as a passenger bombarded me with questions. I just wanted her to shut up. *It's none of your business what happened. I don't care if Craig was in a band with your son. Don't you know I'm only fifteen and have to tell my sister that our big brother is dead?*

My sister's face paled when she saw me walk in without her daughter. All I remember next is her being strong for me as we hurried into the theater's office and she dialed our parents' number.

But I knew they wouldn't answer.

Remember the phones that were attached to cords and hung on a wall? When my parents drank, they argued. Not wanting it to ring and ramp up the nerve-shredding tension or interrupt his sharp-tongued lectures, my dad often hung the phone on the back of a kitchen chair.

I hated them for making me take the call. For making me say the words that broke my sister's heart. More anger layered on a new depth of sadness. I hadn't a clue what to do with any of it.

Later that night, my dad came into my room and sat beside me on the bed. Sorrow seemed to soften and sober him. An already broken man, now shattered. His eyes were empty behind black-rimmed glasses and not quite focused on the floor. He spoke three words I'd never heard him say, "I love you."

It was too late to tell my brother with whom he'd parted on bad terms.

And it was a bit too late for me. Although grateful for the tender words, I needed more. But my dad couldn't give what he didn't have.

Inherited Messages

Born in the late 1920s, my parents were children during the Great Depression and the Second World War. They were from a tough generation and believed psychology is weird, counselors are quacks, and if you ignore pain, it will go away. It's a "suck it up and soldier on" mentality. Authoritarian parenting was common, and "Children should be seen and not heard" was the mantra.

Perhaps you've heard this or a variation of it. It followed my parents into their years of parenting me and my five older siblings. When Dad said it, I believed it and got really good at being seen and not heard.

CHAPTER TWO: WHEN GRIEF CALLS

Friends tell me their reactions differed. Some thought it a joke and kept talking or ignored it and got louder. My friend Sandra remembers, "Children will be seen, not heard" teaching her to not interrupt adults. When her parents let her speak, it showed they respected her individuality and she learned, "Think for yourself. Your thoughts and opinions matter and are valued."

Another friend's experience mirrored mine.

Tracy, a professional counselor, shared, "You did what they said without asking questions. It made me lack self-worth and the confidence to speak up in many situations. I know for those I counsel, authoritarian parents can produce kids who lack confidence in making good decisions." She cites that many adults' "egos and emotional dysfunction" can't handle giving children freedom of expression.

Without knowing it, authoritarian parents punish our autonomy, which is our self-rule and independence.

In my family, "Children will be seen, not heard" was a drill sergeant command expecting unquestioned obedience. To me, those six words dictated how to be safe, valued, and accepted.

Others like, "Respect your elders," "Because I said so," and "Nice job, but…" can shame and devalue a child who's adjusting to her environment. I learned early to get quiet, be agreeable, and conform. In so doing, I developed some messed-up coping skills and was robbed of more than verbal expression.

Although these comments weren't meant to harm me, this is how my child mind translated them:

- Your opinions and feelings aren't valued.
- You're not worth listening to. You have no value.
- Don't speak up. You'll be laughed at, ignored, or punished.
- Comments or questions are disrespect or back talk.
- Those in authority are right. Trust and don't question.
- You are inferior, less than, not good enough.

But our parents weren't alone in shaping us. Birth order, culture, people, and our own personalities also play a part in how we adapted to our childhood environments. Likewise, our parents adopted ways of thinking, good and bad, to navigate safely through their own childhoods. The same, yet unique, factors influenced us all.

Can you see the potential mess of simply being human? It gets messier when we don't realize our value in our God-given identity. While we don't want to connect all our unhealthy thinking to past hurts, it is good to look at what shaped us.

> *"Connecting everything to past hurts is foolish. But connecting nothing there is also foolish." —Dr. Dan Allendar*

Did you grow up with negative messages? You might think of one right away. Sometimes, we have to stop and dig a little. Because a lie is so familiar, and believed for so long, we don't always recognize it. Sneaky little bugger. It's become an ingrained way of thinking—it's how we roll.

Maybe you don't struggle with using your voice. Perhaps you don't hold back anything because proving a point and being right gives you value. Maybe you silence your voice like I did.

Allow me to share another defining moment. Recalling the day my brother died and the first time I heard my dad's "I love you," takes me back a few years earlier, when again words were too few.

Unhealthy Mindsets

My dad loved nature and spending time with family, so he often took us for drives. On one of these outings, my brother Todd and I sat between my parents in the cab of our Chevy truck. Dad parked on a road overlooking a Utah reservoir and my favorite fishing spot. We watched the sun settle behind the mountains. Reds, corals, and yellows sparkled on rippling water.

I don't remember the conversation but it ended right after Mom told us about her two miscarriages and their first baby. My dad's namesake, Edward John, was stillborn back when dads chain-smoked in

CHAPTER TWO: WHEN GRIEF CALLS

waiting rooms. And moms, not allowed to say good-bye to their newborn babes, hugged empty arms to aching breasts. I still wonder what sparked her memory that evening. Was it his birthday?

Imagine the curiosity awakened in two middle-schoolers. "We had a brother before Craig? How did he die?"

But Dad hushed us with a stern look aimed at my mom. "We don't talk about it." The sun sank to gray on our too-quiet silence. And the place I hooked my prized rainbow trout is where I first remember stuffing my voice and internalizing grief.

Perhaps you remember a time when you were hushed by someone who was unwilling to process their own pain. This can make a girl vulnerable—in mind, body, and spirit. That incident confused me and sent some unhealthy messages:

- Some things are too painful to talk about. Ever.
- There's shame in talking about pain.
- Good wives comply without comment.
- Strong people stuff, suck it up, and move on.

My friends, feeling is healing. *Talking* is healing. To pretend a hurt doesn't exist, won't erase it. We must go there to get out of there. Stuffing pain and staying in it, we waste away from the inside-out. Like a parasite in our gut, it slowly sucks the life right out of us.

As I got older, pain added up, and I fell into a victim mindset. Victimhood, which we will look at closer in chapter nine, became comfy and familiar in my teen years and on into adulthood. It gave me the empathy I craved even if I was the only one feeling sorry for myself. It was a twisted sense of comfort and control. Thinking like a victim is a soul-sucking mindset. It stole my joy and stifled my real self.

Science, doctors, and professional counselors agree that if we don't cry, our bodies will. We have to process emotional pain to keep it moving out and make room for physical, mental, and spiritual healing. As we seek peace—and even find purpose—in pain, we identify a bit more with Jesus and who He created us to be.

God gives us courage to feel and heal. Have you read Psalms lately? The authors, including King David, pour out honest fear, anguish, and confession. Like them, may we find strength in knowing God hears us and rescues us.

Bear with me. Or shall I say *bare* with me. It's like seeing yourself in one of those humongous motel bathroom mirrors. There you are in all your naked glory with those lovely florescent lights revealing more than you want to see or have the courage to accept. Being vulnerable is definitely not for wimps.

Baring all clashes with our habit of hiding, our need for comfort, and our desire to keep pride intact. But side-stepping our struggle only cheats us out of who Christ created us to be, whole and free. Persevering—walking right through the middle of pain, fear, and sin—unshackles us because we walk forward in the promise that God heals, holds, and forgives. In Isaiah 43:1–3a, we see His promises:

> *"But now, [Your Name], listen to the* Lord *who created you.*
> *O [child of God], the one who formed you says,*
> *'Do not be afraid, for I have ransomed you.*
> *I have called you by name; you are mine.*
> *When you go through deep waters, I will be with you.*
> *When you go through rivers of difficulty, you will not drown.*
> *When you walk through the fire of oppression,*
> *you will not be burned up; the flames will not consume you.*
> *For I am the* Lord, *your God, the Holy One of Israel, your Savior.'"*
> (paraphrase added by author)

There's such peace in these words for us who believe. They've sustained me through my most difficult days.

I think about my mom and wish she'd been able to fully process her grief. To talk about the loss of those babies. To keep them real and validate their unlived lives. It's sad she couldn't talk freely about Craig either. That was a lot to keep stuffed. She and Dad could have carried their pain together.

If only my dad talked about my brother and allowed healing memories—the good times, the laughing times—to ease his grief. Instead, he replayed the bad and was harassed by pain and regret. His own victim

CHAPTER TWO: WHEN GRIEF CALLS

mindset ate him up. It's humbling to see I'm so much like him. And empathy replaces anger as I understand him a little more.

My dad—my *sober* dad—was a good man. An intelligent, dignified gentleman who shared my nerdy passion for words, my love of loud music, and the need for alone-time, especially on the river. He taught me to drive a stick-shift and trained me in the art of gutting fish. We laughed at sitcoms like *M*A*S*H* and *Barney Miller*.

But there was a tipping point when the booze took over. Easy-to-be-with dad to brooding stranger. Trustworthy to intimidating. I mastered eggshell-walking because I didn't know which dad he'd be when I walked through the door after school.

My friend, unprocessed emotions lie under the surface and fester. They create dis-ease in our bodies and infect our actions and attitudes. Ignored grief, anger, regret, and bitterness is toxic to us and to those we love.

Toxic Grief

A few months after Craig's death, I recall the self-defining moment when I stopped trying to please my parents and fully embraced my party girl image.

Most nights, my dad's drinking and insomnia triggered Viet Nam memories. He also ruminated over his last words to my brother, or about how he was wronged, whether real or imagined. While he kept my mom awake into the wee hours, making his problems her problems, I clung to my brown stuffed bear and cried into its mascara-stained face.

So, on warm weekends and summer breaks, I lugged my bear and bedding to the front yard and slept in our camper. Nestled beneath twenty-foot evergreens and within earshot of the rippling Mississippi backwaters, it was my safe escape. Well, *usually*. I was cleaning it the day that became a defining moment in my adolescent years. One that sparked my deep dive into rebellion.

I swept grit from the camper floor as Ted Nugent screamed from an eight-track tape player. I turned it down when I saw my dad marching across the yard.

Something imperceptible to others, I saw in a split second. His five-foot-nine frame didn't quite match his stride. Like it stretched a little extra, determined to fit into the courage the booze gave him. Arms too stiff. Steps too big. Two men warring in one body. Those eyes, squinting behind black military-style glasses, confirmed what I already knew. I was in trouble. My hopes to perform well and please him plummeted.

Whatever or whoever riled him up, I don't know, but I was his target and my dusting didn't pass inspection. Dad wasn't a yeller. He delivered his words, firm, stern, and packed with dynamite. Knowing any effort to comment, discuss, or disagree was backtalk—I stood there and absorbed the verbal beating.

Determined to hide my tears and thinking his lecture was done, I hurried out of the camper and the aluminum door banged shut. Dad flew out after me with fire on his cheeks and gravel in his voice.

"How *dare* you slam that door on me when I'm talking to you. You're just like your brother." His slap stung my damp cheek and hardened something in me. But I embraced those last five words as a compliment.

I already adored and admired twenty-eight-year-old Craig who called to tease me about boys. Whose name I wasn't allowed to speak and whose instant absence from my life I wasn't allowed to grieve. He was confident, stood up to my dad, and was passionate to pursue his own path. To an angry fifteen-year-old, already finding acceptance and realizing her power in the party scene, his black sheep label fit well.

I learned to speak what musician Rich Mullins calls, "the language of silence." It made him bitter and rebellious. It did the same to me. So, hurricane Robin spiraled further out of control.

On my worst days, when the tension at home was high, I escaped to the peaceful center at the eye of my storm. Sitting on a fallen tree in the woods bordering the riverbank, I sensed a presence. It sparkled in the dew of a lacy spider web and on the white-cresting wave pounding the shoreline. With toes dug into sandy soil and damp leaves, I filled notebooks, giving words to anger and despair and confusion. But the bummer about a storm's serene center is that it's temporary. Chaos's other half was coming.

CHAPTER TWO: WHEN GRIEF CALLS

The next few years, I drank a lot. Even as a football cheerleader in homecoming parades, I rode in the bed of a truck sipping beer from a Tastee-Freez cup. I lied to get to the next party, ditch school, or meet a forbidden boyfriend. The more my parents tried to punish me for failing grades, the angrier I got. I held no respect for their rules.

As a high school senior with no plans beyond the weekend parties, I got pregnant.

Which brings me to my other safe place: my seventeen-year-old best friend and chess nerd, Jeff. Though he knew my baby might not be his, he wanted to marry me. I was scared to say yes because I planned to marry one person. Forever. So, it had to be for the right reasons.

On his way out the door for Army basic training, Jeff proposed for the third time. This time, I was ready. Two months later—eight months after high school graduation—we married. Two days after our vows at the courthouse, he left for more training and three weeks later our son was born. Yes, I'm breathless again.

Justin Lee brought calm and laughter to my parents' home. I don't remember my dad being drunk during the two months we lived there. He adored Justin. Perhaps, a baby gave us purpose. A sweet distraction. Our heartache rested there, under the surface, soothed and forgotten for a while.

Grief Calls Again

Ashley Nicole arrived when spring was new. We were babes ourselves, barely twenty, when I swaddled her in pink and Jeff carried her out of the Army hospital on Fort Riley, Kansas. Sunshine, pink blossoms, and the robin's song were the perfect backdrop. We were happy and excited for our little girl to meet Justin, her fifteen-month-old big brother.

But our daughter was only home two days then hospitalized for a week. I guess those spring robins were asleep the night our neighbor pounded on our apartment's screen door. Having no phone, I hurried next door to take the nurse's call. All I remember is, "Your daughter coded. Code blue. She's okay now…stabilizing her…will transport her…neo-natal intensive care…Topeka."

As we rushed to the hospital, a buck deer bounded out of the dark. Jeff didn't even have time to hit the brakes. It missed us by inches and disappeared into the trees on the other side of the road.

I believed God was like an authoritarian parent, distant and demanding. But that night, when all I wanted was to get to my baby girl, I sensed a protective presence.

The previous days, caring for a toddler while recovering from childbirth, were exhausting. As much as possible, I was with Ashley at the hospital, leaning into her crib and letting her tiny hand curl around my finger. My soft kisses and whispered songs willed her to heal.

Now, in the ICU, there wasn't room to sit among the beeping machines attached to all those tubes, attached to my seven-pound daughter. Ashley, naked except for her diaper, looked peaceful but cold. Jeff and I wanted to hold her, warm her, but the nurse told us they needed to draw blood and directed us to a waiting room.

Assuring us she'd be fine, the doctor encouraged Jeff to leave for the Amtrak station to pick up my sister, coming in to help with our babies.

The next time I saw my Ashley Nicole she was distressed. Not crying but agitated. Her single, delicate whimper prompted my milk to let down and it tingled through my breasts. I reached out to touch her but again a nurse shooed me out.

Hospitals are so freezing cold. I stood in the waiting room in my Daisy Dukes—numb, shivering, and hugging my chest. God bless the chaplain who draped his white hospital coat over my shoulders. After checking on Ashley, he sat with me and closed his eyes to pray about green pastures and quiet waters. I'd never heard such soothing words. Then they took a harsh turn, "though I walk through the valley of the shadow of death" (Psalm 23:4a NKJV).

Wait. What's going on?

The pediatrician walked in and slumped back against the door. His pale face turned toward the ceiling. I stood and waited. The white coat no longer protected me from the chill. It seemed like forever before the doctor exhaled hard and hung his head. Lifting a shaky hand to remove his wire-rimmed glasses, he looked at me. Like he didn't quite

CHAPTER TWO: WHEN GRIEF CALLS

believe what he was about to say.

"She didn't make it."

"No." My head shaking, but my voice firm. "No."

"We couldn't…I'm so sorry." And he was gone.

My legs shook under me. I sat down with my arms tight across my stomach. For nine months, my baby grew and hiccupped inside me. For nine days, all I wanted was to cradle her and comfort her. Now, my arms ached—wrapped tight against an unnatural emptiness.

Alone again. To face grief and to speak words that would break my husband's heart. The one who took our toddler to pick out his little sister's first frilly outfit. And to tell my sister. The one who walked toward me down the hospital hallway smiling, eager to meet her new niece.

Those lying spring robins still sang as unspeakable sorrow settled soul-deep. When Ashley died, I didn't know what to do with all the anger so I silently hurled it at God. Well, at my limited version of Him. And a deeper dive into alcohol numbed my need to be seen, heard, and comforted.

Vices are Temporary Fixes

Maybe you never numbed your struggles by abusing alcohol or other drugs. Some of us lash out or use sarcasm. And social media makes that super easy. Our vices are often more sneaky like gossip, or over-eating, or over-shopping. Sometimes our pain hides in the good stuff like when we work too much or even help too much.

The list is limitless and these temporary surface fixes are like Band-Aids trying to hide a bruised and broken heart. In the moment, we feel better and have a false sense of control. But they infect our insides and our outsides. Our relationship with God and our people.

Vices make room for sin in our hearts and minds. They take up space where God wants to be. The place in us that's created just for Him. Where He is always present with us and all of our anger, sorrow, questions, and confusion. He hears our cries and captures our tears as He walks us toward healing, heart change, and wholeness.

We all have layers of heartache that were painted on in broad strokes. Somewhere along the way, we believed that messy self-portrait is who we're destined to be. Our pain defines us and weighs us down. When Ashley died, all those hurting layers hid my true identity. I was stuck in lies that labeled me victim, voiceless, and less-than.

I'm so grateful we aren't forever named by what we've done, what's been done to us, or how we've coped. We are defined by the Living God. He has the perfect heart of a father and a mother. As we seek this Love, we outgrow the lying layers and reveal our adored divine design, God's masterpiece.

The Promise of a Brighter Day

My friend, this was a heavy chapter. Thanks for staying with me as we went way back from that day in my friend's counseling office. We saw a little girl tip-toeing around in an alcoholic home, now grown into a woman still seeking voice and value. We uncovered a toxic mix that creates a quicksand foundation for making decisions and facing difficulties in adolescence and adulthood.

Will you walk with me through another tough chapter? It's the last of my darkest years and it leads to a brighter day. As we move forward, arm-in-arm, let's look back to see how Mercy worked in our lives even before we met Jesus.

CHAPTER TWO: WHEN GRIEF CALLS

STUDY QUESTIONS

"You may not control all the events that happen to you, but you can decide not to be reduced by them." ~ Maya Angelou

See Your Thoughts

Take a few moments to think about how you talk to yourself. Write down what comes to mind. Maybe nothing comes up right now. If not, pay attention to your inner dialogue as you go about your day. Jot down what you hear and come back to these questions.

The words you say to yourself—are they kind or unkind? Would you speak like that to a friend, a niece, or a daughter?

Where or from whom have you heard these words? Culture? People? Failure? Fears?

In this chapter, we see authoritarian messages like, "Children will be seen, not heard." And we get a peek at a hush-and-stuff approach to grief, "Suck it up and soldier on."

We also see how a child's mind might interpret these messages and be formed by them. Look back at the lists in chapter 2.

Are any of these internalized messages familiar to you? If so, write them here.

How do these thoughts and habits hide your value?

How do they hinder your voice?

Our soul's enemy wants to keep us small and shushed. The father of lies knows we are a powerful force when we own our value and use our voice.

Set Your Mind

See who you are in Christ and renew your mind. Read and reflect on the following Scripture.

"So, let us come boldly to the throne of our gracious God. There we will receive his mercy, and we will find grace to help us when we need it most." Hebrews 4:16

Real people like you and me wrote the Psalms. They are poems and sacred songs inspired by sheer joy and utter sorrow. In the Old Testament, we see God's people use them as hymnbooks, memorize and recite them at celebrations, and sing them on pilgrimages to Jerusalem.

CHAPTER TWO: WHEN GRIEF CALLS

We hear them in today's worship music too.

In Psalms, we see emotions written out in words. Healing words. Angry words. Desperate and worshiping words.

Below, I share some of these ancient songs and poems. Don't feel pressured to read them all. Maybe mix them up a bit and read one from the first row and one from the second. Pray and ask God what He wants you to hear and express. It may help to jot down or highlight a word or phrase that stands out to you.

Anguish, fear, sorrow: Psalms 13, 88, and 51

Joy, praise, thanksgiving: Psalms 103 and 92

Throughout the Bible, we see real people. Made in God's image, they confidently express real and raw emotions. Joy, sorrow, anger, etc.

In 1 Samuel 1, we see Hannah who aches to have a child. She goes "boldly to the throne of our gracious God" and she speaks boldly too. With great faith—*and* with great anguish and sorrow—she cries desperate tears and prays to the "Lord of Heaven's Armies."

In Luke 1:46–55, we see Jesus' mother and her spontaneous song of praise. Mary expresses pure joy and humility in response to Elizabeth's prophetic words about the baby in her womb.

On some level, we can relate to these women. But, I wonder—can we even imagine the emotional pain Jesus expresses in Gethsemane's garden?

In Matthew 26:36–43, we see Jesus' grief. He is anticipating his arrest, torture, and violent death. In verse 38, anguished and already suffering, He says, "My soul is deeply grieved, so that I am almost dying *of sorrow*" (AMP). Jesus pleads with the Father, so distressed in mind and body, that blood literally mingles with His tears.

UNCOVER YOUR DIVINE DESIGN

Yes, God invites us to express our honest emotions. Every single one of them. After all, He *did* create them. So, let's anchor our soul—our mind, will, and emotions—in His promises.

Isaiah 43:1–3 is a powerful promise given to God's people, Israel. We are also chosen to receive Jesus. To root our identity in Him and reflect Him to the world. Since these promises are for you, too, personalize the first verse by substituting your name with the ones I put in bold.

> *"But now, O **Jacob**, listen to the Lord who created you.*
> *O **Israel**, the one who formed you says,*
> *"Do not be afraid, for I have ransomed you.*
> *I have called you by name; you are mine.*
> *When you go through deep waters, I will be with you.*
> *When you go through rivers of difficulty, you will not drown. When you walk through the fire of oppression,*
> *you will not be burned up; the flames will not consume you.*
> *For I am the Lord, your God, the Holy One of Israel, your Savior."*

Seek & Speak What's True

I am defined by I AM. I am safe to express all my emotions to Him. I am seen, heard, and loved.

Because God, _____

_____ , I am _____

_____ .

Celebrate

God of Angel Armies, because You made us in Your image, our value is immeasurable. We are free to enter Your presence with all these intense emotions. We are free to speak and receive from You. Thank You for limitless grace, mercy, help, and comfort. So many centuries ago, You

CHAPTER TWO: WHEN GRIEF CALLS

made a path through the Red Sea for Your people to walk on dry ground. And then in Isaiah 43:18,19a, You said, "forget all that—it is nothing compared to what I am going to do. For I am about to do something new." And You led them out of captivity again and took them back to Israel, their home. Our "something new" is Jesus. He is our path through rough waters and our refreshing river in the desert. He leads us home to our divine design. Thank you. — Your treasured Daughter

CHAPTER 3

When Mercy Pursues: Yes, even then.

"Even when I walk through the darkest valley, I will not be afraid for you are close beside me. Your rod and your staff protect and comfort me." ~ Psalm 23:4

Curled up in the bucket seat of our Chevy Chevette, I cradled Ashley's yellow Care Bear. "Birthday Bear" was a gift from my sister who now sat in the back with Justin. It was three days since Ashley passed.

In the days prior, the shock shifted my mind to slow motion and the unaffected, business-as-usual world spun around me. I was a spectator caught between grieving and living, crying and laughing. I'd kept moving to prepare for our trip home to Illinois to bury our baby girl. I needed to buy myself a dress, wash clothes at the Laundromat, and get snacks and diapers from the commissary.

Just a few nights earlier, we'd rushed to the hospital and almost smashed into that deer. I felt protected—like I was seen and held. It was the same safe presence I experienced in my teen years as I sat on the riverbank. Now, traveling from Kansas to Illinois, I sensed it again.

On Interstate 80, we cruised alongside an eighteen-wheeler. From the passing lane, it suddenly veered across the line toward our car. Jeff swerved a bit then hit the horn and the semi jerked back. The near-collision pounded our hearts but something else grabbed our attention. The car's horn hadn't worked in months. Jeff hit it again and it didn't make a peep. On that unwanted and unexpected trip home, Mercy called to us.

Have you ever looked back to see God's handprints on your life before you knew Jesus? In your darkest times, even in the middle of willful sin, you see Him wooing you into relationship? Some say we earn His attention and unconditional love. But they don't understand mercy. The last time I checked, it's free and shows up when we least expect it.

Mercy's Whisper

A year later, spring blooms and blue skies brought sweet memories of Ashley Nicole. Two-year-old Justin long forgot those first mourning hours when he sensed my pain, crawled onto my lap, and nuzzled my neck. Now, wearing only a diaper and digging tiny toes into cool grass, he scooted along on his wheeled Smurf.

A gentle sadness—triggered by sight, smell, and season—tugged at me. Shaded under fresh leaves and apple blossoms, I put pen to paper:

I picked flowers for you today.
Perfect under spring sun. Bright, delicate, new.
But you far away.

Wildflowers wilted,
lying next to me now.
Tired and dying.

Yet, the robin sings her lulla-bye
and hope scatters seed.

I imagine my soul, someday weightless,
floating to you
like dandelion down cradled on a breeze,
Love still blooms.

CHAPTER THREE: WHEN MERCY PURSUES

Where did that hope and comfort come from? How did they shine through my sadness? In Romans 1:20 (NIV), Paul writes about God's "invisible qualities" being made known by the things He created. The sun and spring blooms, the beauty and order of changing seasons. Like my days sitting by the river, with the dewy spider web and the pounding wave at water's edge, God's presence and power in nature revealed His character to me.

I'm here. Don't give up.

Even when we don't see it or believe it, God isn't far away. Thinking He's distant doesn't change His desire to have a relationship with us. He loves. He woos. He pursues. It's not only what He does, it's who He is. Our Rescuer doesn't quit on us. Ever.

Mercy Pursues

In Genesis chapter 16, we see God pursue Hagar, an Egyptian slave girl. She was an add-on to a marital contract to bear a child for Sarai and Abram. But pride and jealousy complicate any relationship, especially one concocted to speed up God's plan. After Hagar got pregnant, the women became rivals. Imagine that. Competing for top position, they were spiteful and malicious. Hagar ran away and we find her at a desert spring.

Can you see her there, scared and weeping? Perhaps soaking swollen, achy, dusty feet? No family, no women's shelter, no crisis pregnancy center. Zero opportunities. God's mercy reached Hagar in the middle of her mess and distress. *I see your pain. I hear your cry.* She was hopeless until a messenger pointed her in the right direction.

Mercy's message does the same for us.

A year and a half after I wrote Ashley's poem, God reached out to me again.

I stepped onto the icy porch and the winter wind hit my face. Sub-zero air watered my eyes and stung the tip of my nose. Pregnant with our third baby, I grabbed the metal railing to steady myself and saw something that stole my breath. Three-year-old Justin tugged on my shirt. "Mommy, what is it?" Ice crunched and scraped under the box as we shimmied it into our apartment.

Both of us, wide-eyed, knelt beside the box of groceries and lifted out each item: a roasting chicken, canned corn, gravy and corn bread mixes, and a five-pound bag of potatoes. Then Justin giggled and grabbed a bag of candy.

Are you old enough to remember ribbon candy? We used to find them in our Christmas stockings under the apple and orange. Always a bit sticky and covered in fuzz.

The bag crinkled between us as I hugged Justin and cried. The candy wasn't for a Christmas dinner. It was an added treat for my little boy. In that moment, I didn't feel alone. Someone saw my little family and wanted to help.

Stuffed Grief, Stuck Me

After Ashley died, a well-meaning Christian told me, "It's God's will." *Yep. He's a distant disciplinarian.* Inwardly, my anger was the easier part of grief—to feel and to express. And no amount of alcohol or Christian-y answers could fix it.

Though I only held Ashley for nine days, I nurtured her for nine months. We shared kicks and hiccups and afternoon naps. Though we talked about her, Jeff didn't completely understand my oh-so-empty arms and the squeezing ache in my chest. We were both excited when a pregnancy test showed baby number three on the way.

I loved my job as wife, mom, and homemaker, and I was good at it. But society said that wasn't enough. You need college, a career, a *real* job. I often wrestled with that and listened to negative self-talk. My losses, failures, and sin defined me too. Surely, that's how God saw me. So, the real me stayed small and settled for half-living.

Like Hagar in the desert, we need someone to see us and hear us—the real, hurting, messed-up us. Like on that winter morning, when I almost tumbled over the box, Someone sees you, my friend. God looks past sins and struggles and into your potential.

CHAPTER THREE: WHEN MERCY PURSUES

I never knew who left the food box, but I want us all to hear the message it sends to our broken hearts. *I see you. You are not alone.*

Mercy moved a stranger and the compassion moved me. My heart and mind began to change. Maybe my anger toward God was misplaced. Maybe He wasn't mean and distant. His care and closeness became clearer a few months later when Jeff lost his civilian job. We had no health insurance when our son, Preston, was born. Hospital bills weighed heavily on us.

Then God showed up again. A grant I applied for paid our ten-thousand-dollar hospital bill. Every. Single. Penny. I sensed God very, very near. Crying and holding the application check-marked "You are approved" to my chest, I looked up at the ceiling and whispered, "Thank you."

More than three decades later, I remember that moment and still tear up. If I'd known or believed Scripture then, I'd have agreed with Hagar, "I have now seen the One who sees me" (Genesis 16:13b NIV).

You may recall a moment when you were quite aware that something big was happening. Someone greater than you was in the room. Others may hear your stories and wonder or argue (insert snarky tone and raised eyebrow), "How can God be *there*?" Simple. Because that's what His Spirit does. He hangs out with sinners. Jesus, the rebel, defies legalism and the upturned noses of manmade rules. He speaks hope into our brokenness. He is there. He is here. Holding us—knowing us—in the middle of our messes and distresses.

But we struggle to see Mercy, don't we? Sometimes, we think we don't deserve God's attention, then or now.

Are You Defined by a Lying Mental Script?

To hush condemning voices, we need to recognize these Loud Imaginings Appearing Real—the LIARs:
- You don't deserve God's loving kindness.
- You're not good enough.

These mindsets become ground rules for life. Our thoughts wire paths into our brains until they're a natural flow of shame-based thought patterns.[1] Lies squat in our minds so long, we believe them. It takes courage and intentional effort to really think about our thinking. To capture our "rebellious thoughts and teach them to obey Christ" (2 Cor. 10:5).

Let's Flip the Script

Does anyone really *deserve* a father's love when we shake our fist in his face and run from his open arms? But we are dealing with unconditional love, my friend. Beyond our human understanding. Beyond old crusty religion with its squinty eyes and tight lips telling us we're depraved at birth and depraved 'til we die.

Do we still think we have to earn love and attention? That's not from our heavenly Father. Humans are fickle. God's pursuit is a fact. He believes we're more than worth it. We are loved and seen and heard. Dirty little LIARs do not define us.

We are more than good enough. We are valued beyond measure. Our Father God created us with love and good purpose in mind. That rascal King David was God's man and he fell into some deep shame. He penned beautiful psalms out of raw pain, remorse, anxiety, and depression. His sinful choices led to horrible consequences. Yet, he believed, "You made all the delicate, inner parts of my body and knit me together in my mother's womb. Thank you for making me so wonderfully complex! Your workmanship is marvelous—how well I know it" (Psalm 139:13–14).

Do *we* know it? Let's soak in it a bit like a warm, bubbly bath.

Deuteronomy 7:6b tells us we are chosen to be God's "own special treasure." Okay, that one messes with me. But let's keep soaking because unhealthy self-talk will reject our greatest needs to be valued and cherished. Some truths take a tad longer to make it from our heads to our hearts. From knowing to owning. Our brain re-wiring isn't finished yet. Girl, you are God's marvelous, on-purpose creation. You are inferior to no one.

But we get lost in a ranking system, don't we? As if our patient Creator puts those who seem low-maintenance at the top of the list and

CHAPTER THREE: WHEN MERCY PURSUES

us high maintenance beauties at the bottom? Oh no-no-no. He's not Santa. He doesn't double-check a list before He gives. We're not on probation. God not only reaches to us, but He also *runs* to us. That's what Love does. Our good, good Father doesn't play favorites. And He's not only near, He lives in us to guide, comfort, and heal. He sees a heart that wants better. Whether we're naughty or nice, He shows up every time.

When we're bound by unhealthy messages, shame tells us we're not worthy of God's attention. We're designed to be defined by the One who created us. Not by our pain, not by our past, not by our people. When we believe what God sees, we walk forward in ever-reaching mercy.

Sometimes it's years into our journey before we see His pursuit. Why does it take so long? Because condemnation lies as compassion tries to reach us.

The day I wrote Ashley's poem, hope whispered, soft and subtle. I didn't know God was so close. Nearing my fiftieth birthday—thirty years after writing it—I read it for the umpteenth time and finally saw Mercy there. For the first time, clear as a spring sky. Here are my words to Him:

"God, I weep, overwhelmed. Now, I see You with me. How else could I sense hope? You were there, whispering to my soul. All those years, sin and clouded thinking separated us. But it only kept me from finding You. It didn't stop You from reaching to me. That's the only explanation and mercy's purest picture.

A lost girl penning grief under a tree and You there, unseen. You knew it would be a while, so You waited. Wooing me as I ached for my sweet baby. *I'm here. Don't give up.* You were there all along holding out hope."

Child of God, think about a time when God seemed unreachable, when you didn't even know what you needed. Are you surprised to see Him there? Take a minute to sense it and believe it—the love, the mercy, the value of you, worthy of pursuit.

We are Seen and Heard

In the middle of our worst choices and darkest seasons, Father God woos us. When He saw me in bars numbing my pain with beer and attention from men, He saw a beautiful, feisty rebel who didn't know the way to her true self—her divine design and destiny. When He protected broken-me on the highway that day, He saw my potential, the girl He created.

In my teen years, I sensed that presence—a hope beyond my reach—coaxing me out of my mess. Something stronger than religion's rules or my parents' punishment. Something personal. And again, as a young mom, in those rawest days of my grief, God reached out to me.

Compassion continued to nudge me through three more military moves and Jeff's year-long deployment to Korea. In my plunge to rock bottom, grief's weight and shame-filled choices broke me. I could not numb and run anymore. God's pursuit, that gentle tug, became an irresistible pull. Not the yank of a distant authoritarian parent punishing me, but a father wooing me into a relationship.

Six years after my baby's death, Jesus showed me that my husband and children deserved better than what broken-me gave them. And so did I. Mercy led me forward into my brightest days. Join me as I jump from the grave to grace.

"I love the LORD, for he heard my voice; he heard my cry for mercy. Because he turned his ear to me, I will call on him as long as I live. The cords of death entangled me, the anguish of the grave came over me; I was overcome by distress and sorrow. Then I called on the name of the LORD: 'LORD, save me!'

"The LORD is gracious and righteous; our God is full of compassion. The LORD protects the unwary [those with childlike faith]; when I was brought low, he saved me" (Psalm 116:1–6 NIV, paraphrased by author).

CHAPTER THREE: WHEN MERCY PURSUES

STUDY QUESTIONS

God's pursuit is relentless. Especially when our mind and heart are so very far from Him. What if that place where we feel the farthest from God—is actually where we are closest to Him? Because we're just one step, one decision, away from the path that leads from darkness to life.

From abundant grace and mercy, God works in our lives to draw us to Him. He knows us completely and chose us in advance to become like His Son.

"And having chosen them, he called them to come to him. And having called them, he gave them right standing with himself. And having given them right standing, he gave them his glory" (Romans 8:30).

See Your Thoughts

Are you defined by a lying mental script? This automatic, often unconscious thinking tells you who you are. These thoughts define you and dictate how you react.

To hush condemning voices, you need to recognize them.

Does your mind want to reject the message of Romans 8:30? That God chose you and still chooses you. Even…no especially…when you seem far from Him. If so, what condemning words do you hear? What LIARs (Loud Imaginings Appearing Real) harass you?

Do you ever feel like God is distant and demanding?

Write about a time He seemed unknowable and unreachable. In your past. Or maybe right here in your nitty-gritty present.

Like Hagar, who was down and out of options, consider how you've experienced God as the One who sees and hears you.

Think about your seasons of sin, stubbornness, and sadness. How did/does God reach out to you? How and where has Mercy showed up when you least expected it?

Use the following prompts to simply guide your thoughts and perhaps refresh your memory. You don't have to answer all of them. Ask God to give you new insight to see Him there in the midst of your messes and distresses.

In nature:

A friend or stranger:

In Scripture:

An unexplainable sense of His presence and protection:

Other:

CHAPTER THREE: WHEN MERCY PURSUES

Set Your Mind

See who you are in Christ and renew your mind. Read and reflect on the following Scripture.

"We destroy every proud obstacle that keeps [us] from knowing God. We capture [our] rebellious thoughts and teach them to obey Christ" (2 Corinthians 10:5 paraphrased by author).

In the "See Your Thoughts" section, you looked at lies that tell you who and Whose you are. Let's flip the script on the LIARs. Read the following Bible verses. Pause after each one and read it again. Ask God to help you hear His heart—to sense how near He is and how much He values you.

"You are the God who sees me" (Genesis 16:13b).

"[B]e sure of this: I am with you always, even to the end of the age" (Matthew 28:20b).

"'Cheer up and don't be afraid. For the Lord your God has arrived to live among you. He is a mighty Savior. He will give you victory. He will rejoice over you with great gladness; he will love you and not accuse you.' Is that a joyous choir I hear? No, it is the Lord himself exulting over you in happy song" (Zephaniah 3:16b–18b TLB).

Seek & Speak What's True

I am defined by I AM. Because God is renewing my mind, I am able to recognize lies and replace them. I am transformed by Truth.

Because God, _____

_____ , I am _____

_____ .

Celebrate

Gracious God, You love us. And that alone makes us worthy of Your relentless pursuit. Even when we didn't see it or believe it, You did not quit on us. In our messes and distresses—even the self-made ones—You were there calling us to this gift of living loved, seen, and heard. We rest in knowing not only that You are with us, but also that You are already way ahead of us. Like an attentive parent, You know what we need before we even ask. What a joy it is to know we bring You joy and You sing over us. Thank You for always fighting for us. —Your grateful Daughter

CHAPTER 4

When Holiness Calls: A Holy Pursuit

"Nothing in my hand I bring, simply to the cross I cling; naked, come to thee for dress; helpless, look to thee for grace; foul, I to the fountain fly; wash me, Savior, or I die." ~ Augustus M. Toplady

Kneeling at the dark-stained pine bench, I hadn't a clue what to do. All I knew was my gut-aching need to be forgiven and free of guilt. Pastor Mike knelt on the other side. He leaned in to talk to me as the piano clanged, "Just as I Am," drowning out most of his words. I cried and nodded. *Yes, I believe Jesus died for my sin. Yes, I want Him to be Lord of my life.*

Believing Jesus saved me, not only for eternal life, but in my everyday life, I walked out of that little house-renovated-church into a brighter Arkansas sun. Brighter because I wasn't looking at the ground anymore. Forgiveness freed me and lifted my head.

As I walked to my car, my thoughts jumped to the next thing. *Lunchtime. What do I feed my family?* My parents were visiting and the old needing-it-perfect me would have over-thought it and freaked out. But I didn't. Peace replaced panic and I decided that tuna sandwiches were good enough. Boom. God was already renewing my mind.

Though I didn't completely understand what happened to me, I knew

I was new. I had such peace and was hungry for more. After my first taste of freedom, I was determined to die to everything that held me hostage—those pieces of my old self that weren't a part of who God made me to be.

And oh my, there were plenty.

A few months before we moved to Arkansas and I said yes to Jesus, Jeff came home from his deployment to Korea. During our yearlong separation, drinking and loneliness—a bad combination—took me to my lowest lows.

Alcohol intercepts our ability to reason. It actually changes our brain chemistry and takes away our inhibitions. Fearless and daring is fun when dancing or running in the rain, but it's straight up stupid and dangerous when driving drunk. Spending the night in jail with a DUI arrest was embarrassing and humiliating. Especially because I had to call my already-burdened mom to bail me out. More guilt, more shame, more stuffed grief—like dirt being shoveled on top of me.

While grief comes out in wild and risky behavior, it's often subtle and unpredictable too. It makes even small decisions difficult. Like staring into the pantry for five minutes trying to decide which can to grab: corn or green beans. But grief's not-so-small-and-subtle side gets explosive if not processed in a healthy way.

Toxic Release

When sober, I was kind, polite, and responsible—a good wife and mom. But that toxic mix of anger and alcohol created a tipping point when the booze took over. Happy party girl to weepy, angry drunk. Bottled up and shaken up, I exploded. Like the morning I came home after being out all night and ripped three t-shirts off Jeff as he tried to leave for work. Pain will find a voice.

In the months before Jesus, my drinking started on Wednesdays. A few beers while cooking supper seemed like no big deal, but deep down, it scared me. I saw how easily I could slip into drinking every day. It reminded me of my bartending days in the year after Preston was born. I remembered the sick and lonely people who came in every week. Already a bit tipsy, they came in on Wednesday afternoons after their Social Security checks hit the bank. Their alcohol abuse estranged them from their children and grandchildren.

Bottom line: I bottomed out. Shame, guilt, and grief were becoming unbearable. I didn't want pain and alcohol to control my life. But I was stuck in a cycle.

And God knew exactly where in Arkansas to send us and what realtor we were to meet. Sweet Jim Bell found our rental house and did not leave us alone. He checked in on us a couple times a week and never left without saying, "Come visit my church. We're a big family." I'd smile and wave. Nope. No way.

But God's plan won out. For the first time ever, we had nowhere to be on New Year's Eve, so we accepted Jim's invite to his church's party at a Boys and Girls Club. I figured our boys would enjoy it. But we did too. We saw real people having real fun. With no keg in the corner. That was a Friday. Sunday we were in church and three weeks later, I was at the altar with Brother Mike.

No Longer Slaves

When we surrender our lives to Jesus, we identify with His death on the cross and we are no longer slaves to our sin nature. In believing His resurrection, we are resurrected and become a new creation. Our guilt of past sin is nailed dead. Jesus' Spirit walks forward with us to show us our daily sin habits so He can free us from them.

It takes time for us to see and change hard-wired thought patterns. Mine were so familiar and so weirdly comfortable, I wore them like a second skin under silk sheets. In reality, they were steel bars. The real me was locked up tight.

Aren't you glad God doesn't dump all of our stuff in front of us and leave us to sort it out? He walks with us our whole lives, patient in our process of unlocking and freeing the person He created.

Let's look again at John Eldredge's quote from chapter one:

"We are in the process of being unveiled. We are created to reflect

God's glory, born to bear His image, and He ransomed us to reflect that glory again."

When God forgives us and offers us new life, our unveiling and reflecting begins. While His Spirit and Scripture transform the inside, our outward sin habits peel off like old sunburned skin. Sorta like a soul exfoliation. Cleaning up the mind, will, and emotions prompts the shedding of unhealthy behavior. It's an inside-out process. As Brother Mike told me, our *want-tos* change.

We want to honor Jesus and the new person in us by being better, healthier, freer.

As Jesus lives in us—a new resident in our hearts and homes—He is present always. A healthy, sober, best friend.

In that first week, I stopped cussing around Him. And soon after that, I gathered all the alcohol in the house and poured my drink-you-under-the-table party girl image down the kitchen sink. Next came my temper. My angry outbursts over innocent kid stuff like mud tracked in or spilled milk, diminished.

I didn't need constant noise from the radio or television anymore to distract me from my thoughts. With the boys off to school, being alone in a quiet home refreshed me. I never knew that kind of peace was possible.

My new relationship with God ignited a desire to know and experience more. I wanted it *all*. I immersed myself into changing my life for good. I bought a Bible, memorized Scripture, and soaked up Pastor Mike's sermons and discipleship studies. That's where I learned what it means to be a student of Jesus—and this ongoing relationship and sanctification.

Now there's a churchy word.

Sanctification is learning to say no to sin and yes to God. It sets us apart to be used for our sacred purpose—to serve God and others. We aim to become more like Jesus. It's not imitating like an actor, but it's letting His nature and qualities live in us and shine through us. In *My Utmost for His Highest*, Oswald Chambers defines sanctification as "nothing less than the holiness of Jesus becoming mine and being exhibited in my life." All of Jesus. Available to us, all the time. Holiness was created in us and the cross reveals it to us. It's a grace gift.

CHAPTER FOUR: WHEN HOLINESS CALLS

By accepting Jesus' death, which brings us forgiveness, and His resurrection, which gives us new life, our spirits are renewed and empowered by His Holy Spirit. Since holiness was part of our original identity, it's also our redeemed identity. It's Christ *in* us.

Paul tells us that we are adopted "to be holy and without fault in His eyes" (Ephesians 1:4). God sees us blameless—as if we've never sinned. Our holiness is the result of God adopting us into His family. But it's not the reason He loves us. Our holy standing comes from *being* God's child, not earned by doing His work. Our next step to holy living is to surrender and let Him purify our lives.

Perhaps you're thinking, *Is that even possible?* Yes. It's a decision of the will, a holy pursuit. Let's step back again and look at some wrong mindsets about it.

Holiness: What on Earth is it?

"Holy, Holy, Holy…only Thou art holy…" I had no idea what I was singing.

As a child, holiness was inconceivable to me. Hovering somewhere beyond the clouds, it was reserved for God, priests, and popes, not for mere peasants like me. Webster's dictionary even defines holiness as "a title of address used for high ecclesiastical dignitaries and especially for the pope."[1] I sang to a distant being. An obscure word sung to an obscure god.

Outside church, holy was misused and mumbled. "Well isn't she holier-than-thou." I heard other good words—even Jesus' name—twisted ugly and yelled. My sister cautioned me about the careless use of God's name, and I believed her because she seemed to have a connection to Him.

I attended classes, performed the sacraments, checked the boxes, and recited a penitent prayer every night before bed just in case a sin snuck in that I didn't know about. I wasn't taking any chances. A thought process rooted in fear told me that a higher being existed, waiting to zap me with a lightning bolt. Mine was a faraway faith for sure, but it was all I knew.

Holiness remained a superior secret—zipped up tight like it belonged in another world—remote and unattainable. So, I figured if God was holy, He was distant and unreachable too. It was many years and countless tears before I saw my first glimpse of our real God and true holiness.

Holiness: What in heaven is it?

My childhood faith—a simple belief that God existed—and a hunger for change pulled me into that little Arkansas church. The hand clapping was weird, but a welcome weird to a God-starved, spiritually dying young woman. The people were comfortable with God. They knew Him on a first name basis and weren't afraid to stand up and talk about Him. The Father. The Son. The Holy Spirit. They not only enjoyed relationship with Jesus, they aimed to be like Him.

Holiness dawned bright in the light on those sweet Southern faces. It grew skin. It was touchable, huggable. And I wanted it. I hungered for peace to get over my past, strength to get through my present, and hope to get moving on a path with purpose.

Through God's people, Bible-based Sunday messages, and my own Bible reading, holiness—a weird-yet-wonderful concept—became real to me. It floated down to Earth, desirable and doable. Why wouldn't it be? He calls us to it.

A Cloudy Concept Becomes a Clear Calling

"So you must live as God's obedient children. Don't slip back into your old ways of living to satisfy your own desires. You didn't know any better then. But now you must be holy in everything you do, just as God who chose you is holy" (1 Peter 1:14–15).

Peter, a once reckless and fearful disciple, found confidence in his Christ identity. He challenges us to seek sanctification, to take off our old sin habits and put on our new self in Christ. In verse 16, he quotes Moses who quotes God, "You must be holy because I am holy."

CHAPTER FOUR: WHEN HOLINESS CALLS

And remember, Peter and Moses are not picture perfect. Only perfectly imperfect humans. Like us. With hearts set on following God.

Our call is clear. Do you want to live out this holy calling and become a lifelong student, a disciple of Jesus? "The Son is the radiance of God's glory and the exact representation of his being" (Hebrews 1:3a NIV). To know Jesus is to know the Father. To know Jesus is to know the Holy Spirit.

As a brand-new believer, I ate up God's Word. I read about the Spirit's fruit in Galatians. Paul says, "Against such things there is no law" (Gal. 5:23 NIV). My heart made another giant freedom leap. There were options. Holy, guilt-free options. Alternatives to doing wrong and living with shame.

Paul tells us in Ephesians 4:22–24, "You were taught, with regard to your former way of life, to put off your old self, which is being corrupted by deceitful desires; to be made new in the attitudes of your minds; and to put on the new self, created to be like God in true righteousness and holiness." The Message expresses verse 24 this way: "And then take on an entirely new way of life—a God-fashioned life, a life renewed from the inside and working itself into your conduct as God accurately reproduces his character in you."

We don't have to let sin dictate our thoughts and attitudes. Our new nature defines us. The more we seek right living and ask the Holy Spirit to transform our minds, the more we find our true selves. The more we find our true selves, the more peace and freedom we enjoy.

Holiness, once a mystery to me, is the gift that grows us into our Christ identity.

Are you ready to join me and wholly surrender to a holy pursuit? Holiness is a daily, conscious commitment. So, we die to truly live.

Dying? That Sounds a Tad Scary.

In one of my favorite comedy movies, *What About Bob?*, twelve-year-old Siggy Marvin fixates on death.[2] He laments to Bob, who is his father's psychiatric patient. "We're going…to die. We're all…going…

to die." In another scene, Siggy stands on a boat dock, clad in all black, T-shirt and swimming trunks. His father—an uptight, demanding, and arrogant man—is determined to cure Siggy's death phobia. He coaxes him to dive into the lake. But Siggy's fear paralyzes him. His feet are riveted to the edge of the dock.

As believers, we can overcome fear of death because we know it's merely a step into Jesus' presence. But dying daily requires daily surrender. And that's a bit intimidating.

We shrink from this holiness call because we're not quite sure we can measure up. Maybe we rely on approval and balk at diving into something so radical to society's view. We don't want to be different. We want to be accepted.

Perhaps, we dabble in sin because it's fun or simply what we know. We get comfortable in it. Though we might feel guilt, it seems easier than change. Maybe, we don't want to ask God for help and make promises only to fail…again. We may even think we're living large. Fear and pride lie to us and keep us on the dock, riveted to a defeated life.

My friend, letting go leads to sanctification by Jesus, a life-purifying process of understanding and living Christ's victory over our worst fears and our ugliest sin. God's will for us is to be holy, free from sin's control, and set apart for divine purpose. Can you think of a better example of surrender and set apart than Jesus' cross? We must identify with it so we can die to the lingering effects of our old nature and stubborn self-rule.

"We know that our old sinful selves were crucified with Christ so that sin might lose its power in our lives. We are no longer slaves to sin. For when *we died with Christ,* we were set free from the power of sin. And since *we died with Christ,* we know we will also live with Him" (Romans 6:6–8, author's emphasis).

Dead to Self, Alive in Christ

Not long after accepting Jesus, I read about His baptism in Mark 3. My infant baptism was chosen for me. At twenty-six years old, I chose

CHAPTER FOUR: WHEN HOLINESS CALLS

not to perform a sacrament but to celebrate what Jesus did for me. I took another plunge.

I pinched my nose as Brother Mike eased me back into the cold water, a symbol of my old self in the grave, dying with Christ. When he pulled me out, it symbolized being raised to new life. God didn't speak out loud like He did when Jesus was baptized, but I sensed His message: *You in Me, Me in you—we can do this.*

My new brothers and sisters—the ones who first showed me holy—clapped and shouted and celebrated my victory over death. I was loved, accepted, a spiritual baby with a clean start.

My baptism was a step in obedience and a public statement: *No turning back. I'm all in.* It didn't make me a church member or sanctify me. Nor did it erase the nature I was born with, my original sin. Jesus took care of that the day my tears fell onto the dark-stained pine bench. The day my identity was rooted in His death and resurrection.

Our sin nature is dead. Gone. Radically replaced. Christ lives in us. We will die to shackling mindsets and soul-killing habits when we take honest moral inventory and let go of anything that doesn't look like Him. Fear, arrogance, and resentment, for starters. They control our thoughts and ooze out as whining, blaming, people-pleasing, and approval-seeking.

Though old habits linger, the only power sin can have is what we give it. Those unhealthy thought patterns we carry around are dead weight. They are grave clothes. The cross doesn't simply wash them white, it removes them. Why do we insist on wearing them?

We ask ourselves: "Am I willing to reduce myself down to simply 'me'? Am I determined enough to strip myself of all that my friends think of me, and all that I think of myself? Am I willing and determined to hand over my simple naked self to God?"[3]

This is a beautiful transparency—an uncovering—that frees us to think and live as God intended from the beginning. We may wonder about others' opinions. Maybe we worry about what we may have to give up as we allow our new nature in Christ to change us and shine through us.

Anxiety magnifies fear of the unknown.

So Siggy's fear of diving into the cool deep water is understandable. His dad's demands multiply his fear and he can't make the plunge. But we see Siggy again with his feet riveted to the edge of the dock. This time his gentle and patient friend Bob—who shares his own fears and is determined to conquer them—holds on to the back of Siggy's black t-shirt. Now, supported and empowered by a friend on the same journey, Siggy pushes past fear and dives into the refreshing water.

Forward Faith

When we choose holiness, we choose victory. We find our true selves—truly living—abundant and free. Yet, there may be a cost. Not everyone will celebrate our victory. Maybe a fearful friend or a skeptical family member. And we will lose some comfort zones. But be encouraged. We'll also lose toxic thoughts, bad attitudes, and some stinking grave clothes.

I know naked is risky and vulnerable. We will be exposed and at times it will seem we've failed. And that's okay. As long as we don't give up on this journey with Jesus, we fail forward. We move toward our fears until all we see is Jesus and our true self—uncovered, unashamed, and clothed in grace.

Our spiritual re-birth is a re-boot of our original glory. Our sanctification is our beautiful unveiling. It's our "long obedience in the same direction."[4]

CHAPTER FOUR: WHEN HOLINESS CALLS

STUDY QUESTIONS

Before you dive into the questions, pause a bit and pray. Ask God to help you see and think beyond a squeaky-clean right answer. Our hearts need time to consider the questions too.

When and where did you say yes to Jesus?

Read Romans 10:9. Do you believe God raised Jesus from the dead?

Now, read verse 10: "For it is by believing in your heart that you are made right with God, and it is by openly declaring your faith that you are saved."

It's good to be reminded of who Jesus is and what He does for us. He made us right with God. We were spiritually dead, in the grave. We are resurrected too.

"You were dead because of your sins and because your sinful nature was not yet cut away. Then God made you alive with Christ, for He forgave all our sins. He canceled the record of the charges against us and took it away by nailing it to the cross. In this way, he disarmed the spiritual rulers and authorities. He shamed them publicly by his victory over them on the cross" (Col. 2:13–15).

By faith alone, you are re-born and right with God. You are justified—"just-as-if-I'd" never sinned. Father God rescues you from spiritual death and gives you new life. Accepting this gift is the first step in becoming the real you.

UNCOVER YOUR DIVINE DESIGN

The next best decision is to invite the Holy Spirit to lead your daily life and commit to being a student (disciple) of Jesus. This is your holy pursuit and your beautiful unveiling.

When you asked Him to save you, what changed in you?

Take a moment to thank God and to affirm or reaffirm your best decisions ever.

Have I invited Jesus to be Lord of my life? Will I allow His Spirit to teach, guide, and change me from the inside out?

Habits from your old life and sinful nature want to stay in charge. So, in your daily walk with Jesus, it's good to check in with your heart, mind, and your character.

Start with the tough stuff: Is there willful, on-purpose sin in your life? If so, what is it?

What are the unhealthy heart motives—like fear, revenge, jealousy, selfishness—that control your thoughts, attitudes and behavior?

CHAPTER FOUR: WHEN HOLINESS CALLS

What hinders you from letting go of control and letting the Holy Spirit continue to purify your heart and life?

Now for the warm and fuzzy fun stuff: What are healthy heart motives—like love, peace, service, compassion—that free you to reflect Jesus' character?

What healthy habits support you as you continue to let Jesus' Spirit purify your heart and mind?

Set Your Mind

As a Christ follower, seek to grow and mature in your behavior and character. Holiness is becoming more like Jesus. It's a progressive transformation to let His character shine in and through you. It's worship lived out. God's sweet, indwelling Spirit inspires us to lead a life that honors Him.

See who you are in Christ and renew your mind. Read and reflect on the following Scripture.

"And let me live whole and holy, soul and body, so I can always walk with my head held high" (Psalm 119:80 MSG).

What is your first thought when you hear *holy* or *sanctified*?

Maybe it's similar to my old thoughts. Whatever words come to mind, it's good to remember we're created for this holy pursuit.

How can you continue to change old sin habits and grow into your divine design?

Pray and get to know the Father, Son, and Holy Spirit.

Find and read the following Bible truths. I wrote out a few because I like the clarity some versions offer. I pray you will open your heart, mind, and spirit to what God is teaching you. May you hear and heed your call to holy living.

Romans 8:6: What happens to a mind controlled by a sinful nature?

First Peter 1:13–14: This is a call to holy living and to have an alert, fully sober mind. What do you do with your mind?

Now read verses 14–16 in The Message:

"You didn't know any better then; you do now. As obedient children, let yourselves be pulled into a way of life shaped by God's life, a life energetic and blazing with holiness. God said, 'I am holy; you be holy'" (1Peter 1:14–16).

What a blessing and honor to share in this God-shaped life! Will you answer this call and become a lifelong student, a disciple of Jesus?

CHAPTER FOUR: WHEN HOLINESS CALLS

"Since you have heard about Jesus and have learned the truth that comes from him, throw off your old sinful nature and your former way of life, which is corrupted by lust and deception. Instead, let the Spirit renew your thoughts and attitudes. Put on your new nature, created to be like God—truly righteous and holy" (Eph. 4:21–25).

I especially like verse twenty-four in The Message:

"And then take on an entirely new way of life—a God-fashioned life, a life renewed from the inside and working itself into your conduct as God accurately reproduces his character in you."

Wow. Isn't this the best news ever? Our new nature defines us. The more we seek holy, right living—the more we find our true created selves. And there's no better place to search than in God's Word.

Galatians 5:16–18: What two forces are constantly fighting each other?

Verses 19–21: If you live to please the sinful nature, what are some of the results?

Verse 24: What visual do you see of what we do with our sinful nature?

Don't play around. Crucify that joy-sucker, life-wrecker, slave-maker. Romans 6:6–11: What are you dead to? What are you alive to?

You are no longer a spiritual zombie, walking dead. You are no longer a slave, but abundantly free and alive in Christ.

Galatians 5:22–25: When you live empowered by Jesus' Spirit, what qualities does He grow in you?

As God enters your life, it becomes brighter and more beautiful because we are becoming more like Him.

Stasi Eldredge, in her book *Becoming Myself: Embracing God's Dream of You*, reminds us:

"We won't be perfect on this side of heaven. But Jesus is perfect. Always. We are becoming more holy and true. Jesus already is. His name isn't 'Becoming.' It is 'Am.' Perfection isn't the goal. Jesus is."

Seek & Speak What's True

I am defined by I AM. Because Jesus is my Savior I am made whole and holy. I am not defined or controlled by sin. His Spirit empowers me to change my thoughts, habits, behavior, and attitudes.

Because God, _____

_____ , I am _____

_____ .

Celebrate

Holy God, Thank You for Your divine love, grace, and mercy. You are with me even before I know my need. You raised Jesus to resurrect me from the grave too. I am grateful for this gift of being reborn into new life. I surrender and invite You, Holy Spirit, to continue to clean me up from the inside-out. Show me where old sin thoughts and hab-

CHAPTER FOUR: WHEN HOLINESS CALLS

its still hide me. Father, I want my life to honor You and these gifts. In this forward-moving faith, sanctify me—through and through. In You, I find my wholeness and holiness, abundant life in my divine design.

Dear Daughter, this is our holy pursuit. Me in you. You in Me. We got this. —God

CHAPTER 5

When Mercy Calls: We Have the Same Enemy

"Bitterness is the monument you build to your own pain." ~ Author unknown

In the weeks following the best decision of my life, one of the weekly memory verses given to me by Brother Mike really hit my heart and showed me the next right step. Ephesians 4:32 (NIV) challenged me, "Be kind and compassionate to one another, forgiving each other, just as in Christ God forgave you."

Jesus sees people and has compassion on them because they're "harassed and helpless, like sheep without a shepherd" (Matt. 9:36 NIV).

I prayed to see my parents like Jesus did.

The Next Right Step

My parents came into adulthood and parenting with their own hurts, conditioned mindsets, and imperfect humanness. Sin—theirs and mine—did its damage, but I was determined to stop giving it power over my life. So, forgiveness was the next right step. Focusing on the good things about my relationship with them, I chose to forgive my parents.

Since we weren't good at talking, I wrote them a letter. I thanked them for showing me the value of saving money, paying bills on time, and a solid work ethic. In the letter, I said I was grateful they taught me that God existed and thanked them for making our holidays special. Alcohol abuse in the home often ruins holiday gatherings and attaches painful memories to them. My parents made our holidays my best memories.

Warmed by a fire on Christmas Eve, we played Monopoly on the card table and chose prizes from the fireplace mantle. Nat King Cole's "Christmas Song"[1] crooned from the reel-to-reel tape player. We didn't have chestnuts roasting on a fire, but we nibbled on pretzel sticks, homemade fudge, and real not-Velveeta cheese. And we opened our gifts Christmas Eve because my dad couldn't wait.

But I digress. Back to the letter I wrote to my parents. I didn't mention their problems or how the letter helped me forgive them. My aim wasn't that they understand. My motive was not that they change or say sorry. I wanted to bless them for what they did right and mend some of the pain that my rebellion added to their struggle. So, I ended my letter with an apology for the stress I put on them.

It's not always easy, but showing mercy is vital to our emotional, spiritual, and even physical health. "Carrying the hurts and grudges of childhood memories is exhausting, nonproductive, and self-defeating."[2] A couple years after sending the letter to my parents, forgiveness saved me immense sorrow. Grief is difficult enough, without regret and bitterness added to it.

Forgiveness = No Regrets

Jeff, the boys, and I ran to catch our flight to Fort Wainwright, Alaska. Glancing back, I saw Dad a few yards behind us. With a hand on the wall to brace himself, he leaned a bit forward to catch his breath. I ran back to him to say good-bye. I sensed it was our last one.

It wasn't until my family was seat-belted on the plane that my tears started, grief mixed with gratitude. I wouldn't see my dad again, but was grateful for God's gift. The knowing made me hug him a tad longer and gave me courage to say, "I love you, Dad."

Three months later, my mom—worried that he was late for lunch—walked across the road to the river's backwaters. Dad's flat-bottom boat was there at water's edge tied to an oak tree. He'd been bailing out rainwater. It seems he took a break, sat on the boat's bow, then laid on his side to take a nap. His head rested on his hands, his glasses folded neatly next to him.

My forgiveness letter and our airport goodbye gave me peace and no regret. My last words to my dad were probably what he needed to hear and definitely what I needed to say. So, when Mom called to tell me he passed, my conscience was clear.

Forgiveness Sticks

I was eleven to eighteen years old in our family's most turbulent years. My parents were in mid life—late forty to mid-fifty. As I am now. This helps me understand them better. When memories stir up anger, I say, "Nope, I forgave them." They couldn't give what they didn't have. When I think about what we missed, I'm sad. To process this grief, I aim anger at our soul's enemy where it belongs. Sometimes it requires crying and yelling. But when I pause and breathe, my forgiveness foundation sticks. Mercy peels off another pain layer and heals my soul.

My friend, doing the work—feeling what we're feeling—is necessary to grow us into our divine design. The trick is not giving emotions the last word. We come back to simple truth and a raw choice. God forgives. We forgive. I know it's not easy, and it's definitely an on-going process.

The healthier we get in mind and spirit, the more we see messed-up mindsets and the depth of sin's damage. When mercy continues to flow, forgiveness frees us from going back into bondage. Unshackled, we grow further into our true selves. Our whole lives, there will be the daily niggling pet peeves to remind us to be a mercy giver. And we watch for the deep-rooted bitterness that surfaces too.

I pray my first and most important lessons as a babe in Christ empower you to stay in the fight. Come with me now, a few months later, as I'm confronted again with the choice to hold onto anger or give mercy. This time to a total stranger.

Mercy's Call

It was sunshine and softball season in Northern Arkansas. But hovering over me like a storm cloud was news of the recent kidnapping and murder of a local teen boy. I kept my sons, Justin and Preston, closer than usual at the ball field.

The ring of the aluminum bat turned my attention away from the boys just in time to see Jeff running to first base. He and a co-worker, Will, played on our church softball league. Part of a "Big Brother" program, Will was paired with twelve-year-old Anthony who came to the games and played with my sons.

Justin and Preston, now seven and four, loved hanging out with Anthony. They played their own three-person baseball game in the grass behind the bleachers. Anthony enjoyed giving the boys baseball tips. He grinned as he pitched umpteen times to Preston's wild swings. When he thumped Preston's head with a wayward throw, he cried like his heart broke. That kid won my heart that day. After a break with some cool water and comforting words, the boys were ready to play again. Wiping their cheeks with baby wipes, I reminded them to stay where I could see them.

The daily news reported another local boy's murder three years prior and connected it with the current crime. I stayed somewhat detached. It was all too bizarre—something for movies. But even at home, in our quiet neighborhood, I still didn't let my boys wander far.

<<<>>>

Our Thanksgiving plans distracted me until the local TV news aired a mom's plea for leads in her son's death. Her words, cold and mono-

CHAPTER FIVE: WHEN MERCY CALLS

toned, gripped me. Her eyes, unfocused under heavy eyelids, spoke to me. They screamed a sorrow unique to a mother's heart.

Nausea twisted my stomach. Clutching half-folded G.I. Joe pajamas to my chest, I wept for that mom while my boys slept, safe in the next room. Oblivious to the terror unfolding, their biggest concern was who'd wake first to pick Saturday morning cartoons.

Where's Anthony?

Our daily routine continued with softball games, school programs, and grocery shopping. Preston reached to me, bouncing on tiptoes, eager to sit in the cart and chat with our favorite grocery bagger. I'd wait in the longest line to hear Scott delight my son with conversations about Ninja Turtles and Masters of the Universe.

The newscasts eased up on reporting the murders. I prayed for the grieving moms and for the killer to be caught. Then, four days after Thanksgiving, Will showed up at a game without Anthony.

Jeff and I barely greeted Will before Justin dashed up with a bat slung over his shoulder and the extra glove for Anthony swinging from it. Preston raced to catch up with his brother, clutching a baseball with both hands.

Justin tugged on the strap of Will's bat bag. "Where's Anthony? Where's Anthony?"

Will sunk to one knee and rummaged through his gear. "Uh…he…had homework."

"Aw, bummer." Justin waved his arm at his little brother. "Come on, Pres. You'll have to pitch and field."

When the boys were beyond earshot, Will stopped fidgeting and hung his head. "Anthony is missing."

Fear pounded my heart and gnawed my gut. I shook my head. "Will…no. Anthony is not missing. He just hasn't called his mom… sometimes he does that, right?

"It's been two days."

In the hours and days ahead, I worried about Anthony but resisted the worst-case scenario. He'd show up at the ball field as though nothing happened—grinning and asking Justin for their ball game's imaginary stats.

Evil Closes In

For the next couple weeks, news coverage consumed me and stoked my fears. I stopped watching it until a local man was arrested. I sat, stunned, as the news reporter detailed his capture.

Scott, our sweet grocery bagger, was his last victim. Charles Walker, posing as a police officer, abducted him from the Food 4 Less parking lot, a quarter mile from our home. But Scott survived multiple stab wounds by pretending to be unconscious. When Walker unshackled his hands and feet to roll him into a pond, Scott overpowered him and escaped in Walker's car.

Though beyond grateful for Scott's survival, I wanted Walker to be tormented for the rest of his life and rot in jail.

Then, five days before Christmas, Anthony's body was found on the Army base near the airfield where Jeff and Will worked. Details surrounding his death matched those of Scott's story. The news, like a swirling black fog, dizzied me. In the previous weeks, I pin-balled between compassion for the victims' families and fear for my boys and our friend Anthony. Angry and shaking, I ranted. Fueled by hate, I prayed: "God, make this evil man suffer for what he's done to these boys."

As the trial progressed, my disgust for Walker grew so intense I could barely eat or sleep. He confessed to four murders but not Anthony's, which involved the Army base and federal criminal charges. One mother's cast-iron eyes glared at her son's killer as she vowed to never forgive him. I prayed she wouldn't let evil continue to rob her even as my own anger overwhelmed me.

That's when I realized how much this hatred blindsided me. It escalated, churning my stomach, even in prayer. My new faith was tested. Was I going to let this rob me of peace and joy? Would I give what was freely given to me? With evil's footprints so close to my home and my children, I wrestled with giving mercy to Anthony's killer. I begged for help. "God,

CHAPTER FIVE: WHEN MERCY CALLS

I'm struggling with this one. Big time. Please help me with all this hate."

God reminded me that before Jesus, I deserved contempt too. Although I never killed anyone, my sin was disgusting. I was a guilt-ridden sinner living in a self-made prison until "Just as I Am" wooed me out of the pew. God saw me broken, harassed, and helpless. His mercy showered compassion and forgiveness over me—soft and sweet—like a rose petal rain. I didn't earn or deserve any of it.

God coaxed me to see the serial killer with that same compassion. At his core, he was created in God's image. He was someone's lost child, helpless without a shepherd. A weak man, hopeless without a Savior. We were harassed by the same enemy and loved by the same Redeemer. My hatred and anger turned to pity. Not to excuse or absolve him of his vile crimes but to consider what may have caused such lost-ness and depravity.

That horrible season taught me to see people apart from their behavior. Yes, Jesus hates sin, but He died for souls. I am reminded of Romans 5:8, "God showed his great love for us by sending Christ to die for us while we were still sinners." For me *and* Charles Ray Walker. Leaving him to whatever consequences our God and the court system gave him, I was freed from hate. I was even able to pray that he'd find Jesus and seek forgiveness. Mercy transformed my heart and mind.

I'll never fully understand the suffering those grieving moms experienced. And I can't imagine the strength it would take for them to forgive. But I hope they did. For themselves. So they can know joy, peace, and hope. To maybe somehow redeem the pain and use it for good.

Ten Years Later

On August 10, 2000, Scott and the other boys' family members—including the mom whose desperate plea gripped me—watched Walker die of lethal injection. As Psalm 23 was read, he had no comment and showed no remorse.[3]

Anthony's death and two others remain unsolved, but Walker is still the prime suspect.[4] It's sad those boys didn't get justice. At least not how we see it in this world.

I don't know the boys' families or their journeys forward. Their unique struggle in the years before arrest to lethal injection and beyond—unimaginable. I think about them and pray grace for their lives.

Tears still come as I remember Anthony's wide grin and those dirty cheeks streaked by tears. And I'm inspired by Scott's kindness to my son in the grocery store checkout lane and especially by his courage in the face of evil. He said God picked him up and got him the last few feet to the car. "I honestly believe I was a vessel and God used me to stop this methodical killer."[5] Scott didn't remain a victim. His strength and faith defined him.

Is Mercy Calling You?

Not all mercy lessons are this dramatic, but the damage to an unforgiving soul is devastating. Bitterness seeps into our mind, will, and emotions—the core of who we are—and blocks us from knowing our true identity. Persistent anger and hatred toward people don't fit a child of God who wants to live out her divine destiny. In our call to holiness, to transform our minds and hearts to be like Jesus, there's no room for them.

It's time to get mad at evil. Haven't we been robbed enough? We can choose to stop giving people power over our past, present, and future. When we answer yes to Mercy's call, it frees a part of our God-given design. We not only see and empathize with another's struggle but we're also open to see God's compassion in our own.

That's what it did for me.

When mercy reigned, it changed how I see and think about others. But there was more. So much more. Remember, God doesn't dump all our junk in a heap at our feet and leave us to sort it out overnight. It sometimes takes years for His compassion to hush condemning voices.

Our first mercy lessons often deal with the obvious, outermost layers of unforgiveness. God wants us to know a deeper work of His love and kindness. It took fifteen years, walking alongside Jesus, to see I needed to show mercy to my worst enemy.

CHAPTER FIVE: WHEN MERCY CALLS

STUDY QUESTIONS

In your desire to grow and reflect God's character, continue to take inventory of your heart. What unhealthy motives and mindsets block you from living your divine design? A Southern expression from the pastor who led me to Jesus still holds true: "What's down in the well comes up in the bucket." Bitterness and unforgiveness will control your thoughts, attitudes, and behavior.

See Your Thoughts

Pause here and pray. Remember, you are safe in God's presence. He is with you and He is good.

Ask Him to bring to mind anyone you need to forgive.

Maybe it's someone you've forgiven but there's a new layer of hurt God wants to heal.

Are there thoughts that hinder you from even wanting to forgive? If so, write them down.

Maybe your thoughts are similar to the comments below;

"I'll never forgive them."
"They don't deserve it."
"I don't want them in my life."

"They should apologize and ask for forgiveness."
'They haven't changed and they aren't sorry.'
"I just want to forget it and move on with my life."

While these may feel empowering—are they really?

What emotions do these mindsets bring up and out?

How does this emotional loop keep you stuck in bitterness and unforgiveness?

In what ways does it rob you of your present peace?

How does this affect relationships with people you love, including your relationship with God?

Consider how the mindsets listed in #3 and their emotional pull prevent you from forgiving people and hide who God made you to be.

CHAPTER FIVE: WHEN MERCY CALLS

Set Your Mind

Lord, I want to be done with anything that keeps me from experiencing more of You and Your purpose for my life.

Let's dive in and let the Father's heart transform your thinking. Let's look at His mercy, empathy, and compassion.

Read Ephesians 4:31–32. What is the healthiest way to respond to people?

When your heart and mind are set on kindness and compassion, you gain many spiritual benefits like peace and joy. But this verse narrows down your need to forgive to one simple and compelling reason. What is it?

In Matthew 9:36, how does Jesus—our Good Shepherd—see people?

How does His heart respond to them?

See Jesus' sympathy for people's spiritual condition. In seeking to understand mercy and forgive others, consider their spiritual condition too. And remember; we've all been like sheep who lack the ability to make right choices, and we're vulnerable to attacks.

Look up Romans 5:8 and fill in the blanks; "But God showed his _____ _____ for us by sending Christ to die _____ while we were _____ _____" (NLT).

When sinless Jesus died in your place so you could be right with God, what was your heart condition?

Our sin created a chasm between God and us. Jesus died to bridge that gap. He offered this gift before we even knew we needed a Savior. Grace, mercy, and compassion preceded our desire and our decision to follow Him. We didn't earn or deserve any of it.

Read Colossians 3:12–15 below. Keep in mind that Paul is speaking to us about our attitude and behavior toward fellow believers.

"Since God chose you to be the holy people he loves, you must clothe yourselves with tenderhearted mercy, kindness, humility, gentleness, and patience. Make allowance for each other's faults, and forgive anyone who offends you. Remember, the Lord forgave you, so you must forgive others. Above all, clothe yourselves with love, which binds us all together in perfect harmony. And let the peace that comes from Christ rule in your hearts. For as members of one body you are called to live in peace. And always be thankful."

God chose you and gave you a whole new wardrobe. What is your new self supposed to wear?

While these beautiful grace gifts are free, they do come with responsibility. Christ wants to shine in you and through you. Hear what Paul wrote to believers in Corinth:

"What a wonderful God we have—he is the Father of our Lord

CHAPTER FIVE: WHEN MERCY CALLS

Jesus Christ, the source of every mercy, and the one who so wonderfully comforts and strengthens us in our hardships and trials. And why does he do this?" (2 Cor. 1:3 TLB).

So we can be comfy, warm, and fuzzy? Nope. Let's read a bit further.

"So that when others are troubled, needing our sympathy and encouragement, we can pass on to them this same help and comfort God has given us" (2 Cor. 1:4 TLB).

We get to take off layers of bitterness and unforgiveness and put on empathy, understanding, and sympathy. But this doesn't mean we have to allow someone back into our lives. Forgiveness does not always end in reconciliation. In this case, it's for our own mental and spiritual health.

It's important for us to remember that forgiveness is not a feeling, it's a decision. And often, it's a raw choice to choose it every time a name, a thought, or a situation comes up.

So we ask, do I want to stay shackled to people who harmed me? Do I want to keep giving them power over my heart, mind, and life?

We ask God to help us release the need for payback and to stop waiting for an apology that may never come.

Writing a letter to my parents reinforced the decision to forgive them. Decades later, that strong foundation held me up when God revealed more layers. Each time, I forgave a little deeper until I finally empathized with their pain.

Consider writing a letter. You don't have to send it. Even if the person has died, putting words on paper may help you release unhealthy thoughts and painful emotions.

Seek & Speak What's True

I am defined by I AM. I am able to forgive because God forgave me.

Because God, _____

_____ , I am _____

_____ .

Celebrate

God, Thank you for reaching through the darkness of every human heart—including mine. Your compassion, mercy, and capacity to forgive boggle my mind. Teach me to see others as You do. Help me aim anger where it truly belongs—at the enemy of every human soul. I am so done giving people power over my past, present, and future. Thank you for mercy and forgiveness that transforms my heart and mind.

CHAPTER 6

When Mercy Follows: New Every Morning

"As adults we must reach a point of reconciliation with our stories. Eventually we come to a fork in the road when we're faced with a choice. Is our story just a story— or is it who we are?" ~ Barrie Davenport[1]

There I was, at forty-one, typing an email and wailing like a toddler whose ice cream just slipped from her cone. Tears blindsided me mid-sentence as I remembered a girl from my past.

You know the type—lies, drugs, alcohol, careless sex. She disgusted me and wreaked chaos in my life. Reminding me of sin-stained memories, she robbed me of sleep. Even after she embraced God's forgiveness and radically changed, I hated her and tried to forget her. But Jesus wouldn't let me.

I knew other girls, lost and in crisis mode. I counseled them, prayed with them, held their shaky hands and cried with them. Why the struggle to forgive this one little girl?

Because she was me.

Earlier that morning, I read from Proverbs 5. A section entitled "Warning Against Adultery" triggered shame, and I wrestled with condemning thoughts, especially in verse 6 (NIV):

"She gives no thought to the way of life;"
And my inner critic pounced...*I was such a whore*...
"her paths wander aimlessly," ...*a liar and a lush*...
"but she does not know it."
And my mean self-talk got confused.... *Wait... What?*
"*She does not know it*" (author's emphasis).
I let these words linger long enough to really think about them.

My friend, when we hear self-judgment and self-hatred, it's time to stop. It's time to see ourselves through God's eyes and hear with His ears.

So, that's what I did. I dug out my teen writings and spread them out on my bedroom floor. I ran with that girl again down the wooded path to the fallen tree on the riverbank.

Behind the words, let's hear her heart:
What's right? *I want to do right.*
What's the point? *I need to know there's hope.*
What's my purpose? *I need to know why I exist.*
Who am I? *Who I'm becoming is not who I want to be.*
Whose am I? *I ache to belong to someone.*

Pretty deep stuff. Do you sense hope and despair in a tug-of-war here? We all wrestle with these questions. They scream, "This is not the real me! There's got to be more!"

We Don't Know What We Don't Know

We didn't know where to find answers. When we see God as harsh and detached, we aren't good enough to approach Him. We are empty and hungry. So, we reach for whatever or whoever we think will fill us. We cry out for connection, a safe place to give our hearts. Someone who will really see us, hear us, and know us. Someone to trust.

Writing was my voice. Silent and sad, yet strong, it kept my face above water. Yet, even my darkest words mention a light. It was always dim, always distant—something good just beyond my reach.

I didn't know it was God. I didn't know how to get off the crooked path that was leading to spiritual death. I didn't know where to find real love, comfort, and value. So how did I know there was more to life than my party girl image? How did I know I wasn't destined to be tossed aside and brokenhearted?

Because we are created for life, not death. We are made to live—truly live—with God forever. And our soul—our inmost being—knows it.

We Are Made for More

Our Designer didn't make us to satisfy our deepest needs in men, alcohol, attention, or adrenaline. Our good work and our families can't do it for us either. His love is woven into each thread of our DNA so we crave connection with Him. We aren't just body and intellect. We are spirit. God breathed life into us, creating a spirit-to-Spirit relationship. That's where we find our sweet spot, our purest selves. Bonded to the One who knows us from the inside out and is crazy in love with us.

Also woven into our soul is a desire to know the future—to know there's more. Our spirit is made for eternity. The things of time are temporary and cannot fully and permanently satisfy. Ever. They can't fill us or fix our problems. We're wired with these desires to find peace, purpose, and abundant life in our divine design.

Our questions—even our doubts—are normal and healthy and keep us seeking. But being disconnected from God creates chaos in our minds. And living lies on the outside kills us on the inside because we fight against who we're created to be, whole and free. Our original sin nature wars with our original glory. Maybe you relate to my teen struggle—and the adult struggle to forgive yourself.

After analyzing my adolescent mind, my emotions needed a break. I got up from the bedroom floor, left the papers scattered on the carpet, and hurried to my kitchen for some baking therapy. I cranked the volume on the radio. Soon praise music and the scent of cinnamon calmed my heart. Then a news report interrupted the sweet distraction.

"A mother has thrown her children from a bridge..." Surely I heard it wrong. At least that's what I told myself. I kept mixing pumpkin bread until the headline repeated and I couldn't ignore it. I cried for those innocent babies and my fists hit the flour-dusted countertop. Anger and disgust toward their mom welled up. *How could she do that? How could she be so deceived?*

Because, like me, she believed lies, evident through her actions, and they broke her. They might have taken root in her mind. Chaos ensued and dragged her to a desperate place. Though our stories are different, I know how it feels to be deceived and harassed. To make horrible decisions and want death to take away the pain. So, I aimed my anger at evil. The father of lies is the enemy of her soul and mine. Mercy moved my disgust away from her to her sin. Then I prayed for her.

Which Brings Us Back to My Email Meltdown

Before all this emotional work, my interrupted morning email was supposed to be a simple thank you to a friend in Texas who counseled me on the phone the day before. Our recent move to Illinois after Jeff's twenty-one year Army career left me depressed and looking for purpose. God wanted to grow me further into His design, but I needed to get out of the way.

As I typed again, explaining my emotion-packed morning—the Proverbs passage, the looking back, and the outburst in my kitchen—the questions spilled out: "Why is it easier to show mercy to others? Why haven't I shown myself the same compassion?" That's when it hit me. Fourteen to twenty-six-year-old-me deserved mercy too. And my heart broke for her.

I read Proverbs 5:6 again in The Message Bible and personalized it. I didn't have "a clue about Real Life, about who [I was] or where [I was] going" (author's paraphrase). I didn't know a heavenly Father was loving me, seeking me, and patiently waiting for me. With arms wide.

My snarky self-talk changed. *Robin, You weren't horrible. You were human. Simply seeking love and hope, healing and purpose.*

My hands crossed over my chest to keep the words from missing my heart. I closed my eyes to let new thoughts—*true* thoughts—hammer at decades of nasty self-talk. I was a blubbering, self-forgiving, snotty mess. You know, one of those good, ugly cries.

And this was years after finding Jesus and new life in that little Arkansas church. Although forgiven and freed from of a lot of junk, it took over a decade to see and begin to deal with my sneaky self-hatred. Much of my identity was still shame-based, not mercy-based. It was rooted in my old lost self, someone whose sin and situation didn't even exist anymore.

My friend, does self-hatred shackle you to your past? Why does it take so long to forgive ourselves? When we let condemnation shout louder than compassion, shame becomes a liar and a thief.

Guilt + Shame = Good

While they feel terrible, guilt and shame are meant to be good emotions. God wired them into us. Are we sometimes guilty? Yes. Do we sometimes need to feel shame? Yes, in the sense that we feel humiliation or distress when we know we've done wrong or behaved foolishly. It's good we feel bad about our wrong actions, but we aren't meant to stay there. Godly sorrow, sadness for our sin, is healthy. Scripture and the Spirit reveal our wrong so we can turn away from it.

This healthy conviction from the Holy Spirit shows us an action or a thought process we need to change. It inspires hope, offers correction, and opens up the way out.

Of course, guilt and shame have their twisted counterparts. Anything God intends for our benefit, evil perverts. Our souls' enemy uses shame to condemn us so we forget our power and stay chained to our failures. There's no offer of correction or a way out from under it. Guilt and shame plus condemnation point at us and stir up a false sense of hopelessness.

This is how shame tangles truth with lies. Guilt says you did something wrong. False shame says there's something wrong with you. It lines right up with our less-than-others mindset, like somehow we're inferior because we fail. *I'm an idiot. I'm a loser. I'm so stupid.* These shame-based thoughts are automatic and we roll with them.

It's time to slow their roll, get quiet, and listen to why we won't forgive ourselves.

Loud Imaginings Appearing Real

LIAR #1: "I've gone too far."
Child of God, we cannot fall too far. In our lowest low, God is there. His unfailing love—did you hear that? His *un*-failing love. It's *un*-ending, *un*-wavering, and *un*-conditional. It has no restrictions or requirements. Unlike human love, there's no delaying, no hesitating, and no termination date. It's not fickle, never too late, and it won't dump us. God's love rescues us from the deepest, darkest pit. Even the one we dig ourselves.

LIAR #2: "No one else deals with this. I'm alone."
We've all sunk to dirty depths and our own personal hells. Every. Single. One of us. Yes, even her—the one raised in church. She may have the just-right jeans, a huge house, powerful prayers, and the appear-to-be-perfect family, but she battles with something or someone or some thought. You may not see the dirt under her manicured nails from her own pit digging. And if she's out of the pit, she's still smack in the middle of her own messy-beautiful, real-life story.

LIAR #3: "I can't forgive myself because I *did* know better."
Remember the lovable/scandalous hero/villain King David? The one whose lust and power took Bathsheba, impregnated her, and then killed her husband? Yep. That Davie who cracked Goliath's skull and who God chose to be Israel's king. I believe David knew better but fell far. Way far. The Psalms are full of his writing therapy. At his lowest lows, he weeps over his sin and fears and guilt and shame. We see him reclaim his power as he reaches out and reconnects with God. Beautiful, gut-wrenching stuff.

So, we don't need to hang our heads. Shame is not our name. Maybe it's the ninety-seventh time we've cried over the same sin, asking God to forgive us. Maybe we hesitate to ask because we're afraid

CHAPTER SIX: WHEN MERCY FOLLOWS

to fail again. It's okay. We are human. God's imperfect children. His wonderful works-in-progress.

It may be the ninety-eighth time when we're tired enough and wise enough not only to know better, but to grab on to God's best. To not just try to *do* it, but to *be* it. When Mercy called us, He knew what He was getting into. He knew how long it would take for new thoughts and habits to get from our heads to our hearts. And if others learn it the first time? That's cool. They have their own unique stories.

Dear sister in Christ, don't beat yourself up. We make mistakes. It doesn't mean we are mistakes. Our tears show tender hearts and a desire to be better. Our hearts aren't hardened, they're being repaired. Our minds aren't crazy, they're being changed. Rewired and transformed.

But how long will it take us to admit what we're thinking or doing isn't working? How much living proof do we need to see it's not who we are? We tell pride to move aside and ask God to forgive us. And please don't say we can't forgive ourselves. We can, we just *don't*.

It is a raw choice. We forgive even when it doesn't feel all warm and fuzzy. Because we know that self-hatred, self-judgment, and self-punishment don't belong to our divine design.

Don't give up. We're taking our power back. We can recognize and resist the LIARs. We keep moving forward and we remain teachable. As we aim for moral courage and personal integrity, there's always room to grow and *know even better*.

LIAR #4: "If I was a stronger Christian, I wouldn't be tempted so much."

My friend, temptation ≠ sin. We are dealing with powerful spiritual forces. Light against dark. Good versus evil. When I was a baby Christian, my friend Sharon warned me in her sweet Southern drawl: "The devil is as real as you and me sittin' here."

We don't have to look far to see that's true.

First Peter 5:8 shows us that he "prowls around like a roaring lion looking for someone to devour." While we don't want to underestimate the enemy, we don't want to overestimate him either. Because when Jesus defeated death, He knocked those pointy teeth right out of that foul mouth. Like a jealous ex-boyfriend wanting to lure us away from our new love, Satan's quite literally a damned, sore loser. When we ask Jesus Christ to save us and be our daily guide, we beat death and the grave. Empowered by His Spirit living in us, we already have victory. Our enemy is a toothless tyrant, blowing hot air. Tempting and posturing, but not winning unless we let him.

James 1:14–15 tells us, "Temptation comes from our own desires, which entice us and drag us away. These desires give birth to sinful actions. And when sin is allowed to grow, it gives birth to death." And we think our *physical* birth stories are scary. Sin-birth is downright terrifying because it slowly kills our souls. We become spiritual zombies. And it starts in our hearts and minds.

This internal fight—our desires for love, comfort, acceptance—along with pride, greed and self-centeredness get pretty ugly when we let them entice us away from our divine design. Our victory, life over death, is waiting for us to claim. Not just for our minds, but for our identities as God's children.

Our enemy tempts us to doubt who we are and Whose we are. He did it to Jesus too. We hear Satan's harassing words in Matthew 4:6 (NIV). "*If* you are the Son of God…" I emphasize *if* because I imagine that's how he said it.

Does he hiss in your ear too? *If you are a daughter of God…you won't be tempted to think that, do that, say that.*

Temptation is not sin. And while it's not fun, it is good. In *My Utmost for His Highest*, Oswald Chambers explains, "Temptation is not something we can escape; in fact, it is essential to the well-rounded life of a person."

So, let's change how we think about it. Instead of seeing temptation as an attack, let's use it as information. It reminds us of the sewage we'd eventually sink into apart from Jesus. We can take a moment to praise Him for lifting us up and for giving us all the fruit of His Spirit, including self-control. Temptation is good information. It shows us where to take the fight and where to stay vigilant. It teaches us places or people to avoid.

Since temptation is normal and inevitable, we don't need to think of it as a negative thing. It only has what power we give it. We remember it has no claim on us. We resist it, flip it, and use it as a beautiful opportunity to rely on God as we grow in faith, wisdom, and resilience.

Yes, the struggle is real.

We're born with a fallen nature and live in a fallen world. Sometimes, even as God's liberated children, we get distracted and sidetracked. Though aiming for holiness, we simply miss the mark. We pop off with wrong words, motives, actions, and attitudes. I'm grateful for the Holy Spirit who nudges us to make it right. He empowers us to do a one-eighty. We turn from pride, apologize, and ask forgiveness.

Then there's the more serious side of sin. Sometimes, it's a willful choice. That deliberate sin says, "I'm gonna do it anyway." We ignore the Spirit's nudges. Pride pulls us to think we're better than others. We are indifferent and self-indulgent. We gossip and disguise it as concern or a prayer request. We tell *little* lies and get drunk to feel better. We accept an over-eating habit and eat another donut. Fear and jealousy provoke us to hate.

While pleasing our selfish nature, we become our own worst enemy. Will we move forward to grow and know better? Or stay and settle for half-living until we're not really living at all?

Check out another quote from Oswald Chambers' *My Utmost for His Highest*: "Satan does not tempt us just to *make us do wrong things—he tempts us to make us lose what God has put into us through regeneration* namely, the possibility of being of value to God. He does not come to us on the premise of tempting us to sin, but on the premise of shifting our point of view, and only the Spirit of God can detect this as a temptation of the devil" (emphasis added).

That sneaky joy sucker is after our inner life. The core of who we are. If he wins our minds, he gets the rest of us—our will, our emotions, our spirit, and eventually our body. He tempts us to hand over what Jesus gave us when we started this journey. Our new life. Our new spirit, rebooted and regenerated with the power to live free and to lead others to freedom. Evil tempts us away from our holy call and our God-given identity.

See how he does it? Since every sin begins in our mind, we're tempted to shift our perspective and filter thoughts through fear and selfishness. That messes with our beliefs, desires, attitudes, and actions. When we lose our truest selves, we lose the power to lead others to their full redemptive potential. Temptations are an attack on the life of Jesus in us. But we remember that new life He gave us is a done deal. It empowers us to recognize sin and temptation and truly live with a clean conscience, from the inside-out.

Be encouraged. James 1:12 tells us that "God blesses those who patiently endure testing and temptation. Afterward they will receive the crown of life that God has promised to those who love him."

Take back your power and wear your crown, Warrior Princess. Our inner desires and self-talk are sneaky and powerful. Maybe you're thinking, *But you don't know my story.* You are so right. But I do know pain and fear and humiliation. I know confusion and hopelessness and loneliness. And I am with you in this fierce fight for our minds. We aren't that different. We will be stronger on the other side of our battles, if we don't give up.

God promises. God provides. He is present and He is our Defender.

By faith, we ask the Holy Spirit to help us. W. Phillip Keller, in his book *A Shepherd Looks at Psalm 23,* says, "I invite the Holy Spirit to come into my conscious and subconscious mind to monitor my thought-life."

Life in the Spirit

"So now there is no condemnation for those who belong to Christ Jesus. And because you belong to him, the power of the life-giving Spirit has freed you from the power of sin that leads to death. The law of Moses was unable to save us because of the weakness of our sinful nature. So God did what the law could not do. He sent his own Son in a body like the bodies we sinners have. And in that body God declared

CHAPTER SIX: WHEN MERCY FOLLOWS

an end to sin's control over us by giving his Son as a sacrifice for our sins. He did this so that the just requirement of the law would be fully satisfied for us, who no longer follow our sinful nature but instead follow the Spirit.

"Those who are dominated by the sinful nature *think about* sinful things, but those who are controlled by the Holy Spirit *think about* things that please the Spirit. So letting your sinful nature control your mind leads to death. But letting the Spirit control your mind leads to life and peace" (Romans 8:1–6, author's emphasis).

Hallelujah! Willful wrong choices don't have to be a constant part of our lives. We are no longer slaves. The roles are reversed. We master sin. It listens to us and Christ in us. When Jesus' Spirit convicts us and our minds stay connected to our power source, the life-giving Spirit, we choose abundant life, free from sin's control.

We don't want to excuse sin, but we can't let it condemn us either. Let's not make our soul's enemy too little or too big. The devil doesn't make us do it. We are not puppets or victims. Our thoughts and self-talk determine what we do with guilt and shame. What we do with guilt and shame determines how we define ourselves. We can't let condemnation shout louder than compassion.

Defined by Mercy

Romans 8:1 is worth repeating: "There is no condemnation for those who belong to Christ Jesus." Zilch. Zero. Left unchecked, shame says, *"You're hopeless."* And we imagine our Father with folded arms and furrowed eyebrows. He's tapping a foot and shaking His head. Maybe our earthly father would do this, but not our God.

The Holy Spirit's conviction has a good purpose. It convinces us of sin and compels us to repent, to turn away from it. It's a check in our spirit to direct us—not to defeat us or define us. We use that conviction to repent, to turn away from sin. *I shouldn't have done that. I'm so sorry. Oh God, help me.* We see our Father run to us with arms wide. "My daughter, don't be afraid. Come, sit with me." Nestled into God's high opinion of us, our identity is rooted and nurtured in mercy. We're defined and protected in the eternal grip of unconditional Love.

We are unstoppable when we know who we are and Whose we are. The enemy of our soul knows as we grow and live in our divine design, he loses. Big time.

When our self-talk transforms to God-talk, it changes everything. If you hear, *You're not good enough*. Jesus says, *Yes, you are more than good. You are loved, accepted, and adored. Let go and forgive.* No one benefits from self-hatred, self-punishment, and self-judgment.

Transformed by Truth

The day I began my self-forgiveness journey, my mind was changed. When truth trickled into my heart, I didn't see myself defined by my sin. A lush running after false peace with mind-numbing chemicals. A liar using deceit to get temporary fixes. A whore finding counterfeit love. I saw a scared girl. Not weak, but resilient and determined to be better. Not a casualty, but a survivor wise enough to sense her Creator in nature's horizon light.

Thirty years after my teen writings, I finally saw the real me—a good person, spiritually dying. I found a fighter and a strong rebel. Those are pieces of me I don't want to run from anymore but to remember and embrace.

Do you catch yourself cringing at certain parts of your life? That person reminds us that the fight is fierce and we are made for more. We respect her for hearing Mercy's call above the chaos and for knowing someone better was hiding under lying layers. Our God-given identity grows as we accept our rebel side, take back our power, and let God use it.

Driving around my old stomping grounds, I used to see what I was running *from*. Now, the bars, dirt roads, and my wooded path remind me Who I was running *to*. I remember fishing calm waters under autumn sunrises. I remember choreographing pom-pom routines and disco dancing and rolling backwards down a ditch on a country road when I was too far from a bathroom. Then there's the Tastee-Freez where fifteen-

CHAPTER SIX: WHEN MERCY FOLLOWS

year-old Jeff flipped burgers and told my brother he'd marry me someday.

I don't know if that little river town will ever feel like home, but that's okay.

If people and places trigger bad memories for you, I challenge you to see the good and choose to remember the One you were running to. Our past was our zig-zag journey to Jesus. The next time our thoughts go on auto-play, we interrupt them and attach new thoughts to old haunts. In doing so, we show up grown-up and reclaim our power.

It's often years into our journey before we see God's past pursuit. To understand our lost self is to see how we layered up and limped into adulthood. We look back only to move forward. We go there so we can get out of there.

We don't have to know where shame and self-hatred started. Or how or when they covered us like old wool blankets from a moldy basement. What's more important than their origins is that we now see them and heal them.

God's invisible qualities still pursue us. He is relentless. Our lives aren't without pain, but we know the Light that always shows up. Jesus is our steady hope and abiding peace. Not only reachable, but abiding with us.

Remember the poem I wrote for Ashley Nicole? Reading it decades later, I see myself different. God didn't reject me, I rejected me. When I see Him there with me, I look past my problems and into my pain. I see the hurting girl. No condemning voice. No negative emotions or nasty self-talk.

In this process of self-forgiveness, we remove judgment from memories. We change how we think about them, and they help us see how God sees us. We learn to recognize lies and love ourselves. This is a gentle exfoliation of another dead layer. As self-forgiveness replaces shame, we continue to change unhealthy mindsets and reveal more of our divine design.

STUDY QUESTIONS

"As the trees show us the beauty in letting go of their leaves, let us show the world our own beauty by letting go of all that holds us back from becoming who we truly are." — Siobhan Kukolic, "How Beautiful Letting Go Can Be"

Do you label yourself with words God has never spoken about you?

Since we're created in His image, does harsh self-criticism insult God's workmanship?

See Your Thoughts

Before Jesus, you didn't know your path was leading you to spiritual death. Rebellion—whether you know Jesus or not—slowly kills your soul. Sin pulls you away from the person God created. You feel guilt and shame because, deep down, you know you're made for more. When you ask God to forgive you, He does. But you often don't forgive yourself. It's time to slow your roll, get quiet, and listen to your thoughts.

When you think of yourself—past or present—what do you say to her? Write out your thoughts.

CHAPTER SIX: WHEN MERCY FOLLOWS

Are these words healing or harmful? Graced-based or shame-based?

I hope your self-talk is good, healthy, and true. But if it's more like the shaming names I used to call myself, I pray you will pause here and consider these questions:

Is it easier to be kind to others than to yourself?

In what ways do you hold yourself up to a perfect standard?

Do you need to give yourself some grace and forgive yourself?

If you won't forgive your own humanness, you disagree with God as though Jesus' sacrifice wasn't sufficient for you. When you let condemnation shout louder than compassion, shame becomes a liar and a thief.

If you hate and berate parts of yourself, you allow your soul's enemy to define you. And you know he has absolutely nothing to add to your divine design. He only steals, kills, and destroys. So, ask yourself:

Am I allowing the Holy Spirit to monitor my thought-life? Or am I letting it run around like unsupervised toddlers on a busy street?

UNCOVER YOUR DIVINE DESIGN

Who defines me? Is my identity rooted in sin's shame or God's grace?

When you hear self-judgment and self-hatred, it's time to stop. It's time to see yourself through God's eyes.

Set Your Mind

See who you are in Christ and renew your mind. Read and reflect on the following Scripture.

"So now there is no condemnation for those who belong to Christ Jesus. And because you belong to him, the power of the life-giving Spirit has freed you from the power of sin that leads to death" (Romans 8:1–2).

In John 8, we see the beautiful story of a woman caught in adultery. Read it in verses 1–11. Watch how Jesus ministers to her.

Let's see how Jesus protects her and cares for her soul, beginning with verse 3:

"As he was speaking, the teachers of religious law and the Pharisees brought a woman who had been caught in the act of adultery. They put her in front of the crowd.

'Teacher,' they said to Jesus, 'this woman was caught in the act of adultery. The law of Moses says to stone her. What do you say?'" (vv 3–4).

Jesus knelt in the sand and wrote in the dust with his finger. The men demanded an answer so He stood up and said,

"All right, but let the one who has never sinned throw the first stone!' Then he stooped down again and wrote in the dust" (v 7).

Can you hear the stones hitting the sand as her now-silent accusers drop them and slip away…one by one? Until it's just Jesus and the woman in the middle of the crowd.

"Then Jesus stood up again and said to the woman, 'Where are your accusers? Didn't even one of them condemn you?'

"'No, Lord,' she said.

"And Jesus said, 'Neither do I. Go and sin no more'" (vv 10–11).

When you don't give yourself the gift of forgiveness, who is holding the stone? Who is your accuser?

I wish we knew what Jesus wrote in the sand that day. Some guess He wrote the names and sins of the men who pushed the woman to the front of the crowd. I like that.

I also like to believe Jesus wrote a message something like this to the woman and to us:

"I see your humiliation. Do not be ashamed. Drop the stone."

Seek & Speak What's True

I am defined by I AM. Because I am made in God's image—whose thoughts toward me are always compassionate, never condemning—I am able to love and forgive myself.

Because God, _____

_____ , I am _____

_____ .

Celebrate

"The faithful love of the LORD never ends! His mercies never cease. Great is his faithfulness; his mercies begin afresh each morning" (Lamentations 3:22–23)

Forgiving Father, I am grateful that no matter how a day unfolds, I can hit the refresh button. Your kindness is always with me. When my mind labels me with words that You wouldn't say, remind me to replace them with the truth: I am free forever from condemnation and can never be separated from Your love. Please continue to teach me to be kind and patient with myself—to hush my inner critic and harsh self-judgments.

CHAPTER 7

Life Interrupted: A Holistic Meltdown

"As a general rule, if you are prone to melodramatic meltdowns, please avoid purchasing a webcam for any reason." ~ Ray William Johnson, Comedian & YouTuber

Ever feel so tired and so done that you think you'll never get unstuck? Problems and pressures squeeze you tight and you almost lose your mind? Me too. Right smack in the middle of telling you my story, I hit a transition in birthing this book baby, and it turned sideways in the birth canal. Yes. Ouch.

I pushed and strained and cried and screamed. But sheer willpower and raw stubbornness weren't enough to squeeze out my next chapter. All I did was rearrange the mess and stare at the computer screen. It had to change, but I just wanted it done, wrapped up and kept in a safe little box.

Change is scary, isn't it? That's why we fight it.

It's four years since I heard the question that left me speechless and wondering: If I woke up tomorrow and could do the one thing I've always wanted, what would I do?

I left the counseling room that day all smiley and excited to find out who I was under all those unhealthy childhood messages and mindsets. Looking in my mini-van's rearview mirror, I had an epiphany. "I'll write a book."

What was I thinking?

"God, I'm tired. I'm done. So done with giving and giving and grieving and loving and living with fear and people and messes and a neurotic cat and writing about hard stuff…I quit…please let me quit."

Empty and exhausted, I burned out. I hit a holistic meltdown of mind, body, and spirit. A desperate face-to-yoga-mat moment. And all I could do was stop.

How did I get there?

The same way we all do. It all simply becomes too, too much. Crises come and shake us to our core. In the months before my meltdown, life shifted big time.

By this time in my story, my mind and body were fueled by an inner fire. I was the poster girl for peri-menopause, eight years into what my mom's generation calls *The Change*. Biggest. Understatement. Ever. *The Chaos* is more like it.

Those lovely ebbing hormones hit us with a whirlwind of confusion and the inside-out burn of a volcano. As my hot flashes, night sweats, and sleeplessness subsided a bit, my emotional symptoms intensified. My moods were in full swing and it was hard to focus on anything.

Then in the first couple weeks of December, life kicked up a few degrees. My sister, diagnosed with aggressive breast cancer, almost died from her first round of chemo. This came as I started to see and accept the reality of Mom's dementia.

She called every day for a week to ask why I wasn't there. Though I wrote my next visit on her calendar, she waited and worried. Then she just forgot how to use the phone. It's heart breaking, isn't it—to lose them in bits and pieces?

My friend, even when we know God and the peace that passes understanding, we all have a breaking point. A shift so extreme it stretches us to a whole new level of faith. Mine came right smack in the mid-

CHAPTER SEVEN: LIFE INTERRUPTED

dle of this crazy changing season. Just as Jeff and I were getting closer to an empty nest.

With Hannah, our adventurous and independent daughter, living in Italy for a few months, we got a peek at how life would be in a couple years when she'd graduate college. And we liked it. A lot. Small messes, lots of quiet, calm routine, and walking around in our undies. Yes, sign me up.

But two days before Christmas, our life careened from calm to chaotic. Three simple words rocked our world and my faith. "Mom, I'm pregnant." Hannah sobbed and something in me broke. Hugging my girl, I dug deep. Because that's what mommas do, right? We fix and protect and nurture. We make everyone and everything okay.

Hannah's due date gave us seven weeks, but little Alexander Saul gave us only three to prepare our minds and our almost-empty nest. One moment life was slow, cozy, and predictable, then BOOM. It wasn't.

I know you've been there. Life's sudden and unplanned events spin your head and break your heart. Knocked dizzy, you're plopped into an unwanted season. Perhaps you went into fight mode, like me. Momma Bear took over. To help my baby-girl-now-mom care for a newborn and make room for diapers and bottles and a crib, oh my. But we'd made it through tougher times, right?

I figured I'd take a year off from all other commitments. From leading teens and Bible studies and volunteering for events. Surely by then we'd conquer and have it all together, neat and tidy. I knew how to manage a home and was a pro at managing family crisis. We survived thirteen household moves and Jeff's deployment to Iraq. And when our sons, in their own crises and life transitions, moved their families in? We nailed that too.

I knew how to process pain and shattered hopes. After all, we buried a child. So, I held on to past proof of God's grace and its promise that we would be okay. We'd soldier on and get through this.

I plowed forward to get ahead of it all and do it all perfect. To blog and write a book and a newspaper column and to organize my home and balance my pinging hormones and be a good wife and a strong Christian and help my sisters with my mom and care for Alex and Hannah and be there for my sons and their wives and those four grandbabies and work hard at the candy store and…and…I didn't slow down enough to really process the broken pieces in me.

Warrior to Worrier

When we strive to simply survive, our blessings become burdens. In the months after Alex was born, the struggle got very real. This good fight collided with all of my unhealthy mindsets. Voiceless, victim, chameleon, and scarcity hung on tight. My need to be valued and to speak up and be heard was at an all-time high and it was an all-out battle. Parts of me felt like a little girl again. Powerless and paralyzed in managing my home, my writing, myself. I felt stuck, exhausted, and closed-in.

Fighting not to shrink back and stay under the struggle, I swung from low lows to high highs. My temper came back, explosive and irrational, like when my boys were small. When alone, I vented. When not, I stuffed. Resentment boiled in me when my daughter's cat yacked on the carpet or meeeyyoowwwed at zero-dark:30 BC (before coffee).

I tried hard to get ahead of the messes, the sadness, the confusion, the chapters. It seemed that everyone and everything worked against me. My changing body, once predictable, wouldn't cooperate. The book was changing and it scared me. I was changing and it scared me. My future plans were changing and it ticked me off. I couldn't fix it or figure it all out.

So, this strong Christian woman who took pride in not being a worrier—became one. Big time. This girl, who was told she has a non-anxious presence, lost it. Even Wonder Woman has her limits, ya'll. I gave 'til I gave out. This warrior slipped from attack mode into survival mode.

<<<>>>

Underlying tension and anxiety tell us our chaos is our new norm. We'll *never* get ahead of the messes. We'll never get ourselves or our families balanced out. Nothing will ever feel safe and predictable again. LIARs are loud, aren't they? They drive us to a good ol' face-

CHAPTER SEVEN: LIFE INTERRUPTED

to-the-floor meltdown.

Mine went something like this: "God, I quit. Plleeaasse let me quit. This wasn't supposed to be our story. This wasn't supposed to be her story."

When sadness and anger come from a deeper place, it's time to be seen and heard and healed there. We need to slow our roll and deal with our inside messes.

My friend, sometimes the next right step is to stop stepping. When we started this journey, I invited you on a soul-deep search that wouldn't always feel like daisies and rainbows. But I did not know how much it would feel like a punch in the gut and hyperventilating. I started in let's-punch-evil-in-the-face mode and then slipped into fight-to-survive mode. It's a fearful place and a frantic pace where we over-work and over-think and hold all that stress in our mind and body.

So, it's time for a deep breath…to inhale courage and exhale fear.

When I saw grief and resentment coming from a deeper place, I knew it was time to go there so I could get out of there.

Striving to Surrender

In my first therapy sessions, I verbally vomited the chaos in my head. Renee, a professional counselor and art therapist, encouraged me to focus on how emotional stress feels in my body and asked me to draw it. I drew a black rectangular box. It looked exactly like a casket. *God, no. You already saved me from the grave.* So, it wasn't about what was happening around me and to me—it was all about what was happening in me.

Even when we stop the outward rushing, inside we stay wound tight and are blocked from becoming who God created us to be. Research shows that unexpressed emotions and trauma stay in our bodies. We stay stuck in self-protective habits.

Those sneaky, underlying tensions create internal chaos. Like our conditioned mindsets, our conditioned responses to fear are automatic. We accept them as part of who we are because they feel normal to us. They seem safe until we want to be free and they squeeze us tighter.

Has anyone ever repeated back to you all that's going on in your life? And you think, wow, that is a lot. Renee did that for me. She reminded me to be kind and patient with myself. To hush my inner critic and harsh self-judgments. To breathe deep and calm the inner turmoil—the same advice I gave to everyone else. Talking about or even making a list of all that's happening helps us see the magnitude of multiple life shifts. It reassures us that we're doing better than we think.

Be reassured, my friend, by my therapist's words: "Stuck is part of any creative process." In art and in the rebirth of our divine design, God's masterpiece. We aren't really stuck, we're just stopped because we're on the brink of a strong breakthrough. This birthing process is painful, exciting, and sometimes scary because we don't get an epidural. We have to feel it to heal it. That means trusting God, wise counsel, and ourselves. We learn to live more from our created core. The parts that God put there.

I left the art studio/counseling room seeing my complete and utter meltdown. *Wow, I'm really messy but so ready.* To stop doing, doing, doing. To wallop some unhealthy thought patterns and learn to simply be still. It was time to dig out some research I'd stuffed away.

Self-Defeating Mindsets and Habits

"Adult children of alcoholics have learned that their feelings and actions are not governed by outside events but by attitudes and thoughts from childhood." —Douglas & Deborah Bey, Loving an Adult Child of an Alcoholic

Even if we don't have the same history, I believe some of this will resonate with you. If it does, it might help to tell yourself, "This is my habit but it's not who I am." Or just skip it for now and come back to it like I did. Digging out this research, I was ready—yet not ready—to deal with this list. Reading it again, I ugly cried and highlighted almost every single one of the twenty to thirty thought patterns listed for adult children of alcoholics. Here are a few:

CHAPTER SEVEN: LIFE INTERRUPTED

- An ever-present undercurrent of tension and anxiety[1] = Do it NOW, figure it out and fix it NOW.
- Fear of conflict[2] = Sshh…Don't rock the boat. Keep the peace. Please and conform or stuff and run.
- Distrust, fear of abandonment, and sensitivity to criticism[2] = Put up walls. Avoid conflict. Don't speak up or you might get hurt.
- An over-inflated sense of responsibility[3] = Figure it out. Fix everything and everyone. A false sense of control. I can prevent negative outcomes.
- Overreact to changes over which they have no control.[4] = Fear, regret, anxiety, and anger. Ruminate and wish things were different. Feeds victimhood.
- Low self-worth/self-esteem[5] = Live small, inferior, less-than. Perform and conform to be valued and accepted.
- Depression[6] = An underlying current of mental and spiritual exhaustion.
- Addicted to chaos and drama[7] = An adrenaline fix, a sense of power and control.

Wow. That's a lot. See how it's easy to lose ourselves?

Though it's difficult to see ourselves here, it helps us understand why we often struggle with everyday challenges of co-existing and communicating with people—whether we manage a home or workplace or both. They also explain why it's hard to believe our value and trust our voice. To stand firm with our needs, opinions, and preferences.

I hate labels. And whining and blaming and making excuses for bad behavior. That's not what this is. We can say without shame, "I am an adult child of an alcoholic," or some other family dysfunction because we're simply stating a fact. We accept and own this part of our story. Our childhoods—especially those high-stress adolescent years—were impacted by traumatic events. That little girl's becoming was interrupted; her growth was stunted. And since she'll always be a part of us, it's time to listen to more of her pain. So we can show up, grown-up.

My friend, what kept us safe in crisis still shows up when we are stressed, pressured, and threatened. This list may explain parts of our thinking and behavior, but it doesn't define us or condemn us. We are not voiceless victims controlled by past events. This may be our history, but His story in our lives is not done.

Pray and ask God to help you take all of this in for what it is: information. Empowering information. We now understand why we are stuck in learned conditioned responses, childhood thoughts, and childish reactions. Our protective parts show up because they don't know our age or our resources.

When you read these habits formed by living in an insecure environment, did you feel a physical reaction? I did. Big time. Tight chest, throat, and head. I even stomped my feet on the floor under my desk. This panic is a wired-in habit of fight, flight, freeze, or fold. To which I add: freak-out.

As I read the list, I flashed back to eighth grade PE class. With the air knocked out of me, I'm dizzy and angry and punching the jerk who slammed the basketball into my gut and then with a creepy smile asked, "Can I give you mouth-to-mouth resuscitation?" I hear the laughter and the sting of humiliation but refuse to be small. Adult-me shows up and says, "Nope. Not today."

Grabbing on to God's grace, we sit with discomfort, fully present and protected in our grown-up selves and our adult reasoning. We breathe deep and exhale long. Though exhausted with this old battle, we resist the lie, *I should be over this.*

Remembering who and Whose we are, we break through. Jesus in us, we find our fight. As we learn how to take charge of anxious moments, we open spaces for peace to dwell.

Child of God—woman of God—walk into your power. Even if it feels like a baby step. Go forward, in Jesus' name. Let's paraphrase my go-to verse in these moments: God, the Spirit You gave us does not make us timid or afraid but gives us power, love, and a sound mind (see 2 Timothy 1:7).

Our Savior freed us from our past. He gave us a new heredity and we claim our birthright. We are daughters of a good, good Father. We

CHAPTER SEVEN: LIFE INTERRUPTED

are changing our attitudes and thoughts from childhood. Let's press in to feel and heal. Not as timid girls but as empowered women. And remember, there's a difference between knowing and believing. We have to let Truth trickle from head to heart.

Ever had a Scripture appear everywhere and realize you need to pay attention? During my meltdown, God used Psalm 46:10 a lot. Here's my version. Like a little love note, read it slowly. Savor it and allow it to flow from your head to your heart to your toes.

Dear Daughter,
Be still. And know I AM. —God.

He calls us to rest. He's with us every step of this windy way. So, we slow down and surrender to the meltdown. To get out of our head, free our body of tension, and live more from our spirit.

Don't Quit

God never quits in the middle of anything and neither will we. Though pressed from every direction, we have all we need at the core of who we're created to be. All of God's rich resources. His presence, promises, and redemptive power.

When we feel like we're stuck, there's a reason. We're about to begin a brand-new season. When we sense we are on the brink of a complete nervous breakdown, it's because we're kneeling on the threshold of healing. When we meet God there, we find deeper trust, deeper faith, and higher awareness.

We don't have to figure it all out, get it all together, or keep it all together. Striving to get ahead and stay ahead leaves us breathless. We can't give what we don't have. And when we try, we're like a little robot smacking up against a wall with its arms and legs moving but going nowhere.

The walls that used to protect us, now simply block us. But they have a door. When we feel like we're stuck, we're not. We already know the Way through. Jesus, our absolute need, is on the other side.

The unknown and the unseen is scary. Transition labor is the most painful yet most productive—and most welcome—part of childbirth. It takes time to let go and surrender to a new life flow. Creating a fresh rhythm in a new life season takes time. It may look like chaos, but messy progress is still progress. A tad erratic, but moving forward. Life doesn't unfold in a neat straight line, does it? Neither does our healing. We are called to surrender to the ups, and the downs, and the sideways. It won't always feel safe, but such is life where joy and pain coexist. And it's all good.

So, I'm asking you to be disillusioned. To accept that our lives will have sharp zig-zags and meandering loops without neat and tidy edges. They aren't easy and conventional and normal…whatever that is.

The challenge is, we crave safety and stability—those days when all feels right and good and easy—without conflict and dead car batteries and emergency room visits and pinging hormones.

But staying in fight/survival mode exhausts us. And though we want quieter seasons back, it's time to move forward.

Help us, Jesus, to release the unrealistic belief that life is to be easy and uncluttered.

We won't receive until we release. We can't let in until we let go.

And today, God whispers, "Open up, Dear one. You've worked hard on your mind. Now, slow down and breathe. Trust, rely, release."

Let's surrender to the chaos. We hit the end of our willpower and boom—there's Jesus. Right smack in the midst of our scary life changes is our calm center. He's been there all along. Christ, our source of peace.

Depleted but Not Defeated

I pray you'll join me in a holistic meltdown as we continue to uncover our God-given identity in the middle of life transitions. I hope something in my story helps you take another step forward in the process of becoming messy, beautiful you. Our meltdowns take us to a new level of vulnerability, a deeper soul search. What is still hiding? Who is still hiding?

Birthing takes time and patience. But we do it because on the other side, we'll be better, stronger, freer of some unhealthy core beliefs. Like

CHAPTER SEVEN: LIFE INTERRUPTED

in transition labor, we're so ready to be done but we can't push too soon.

Let's see what we learn in the middle of our paradigm shifts. The meltdown of mind, body, and spirit isn't all pretty, but it's all good. It's our chance for a soul-cleansing breath.

Are you stuck sideways in the birthing of who God made you to be? To free our boxed-up pieces, we surrender to our deeper need for Jesus.

STUDY QUESTIONS

"When I understand that everything happening to me is to make me more Christ-like, it resolves a great deal of anxiety." —A. W. Tozer

Have you ever experienced a holistic meltdown—a time when life becomes too, too much and you hit a wall of mental, physical, and spiritual exhaustion? Maybe that time is now.

Things are shifting and change is scary. You want calm. You want control. You try to keep up but simply cannot.

See Your Thoughts

In your meltdown, what was or is going on in your life?

Now, read what you wrote. Whether it's one difficult thing or many, slow down and really see it. Maybe you need to take a deep breath and exhale and tell yourself, "Wow, girl. That's a lot."

But sometimes lies block self-compassion.

It's no big deal.
You don't need help.
You're responsible for everyone and everything.
Hold it together. If you don't keep up, it all falls apart.
It has to be perfect.
You gotta fix this before it gets worse.
What is wrong with you? Don't be a wimp.

CHAPTER SEVEN: LIFE INTERRUPTED

You're tough. Suck it up and drive on.

Underline any of the above that are true for you. If you have other thoughts, write them here.

In this chapter, I shared a list of characteristics found in adult children of alcoholics. While they don't define me, they helped me understand why the sudden changes in my life completely overwhelmed me.

Dr. Janet Woititz, in her book *Adult Children of Alcoholics,* says these traits also apply to other household dysfunctions. Like living around other compulsive behaviors—gambling, drug abuse, or overeating. And those who grew up in foster care or in a home with chronic illness or strict religious attitudes might identify with this list as well.

When chaos comes into our lives, our feelings and actions might be controlled by habits and mindsets formed in childhood. While they don't define us, they keep us stuck and block us from knowing and living our divine design.

If you go back and read the list again, take a moment to pray and become aware of God's loving presence with you.

Does the list shed light on why you respond to pressure the way you do?

Eighteen to twenty percent of American adults were raised by alcoholics. Add in other dysfunctions of family and messages from the world and it's feasible that most humans have at least one of these characteristics. So, we are definitely not alone. Please don't try to do it all alone.

If you see yourself deeply affected by your experiences, please seek professional counseling. Alongside my faith, it helped me understand and get me through my meltdown season.

Set Your Mind

God, we rely on Your sustaining promise in 2 Timothy 1:7. We already have a spirit of power, love, and a sound mind. We may not feel it now, but we know it's true. When we choose faith over feelings, You calm us and comfort us, lead us and grow us through the chaos.

See who you are in Christ and renew your mind. Read and reflect on Psalm 46:10–11. Do you hear the call to be still? Not to strive and worry, but to surrender, trust, and rest in your Safe Place— the Lord of Heaven's Armies.

In Exodus 14:10–14, the Israelites are panicked and terrified. They are stuck. Hemmed in by overwhelming, insurmountable obstacles— will they die by drowning or be captured by Pharaoh's army? Their resilience wavers. Weren't they better off as slaves back in Egypt?

"But Moses told the people, 'Don't be afraid. Just stand still and watch the LORD rescue you today. The Egyptians you see today will never be seen again. The LORD himself will fight for you. Just stay calm.'"

Even if you already know this story, I encourage you to read it again. With fresh eyes, see the powerful miracle—how Moses and over two million Israelites walk through the Red Sea on dry ground. And their oppressors? Swallowed up by seawater. Never to be seen again.

What does this story of God's power, protection, and provision say about your situation—about what seems to be an insurmountable obstacle in your life?

CHAPTER SEVEN: LIFE INTERRUPTED

When life shifts big time and we're boxed-in by a dilemma or two or three…we stop. We stand still and shift our thinking. We aren't going back into what God saved us from. We aren't staying blocked by a raging sea of unhealthy thoughts and habits. In trust and obedience, we surrender our false sense of control and let God, our Rescuer, fight for us.

> *"When you're up against Pharaoh, you're going to need someone that's so self-sufficient He can be whoever you need Him to be. That is I AM." —Pastor Tony Evans*

Seek & Speak What's True

I am defined by I AM.

Because God, _____

_____ , I am _____

_____ .

Celebrate

God, this life is full of difficult surrenders, but we are grateful. You are patient and trustworthy. You give us breath and courage to keep changing into who You created us to be. It is a miracle how You calm our inner turmoil—our mind, our body, our spirit. You are not the author of confusion. Because You are a fortress and strong tower, we're able to let go and stop trying to fix it all. We release, rely, and rest.

CHAPTER 8

Rise Strong: Reclaim Your Power

"We were under great pressure, far beyond our ability to endure, so that we despaired of life itself. Indeed, we felt we had received the sentence of death. But this happened that we might not rely on ourselves but on God, who raises the dead." ~ 2 Cor. 1:8b–9 NIV

Remember I told you that something inside me broke the night I heard, "Mom, I'm pregnant"? All the extreme and sudden life shifts, not only burned me out, they broke my heart. My peace, trust, and a piece of my identity were still rooted a bit too much in a desire for my family—especially my kids and grandkids—to live perfect, pain-free lives.

Who among us doesn't get tired and want to be done with sadness and struggle? We know pain-free isn't possible in this world, but hope is automatic. It's what we do. When our hope gets rattled, it shakes our faith foundation. It's a desperate place where our desires are dashed and we tumble into a spiritual crisis. Peace, hope, and joy trickle off the raw and jagged edges of a broken heart. Doubt, cynicism, and resentment seep in. *God, this is not how our story is supposed to go.* When we run on spiritual fumes, everyone and everything—even our faith—become an endless and heavy to-do list.

I'd spent months in therapy with Renee to process emotional pain and months in physical therapy to fix a frozen shoulder. Because I was healing well in mind and body, it was time to focus more on my spiritual health. Then sudden back pain pulled me down. Would I ever get above pain and struggle? I didn't know it was possible to be that empty and depressed. Like in my teen years—but a deeper despair and a brand new, heart-pounding anxiety. Many days, I was on the edge of a complete stay-in-bed breakdown.

In this journey to become who God created us to be, we often come to a crossroad—a point of decision. Will we continue to move forward toward wholeness and holiness? Or will we stay where we are and settle for half-living?

The Chinese word for *crisis* is made of two symbols. One is *danger*, the other is *opportunity*. I love this. Spiritual crisis is a door inviting us to more. With our faith so shaky, we have to get back to the basics. Just us and Jesus.

Hardest. Questions. Ever.

Though we work hard on our mental and physical health, we'll always be out of balance if we ignore our spiritual well-being. It took a year of hindsight for me to see and accept my faith was in crisis. I resisted the deeper spiritual work by avoiding some scary questions because the answers might crush me and keep me in the dark. They could make me a fool and the last thirty years of my life, a joke. My lovable skeptics and atheists would all be right.

It was a dangerous crossroad and it demanded decisions. *Am I really a Truth-seeker? How bad do I want my peace, hope, and joy back?* Opportunity knocked and knocked and knocked until I finally faced the tough questions.

Was my salvation experience real?

What I experienced back there in that little Arkansas church, was it even real? Sweet God of mercy, the answer was a quick and quiet yes.

CHAPTER EIGHT: RISE STRONG

It was settled. I wasn't just caught up in emotions that day. I was free. My head was lighter and the sun was brighter because those few simple answers to Brother Mike's questions lifted my burden.

God knew all of my sin and guilt. He saw my heart open and my head nod: *Yes, Jesus save me. Yes God, take charge of my life.* It was a spiritual transaction. The peace, power, and presence of God the Father, God the Son, and God the Holy Spirit made me new. In that moment, my mind started a dramatic, one-eighty death-to-life transformation. Boom. Yes, my faith is real. With that settled, I moved on to the next tough question.

Do I Really Believe God Is Good?

I'm not gonna lie. I hesitated on this one. Danger and opportunity tangled a bit. I was tired and bitter, wrestling with the illusion that someday my life and family would stop being interrupted by pain and difficulty. Anger surfaced about past situations when my kids were hurt by Christians. And deep sadness too—that in my sincere desire to protect them and break unhealthy cycles—I messed up and caused them pain as well. All this fueled my anger and I vented at God.

But deep down, I knew. He's always good—not only when good things happen. He isn't a puppet master who orchestrates each detail of each circumstance. People make choices and choices have consequences. Humans are often unreliable and life events unpredictable, but God is trustworthy. Yes, God is still good.

When we're in this questioning place, it helps to write down our blessings and milestones—the moments and memories when all we can say is, "That was totally a God thing." It's good to remember how He cared for us in our messes and distresses; how He rejoiced with us in every joy and celebration. Seeing our track record with God reminds us to be grateful. Gratitude helps us live from our healing, not our hurt.

God's promises sustain and strengthen us. Always there, as they say in the South, to bless our socks off. In my darkest days, He used several promises from Isaiah to sustain me. Verse 41:10 popped up everywhere. In just eight days, I read it in my Bible and heard it on the radio and in a Sunday sermon. I found it printed on a bookmark and on a journal my husband gave me. The Bible verse showed up in a friend's text and on a Facebook meme. And if that's not enough, it scrolled across a computer screen as I reclined in a drafty hospital gown and sexy no-slip socks waiting for ear surgery.

God's persistent whisper came loud and clear:

> *"Don't be afraid, for I am with you. Don't be discouraged, for I am your God. I will strengthen you and help you. I will hold you up with my victorious right hand" (Isaiah 41:10).*

Love, abundant and overflowing. I can't tell you how many times I read this, reached my hand up, and imagined His strong hand gripping mine. God, You are good. So, so good.

My friend, we won't always feel strong or sense God's loving presence. Moment by moment, we must make a raw decision—a pure act of the will—to lead with the facts and not the feelings that surround our situation. Emotions, though good gifts, are terrible guides. They yank our mind up, down, and sideways. In a nanosecond, automatic and fear-filled reactions overshadow our faith. We burn out, fall into despair, and aren't fully equipped to fight anything. Thoughts tug us toward hopelessness. *Will I ever feel right again? Will I ever feel God again?*

Reclaim Your Power

> *"And although these kinds of gifts don't come with confetti, distress, heartache, and loss can be gifts too. Because it is our emptiness that precedes our filling. It is in our moments of desperation when we see our deep need for someone beyond ourselves. Desperation draws us to our knees where Jesus meets us and picks us up to carry us. We move forward not in our own strength, but His." —Brooke Frick*[1]

God hears us and loves us. He reaches us wherever we are by whatever means available. Sometimes, He speaks to us in dreams. Many are

CHAPTER EIGHT: RISE STRONG

random, products of a brain that doesn't sleep. But a few of my dreams have been so clear and compelling I know they're another Love note.

After a year of physical therapy and being a functional depressed person—digging deep to get out of bed, to smile, and to do the next right and needed thing—I had a dream that lifted my whole perspective.

There was this evil presence. No form, just a swirling gray-black mass. Like the gloom and doom poop cloud I walked under for so long. But now it was distant. And I was above it, pointing my finger. "You will not win. I belong to Jesus. You have no authority in my life."

I started to wake and heard myself whisper, "Jesus…Jesus…Jesus." No fear. No anxiety. No tight chest or racing heart. No weight of despair. I kept my eyes shut to soak in the moment and process what was happening. Inexpressible peace. Infilling power.

From this higher perspective, fully present in God's presence, fear is absent. When fear is absent, oppression is gone. Our full fight begins to come back and our upward call is clear. To believe again in abundant life and redemption—that beauty still rises from ashes.

Girl, my weary spirit sparked. It was the beginning of a major comeback. When I got out of bed, I stepped into my power. Jesus in me. With my spiritual vision raised higher, I reclaimed my position as God's daughter and laser-focused on staying in His presence. To quiet my mind, open my heart, and rest my spirit. I reclaimed my peace in Jesus. Only Jesus.

"Are you tired? Worn out? Burned out on religion? Come to me. Get away with me and you'll recover your life. I'll show you how to take a real rest. Walk with me and work with me—watch how I do it. Learn the unforced rhythms of grace. I won't lay anything heavy or ill-fitting on you. Keep company with me and you'll learn to live freely and lightly" (Matt. 11:28–30 MSG).

That's how we fight. We trust and rest in that sweet spot where our human limitations meet His limitless power. Where our fears and faults open up to the Light and remind us where we'd be without Jesus. You see, those cracks in our courage work for us. They call us into this higher, deeper, wider awareness and abiding. To know we are loved, held, and shielded—in unhurried and unworried rhythms of grace.

Exhausted in body, mind, or spirit, we are susceptible to attack. All our fears show up like mean girls who won't stop whining and yapping, and they bring their mean menopausal mother with them. Doubts, cynicism, and futility grip us. But we're ready for them. With patient and deliberate focus, standing in the victory Jesus already won for us, we go forward with grit and walk in grace.

Doubt

In the Gospels, we see the ministry of John the Baptist. The one who jumped in Elizabeth's womb when Mary, pregnant with Jesus, showed up on their doorstep. John grew up and fulfilled his calling to preach, prophesy, and pave the way for the Way.

Can we even imagine what it was like when John saw Jesus walking toward him? The long-awaited Messiah getting ready to redeem the world—coming to *him* to be baptized. Imagine the awe and wonder as John lifted Jesus from the water, heard the flutter of dove's wings, and then the booming voice from the heavens, "This is my Son, whom I love; with him I am well-pleased" (Matt. 3:17 NIV).

What a stunning, miraculous experience. This was the grand finale of John's mission and the official beginning of Jesus' ministry. I imagine they laughed and clapped and danced, celebrating this exclamation point on a job well-done and the anticipation of God's promised deliverance.

Fast forward and we see outspoken fearless John, baptizer of Messiah, locked up in prison. Dirty, tired, and hungry. It's likely he was imprisoned for over a year and knew he'd be executed. It's no wonder his mind fell under attack. We don't know his mental state exactly, but we do know this man, who once called himself "thunder in the desert,"[2] wrestled with doubt. And for good reasons.

John's life and the redemption of Israel wasn't going at all like he imagined. And the majority of Israelites and their leaders strongly rejected Jesus. So, yes, doubt niggled in. John sent a message to Jesus: "Are you the Messiah we've been expecting, or should we keep looking for someone else?" (Matt.11:3).

CHAPTER EIGHT: RISE STRONG

Here we see John's crossroads moment. This powerful prophet still empowers us by pointing us to Jesus. He shows us courage to ask the tough questions. He risks dying a fool. His whole life mission, a waste. Just another crazy zealot out in the desert eating locusts and honey. All those ornery people would be right. But John was a Truth-seeker. He persisted against all popular opinion and decided to duke it out with doubt.

Our gracious Father welcomes this honesty. In fact, He invites it. No distance and no lightning bolts. Jesus sent the messengers back with words to assure John that hope was not dead. He had accomplished his life purpose.

In Matthew 11:4–5 (MSG), we hear Jesus:

"Go back and tell John what's going on:

The blind see,

The lame walk,

Lepers are cleansed,

The deaf hear,

The dead are raised,

The wretched of the earth [those who are heartbroken and in despair] learn that God is on their side." (brackets added)

Encouraging, right? But that's not even the best part. Jesus loved John. He knew the heart of the questioner and the trial he was enduring. He used the doubts and questions as an opportunity to remind the crowd of John's powerful preaching. No rebuke. No shame. "I tell you, among those born of women there is no one greater than John" (Luke 7:28 NIV). Now that's quite an endorsement. Not just for John, but for his ministry and his message. The message of repentance—to turn away from sin and prepare our minds and hearts for the Way.

Cynicism

Spiritual crises can make us cynical. At the root of cynicism is distrust. It's a mindset that makes us negative, suspicious, and pessimistic. Sometimes it's wise to be wary of people's motives because this world gives us plenty to be suspicious about. But if we aren't careful and prayerful, cynicism becomes the filter for everything. Even how we view God.

This spiritual sickness snuck up on me. I was caught up in its perfect storm. Depression, back pain, resentment, self-reliance. Oh, and did I mention it was during the 2016 presidential elections? Yep, that'll do it. I thought like a cynic, saw through the eyes of a cynic, and heard through a cynic's ear. This filter corrupts our perspective. When we're in pain and the world is loud, our spiritual senses are dulled and God seems unreliable. He whispers but we can't hear it. Light shines but we can't see it.

When my cynicism was raw and snarky, well-meaning Christians and their Christian-y platitudes ticked me off. I was suspicious and weary of them and all the worn-out clichés and Scripture-ish phrases:

"It will all work out for your good."

"God doesn't give us more than we can handle."

"I'll pray for you."

"God's got you."

"There's a reason for everything."

Until all I heard was blah, blah, blah, blah, blah.

Christian music, Christian teaching, and Scripture memes become stale and hollow too. It's all just words. Way too many words when our minds just need quiet. Sometimes, we have to unplug, switch off the voices, and soak in silence until Jesus becomes our thought filter.

Futility

Cynicism has a heartless friend. When we're down, futility hits us with a one-two-three punch. Emptiness, hopelessness, meaninglessness. Our setbacks tell us we'll never feel right and whole again. We'll never feel God again. Hopelessness is scary. We see no glimmer on the horizon, and we no longer sense the familiar promise that everything will be okay. It's a dark and shaky place where it seems God is gone.

In a spiritual crisis, it's easy to focus on everything that's going wrong. Our mind magnifies pain and problems as if they're bigger than God and His Spirit in us. Where our focus is, our mind is. Where our mind is, our actions follow. Distracted by a sin-sick world and our own struggle, we forget evil is not winning. We forget about redemp-

CHAPTER EIGHT: RISE STRONG

tion. Our thoughts pass through this futility filter.

What's the point of trusting and living as a Christ follower? Of sacrificing and working hard and holding on to dreams for ourselves and our children? It's like the good we do—the good we seek—it's all for nothing.

It's horrible to see and hear like someone who doesn't believe in Jesus, redemption, and abundant life. Because we know that is not who we are and not how we're designed to think. Here's one of my tearful and desperate prayers:

"God, I hate this person I'm becoming. God, I hate my life."

These are startling thoughts sliding down a slippery slope. They hold dangerous potential and beautiful opportunity. Right above our feelings is rational thought. We set our minds higher to remember what is true and we speak it, "I know this is not who I am and this is not the abundant life Jesus gives." Clinging to God's promises, we pray as though our lives depend on it. Because they do.

Ephesians 6:12–18 sums up what we need to remember during our struggles: "This is for keeps, a life-or-death fight to the finish against the Devil and all his angels. Be prepared. *You're up against far more than you can handle on your own.* Take all the help you can get, every weapon God has issued, so that when it's all over but the shouting you'll still be on your feet. Truth, righteousness, peace, faith, and salvation are more than words. Learn how to apply them. You'll need them throughout your life. God's Word is an indispensable weapon. In the same way, prayer is essential in this ongoing warfare. Pray hard and long" (MSG, author's emphasis).

Dear daughter, be still. And know I AM. —God

Some days it's hard to pray and stay focused. The phone pings, the cat pukes, the to-do list screams. Often the interruptions are way more subtle, and the to-be list is under attack. Be fearful, be confused, be stressed. Worry and anxiety squeeze our heart and nameless dread casts a shadow across our mind. Our spirits are squished and we feel small. So, it's important to remember who we are and Who we're praying to. We reclaim our peace, position, and power in the promises of I AM.

God calls Himself I AM. He is unchanging, eternal, and ever-present. He is complete and all-sufficient, and He is crazy in love with us. This perfect love is hard to understand, but it is our aim. We are God's daughters, made in His image. So, as we seek Him, we find ourselves in the heart of an unshakable, loving Father. We find our I ams in the I AM.

> God, Because You don't shift with my emotions and circumstances, I am able to trust You. I surrender all my tomorrows because You are already there working things out. Every time worry and anxiety bubble up, I remember You fill my spirit with power, and I have a strong mind. You are always present and hold me in perfect peace. You are my defender so I need no other hero. Because Jesus' Spirit is in me, I have everything I need. In Him, I stand above all that tries to trip me up and pull me down. —Your grateful Daughter

Focusing on our Father's character and promises is powerful. It reminds us we are complete. He heals the heart and mind of the girl who desperately needs love and to be assured she is safe, she can trust, and she'll be okay.

Pray. Receive. Repeat. As often as it takes to root your faith and cast-off fear. We are cared for and defined by the Father we always needed and Who never leaves.

We can trust God's heart. Ask the questions. Do the wrestling. Remember the message Jesus sent to John the Baptist? Attached to that list of miracles was this: "God blesses those who do not turn away because of me" (Matt. 11:6).

I sense Jesus assuring us too.

My work in you and in your family's life is not going like you imagined. But it doesn't change who I AM. Do not give up hope. My Way is way better than what you expected or will ever imagine.

We are designed to be in constant connection with our Creator. The

CHAPTER EIGHT: RISE STRONG

world's stuff and sadness distract us. The sin nature we inherited from humanity's fall wants to be in charge. Our original sin still wars with our original glory. But Jesus changed our heredity and gave us a new nature. Boom. One and done. So, we are patient. We have a new spirit, but our mind is still transforming and conforming to Christ in us.

The really good news is, God formed us before sin showed up. And He continues to reveal the beauty of that original glory, our divine design. My friend, we are rising strong. We are rescued and being restored. Not back to something we lost, but growing forward into a deeper Spirit-to-spirit connection where we root our identity in Jesus. Only Jesus. Not in feelings or circumstances, people, or performance. We set down our to-do list and pick up our to-be list.

Be quiet.
Be humble.
Be open.
Be loved.
Be courageous.
Be empowered.
Surrender to more of Jesus and be you.

STUDY QUESTIONS

"The father of lies twists the truth and distorts reality. He is the author of cynicism and skepticism, mistrust and despair, sick thinking and self-hatred. But I am the Son of compassion. You belong to Me, and no one will tear you from My hand." ~ Brennan Manning, Abba's Child

Desires are dashed. The heart breaks. Peace, hope, and joy trickle out. Sadness, cynicism, and resentment seep in.

"God, this is not how our story is supposed to go."

Change is often scary, isn't it? We resist it and might even resent it.

See Your Thoughts

Do you expect things to go your way and get angry when they don't? If so, give an example:

How might you have a do-it-my-way mindset with God?

CHAPTER EIGHT: RISE STRONG

What parts of life are you trying to control? (aka being self-reliant)

In what areas have you surrendered control? (aka being Savior-reliant)

Are you cynical (negative, suspicious, pessimistic)? If so, what reasons come to mind?

Do your thoughts tug you toward hopelessness or emptiness? What are they?

On a scale of one to a kajillion, how bad do you want your peace, hope, and joy back?

Set Your Mind

See who you are in Christ and renew your mind. Read and reflect on the following Scripture.

"You will keep in perfect peace all who trust in you, all whose thoughts are fixed on you!" (Isaiah 26:3).

Write down Bible verses or other truths that come to mind often.

These are God's persistent whispers to sustain and strengthen you. Pause and read them again. Let the compassion of your ever-present Father trickle from your head to your heart.

> *"God speaks to the deepest reaches of our soul...*
> *and takes us through the night into the daylight of*
> *His truth." —Brennan Manning,* Abba's Child

Read the following Scripture. Ask God to show you what they say about the "daylight of His truth."

"'For even if the mountains walk away and the hills fall to pieces, My love won't walk away from you, my covenant commitment of peace won't fall apart.' The God who has compassion on you says so" (Isaiah 54:10 MSG).

What does the above verse say about God's compassion, love, and peace?

CHAPTER EIGHT: RISE STRONG

Matthew 11:28–30. What does Jesus say to your weary and burdened mind?

Isaiah 41:10. What is God's promise when you're afraid and discouraged? Where does He hold you?

Ephesians 1:19–21. We are not equal to Christ. But what does this passage say about where Christ is seated and the power for those who believe in Him?

Imagine yourself there with Jesus. Wrapped in His peace, safe and empowered in His presence.

Far above sadness and oppression. Far above all fear, despair, cynicism, and self-reliance. Everything your soul's enemy throws at you— lies, sin, and death— Jesus already defeated. And He gives you "authority over all the power of the enemy" (Luke 10:19).

Therein, you find your fight.

Yes, this is spiritual warfare. And you stand in the victory Jesus already won for you.

With patient and deliberate focus, we stand with grit and walk in grace.

Here are some habits that helped me stay aware of God's presence and rise strong.

Look up Philippians 4:6–8 and read through it.

On sleepless nights, this was my go-to. Putting these timeless principals into practice disarms our anxious thoughts.

"Don't worry about anything; instead, pray about everything" (v 6).

Even if it's silent or whispered, prayer is a weapon. Tell God what you need and pray for others too. Praise and gratitude are weapons. Thank Him for what He's done and is going to do. Refocusing our thoughts on all that is good and beautiful is a weapon. And so is the peace that's truly beyond human understanding.

Deliberate, determined, and unhurried. This is our strong and quiet fight.

Another habit that helped me was making lists. Whether you're a list-maker or not, I hope this helps you.

When we're tired, our minds and emotions are especially vulnerable. So, at bedtime—already anxious about the next day—I made a list.

Get up. Brush teeth. Decide the next needed thing.

Or

Get up. Make coffee. Drink coffee. Decide the next needed thing.

It may seem silly, but the next morning, when my first lucid thought was sad or anxious—this simple list of baby steps got me up and moving.

What does your simple list look like?

Another way we refocus the mind is to make a list of moments, milestones, and memories. When we look back and say, "That was totally a God thing." Gratitude helps us live from our healing, not our hurt.

Make a list. And don't forget your current blessings too.

CHAPTER EIGHT: RISE STRONG

The Author of our story is good and faithful. He is trustworthy so let's be done with the sin of self-reliance that says, *I'll do it myself because this is not how my story is supposed to go.*

Set down your stubborn self and her to-do list. In fact, shred that baby. Pray for forgiveness and pick up your to-be list.

Be quiet. Be humble. Be loved.

Be courageous. Be empowered. Surrender more to Jesus and be you.

Seek & Speak What's True

I am defined by I AM.

In Judges 6, we see Gideon who is a judge, prophet, and military leader. Pretty powerful, eh? Yet we find him threshing wheat at the bottom of a winepress hiding from the Midianites.

In verse 12, God calls him out, "The Lord is with you, mighty warrior" (NIV).

Gideon's like, "Uh, excuse me? If you're with us then why did all this destruction happen? Where are your miracles now?" (verse 13, author's paraphrase)

Hmm. Doesn't sound very mighty. But God sees through Gideon's fear, doubt, and questions. He sees the strong warrior He designed and calls him out to fight.

Do not be mistaken, my friend. God is not silent. He sees you too, strong warrior. And He calls you out of hiding—out of the weary wounds that hide the warrior in you.

"When doubts filled my mind, your comfort gave me renewed hope and cheer" (Psalm 94:19).

Because God, _____

_____ , I am _____

_____ .

Celebrate

God, life is not going like I planned or imagined. These changes are scary but I'm grateful that my fear doesn't change who You are. You are the Author of life—all life—so I give You back the pen. Trusting You to write our story, I find peace, hope, and joy.

CHAPTER 9

Victim Mindset: Reclaim Your Victory

"When I was a child, I talked like a child, I thought like a child, I reasoned like a child. When I became a [woman], I put the ways of childhood behind me." ~ 1 Cor. 13:11 NIV, bracket added

When I was eight, my mom taught me how to wash my thick, waist-length hair. Once a week, I'd lather, rinse, repeat, condition. In my adolescent years, my showers were hurried. A sharp knock on the bathroom door reminded me not to waste water or put wear and tear on the septic system.

Thirty-eight years later, midway through lather, rinse, repeat, condition, a new thought trickled in, *wait...why am I still washing twice and turning off the water in-between?*

Do you see the staying power of a learned mindset? It can take decades to think and respond like a grown woman. Some life lessons cause us to react like we did as kids. But once we see these conditioned thoughts wired into our brains, we can unlearn them. We create new passageways to take us on the high road.[1]

In the middle of my shower epiphany, a thought tried to take the low road and tell me, *you're such an idiot.* But I smiled and crushed it. "Robin, you don't need to lather twice or shut off the water. You're a grown woman and can think for yourself." Boom. I busted an old thought pattern and transformed my mind.

Aren't you grateful we can experience the promise and power of God's Truth? Me too. Because I'm quite aware of my history with a mindset that's way more serious than a hair washing habit.

Walking Wounded

"Victim mentality is a learned personality trait in which a person feels powerless and unable to cope or take action in difficult situations. This person tends to see him/herself as a victim of the negative actions of others, and continues to feel this way even after the negative situation or actions are no longer real or relevant. Quite often, the sense of powerlessness is learned behavior originating from childhood when core needs were not met adequately. That's why this mentality becomes so ingrained—it's had lots of time to simmer.

"But any negative, traumatizing event that makes us feel powerless can foster a victim mentality. It becomes a coping mechanism to survive fear, pain, and to reclaim our basic psychological needs of safety, love, affection, belonging, and self-esteem."[2]

Wow, that's a lot. No matter who we are or what our history is, we all have the same core needs. When we lack basic needs, everything can feel like rejection. And because rejection hurts, we build defenses against it.

In those difficult years with my dad and my brother's death, I sank into a victim mentality. I had this gaping wound that screamed for help, but no one talked about it. I sat in school day after day with Craig's former teachers and coaches, but it was like his death never happened. Just like at home. And I get it. Grief isn't easy to talk about. Especially then, we lived in such a stuff-and-hush culture. Maybe someone wanted to reach out but just didn't know how. At the time, it seemed like they didn't care. So, as some teenagers do, I pretended I didn't care.

Wanting someone to see my pain, I often wore Craig's khaki-green Navy jacket and got quiet and gloomy. Some days, I was the angry rebel, skipping school, refusing to do schoolwork, or mouthing off to

CHAPTER NINE: VICTIM MINDSET

teachers. My coping mechanism lied; *I don't need you anyway.* Two girls warring in one body. These please-see-me cries for help probably pushed people away.

With extreme inner turmoil coming at an age when we're trying to figure out who the heck we are, our identity gets wrapped up in a victim-skin. It's a soul-killing, toxic comfort zone. It gives us the sympathy we crave even if we are the only one feeling sorry for ourself. We may not remember why we started to think this way. We are simply in the habit of feeling and behaving like a victim. But that's not who we are created to be.

"If we continue to allow our childhood pain, or any pain for that matter, to define us and serve as the reason for living a compromised life, then we'll forever be stuck in a victim mentality."[3]

Even after I met Jesus, this mindset often stole my joy and peace. Years ago, my pastor taught a series called "Victim to Victor" and I kicked it to the curb. Or so I thought. In my meltdown season, as I focused on healing physical and emotional pain, my mind spiraled into this old protective pattern and it came back strong.

In our striving to fix every little thing, while pain piles on top of pain, and it feels like everything's against us, old reactions to stress back us into a corner. Some of us come out swinging. Some of us stay there.

My friend, victimhood keeps you from finding and living your God-given identity. But do not let your past as a victim steal your present victory.

Jesus explains our challenges and His promise in John 10:10. This is my version of it: The thief only comes to steal, kill, and destroy. I have come that you may have life, *more abundant life.*

Our soul's enemy wants to kill Jesus' spirit in us because he knows our power and potential in Christ. He wants us small, crushed in spirit, and boxed up in a little casket of pain. So, we have to make decision.

Do we want burdened lives or abundant lives? Remembering our positions of victory and relying on our power in Jesus, we demolish anything that comes against us. "[W]e take captive every thought to make it obedient to Christ" (2 Cor. 10:5 NIV).

Our thoughts, once soul-killing, become life-giving.

Let's take a closer look at ways we might think like victims. As we open our hearts and train our minds, may we learn to see them until we can't un-see them.

Oh, Poor Me. Life Is so Unfair.

When a victim mindset is in charge, we expect the worst so that's what we see: the negative, the lost opportunities, how our lives are lacking. Confirmation bias is a booger, isn't it? Everyone else is luckier, happier, and has it all together. We have imagined an ideal of what's perfect and normal, and we've already decided that we will never have it. Life is just so unfair. We attract and create negative situations with a snarky attitude or we simply give up because of our *bad luck*.

If we filter relationships and life events through the baseline belief that everything's against us and nothing ever goes our way, that's what we will see. Again, there's confirmation bias. *The rain came to spoil my picnic plans. My flight was cancelled to ruin my vacation. My water heater broke and I'll never get ahead. My child is struggling so I'm a terrible parent.*

My, my, my, oh me.

The truth is, there's no cosmic, global conspiracy working against us. We all experience everyday problems and excruciating crises. And we know that. But a me-first, victim mentality ignores it or refuses to see it because our story is always the worst. Is life often unfair, unjust, and unreasonable? Our sinless Savior suffered and died to bridge the chasm our sin created. So, yes. Yes, it is. And a victim mentality is unfair too. Especially when we expect someone else—besides Jesus—to fill our basic psychological needs.

Unrealistic Expectations

When we think like a victim, we cling to unfair and unrealistic expectations of life and people. Like little beggars, we hold out our emotional tin cups, but they never get full enough. If we look to people to complete us—to meet all our needs for love, self-worth, safety, affection, and belonging—we will always be empty.

When my dad came home from Viet Nam, he was weary, and his emotional pain was beyond what any of us could understand. Once home, he thought he'd find peace—retire at forty-eight, enjoy his family, and fish the Mississippi. He expected something or someone to settle his soul and his questions.

"Why can't we just be a normal family?" I now see this came from a desire to satisfy his core needs and to be done with struggle. He wanted to move on and into the life he imagined. But back then, his question confused me. Was he blaming us for his unhappiness? My dad had serious emotional problems that created major stress and dysfunction, but we had a good family. Why weren't we good enough? We were all hurting, but he couldn't see past his own pain.

If we think *normal* is a perfect problem-free life and family, as we imagine everyone else has, we will never be content. We will grumble, blame, and complain. In this fairy tale with its imaginary standard, we, our lives, and our families, will never measure up.

What is *normal* anyway? Let's re-think it.

Normal is messy. Normal is problems and challenges. Normal is difficult relationships and heart-breaking circumstances. Yes, all that and more. So, let's pause a moment. Let's take comfort and find courage in knowing Jesus said it would be so.

"Here on earth you will have many trials and sorrows. But take heart, because I have overcome the world" (John 16:33).

With Jesus in us, we overcome too.

I'm Offended.

Alongside unrealistic expectations, a victim mind is easily offended. Our low self-worth gets triggered by people's comments, actions, inactions, or opinions. Walking around wounded, we carry these as personal attacks. Offenses are often a product of our imagination. They are exaggerated, way too important, and should not get so much of our emotional energy and brain space. But that's the nature of a victim mentality.

We carry around dead weight, replaying words or situations over and over until we're caught in a loop: anger, hurt, and self-pity. Owning an offense puts us on the defense. Depending on our personality and past experiences, we either fight or fold it all up inside. We attack or retreat with our wounds.

I'm not saying we pretend words don't hurt, because they do. People say and do truly mean and insulting things. But we think above our emotions and learn to discern what to shrug off and what's worth addressing. And we stay aware of our tendencies to absorb hurtful words because even when we walk strong and confident, victim thinking can sneak up and make us feel small.

Years ago, driving home from the grocery store, I stopped behind a school bus. Parked across the street from my driveway, its door was closed and its engine turned off. Inside, the driver waited for my neighbor to bring out her son in his wheelchair. Knowing it might be five to ten minutes, I inched around the bus—not passing it—and pulled into my driveway. As I opened the car door, a loud and angry voice startled me.

"What the [blankety-blank] is the matter with you, passing a school bus..." and blah, blah, blah, blah, blah. It was the bus driver. A sixtyish, gray-bearded man with dark-rimmed glasses and a gravelly voice.

My gut twisted and my face flushed hot. I yelled back, "Who do you think you're talking to?" Though I spoke up, his tone of voice triggered old reactions inside me. Forgetting the groceries, I shut my car door and hurried to the house. Once inside, I worked through it. I shook, paced, cried, yelled, and prayed. Snot, tears, tissues. Yep, a good, ugly cry. Fear, that feeling of being unsafe, stirred up my insides and it needed to come out.

When threatened and overwhelmed by stress, our default reactions show up. But remember, they don't know our age or our resources. We are grown women who have Jesus and rational thoughts. Determined not to give fear our power, we tell ourselves what's true. People's harsh words and reactions come from their own inner conflicts. And, fact is, some humans simply like being mean. But we don't have to own it. Will

CHAPTER NINE: VICTIM MINDSET

we continue to give them our power? Will we choose to be offended or free? Woman of God, small and powerless is not who we're created to be.

I Gotta Know Why

Why questions are honest and healthy. The brain wants to make sense of pain and problems. But keeping *why?-why?-why?* on a continuous loop keeps us wound up and bound to victim thinking, unable to move forward.

My friend Holly showed me a healthy way to answer the whys. Her daughter, Angie, died unexpectedly from an asthma attack. A happy newlywed expecting her first baby, Angie's whole beautiful life was ahead of her. Of course, Holly asked, "God, why her?"

My friend's answer came in those first raw hours after losing her precious daughter and grandbaby. "With all the suffering in our world, why not her?"

Wow. That's amazing, powerful faith, isn't it? By accepting that no one is exempt from pain, Holly did not betray Angie. And she did not disregard her own grief. Acceptance helped her begin to walk forward with it. Holly's huge heart and soul question did not pull her into victimhood, it helped her suffer well.

Another good and legit question is: "Why is this happening to me?" To avoid thinking like a victim, we must think above it. We take the high road and surrender to a new question. "God, what do You want to teach me?" Now, that's redemption power too. When we believe we can find purpose in pain, we reroute our mental scripts. We know it's not happening *to* me, but somehow it's working *for* me.

When everything in us wants to rewrite our story, we humbly surrender our *whys*. God is the author and finisher of our faith. Our sorrows do not define us as victims. God says we are victors. When we walk in that Truth and give Him the present and our histories, He creates His story.

Do we want the hurting parts of our stories to define us? Or will we let them refine us?

Charlie Brown, of *Peanuts* fame, is a lovable loser. Despite his childlike trust and good intentions, he gets knocked down. A lot. Rocks in his trick-or-treat bag. Hassled by pretty much everyone, especially Lucy. Time after time, she pulls away the football, and he's on the ground again.

Though bad luck seems to follow Charlie Brown around like a cloud, he does not play the victim. He doesn't give up on life or people. Why does he keep showing up for all that humiliation? Because this lovable loser is actually a brave leader. Charlie Brown rises above disappointments. He doesn't use failure, insults, or offenses as excuses to whine, blame, or quit. He doesn't give up trick-or-treating to avoid all the rocks. Charlie Brown is a team player.

As we seek our divine design, it's freeing to know it's not us against the world. We look beyond a me-attitude and grow into a we-attitude. We remember who our real enemy is and stop criminalizing people. Especially those we live with—we need to see them as blessings, not burdens.

Our people—those who know us and love us best—want to help. Often, they just don't know what to say or do. We may have even conditioned them to clam up because our defenses are up. We dig deep, put on a thick skin, and listen to our loved ones' concerns or corrections because their hearts want to help us, not hurt us. We are humble, honest, and remember we are all on our own zig-zag journey. We let people be people. And as God intended from the beginning, He put us together so we can figure it out together.

When I saw myself sinking into a victim mindset again, I talked to my people. I told Jeff and talked about it in my therapy sessions with Renee. Eventually, I asked an older woman of faith to meet with me and mentor me on my rise up.

Remembering their role is to support us, we let go of demands. We don't expect them to fix us or fill us.

Friends, husbands, children, parents, or pastors are wonderful, but they can't make us whole. God puts people in our lives to walk alongside us. But these good gifts are idols when we put them first in our thoughts and in our appeals for healing. That space is created only for the Father. He alone hears our soul-deep cries and soothes those raw and hurting places.

CHAPTER NINE: VICTIM MINDSET

Every single one of our unfulfilled longings—our healthy, legitimate needs to be seen, comforted, and understood—are met in Him. We fill our cup with Him first. So our people and celebrations are the overflow of blessings. Lavish, abundant gifts from a generous Father. Not the clinkety-clink of pennies in a tin cup but the whole treasure trove of His glorious riches. To have this abundant life Jesus promises, we choose to see what is true. Scripture teaches us to recognize unhealthy thought patterns and replace them. When we change our attitude and behavior, it's a full-blown miracle.

Don't we owe it to ourselves and our loved ones to heal a victim mindset? We decide today who we want to be and interrupt our thoughts when they get caught in the loop of our woe-is-me stories. Remembering our position and relying on our power in Jesus, we demolish anything that keeps us from our victories.

Wounded to Warrior

We see how our needs can take us to unhealthy places. A victim voice says we're powerless, and we're tempted to believe it. Like angry, defensive teenagers, our problems define us and we blame others for our issues.

When our mind tricks us, we think, instead, on what is true. We turn our thoughts from the worst and focus on God's best. We flip our mental script with Scripture.

"And now, dear brothers and sisters, one final thing. Fix your thoughts on what is true, and honorable, and right, and pure, and lovely, and admirable. Think about things that are excellent and worthy of praise" (Phil. 4:8).

In Ephesians 1:19–20, Paul prays for believers to "understand the incredible greatness of God's power for us who believe him. This is the same mighty power that raised Christ from the dead and seated him in the place of honor at God's right hand in the heavenly realms."

Wow. The power that God exerted when he resurrected Jesus? That same death-to-life power is in us. Jesus already fought the battle with sin and our soul's enemy. When He duked it out with death and won, we did too. It's a done deal no matter how we feel.

Jesus' victorious Spirit lives in us and surrounds us, so we are more than conquerors. We already have victory over victimhood. We stand in our power and in our rightful places with Jesus. And when we fight, Scripture tells us He stands on the necks of our enemies (see Joshua 10:24–25).

Mighty Warrior, remember who and Whose you are.

"I pray that from His glorious, unlimited resources he will empower you with inner strength through his Spirit. Then Christ will make his home in your hearts as you trust in him. Your roots will grow down into God's love and keep you strong. And may you have the power to understand, as all God's people should, how wide, how long, how high, and how deep his love is. May you experience the love of Christ, though it is too great to understand fully. *Then you will be made complete with all the fullness of life and power that comes from God.* Now all glory to God, who is able, through his mighty power at work within us, to accomplish infinitely more than we might ask or think" (Eph. 3:16–21, author's emphasis).

Now, that's a lot of power and abundant life.

When our mind is set where we belong—in the Spirit and heart of our loving Father—we are seen, safe, and cherished. Our self-worth is complete, and we are free to let go of unfair and unrealistic expectations. Filled up, we choose to be un-offendable. Blessed to be blessings, our cups overflow to others.

My victorious friend, I know this journey to your truest self is not easy. It stirs up a lot of stuff. So, it's good you're not alone. Supported by each other and empowered in Christ, we step forward together into more of our divine design.

CHAPTER NINE: VICTIM MINDSET

STUDY QUESTIONS

"Healing from a deep loss is not about recovery and returning to the way things were. Rather, it's about allowing ourselves to keep on changing and becoming amidst the pain." —Robert Zucker

See Your Thoughts

What self-talk pulls you toward thinking like a victim? For example: "My life is unfair." "I never get a break." "I have the worst luck." "Why me?" "Why my family?" Write your thoughts here:

Do you want your hurts and setbacks to define you as a victim? How do these thoughts hold you back from growing into your God-given identity?

What are your *why* questions? Are they me-centered: "Why is this happening to me?" Or are they God-centered: "God, what do you want to teach me?"

We may never get answers to our *whys* this side of heaven. So, how can you change your mind and get off the mental loop of "why, why, why?"

A me-centered world keeps us small and boxed-up. So, we have to remember who our real enemy is. It's not people. It's not even our difficult circumstances.

Set Your Mind

Read John 10:10 and see what Jesus, our Good Shepherd and Protector, says to you.

Who is the thief, and what is his sole purpose?

What does Jesus give you?

CHAPTER NINE: VICTIM MINDSET

Satan steals, kills, and destroys. Jesus gives life—satisfying and abundant life. He did not create you to be a victim, stuck in small-living.

Read John 16:33. While it's true Jesus gives abundant life, what will you also experience?

Jesus tells you to have courage. Why?

Jesus overcame the world of trials and sorrow. His suffering, which seemed like a horrible defeat, became the ultimate victory—for Him and for you. But you still live in this world where the enemy schemes. So, armor up.

Read Ephesians 6:10–18. What pieces of body armor are we to put on?

In the New Living Translation we see, "stand firm," "standing firm," "stand your ground." We stand in the victory already won for us.

In Joshua 10, we see Joshua lead Israel's army to miraculous victory over five enemy armies. He has the five kings brought to him and gives the battle-weary soldiers a visual of what God does for them.

"When they had them all there in front of Joshua, he called up the army and told the field commanders who had been with him, 'Come here. Put your feet on the necks of these kings.' They stepped up and put their feet on their necks.

Joshua told them, "Don't hold back. Don't be timid. Be strong! Be confident! This is what God will do to all your enemies when you fight them" (Joshua 10:24–25 MSG).

My friend, the next time your mind pulls you toward thinking like a victim, imagine God standing on the neck of your enemy.

Mighty Victorious Warrior, remember who and Whose you are.

Seek & Speak What's True

I am defined by I AM. Jesus, the King of Kings, raised me to a new and empowered life with Him. I am defined by that victory, not by thoughts that tell me I'm a victim.

Because God, _____

_____ , I am _____

_____.

Celebrate

Father, thank you for this abundant life You give! Though trials and sorrows come, I am grateful they do not define me.

CHAPTER 10

Scarcity: Reclaim Your Value & Voice

"One of the most serious and rewarding activities of life is that of trying to discover who we are, why we are the way we are, and—if we don't like what we see—what we can do about it."
~ Lucille Forer & Henry Still, The Birth Order Factor: How Your Personality is Influenced by Your Place in the Family

Rain drizzled on my pony tail as I stood on the riverbank with my tennis shoes squished into Tennessee mud. Jeff, standing at the edge of the churning rapids, plopped onto the front of a raft. My heartbeat pounded my ribs, squeezed my throat, and echoed in my ears. *Are you crazy? Right up front?*

That red devil had no seats and it looked really bouncy. Like bouncy-house bouncy. And that river? It was narrow and the whitewater twisted and clawed at the air above it. Not at all the rolling whitecapped waves of my beloved Mississippi.

My dad taught me about the dangers of a river's undertow. How even under peaceful waters, it hides silent, ready to grab and pull you under. So when our river guide/mountain man spoke, I listened. Birdman, with wild eyes and a wide grin, warned me, "If you fall out, don't let your feet touch bottom, it *will* grab you and it *will* hold you under."

What? How will I know where my feet are? Oh, heck no. I will drown. I will die. And the chafing! Water soaked through denim shorts. Nope. Chilling on the riverbank is cool with me. Safe, comfy, dry…ish.

The rafting trip came a few months after talking to Diana in her counseling room. God invited me on a soul-deep surrender to unstuff my voice and value—to unstuff *me*. Determined to be free, I said, "Bring it on." I stepped all-in to find abundant life in my divine design.

But whitewater rafting? What was I thinking?

Fear of catapulting down a dangerous river is quite rational. But fear that keeps us stuck in the mud of unhealthy thought patterns is not. A scarcity mindset tells us to stay small and don't take risks. It drowns out our value and our voice.

- I can't. I shouldn't. I'm not enough.
- Ssshhh…waves are scary. Don't make waves.

These LIARs whisper words that make us inwardly timid. They create an undercurrent of tension and anxiety. This persistent and subconscious reaction to our environment drags us in the opposite direction of the abundant life Jesus promises. But our subconscious selves want and need to be heard. God stirs us up because we aren't made for small-living.

Come on. Let's jump on the raft. It's time we unashamedly reclaim our God-ordained value and voice.

> *"This is for the kids who know that the worst kind of fear isn't the thing that makes you scream, but the one that steals your voice and keeps you silent."* —Author Abby Norman

Our voice is:

A. "[A] medium or agency of expression. To give voice to one's feelings."[1]
B. "The right or opportunity to express a choice or opinion or participate in a decision."[2]

CHAPTER TEN: SCARCITY

There are countless reasons why fear and shame might block the ability to form and use our healthy voice. For this chapter, we'll focus on messages we picked up from living with authoritarian parents, which creates an environment with strong adult superiority. We aren't looking for someone to blame. We want to see what formed us so we are informed and growing forward.

Here are a few characteristics of authoritarian parents:

- They are obedience oriented and are "to be obeyed without question."[3] Because I said so.
- They don't encourage discussion. We don't talk about it. Children should be seen and not heard.
- They do not allow verbal give-and-take.[4] Don't share your feelings or opinions.
- They are low on warmth and high on control.[5] Suck it up, soldier on.

I think of warmth as grace, and control as shame. Grace fosters freedom to become who we're created to be. Shame demands we conform and blocks our unique development. When individuality isn't encouraged, we may lack self-worth and confidence. In a domineering presence, we aren't free to express ourselves or encouraged to think independently. We often become perfectionists and people-pleasers. See how we get lost in what we do and who we do it for?

Controlled by external pressure, we lose autonomy and become subordinate. It's hard to trust ourselves, so decision making becomes difficult. Always deferring to others' wants, needs, and preferences becomes a habit.

This is a bit embarrassing to share, but until a couple years ago, I used to stress about changing the thermostat in my own home. I wrestled with the subtle external control of an authoritarian, waiting to zap me for stepping out of line. Rational, healthy thinking finally woke me up. "What is going on, Robin? You're a grown woman and this is your home. It's totally okay to do this."

We see why marriages and families led by an authoritarian don't do healthy conflict and communication. Some of us, despite being hushed, learned to get loud and fight. But many of us learned to get quiet and submissive around demanding, domineering people, aka bullies.

Long after we live in this environment, it still affects us. Caught up in scarcity's silent undercurrent, our conditioned responses remain. Stay safe. Conform. Don't make waves. Suck it up.

Fear and Shame-based Messages:

- My opinions and emotions aren't important.
- My words aren't valued = I'm not valued.
- Don't speak up. I'll be laughed at, ignored, or punished.
- Comments or questions are disrespect or back talk.
- Snap in line. There is no room for error.
- Something is fundamentally wrong with me.

Sheesh. That's a lot. Does any of it resonate with you? These messages can make it impossible to speak up. We might even feel inferior to others. It's a habitual response so automatic it bypasses our conscious thinking. No wonder we have irrational fear and avoid conflict at all costs. And the cost is often too, too much.

> *"When children are shamed for expressing normal needs, valid emotions, or personal opinions, they survive by learning 'Deny your needs, ignore your feelings, and don't have an opinion, or things will get even worse.' As adults, they then discover that they have lost touch with their core—they don't know what they feel, need, or truly believe. What helped them survive abuse—underreacting—now costs them dearly as adults. Ultimately, underreacting to life out of fear costs the most precious thing you have to offer: yourself."* —Paul Coughlin & Jennifer D. Degler, Ph.D., No More Christian Nice Girl

Do you hear the scarcity? Deny, ignore, don't have, don't know, under-react, costly. Heavy stuff. These internalized fears and habits come

CHAPTER TEN: SCARCITY

to the surface in our relationships and our jobs in and away from home.

In that busy, shifting season after Alex was born, God showed me how much my value and voice were still wrapped up in what I did and who I did it for. As my roles and responsibilities as a mom changed, my irrational fears and inferiors showed up big time. Alongside the over-inflated sense of responsibility for everything and everyone, my battle to be who God created got really real. Major on-the-job-training.

Our normal family arguments and disagreements stirred up an internal heart-pounding panic. My drive to get things tidy and under control—to fix it all—made unmet requests for help seem like push back and disrespect. Being unheard, I felt small, blocked, and claustrophobic. People-pleasing showed up strong. I didn't want to make waves and have anyone feel mad or sad, uncomfortable or inconvenienced. Even though I was. Speaking up to break fifty-plus years of unhealthy habits was harder than ever because they were about to be brought to the Light.

At just the right time, our gentle Father lifted my head and held my hand, "Come on, it's time to deal with some more mental strongholds."

The Tenacity of Scarcity

As I charged forward to write about being stuck, I got stuck. That boxed up, not-able-to-move feeling sparked painful flashbacks. My arms hung heavy, and I rested my forehead on my desk. Remembering my therapist's advice, I pushed away from my computer to practice some self-care.

Grabbing a backpack, snack, journal, and colored pencils, I drove across my noisy Chicago suburb to a patch of woods behind a Franciscan convent and retreat center. As I approached the walking path, I prayed a risky prayer. "God, take me to the depths so I can reach the heights." I resisted thinking about anybody else. I was there to enjoy the sun on my skin, the smell of wet leaves, and the rippling water in the creek. To rest and receive whatever God had for me.

At the end of the trail, I sat under a tree, opened my journal, and dumped my thoughts. God revealed how much I was still bound to internalized childhood trauma. He showed me why I struggled to write and manage my home. Why I reacted to push back by shrinking back. At fifty-three years old, I was still a pro at eggshell-walking.

It frustrated me to see how I still reacted like a timid girl tiptoeing around an alcoholic, authoritarian parent. How I adjusted to the mood in the room to avoid conflict. How I still read people so I wouldn't rattle them. Back then, there were angry silences and razor-sharp words. And some days there weren't. But the stress and self-protective habits remained in me.

Do any of these things ring true for you? These hyper-vigilant behaviors and unpredictabilities create undercurrents of stress and anxiety. When feeling threatened, our insides ramp up and we stay in problem-solving mode.

Wayne Muller, from his book *Legacy of the Heart: The Spiritual Advantages of a Painful Childhood,* encourages us:

"You are not broken; child suffering is not a mortal wound, and it did not irrevocably shape your destiny. You need not remove, destroy, or tear anything out of yourself in order to build something new. Your challenge is not to keep trying to repair what was damaged; your practice instead is to reawaken what is already wise, strong, and whole within you, to cultivate those qualities of heart and Spirit that are available to you in this very moment."

If I have to claim one life verse, it's 2 Timothy 1:7:

"For God has not given us a spirit of fear and timidity, but of power, love, and self-discipline." The New King James Version ends with "a sound mind." This promise from our Creator makes us resilient. We are not timid. We persevere, determined to face our fears. It is good to see when we react from low value and learned voicelessness. We get to decide what to do with these ingrained thoughts and habits.

For me, it meant facing the place where I learned to eggshell-walk.

It's Time to Make Some Waves

Before my mom could downsize and sell her home, she moved into an assisted living apartment. After visiting her, I'd stop by the house

CHAPTER TEN: SCARCITY

to sort through stuff. But being back there brought it all up. The flashbacks, the anger, the tears, the tension. Too much to sort through in one day. So I never stayed long.

On an especially difficult day, I hurried through the kitchen to leave. Passing the table and my dad's empty chair by the window, I saw him with his eyes squinted and jaw tensed. My heart rate ramped up and my chest tightened. I recalled teen-me rushing to the door. *Breathe, Robin.* God's Spirit reminded me of 2 Timothy 1:7, and it flipped my mental switch. So I spoke up.

"Oh no. I'm not that little girl anymore. You will not win today. I'm not leaving like this." Determined to clean out and unbox myself, courage met rage.

Turning around, adult-me showed up. Not to read the room and walk on eggshells. Not to sense if it was safe and hurry past an unpredictable dad. Letting myself feel the discomfort, I sobbed and gave pain a voice. I yelled at the empty chair. "You were supposed to protect me! You played the victim and didn't even try to get help for yourself!" There were more colorful words I won't share here—stuffed for decades, fueled by anger and a profound sadness.

Then that fine line between hate and love shifted a bit. I saw Dad there, shoulders relaxed, holding my baby boys as they cooed and he smiled that big close-mouthed grin. But my anger wasn't done.

I shouted at the house. "I hate you! You were supposed to be a safe and happy place!" I forced myself to think past the junk and a few more memories stirred. Jeff's marriage proposal at the front door, our engagement ring hidden in my bedroom, my sister's marriage ceremony in the living room, nieces and nephews running around. Wanting more but exhausted, I gave myself grace. Walking out, I slammed the door, twisted the bolt-lock in place and smiled.

Brené Brown's words about vulnerability explain exactly how I felt in that moment: "You'll…wonder how you can feel so brave and afraid at the same time…brave, afraid, and very, very alive."[6]

A couple years later, my sisters and I signed the house over to a new owner. I walked through one last time and realized I'd already made peace with it. All those years, all those empty rooms. They no longer stirred an undercurrent of fear, tension, and anxiety. Emptied of stuff, it was just a good house. It still didn't feel like home, but that's okay. Because I was free.

<<<>>>

This newfound strength and freedom did not come easy. It took a few years and multiple visits to that old house to let myself feel all the emotions—bit by bit. I gave myself no time line on when to be done with the pain, anger, and sadness. I just let them be.

My friend, this is hard work. So we love ourselves through the process with grace and patience. Because if we soldier on and suck it up, we stay bound. To re-awaken our voices and self-worth, we need less inner combat and more self-compassion.

We Are Made for More Than Less-Than

"One of the great sorrows which came to human beings when Adam and Eve left the Garden was the loss of memory, memory of all that God's children are meant to be." —Madeleine L'Engle, Walking on Water: Reflections on Faith and Art

When we seek our value and strong voice, God sends us love notes. As I did the work to stop tiptoeing around my life, I received a Facebook message from my brother Craig's widow. Debbie shared a sentence from a letter he sent from Saigon, Viet Nam, circa 1970. I was six years old. In it, he responds to a family picture.

In the quiet of my home office, I sat on the floor by the window and read my big brother's words, over and over—slowly soaking up each word. "Robin looks a little older but she still has that devilish gleam in her eye 'cause she knows that no one better mess with her and if they try, they won't even know what hit them."

I heard Craig's gentle voice. His humor, his teasing, his love of fam-

CHAPTER TEN: SCARCITY

ily—his love for me. I cried happy/sad tears and thanked God for the gift. He showed me who I was before Viet Nam shredded the best of my dad. Back when we still took Sunday drives, threw Frisbees at family picnics, and watched Marlin Perkins' *Wild Kingdom* on our black and white TV.

My friend, sometimes we forget who we were before the wounding years because so much of us went into hiding. God gave me a peek at my six-year-old self. I see the child, strong and feisty. And I remember the teen rebel, smart and resourceful. And the woman, capable and stronger than I think.

Whom does God want you to see? You were not a problem to be solved. You were not weak—you were a child. A survivor who figured out how to feel safe in situations you didn't understand and were not responsible for.

So, we respond to her like a loving, listening, nurturing parent: "You are safe. You don't need to hide or be afraid. Thank you for being so strong, but I've got it now." This self-talk flows from love, kindness, empathy, and compassion.

I doubt my sister-in-law knew the impact my brother's words would have on me. But God did. He knows what we need to heal our inner conflict and find our resilience. Our Creator reminds us we are made in His image. With power, love, and the healthy mind of Christ.

Power-Walking

Duking it out with fear empowers us with self-respect. Dealing with inner conflict, we can deal with outer conflict. We move forward to communicate better in our normal day-to-day interactions. As we value ourselves and find our confident voice, we get to stop letting our past and our people define us as less-than.

And life gives us plenty of voice lessons, doesn't it? Whether we manage a home, an office—or both—speaking up for our ideas, opinions, and preferences is important because we bring value to the table. We deserve to be heard.

Free of tiptoeing around my past, it was time to break the daily habits with my family. But we were all adjusting to our new season and the stronger-me emerging. For decades, I conditioned them to respond to a more wishy-washy, people-pleasing me. Outspoken one day, giving in the next. Because sometimes it's just easier to do it ourselves, isn't it? But being inconsistent sends a message that our requests aren't important to us. So, why do we expect others to take them seriously?

And why don't we hold them accountable to follow through? Because it's mentally exhausting and sometimes our emotions get too wrapped up in our conversations. Each unmet request presses on our less-thans and being unheard feels like being unvalued or even rejected. Then, whether we blow up or hush up, we focus on the failure and frustration and the cycle continues.

Until we remember that people are not responsible for our lack of self-worth and our emotional responses. We are. That's why rooting ourselves in our Creator God is so vital. His Holy Spirit empowers us to keep showing up. Because if we come to a conflict already inferior and defeated by our thoughts and emotions, everyone loses. We all miss out on growing ourselves and our relationships.

But here's the tricky part—if we didn't learn healthy conflict, we don't know what it looks like. Disagreeing always feels unsafe because we fear others' responses and reactions. We don't want to create division, make waves, or hurt feelings. We don't want to make anyone mad or sad, uncomfortable or inconvenienced. Even though we are.

As I mentioned before, arguments and disagreements with my husband and grown children used to toss me into a panic. Conflict seemed to create distance between us and it gutted me. But I learned to stand in the discomfort and tell myself the truth. "Robin, this is normal. Couples argue. Parents and children disagree. It's okay. This is healthy. It's how we grow." I ask, *Are my motives right? Yes. Is this worth the fight? Yes. Then hang in there.*

If people agree all the time, someone is eggshell-walking.

Another thought pattern that reinforces a habit of acquiescing in conflict and communication is the lie that Christ followers have to be

CHAPTER TEN: SCARCITY

nice. While we are called to be good, we won't always be perceived as nice. Yes, we grow a gentle, quiet spirit like Jesus. But even He spoke up with firm and sometimes scandalous words to defend truth, goodness, righteousness, and the outcast. He is a protector, not a pleaser. Love does not always look or sound nice. And sometimes by playing nice, we're vulnerable to those who don't fight fair. We let them roll right over us.

And that's what bullies do. They steamroll over everyone. They are blamers and shamers. We find them at home, at work, and even on our church committees. Maybe they enjoy being mean, rude, and insensitive. Maybe their tough outspokenness is their self-defense habit to hide their own issues. But we—my strong friend—were not created to be doormats.

I so admire women who exude confidence and articulate well. I used to compare myself to them and thought there was something wrong with me. But nope. Now, I know being an introvert is okay. Quietness is a strength too. Extroverts have their own set of skills. We're all learning to balance the strengths and weaknesses of our personalities.

So we do need to learn to discern who's strong and who's just a loud bully. The bully is the one who won't hear you because she speaks over you. Saying the same thing over and over, only louder and louder. She pushes her way and has to prove you wrong in front of her minions—her "yes-women." She's also good at placing blame, so we say, "Nope, you can't put this on me." And if we call her out and try to elevate a conversation, it backfires. Because a bully needs to be right and she has to have control.

Remember my friend, people do not give us our value and we cannot give them our voice. Their words are simply *their words*. We won't let them shrink wrap us to fit their world of scarcity. We will not give them that power over us anymore.

As author and first lady Eleanor Roosevelt said, "No one can make us feel inferior without our consent."

Raise Your Sight and Your Thoughts

No matter how well we articulate or how others respond, we are children of the Most High God. In His presence, we are safe. Rooted in who we are as God's child, we stand our ground and no longer walk around timid.

We are so done with adolescent responses to adult opportunities. We are so done with an undertow of shame telling us we're somehow inferior to others—that we are weak, or voiceless, or unvalued. We are grateful that God reveals scarcity thinking so He can heal it. We get unstuck from the mud and see it's okay to make some waves. We plop onto the raft, face our fears, and find abundant life in our divine design.

My friend, do not relinquish your God-given authority to any fear or anyone. Remember to reclaim the power we talked about in chapter eight. That death-to-life power redeems pain for good.

Now, I use my old eggshell-walking habits to connect me, not control me. Reading the room, studying people, and knowing when to be quiet and when to speak are gifts of discernment. To listen and learn, to comfort and encourage.

With our confidence rooted firmly in the mind of Christ, we bring our whole selves safely to any situation, especially our socially awkward parts. They make us 100 percent human, 100 percent our true selves. They belong. We belong.

> *"Your life is not a problem to be solved, but a gift to be opened. Just as the pain, hurt, and suffering that came to you as a child were powerfully real, so is the tangible resilience of your spirit equally vital and alive."* —Wayne Muller, Legacy of the Heart: The Spiritual Advantages of a Painful Childhood

Jesus' Spirit reawakens the resilience of our God-designed spirit, and we find our place of safety, belonging, and peace.

CHAPTER TEN: SCARCITY

STUDY QUESTIONS

"When we make ourselves behave other than the way we were accustomed to act, we are changing our identity." ~ Douglas & Deborah Bly, Loving an Adult Child of an Alcoholic

Remember how fear kept me stuck on the muddy riverbank in Tennessee? Tired of playing it safe, I finally sat on the front seat of that bouncy raft and hurled down the raging whitewater. It was the most terrifying, exhilarating, horrible, and fun ride of my life.

Kinda like this journey to find our divine design, eh? In times of stress and conflict—with self or others—we need to be battle-ready. And because our mind is a battlefield, that's where we stop the undertow and silence anxious, irrational thought.

See Your Thoughts

God offers you real life—an enJOYable, satisfying, abundant life. Is your lack of self-worth stealing this gift from you—as if you somehow don't deserve it?

Is there something you want to do, but you're stuck in the mud of fear and indecision? Whatever comes to mind—however small or big it seems—write it down.

Now that you see it written out, read it. What do you feel? Not just an emotion, but do you actually have a physical reaction? If so, describe it.

Does your mind hear encouraging words? Are there LIARs present? Write out your thoughts.

The Cheerleaders tell me:

The Loud Imaginings Appearing Real tell me:

Who's in charge? Is fear louder than your confidence? If yes, in what ways do you think it hides your value and/or hushes your voice?

How do I do conflict?

CHAPTER TEN: SCARCITY

For the next questions, think about your everyday, ordinary conversations with friends and family.

What do you do when you disagree or have a different opinion?

    Stuff my words

    Blast my words

    Express my thoughts and opinions with calm, confident words

What does a healthy conversation look like to you?

Have you seen healthy conversations and minor conflicts handled well? If so, who modeled that for you?

If normal healthy conflict and conversations don't feel safe—even with people you trust—write down the reasons.

When discussions get difficult, how do you react?

    Avoid: deny, deflect, run

    Dominate: explode, interrupt, intimidate

    Eggshell-walk: don't make waves

    Other: _____

Which of the following statements are true?

> A disagreement feels like rejection.
>
> I take control by being loud and/or using hurtful words. Hurt them before they hurt me.
>
> Silence is my superpower. I can give the silent treatment for days.
>
> I'd rather hush and please people than openly disagree with them.
>
> Other: _____

Self-protective, people-pleasing habits are costly. We are dishonest with others and disloyal to ourself. This harms our inner life and hides our divine design. And self-betrayal feels icky because in our gut we know we're made for more than small-living.

Set Your Mind

God, I accept this gift of abundant life. I want to see my value and have a healthy, confident voice.

A scarcity mindset tells us we are lacking, so we need to know and believe our worth. We need a true and healthy assessment of who and Whose we are.

Read Psalm 23:1. "The LORD is my Shepherd, I lack nothing" (NIV). What do you lack?

Now read the whole psalm. This is an intimate, safe, trusting relationship. What words stand out to you and why?

Your Gentle Shepherd loves you and leads you. What words or phrases show this?

CHAPTER TEN: SCARCITY

Even correction comes from a tender, loving heart—to protect and comfort. Father God cares for what He highly values: you.

We walk in God's ever-presence, provision, and peace. From this place of wholeness—not lacking one good thing—we turn from living in lack to abiding in abundance.

Read Psalm 139.

David describes a deeper, detailed intimacy here. Watch for words and phrases that show how well God knows you. Write them down.

Now write the words that describe where God goes with us:

What does this say about your value and worth?

Verses 13-14 show Creator God knitting and forming you in the womb—shaping who He already imagined you to be. This is your beautiful intrinsic value. And it never changes. Ever. You are a "wonderfully complex" and amazing creation. David says, "How well I know it."

Do you?

Since the first sin-choices in Eden's garden, we have fought to believe our value and to have our own true voices.

Maybe you need to sit with this a bit. Your head might know this to be true, but what about your heart? Pray, write your thoughts, or just simply be still.

I hope these next practical exercises help you. Use them to reveal lies, renew your mind, and reclaim your resilience.

Our mind creates some sketchy stories about us. While we focus on our perceived less-thans, others see our strength and moxie. We need an outside perspective. So, I know it's awkward, but ask someone to share the positive character traits he or she sees in you.

And while you're at it, what do you value in yourself? This isn't bragging. Part of our self-care is being self-aware. So hush your inner critic's negative self-talk and go for it.

Positive traits others see in me:

Positive traits I see in me:

These good qualities of your heart and personality reveal your divine design. Enjoy this visual of your strengths. Keep it in your phone, on the fridge, or taped to a wall. May these words—these true words—replace lies and renew your mind.

A Healthy Voice

Healthy communication is a common challenge. Too often, we fear how others will react or what they will think about us. This habit might be from past experiences, but current relationships can reinforce it too.

We're all still learning how to listen, speak, and react well to each other because nobody is exempt from traumatic life events that produce pain or psychological injury. No wonder God tells us the way to healing is by changing the way we think.

Here are some in-the-moment questions that trained my brain to think higher and respond better to every day stress.

Awareness: What is happening in my body?

Our body often reacts to stress before our mind does. It alerts us to perceived danger. This fight or flight reaction is automatic. If we don't stop and think about it, our emotions take charge. Noticing our body's alarm system helps us take back our power. We intercept emotions and ask good, rational questions.

Arrest the thought: What am I thinking?

In the See Your Thoughts section, we looked at how we do conflict. Remember, you have the mind of Christ (see 1 Cor. 2:16). Take lies captive and tell them, "No! This is not who I am."

Anything contrary to Jesus' character is not part of our divine design. So, we also check in with our hearts.

Ask: What are my motives in this fight with myself or others?

Let's look at Psalm 139 again. David begins and ends this psalm with an open invitation for God to check his motives. He reciprocates the intimate relationship.

"GOD, investigate my life; get all the facts firsthand. I'm an open book to you…Investigate my life, O God, find out everything about me; Cross-examine and test me, get a clear picture of what I'm about; See for yourself whether I've done anything wrong— then guide me on the road to eternal life" (vv 1, 23–24 MSG).

David trusts God to deal with his enemies and his own heart issues too.

When we listen to our bodies, arrest our thoughts, and check our motives, we change how we respond to fear and stress.

Awaken God's Warrior Spirit: Who am I in Christ?

You know who she is. She roots her confidence in her God-designed intrinsic value. She's there even when she doesn't feel all warrior-y and battle-ready. Dignified, with a side of sassy, she faces fear and power-walks right through difficult moments.

Your voice is strong too. You speak when you text a friend or take food to a neighbor. Others hear it when you hush and really listen. So speak strong, my friend. With or without words.

Lean into this intimate, trusting relationship with your Creator.

Seek & Speak What's True

I am defined by I AM.

Because God, _____

_____ , I am _____

_____ .

Celebrate

"How precious it is, Lord, to realize that you are thinking about me constantly! I can't even count how many times a day your thoughts turn toward me. And when I waken in the morning, you are still thinking of me!" (Psalm 139:17–18 TLB).

Father, thank You. In You, we reclaim our value and confident voices. Where we see our deficiencies, You see our sufficiency in Christ. Where we live in lack, You wait for us to enjoy abundance. Because we are on-purpose creations, we are valued beyond any human measure. All Your creation is marvelous, so we believe we are pretty amazing too.

CHAPTER 11

Chameleon: Reclaim Your Place

"We've been taught by life that being ourselves is dangerous, risky, wrong. We've been hurt, scarred, disappointed, and wounded… so like a turtle retreating to its shell, we've retreated behind our walls." ~ Alexandra Headrick, Remembering Original Glory

At my first writer's conference, I ran and hid in my hotel room. Well, I didn't really run. More like walked awkwardly fast in new heels because I couldn't process in public what was happening inside me.

A few days prior, I arrived at the five-star hotel where a concierge escorted me and my suitcase to a room. Excited but intimidated by this new experience, I fumbled for words and forgot to tip. Praying through the you're-so-dumb moment, I ate the chocolate mint from the pillow and put on the fluffy white robe. I'd find the concierge later and make up for my blunder.

Hanging up my new clothes, I decided what to wear the next day and set my morning alarm. Then I re-decided what to wear, arranged pens and notebooks, re-read the schedule, and re-checked my alarm.

The following days, I met other word nerds, ate amazing food, and took notes from well-known authors and other writing professionals. There was so much to digest. Each night, I plopped on the bed, with my head loud and spinning. Then the third day, as I sat at a round table draped in white and long-stemmed water glasses, it hit me. An overwhelming sense that something terrifying was about to happen. Not around me, but *in* me.

That's when I escaped across the long courtyard to the hotel. Once in my room, I considered hiding for the next two days. I could get room service, enjoy the view of the Colorado mountains, and call it a vacation. "Sheesh, Robin. What's your problem? Get it together." Resisting that shaming voice and the cute little wine and liquor bottles in the cabinet, I grabbed my journal and sank into the garden tub.

Up to my neck in hot water, I sobbed and prayed. "What is going on? Why am I freaking out?

<<<>>>

We all have basic human needs to be loved and accepted, and to belong somewhere and to someone. We deeply desire to be seen, heard, and known. But it's hard to trust. So, whether on purpose or subconsciously, we build walls and develop a habit of hiding. Like chameleons, we change to fit into our surroundings because being real—showing up with our awkward, imperfect self—is risky. People might not like us. They might misunderstand us. We might fail. And it all feels like rejection. Yes, expressing our true selves is absolutely terrifying.

So sobbing and soaking my scared self in the garden tub—I breathed deeply and sank under the water. God spoke to my spirit. "You've hidden long enough." This was my first hint at what would be revealed in counseling a few years later; I'd been hiding for most of my life.

I raised my head above the water and grabbed my journal. Dripping water onto paper, I scribbled: "I see this generational habit of hiding. 'We look okay, so we are okay.' I don't want safe, shallow relationships. I don't want to be friendless, boring, and predictable. God, You didn't create me to play a role or prove my worth. I don't understand all of this but something new is happening, like a re-birth. And tomorrow's my forty-fifth birthday. God, You are a Poet."

God calls us out. Out of the shallows to show our real selves, pro-

CHAPTER ELEVEN: CHAMELEON

cess real emotions, and make real connections—to live a *real* life. We aren't created to conform to outside pressure but to live from His Spirit in us—from the inside out. It's time to get real or go home. To stop hiding, start trusting, and step into our calling. To love God, ourself, and people.

Going into Hiding

With love and belonging as our greatest needs—our greatest fear is rejection. We may experience it after divorce, job loss, broken promises, a loved one's death, shattered friendships, etc. Someone or something didn't come through for us. Abandonment creates mistrust. Mistrust creates walls. Walls block our ability to form attachments, the healthy relationships we need.

We're most vulnerable to rejection with those we need the most. My dad came back from Viet Nam so overwhelmed by his traumatic experiences that he retreated inward and kinda checked out.

I'm not sure what's worse—watching our heroes plummet or not being able to shake our need for their affirmation—an "Atta girl," "I love you," or "I'm proud of you." So, we retreated behind walls and acted like we didn't need them. This creates inner tension with our need for intimacy: *See me, don't see me. Love me, don't love me.* An inner warring against our truest self, the person who's purpose is to fully live and fully love.

With psychological injury somewhere in our history—recent or long ago—our brains decided to protect us. We retreated and found our need for acceptance in appearances and perfect performance.

My friend, we have hidden in plain sight long enough. This chameleon skin we're in wasn't made for us and we know it. We are created to be real and belong. Vulnerability is raw and terrifying, but it's so worth the risk. Hiding is a habit we can break.

Let's look at lies that hide us and disconnect us from our most vital connections.

Created to Connect with Our Creator

Here's the lie we believe: If I wear the right clothes, perform well, and acquire cool stuff people will accept me. *Then* I have value and I belong.

This is the outside-in thinking we inherited. Since Eve and Adam had it backwards, all humanity does too. We are tempted to fix and fill our core needs with outside things, voices, and people.

Let's flip the lie and tell ourself the Truth: I'm already valued, already accepted, and I already belong. My Creator satisfies my core needs so I am already whole and free to live from the inside-out, to let my true self be seen and make authentic connections.

Healthy relationships start with this solid truth. We belong to God. Period. Final answer. God's love does not let go, check out, or leave us. We. are. His.

Our relationship with our Creator is designed to be a constant connection. But the very first lie and the very first sin-choice created fear, shame, and self-centeredness, and humanity went into hiding. This created a chasm between God and us. In the process, "we've lost something precious, and we know it. It's embedded into our souls; before original sin there was original glory."[1]

Jesus reconnects us to our original glory—a right relationship in God's constant, safe, and loving presence. While His end of the connection is quite secure, ours gets a little shaky. Trust does not come natural to us humans, especially when we're deeply wounded.

When we experience loss and abandonment in a child-parent relationship, we often attach human faults to God. If a parent is absent, angry, distant, and demanding, we might assume God is too. We subconsciously hold on to shame habits in our relationships. Shame births perfectionism. Hello, outside-in thinking.

If I'm good and follow the rules, then you'll love me and won't leave.

We create the perfect do and don't list because performance is tangible. Something we can control. We can see it and do it. And we just might get an "atta girl."

CHAPTER ELEVEN: CHAMELEON

We even bring our do and don't list into our relationship with Jesus. What does a Christian look like and what does she do? *I'll be the perfect Christian, the perfect parent, the perfect friend, the perfect homemaker, the perfect employee.* A tidy list gives us clear, concrete instructions on how to perform well, but it leads to burn-out. Performance—no matter how perfect—is a stressful, shallow experience and does not satisfy our deeper, spiritual needs.

Unconditional Love = God is Already Pleased with You

My friend, before you do or don't do a darn thing, God not only accepts you, He delights in you. We see this illustrated in our Savior's baptism, the official beginning of His ministry.

As Jesus came out of the water, His Father was the first to celebrate. "You are My Son, My Beloved, in You I am well-pleased *and* delighted!" (Luke 3:22b AMP).

Jesus had not yet performed any official ministry work. Scripture tells us the Holy Spirit descended like a dove and immediately led Jesus into the desert to wrestle temptation. How painfully hungry, thirsty, and lonely He must have been.

For forty days, the deceiver offered Him the whole world of pleasure, power, and popularity. But Jesus resisted, because He knew to Whom He belonged. One hundred percent. I imagine Jesus clinging to God. Walking and talking, relying on the words He heard from the Father at His baptism. *My Father, I know I am Your Beloved and You are well-pleased with me.*

In those desert days, it's likely the Psalms ministered to Jesus as they do to us.

"I cling to you; your strong right hand holds me securely" (Psalm 63:8).

"Let [us] praise the LORD for his great love and for the wonderful things he has done for [us]. For he satisfies the thirsty and fills the hungry with good things" (Psalm 107:8–9 paraphrase added).

We are God's beloved children. Held, cherished, satisfied, and dearly loved.

"Since, then, you have been raised with Christ, set your hearts on things above, where Christ is, seated at the right hand of God. Set your minds on things above, not on earthly things. For you died, and *your life is now hidden with Christ in God*" (Col. 3:1–3 NIV, author's emphasis).

By grace, we are "hidden with Christ in God." Jesus + nothing. That's a connection we can trust. So, dearly loved ones, we are safe to open up and trust ourselves.

Created to Love and Accept Ourselves

In Matthew 22:37–39, we read this commandment: "'You must love the Lord your God with all your heart, all your soul, and all your mind.' This is the first and greatest commandment. A second is equally important: 'Love your neighbor as yourself.'"

We can only genuinely love others when we love ourselves. If we don't accept ourselves unconditionally, we reject parts of us. And we will always be longing to belong. When disconnected inside, how can we be whole, secure, and settled? If we want to be healthy and wholly love like Jesus does, we have to stop shaming ourselves for being ourselves.

To deal with traumatic events, we learned to detach from people and unsafe situations. As our identity was forming, we detached from ourselves too. We retreated into our heads because we didn't know how to process all of the scary emotions. We may have stuffed all the fun and fluffy ones too—all those beautiful and essential parts of us. When we hide them, we hide from ourselves. So, maybe we don't trust ourself because we haven't expressed her enough to really know her.

Do you remember when my art therapist asked me to draw what emotional distress felt like? I drew a black rectangular box. A tiny, tight casket of trauma and turmoil. I didn't know so much of me was still bound tight. It's easy to hide until Jesus' promise of abundant life calls us to rise up and go forward. And yes, it's risky and scary.

Author and sociologist Brené Brown describes it well:

"Yes, we are totally exposed when we are vulnerable. Yes, we are in the torture chamber that we call uncertainty. And yes, we're taking

CHAPTER ELEVEN: CHAMELEON

a huge emotional risk when we allow ourselves to be vulnerable. But there's no equation where taking risks, braving uncertainty, and opening ourselves up to emotional exposure equals weakness."[2]

God created emotions and He wants us to express their whole spectrum. Joy is as much a part of us as sadness. But we can forget—or maybe never learned—how to express it. When we release honest emotions, we stop under-reacting to the good things in life. We stop stuffing the good stuff.

A few days before my son Justin graduated from Air Force basic training, I realized what I needed to un-stuff. I wanted to feel and express all the joy so he wouldn't just hear, "I'm proud of you." He'd see it, feel it, and remember it. So despite the humidity of Texas' triple digits, I hugged that kid. I opened up my heart and let tears mingle with sweat and mascara. It didn't matter that everyone else was more quiet and composed. And I did not care how I looked or what anyone thought. I ugly cried. Because it was our moment.

Being real, I showed up for my son and myself. An intimate, genuine connection. That was the beginning of an intentional effort to let myself feel the whole spectrum of God-given emotions. Sometimes, I still have to remind myself to feel, to enjoy, to be present, and not to detach.

We are created for joy and celebration. Let's not miss the moments and memories.

Created for Community

"I define connection as the energy that exists between people when they feel seen, heard, and valued; when they can give and receive without judgment; and when they derive sustenance and strength from the relationship." —Brené Brown, The Gifts of Imperfection: Let Go of Who You Think You're Supposed to Be and Embrace Who You Are

Have you ever wanted deeper friendships but shrink back?

Brené Brown has researched shame and vulnerability for decades. In her book I quoted above, she says, "Until we can receive with an open heart, we are never really giving with an open heart."

We are not created for shallow living. We're made with a brain that's neuro-biologically hard-wired to connect with others. But we self-sabotage because it's also wired to protect us. We struggle to trust and a part of us detaches. We want to get close but push people away.

My time in art therapy revealed my fear of attachments and how I avoided them. A friend would say, "Let's sit at our booth." or "We love our coffee, don't we?" and I didn't know how to respond or how to receive it. It created inner panic and a very awkward moment. Stay shallow. Stay safe. Her bonding words bounced right off a protective wall.

Some adult children of alcoholics find it difficult to trust. We struggle with intimate relationships because we feel like we lost control. We often have to guess what normal, healthy emotions and relationships look like. Up until a few years ago, my protective walls were high and strong.

During my season of deep depression and profound loneliness, God showed me how to begin to build healthy friendships. Connecting with God, myself, and others—in that order—lifted me out of darkness.

In talking to women, I see we also self-sabotage deeper connections by rejecting compliments. Why do we remember more put-downs than praises? Think about it. I bet you remember a negative criticism from years ago and barely recall kind words from yesterday.

Our automatic self-talk tells us irrational and ridiculous stories. Even those of us who are strong encouragers struggle to receive kind words.

Give + Receive = Connection

Sitting in my Honda Pilot in the Office Max parking lot, I read a Mother's Day card from a woman who was a fan of my newspaper column. We never met but corresponded for years via snail mail. I read her words and battled self-sabotage.

"My Dear Girl…" My heart warmed a bit but as I kept reading, my mind started its mean story. Why would she send this? She probably had no one else to send it to. Absurd, irrational, and downright ridic-

CHAPTER ELEVEN: CHAMELEON

ulous thoughts are clues that a mental fight is on like Donkey Kong. I stopped and started over. Slowly.

"My Dear Girl, Robin. You are a blessing in this world." Instead of deflecting her words, I held the card to my chest and let them sink in. Her sweet heart melted walls of mistrust and suspicion and connected to mine.

The same day I read the letter, self-sabotage showed up again in two separate conversations—one with my husband and another with a friend at church. As they spoke to me, a mental fog created a wall, and I heard, *blah, blah, blah, blah, blah*. Kinda like the teacher in Charlie Brown's classroom. But instead of letting my brain fog over, I actually interrupted my people mid-sentence. "Can you please repeat that? Because my brain is trying to reject what you're saying to me."

If we aren't aware of our self-talk and don't arrest this habit of deflecting love and compliments, we'll miss real heart-to-heart connections. When we accept the gift of encouraging words, we disarm lies in our head and learn more about our true selves.

"Sometimes we are scared to let our authentic selves become uncovered. We think we need the status and the look and the friends and the degrees and the lifestyle. But once all that is stripped away and the person we truly are is unveiled for the world to see, we learn one thing. The people who like us will like us. And the people who don't, won't. But we have gained strength in knowing that, like the trees, we have let all the excess go and are still standing strong. Seasons will change and we will bloom again. Without pretending."[3]

Receiving love from God and others gives us self-respect. Self-confidence is important because not everyone will affirm and accept us. That's a fact of life. To expect otherwise is unhealthy and keeps us in chameleon mode. So, we choose our inner circle wisely because we can't and shouldn't trust everyone. Playgrounds aren't the only place we find bullies, takers, and joy suckers. They are neighbors, family members, and fellow Christians.

When we know and own our worth, we recognize takers. Those who grab what you give but don't give back to the relationship. They lie to you but expect you to be perfect. They dump, dump, dump their problems on you but don't listen to yours. They have to be right, they ignore your needs, and steamroll right over you. What we give them is never enough.

Takers cannot and should not be trusted, so we guard our heart, mind, and spirit. Not with walls but with boundaries to protect our peace and joy. We limit our time with takers and are careful what we tell them. As much as I hate small talk, some conversations need to stay there.

Fully accepted by God and ourselves, we also recognize bullies. I mentioned her in the last chapter. She's the one who doesn't hear you because she talks over you. Repeating herself over and over, louder and louder. And there are quiet bullies too. They use charm to subtly get their way, to prove you wrong, and make you doubt yourself. Even the quieter ones are verbally and emotionally abusive. It's called gas-lighting. They shame and blame because nothing is their fault. Ever. And if we call them out, it backfires. Because a bully has to dominate.

In Christ, we are confident and wise. With healthy boundaries, we know when to speak up and when to walk away. We know when to ignore their calls and texts, and when or if we re-engage. We pray for them and let go of our need to friend them or fix them.

"To be nobody-but-yourself in a world which is doing its best, night and day, to make you everybody but yourself—means to fight the hardest battle which any human being can fight—and never stop fighting" (E.E. Cummings, *E.E. Cummings: A Miscellany Revised*).

Sister in Christ, we weren't made to be copies or chameleons. We were born to be originals and called to be different. To be rebels, like Jesus, who go against culture's flow. So when we come to a crossroad, we don't turn to the right or the left. We blow right through on the road less traveled. That, my friend, is where we find abundant life.

Honest with ourselves and fully belonging to God—we fit into our rightful place. We come out of hiding and allow Him to reveal the naked truth of who we pretend to be. How we posture, conform, and perform.

Seeking our divine design—our truest selves—empowers us to show up, reject, and replace the deceiver's lies. Author McNair Wilson, speaking at a writer's conference, explains why we do this. Because "if you don't do you, you doesn't get done and creation suffers."

CHAPTER ELEVEN: CHAMELEON

When we reject pieces of ourselves, we tear apart our soul and we suffer. And because we're created to connect with each other, the world suffers. It's forever robbed of our unique contribution. If we continue to hate, harm, and hide, we shame ourselves and shun God. It's as though we say, "You didn't know what You were doing when You made me."

He knew exactly what He was getting into when He created you. Beloved, He is well-pleased and delighted with you. So today, decide. Make the conscious choice to stop hiding, as often as it takes to stop stuffing yourself into a tight little mold. If you don't get comfortable in your own skin—let your authentic self be seen and heard—how will others really get to know you?

We know some people just won't like us. Some will misunderstand us, and we'll definitely disappoint others. But take heart, Jesus experienced all of that too. He was rejected by the world yet completely accepted by the Father. Securely attached to our Creator, we come confident to any table—already whole, loved, and accepted. We are "hidden in Christ," our strong defender. It's from Him we hear our "Atta girl. I love you and I am proud of you."

Instead of giving up and going home, we come home where we belong—safe and accepted. Resting in our Father's heart, we find ourselves in the One who never leaves.

Dear Daughter,

You were in my mind and heart before I designed you in your mother's womb. I created your inmost being. I see you, I know you, I celebrate you. Your entire life, you've belonged to Me. You *are* mine. Holy and wholly loved. Now rest because I'm not going anywhere. —God

"I am at rest in God alone; my salvation comes from him. He alone is my rock and my salvation, my stronghold; I will never be shaken" (Psalm 62:1–2 CSB).

STUDY QUESTIONS

"Define yourself radically as one beloved by God. This is the true self. Every other identity is illusion." ~ Brennan Manning, Abba's Child

See Your Thoughts

Wall up. Look good. Perform well. And all will be well, right? Not so much.

Our Creator calls us to tear down walls and bust out of boxes. He made us for authentic connections—to trust, open up, and receive.

Who has had hero status in your life's story but has let you down?

Have you forgiven him/her?

"Forgiveness is first for you, the forgiver…to release you from something that will eat you alive; that will destroy your joy and your ability to love fully and openly." —William Paul Young, The Shack

Do you struggle to trust people—even those who stuck by you and proved they are trustworthy? If so, what thoughts hinder you from trusting others?

CHAPTER ELEVEN: CHAMELEON

Do you sense an inner conflict of wanting more intimate relationships but find yourself hiding? "See me, know me…but don't get too close."

If this is true, what thoughts hinder you from opening up to deeper connections? What creates panic in you?

If you deflect compliments, practice how you will begin to receive them. What can you say the next time this happens?

To yourself:

To the other person:

Have you projected human attitudes and actions onto God? If yes, write your thoughts.

Have you ever been in a situation where you felt so out-of-place you panicked? Describe it.

What thoughts create this panic in you?

Do you struggle to let others see the real you? If so, what would it look like to trust yourself—to simply be yourself?

At Home:

At Work:

At Church:

With Friends:

We are created for constant connection with our Creator. The first humans had it. They walked complete in their naked, true selves—one

CHAPTER ELEVEN: CHAMELEON

hundred percent unashamed. Then sin slithered in. Satan deceived Eve by implying that God was holding out on her. She believed what was created in her and for her was not enough. Listening to this outside voice, she made a lethal choice.

"A lie was told. A lie was believed. The circle of love and trust was broken." — Timothy R. Jennings, M.D., The God-Shaped Brain; How Changing Your View of God Transforms Your Life

Let's flip the lies and tell ourself the Truth.

Set Your Mind

Healthy connections with God, ourselves, and others begin with this foundation: we belong to our Creator. His love does not let go, check out, or leave us. We. are. His.

See who you are in Christ and renew your mind. Read and reflect on the following Scripture.

Read Luke 3:22. "You are My Son, My Beloved, in You I am well-pleased and delighted!" (AMP). Let the Father's words to Jesus belong to you too.

Put your name in the blank and read God's love note to you: _____ , you are My daughter, My beloved, in you I am well-pleased and delighted.

Read Psalm 63:1–8. In verse 8, what does God do when we cling to Him?

Read Jeremiah 17:7–8

"But blessed are those who trust in the Lord and have made the Lord their hope and confidence. They are like trees planted along a riverbank, with roots that reach deep into the water. Such trees are not bothered by the heat or worried by long months of drought. Their leaves stay green, and they never stop producing fruit."

When you trust God and plant yourself firmly in His Word and in His love, you are safe and satisfied. You come out of hiding because outside forces are not in charge of you.

Look up Matthew 22:37–39 and see what Jesus says about loving God, ourselves, and others.

How are we to love God?

What does He say is second and *equally* important?

"Since, then, you have been raised with Christ, set your hearts on things above, where Christ is, seated at the right hand of God. Set your minds on things above, not on earthly things. For you died, and *your life is now hidden with Christ in God*" (Col. 3:1–3 NIV author's emphasis).

Seek & Speak What's True

I am defined by I AM

Because God, _____

_____ , I am _____

_____ .

In Christ, I'm already accepted, already approved, and I already belong.

CHAPTER ELEVEN: CHAMELEON

Celebrate

"Here's a radical thought. Wouldn't it be refreshing if we collected our masks and had a bonfire? We could bring hot dogs and marshmallows and revel in getting to know each other…the way God intended us to know each other. The way He knows us. We could talk, really talk. And listen, really listen. And maybe we'd find that under our masks we're still His beloved children, made in His image. We'd see that the masks we hide behind are just cheap imitations of the faces and souls He gave us–and that those flimsy masks can never cover the pure gold He's already spun into us."[4]

CHAPTER 12

Identity Found: Coming Home to the Father's Heart

"There is something sacred about going full circle, the end making sense of the middle." ~ Blogger Laleña Leigh[1]

We all hear them. Those parent-child stories wrapped in warm fluffy blankets. About moms and dads who weren't perfect but loved their children well. The bonds they formed with sons and daughters are foreign yet so attractive.

Though heart-warming, these stories are hard to hear because they are not what we experienced. They magnify the relationship we missed. But as our hearts melt, they also mend. God redeems sadness as "a call to return home and discover there your true belovedness."[2] God is our home. He is the perfect parent who embodies the protective heart of a father and the nurturing heart of a mother. Immeasurably more than even the best earthbound parents, He's the Father who doesn't leave us and doesn't forget who He is, like we humans do.

He knows us from our head to our heart to our toes to our soul. Forever held, "in him we live and move and exist" (Acts 17:28). God lives "outside of time and space yet is closer to you than your own breath."[3]

There is no tighter bond than this. How do we even fathom it?

To belong to such a limitless and loving Father is mind-boggling.

There are not enough brain cells or ink or paper or words to explain this complete, all-encompassing, and eternal love. Yet, that's where we find ourselves. At home in the mind and heart of God. Right where we started.

"Long before he laid down earth's foundations, he had us in mind, had settled on us as the focus of his love, to be made whole and holy by his love. Long, long ago he decided to adopt us into his family through Jesus Christ. (What pleasure he took in planning this!)" (Eph. 1:4–5 MSG).

"It's in Christ that we find out who we are and what we are living for. Long before we first heard of Christ…he had his eye on us, had designs on us for glorious living, part of the overall purpose he is working out in everything and everyone." (Eph. 1:11-12, MSG)

So, our identity search brings us full circle because we were never truly lost.

It's the middle of the story—walking through the hurt to get to the healing— that's a bugger. But "pain travels through family lines until someone is ready to heal it in themselves."[4]

My friend, you did just that. You intercepted pain with courage and moxie, grit and grace. Now, you can stop looking at your past sin, and others' sin against you. You're no longer stuffed into boxes that bind you or wear labels that define you. You are God's child. And He is patient as you continue to mature in your wholeness and holiness.

We read in Acts 17:30 (GW), that God's grace "overlooked the times when people didn't know any better. But now he commands everyone everywhere to turn to him and change the way they think and act." And thank You, Jesus. We do know better. We are learning to define ourselves and others—not by our worst choices and characteristics—but by who You say we are.

I hope you see no villains in my story. This identity search that finds us in the mind and heart of God taught me to understand some of my dad's heart. Not just the human faults and willful sin but the tender, wounded parts too. I humbly see the traits I share with him, the good and the ugly.

CHAPTER TWELVE: IDENTITY FOUND

Letting go of the need for others to be our heroes brings us home—complete and content—in the Father's love. Even the best parents will never replace that.

Where you've healed mindsets and habits, I pray you savor the silences. Where there used to be toxic, harassing thoughts that hid the real and redeemed you, there is now peace. I pray you accept your story for what it was and for the beauty of what it is. Your strong story—surrendered and transformed. Redeemed for good.

We are rebels rising, and this is our amazing comeback. We get to display Jesus' power as He gives "beauty for ashes; joy instead of mourning; praise instead of heaviness. For God has planted them [us] like strong and graceful oaks for his own glory" (Isaiah 61:3 TLB, bracket added by author).

I pray God ignites our passion to stay on this sacred and transparent journey with Jesus. With our identity rooted in Christ, first and foremost, we remember and believe who we are and who we aren't. So when we're tired, harassed, or discouraged by overwhelming thoughts, events, and emotions, we refuse and refute anything that comes against the truth of who and Whose we are.

Daughters of the Most High God, we come home to our core desire and design: to live and love like Jesus. The One who shows us the Father's heart.

"The Son radiates God's own glory and expresses the very character of God, and he sustains everything by the mighty power of his command. When he had cleansed us from our sins, he sat down in the place of honor at the right hand of the majestic God in heaven" (Heb. 1:3).

In Christ, we are seated there too. In our position of power, abundance, and belovedness, forever in God's presence. Though we've come full circle, our becoming is just beginning. We get to bring God glory in our unfolding story—this lifelong pursuit to live out our God-given identity. It is our joy and honor and privilege.

"When I think of all this, I fall to my knees and pray to the Father, the Creator of everything in heaven and on earth. I pray that from his glorious, unlimited resources he will empower you with inner strength through his Spirit. Then Christ will make his home in your hearts as you trust in him. Your roots will grow down into God's love and keep you strong. And may you have the power to understand, as all God's people should, how wide, how long, how high, and how deep his love is. May you experience the love of Christ, though it is too great to understand fully. Then you will be made complete with all the fullness of life and power that comes from God.

"Now all glory to God, who is able, through his mighty power at work within us, to accomplish infinitely more than we might ask or think. Glory to him in the church and in Christ Jesus through all generations forever and ever! Amen" (Eph. 3:14–21).

Dear Reader

This journey to find ourselves in the Father's heart seems incomplete without talking a bit more about my earthly father. As I said before, there are no villains in my story. Just us human beings figuring it out as we go—how to live, love, and be loved in this often crazy complicated life.

As you and I choose to stop defining ourselves by our worst choices and characteristics, we aim to do the same for others. As we live out this compassion piece of our divine design, we see their human, tender, and wounded parts too. We may even be humbled to see similar traits in ourselves.

My dad was a good man who loved deeply, but whose pain often went deeper. It hid him—like mine hid me. He came into adulthood with his own childhood wounds that gouged a gaping hole in his soul too. The longer I live, the more I understand and see myself in him.

In these last few pages, I share about an ordinary day when grief hit me hard. A simple household task helped me unpack sadness and anger. It also revealed my dad's heart to me and deepened my work of forgiveness. So many memories processed through so many tears—twenty years after he passed away while resting in his boat.

I pray this little ditty helps you pause and see people a bit different-

CHAPTER TWELVE: IDENTITY FOUND

ly. Under their pain is a whole person God created. Perhaps they just haven't understood that yet. Let's pray they do.

Remember the Treasure

My Noritake china came in the mail from Saigon, Viet Nam, when I was ten years old. I remember thinking it wasn't as pretty as my mom's and sisters' dishes—but it was cool. Blue skies beckoned me outside to play hopscotch, ride my bike, and stomp in the creek. Mom put my boxes of china in the basement as I skipped off to leave no rock or insect unturned.

It stayed boxed and packed away for decades, through my family's move to the house on the Mississippi backwaters and our turbulent years after Dad's second tour in Viet Nam as a civilian ammunition inspector.

When I married Jeff, the boxes of china followed us through most of our military moves. They accumulated dust in closets, attics, and for a while in my mother-in-law's spare room. Sometimes at Thanksgiving, I used a few pieces—plates, coffee cups, the gravy boat—but I never fully unpacked the whole set.

Maybe, deep down, I knew I wasn't ready.

Forty years after ditching the china to play outside, I unpacked the white silver-trimmed dishes. I imagined Dad sitting there in my living room because he always delighted in watching us kids open presents. At Christmas, his unopened gifts stacked up next to him because he didn't want to miss a thing. Our smiles made him smile, and our laughter made him laugh.

As I pulled out plates and platters from the original cardboard boxes sent from Saigon, I remembered Dad's stories of his first civilian tour in Viet Nam. I recalled the Vietnamese wedding feast and the boiled dove, served with feathers and all. Dad, a gentleman and not one to offend his host, picked up his chopsticks and dug in. Though he enjoyed talking about food like fried fish and Chicago-style hot dogs, the memory of boiled bird still gave him the willies.

Unpacking shiny bowls from dusty boxes, I remembered my dad's stories about his Vietnamese driver, Huang. Dinners in his home was where Dad got his kid-fix. Huang interpreted as his seven children bounced around my dad curious about the American children in the pictures he pulled from his wallet. They sang, danced, and displayed their drawings. In their smiles and personalities, Dad saw my five siblings and me. For an evening, he'd forget how much he missed us.

Telling me about Huang's kids, Dad laughed himself breathless. That head-back-and-slap-your-knee kind of laugh. He'd pull out a handkerchief from his pants pocket, take off his glasses and wipe his tears, pat his receding hairline, and blow his nose.

It took a minute or so to reclaim his breath. His loud laugh reduced to a chuckle, he'd shake his head and sigh. Slipping across that fine line between joy and sorrow, he'd gaze out the window. Birdwatching and weather-forecasting, a sudden priority. Memory's crushing undercurrent often swept him into his second Vietnam tour.

Sometimes he stayed quiet. Sometimes he told me more stories about the street children. With dirty hands, they begged or offered him fruit for sale. But they were known to give an American a hand grenade along with a ripe papaya. It grieved my dad to refuse them and walk away.

I remember the day Dad called my mom after he found a newborn in a trashcan. He wanted to adopt the baby boy. But a Vietnamese woman wanted him and, at the time, it seemed like the right thing to do. Of all the stories he shared with me, Dad never talked about that one.

In my research, I learned there was so much more to that second tour. No wonder Dad had post-traumatic stress. For almost two months, the brutal North Vietnamese Army advanced toward Saigon forging a path of death and destruction. I can only imagine that final chaotic morning when explosions rocked the city. Irving Berlin's "White Christmas" blared from radios signaling American civilians to evacuate.

With the airport overrun by enemy soldiers, Operation Frequent Wind was underway. My dad grabbed his pre-packed suitcase, leaving family gifts behind. Huang drove him to the hotel where he waited in line to get to the rooftop and a seat on an evacuation helicopter. Small arms and anti-aircraft fire blasted from neighboring buildings. Pan-

CHAPTER TWELVE: IDENTITY FOUND

icked crowds swarmed the streets. Vietnamese parents begged Marine guards to take their children to safety. Some even tried to throw them over the twisted barbed wire around the American embassy.

I wonder if my dad's heartbeat kept time with the helicopter propellers. The fear for himself, his colleagues, and friends—I can't even imagine. He couldn't help Huang and his wife or the children who'd eased his homesickness. He hoped they were evacuated too. Not knowing his friends' fate kept my dad awake at night. He drank to numb the pain.

As a teen, I couldn't understand the stress of his Viet Nam tours and the trauma of surviving Saigon's fall. None of us could. And now I see the timeline. Those difficult years of my adolescence started just a few months after his emergency evacuation from a war zone. Now I see why he drank and how his introspective, melancholic personality made it easy to sink into depression. While this doesn't excuse his behavior, it helps me empathize. I'm so much like him.

I realize our good days were healing for my dad. I'm grateful for mornings in his flat-bottom boat on the backwaters of the Mississippi River. He was content there. To catch fish or simply cast a line and "drown a few worms."

Just before dawn, as the moon still sparkled the water, we'd push away from shore and float a bit before turning on the motor. I remember a cool silent October morning when six Canada geese glided over us in their V-formation—so close I could have touched them with the boat's oar. We froze. Captivated by nature's gift. When the geese passed out of sight, we smiled and spoke few words.

Then the motor hummed and Dad pointed the front of the boat toward the tree-lined bluffs on the horizon. He steered us through the stump field by aiming straight at a silo that jutted up from trees draped in autumn's gold, red, and green. Perched up front, I watched for floating logs.

Arriving at our fishing spot, we dropped anchor. Since a real fisherman baits her own hook, I dug through the dirt of the Styrofoam box for a fat and slimy night-crawler. As the juicy worm and I squirmed, Dad just laughed. Head back, hand slapping his leg. Glasses off. Handkerchief out. Well, you get the picture.

On our return home, I sat on the boat's bench to get a lesson in navigating the stump field. Dad sat next to me and put his hand over my hand on the motor's throttle. His whiskered cheek tickled mine. "Don't jerk it—finesse it, like this." He eased the handle to aim the boat's bow at a red and white buoy swaying in the water.

Decades later, as I unpacked my priceless Noritake china, I recalled these treasured memories.

My dad's hurt went deep because his love went deep. Though he often struggled against memory's rushing flood of sorrow and regret, he still found reasons to laugh.

Wiping the china pieces, I uncovered memories that my anger locked away. These freed me to understand and forgive my dad who, at his core, was just a man wounded by war and difficult life situations. Do I wish he would have navigated life's pain like he did the stump fields of the Mississippi backwaters? Of course. But that's not our story. And now I'm okay with that.

Like the sacred moment of geese gliding over us at sunrise, unpacking my china was a gift. The love, the stories, the laughter. These are the treasures I choose to remember.

Endnotes

Chapter Three

1. Art Nichols LCPC & Tracy Bell MS, LCPC. *Passageway: Learning the Skills for Life's Journey*, Passageway Resources, Inc.

Chapter Four

1. *Webster's II New Riverside University Dictionary*, (Boston: Houghton Mifflin Co., 1984).
2. *What About Bob?*, Frank Oz (Director), L.A. California: Touchstone Pictures, 1991.
3. Oswald Chambers, *My Utmost for His Highest* (Grand Rapids, MI: Discovery House, 1992).
4. Eugene H. Peterson, *A Long Obedience in the Same Direction: Discipleship in an Instant Society,* 2nd Edition, (Downers Grove, IL: InterVarsity Press, 2000).

Chapter Five (Names were changed to protect families on pages 48-52)

1. Robert Wells & Mel Tormé, "The Christmas Song," 1945.
2. Dr. Kevin Leman & Dr. Randy Carlson, *Unlocking the Secrets of Your Childhood Memories.* (Nashville: Thomas Nelson, 1989).
3. Bobby Ross Jr., "Escaped Victim Watches Killer's Execution," August 11, 2000, https://www.oklahoman.com/arti-

cle/2707369/escaped-victim-watches-killers-execution, (accessed January 25, 2022).
4. Jimmy Tomlin, "George Kent Wallace Faces Executioner," May 5, 2016, https://www.swtimes.com/article/20160505/NEWS/305059907, (accessed June 8, 2022).
5. Bobby Ross Jr., "Escaped Victim Watches Killer's Execution," August 11, 2000.

Chapter Six

1. Barrie Davenport, "Victim Mentality: The Mindset That's Kicking Your Butt," February 28, 2014, http://liveboldandbloom.com/02/self-confidence/victim-mentality (accessed December 3, 2021).

Chapter Seven

1. Janet Woititz, *Adult Children of Alcoholics,* (Deerfield, FL: Health Communications Inc, 1983).
2. Douglas Bey, MD & Deborah Bey, RN *Loving an Adult Child of an Alcoholic,* (Lanham, MD: M. Evans, 2007).
3. Ibid.
4. Woititz, *Adult Children of Alcoholics*; Gilda Berger, *Alcohol and the Family*, (New York: Franklin Watts, 1993).
5. Berger, *Alcohol and the Family.*
6. Bey and Bey, *Loving an Adult Child of an Alcoholic.*
7. "Adult Children of Alcoholics," https://theretreatinitaly.com/adult-children-of-alcoholics/ (accessed December 16, 2021).

Chapter Eight

1. Brooke Frick, "Reimagining 2020," *Brooke Frick* (blog), https://brookefrick.com/2020/05/21/reimagining-2020/, (accessed December 3, 2021).
2. John 1:23, MSG.

ENDNOTES

Chapter Nine

1. Art Nichols LCPC & Tracy Bell MS, LCPC; Passageway: Learning the Skills for Life's Journey, Passageway Resources, Inc.
2. Barrie Davenport, "Victim Mentality: The Mindset That's Kicking Your Butt." February 28, 2014: http://liveboldandbloom.com/02/self-confidence/victim-mentality (accessed December 3, 2021).
3. Ibid.

Chapter Ten

1. Webster's II New Riverside University Dictionary, (Houghton Mifflin Company, 1984).
2. Ibid.
3. Gwen Dewar, PH.D "The Authoritarian Parenting Style: What does it look like?" www.Parentingscience.com, 2010-1018 (accessed January 25, 2022).
4. Ibid.
5. Ibid.
6. Brené Brown, *The Gifts of Imperfection: Let Go of Who You Think You're Supposed to Be and Embrace Who You Are*, (Center City, MN: Hazeldon Publishing, 2010).

Chapter Eleven

1. Alexandra Headrick, "Remembering Original Glory"
2. Brené Brown, *Daring Greatly: How the Courage to Be Vulnerable Transforms the Way We Live, Love, Parent, and Lead*, (New York: Avery, 2015).
3. Siobhan Kukolic, "How Beautiful Letting Go Can Be" https://www.huffpost.com/entry/how-beautiful-letting-go-can-be_b_59d-21d32e4b034ae778d4c27 (accessed January 25, 2022)
4. Deb Gorman https://debggorman.com/2021/03/01/masks/

Chapter Twelve

1. Laleña Leigh "Old Oaks" https://www.fallingforward.life/reflections/old-oaks (accessed January 25, 2022).
2. Henri Nouwen, *The Inner Voice of Love: A Journey Through Anguish to Freedom*, (New York: Doubleday, 1996).
3. Pastor Tony Evans, *The Tony Evans Study Bible Commentary*, (Nashville: Holman Reference, 2019).
4. Dani Stevens, *TheMindsJounal*, meme, https://themindsjournal.com/pain-travels-through-family-lines-until-someone-is-ready/ (accessed January 25, 2022).

About the Author

Robin Melvin is an award-winning author, freelance writer, and fulltime wife, mom, and gramma. Her six grandbabies call her Meema.

Robin writes nonfiction to inspire women to find themselves in the abundance of their divine design, their true identity in Christ. Sharing biblical truth and her transparent story, she walks alongside women as they transform unhealthy habits and mindsets to become who God created them to be, whole and free.

She is a firm believer in God's Word and the Holy Spirit's power to change us from the inside-out. Our forward-moving faith—to become more like Christ—is not only our calling, it's a privilege and a beautiful lifelong journey.

Robin is a former military wife, married almost four decades to Jeff, her resident computer geek. She loves rocks, wildflowers, driftwood, hiking, and camping. Basically, anything outdoors as long as it doesn't require running. A word nerd, Robin loves how words look, feel, and sound. Some of her favorites are: Anomaly, serendipity, and discombobulated.

RobinMelvin.com
Facebook.com/RobinMelvinAuthor

Answers, gifts... love and promises...

Abba's Devotion series

Available in bookstores and online retailers.

More great books from...
CrossRiverMedia.com

An Unnatural Beauty

Holiness is not an endless list of "thou shalt nots." It's not how we behave, what we think, or how we react or respond to life and the people around us. You'll discover foundational truths from Scripture, the path to a deeper, more intimate relationship with God, and why holiness can't be achieved through our own efforts. With relatable stories, Esther reminds us that Holiness is not a what, but a glorious Who, and He's inviting you to share in His divine nature.

Unshakable Faith

With Unshakable Faith, you'll build an indestructible foundation to your faith and crush your doubts. This 7-week Bible study contains 5 to 6 lessons per week, each lesson designed to be completed in 20 minutes or less. Topics covered include your kingdom identity, faith fundamentals, your authority and power, and your weapons and armor. You'll grow and strengthen your faith, learn faith fundamentals, and learn to command the power and authority God has given you.

Growing in Christ

When Pauline and her husband, Tom sold their charter fishing boat and house in sunny Florida to move to a tobacco farm in North Carolina, they had a dream of growing their own food. They have experienced a few successes but mostly failures. However, God's economy is never wasted. He wove their mid-life-change-of-life into a tapestry of His grace.

Books that ignite your faith.

If you enjoyed this book, will you consider sharing it with others?

- Please mention the book on Facebook, Instagram, Pinterest, or another social media site.

- Recommend this book to your small group, book club, and workplace.

- Head over to Facebook.com/CrossRiverMedia, 'Like' the page and post a comment as to what you enjoyed the most.

- Pick up a copy for someone you know who would be challenged or encouraged by this message.

- Write a review on your favorite ebook platform.

- To learn about our latest releases subscribe to our newsletter at CrossRiverMedia.com.

A Clear Picture of the World

A NOVEL BY

Everett Heath

Reader House Publishing
A Clear Picture of the World©
Photograph and Cover Design by Charles & Charlotte Masters

Everett Heath was born in Texas and lives in Hawaii.

Leave of Absence
The American Savior
The Handyman's Habit of Larceny
Quincy

1

Birdy Wire lay staring at a trillion stars--on a tight woven grass mat the size of two side-by-side California king beds, smothered thick with a layer of drying cinnamon, on a bare spot on a large hill on Pemba. There must be trillions of stars, he mused, not only to observe and speculate upon for a time, but to provide witness to all of it, and to have memory of the same. He had no idea what a trillion stars looked like. From his view, a trillion were above him. Witness and memory of all of it, Birdy too, until they too died.

He reeked of Zanzibar cinnamon. The olfactory immediacy of that indescribable scent--Birdy laid there for two hours. Long sleeved linen shirt, buttoned up to the neck and tucked into travel trousers, which were tucked into cotton calf length socks, all which rented some assurance to ignoring the biting and sucking insects, and so too the echoing moans, laments, and alarming calls from the forest's animal inhabitants-- never pleased to be around humans. Whereas the black and green mambas, and puff adders? Now that was how powerful cinnamon's aroma was to Birdy. In Pemba, cinnamon was his snake protector, whose venom's neurotoxins and cardiotoxins could send his heart into off-beats of particular bad rhythms and paralyze his respiratory system. But they lay elsewhere, thought Birdy, not waiting for him. Plus, he always carried his mojo beads, and on Pemba, his tapered, thick walking stick. And at night--a blinding bright flashlight.

Not often, but often enough. And this was one of those times. And why not? He was here again, wasn't he? How many more visits were probable? No certainty. Birdy never recalled worrying about certainty--that was for certain. He was a ruminator sure, but never about uncertainty. Maybe he obsessed rather than ruminated. No--he could definitely obsess while ruminating. And he loved to obsess, or ruminate, on the power of the indescribable scent he found himself immersed in.

"P-shoo," he whispered, while aiming his finger at every meteor arcing across his field of view. So many his arm fatigued. Now the leaves rustled on their branches with such fervor as to mask most forest sounds. It was comforting cool trades that encouraged Birdy to drift off as he rolled over onto his side. Just before sleeping he thought of Vanmeter Symthe, wondering how he would handle the mambas and puff adders. Vanmeter hailed from West Virginia, and his granddaddy was a snake handling preacher. Rattlesnakes mainly, Vanmeter said.

At nine years old he was put in charge of care and feeding of the snakes. Got bit by a baby rattler his first day. His thumb swelled more than twice the normal size. The red streak stopped finally, just below his elbow. A wasp sting hurt more, Vanmeter said. He kept the job.

Funny where college sports recruiters find their prizes, thought Birdy. He rolled over on his back and his snoring was camouflaged by the stiffening breeze swooshing the trees.

Adding black peppercorns and vanilla beans to the cinnamon Birdy had one hundred and fifty pounds to take home. The co-op leaders were satisfied with the payout. They liked Birdy, or at least he liked to think so. Waswahili people. Sunni. This trip they welcomed dollars. Last visit was Euros. He always had to be prepared to pay with either. The price included whatever bribes the co-op leaders felt necessary to distribute locally in order to get Birdy access to the farms with no hassle. They were friendly enough. They let him sleep atop the drying cinnamon. They thought he was trying to assimilate. Stupid thing to do, they all agreed. Birdy didn't have an opinion one way or the other about being Sunni. But he did keep it to himself he was going to Old Stone Town to meet up with Freida Wassergold at St. Joseph's Catholic Cathedral.

Pemba's the kind of place where you have to reconcile with never ending sweating. With the trades present, the breeze ballooned his wet shirt from his back, bringing welcome relief. He carried bandanas to wear as headbands, and one around his neck drenched in water from any spigot he could find--as long as he saw locals use it too.

The island farms were choked with cloves--the big-time spice traders prime source for top quality. No cloves for Birdy--the scent made him nauseous. It was a rare visited aunt's clove cigarettes that did it. He vomited when she made him take a long drag. She might have been a real sweet lady for all he knew, but his trailing memory was retching off the front porch rail and into her long box of begonias. She loved begonias.

The East Africa Coast Hospital Ship was docked in Zanzibar City, too large by inches to fit in the small port. But here it moored. It seemed a big event to have the E.A.C.H.S. Maybe because of certain promises made. Frieda Wassergold didn't know much of anything about ships, ports, harbor masters, or even the ocean, other than a few times visiting Florida while in high school. Medical school, residency, and the fellowship stole all the time away, only to deposit it into endless days of memorization, labs, lectures, on-call, and practice, practice, practice.

Endless days that stretched to years, all ten of them. Now a pediatric surgeon aboard the E.A.C.H.S. Her first job--it seemed liked a vacation.

The hospital ship owners helped defray her school costs by fifty percent for a two-year commitment. Frieda's parents insisted they pay for medical school.

Her mother felt more than a little guilty nudging her only daughter into being a doctor. But Frieda was relieved to know she wouldn't have to go into the family business.

Restaurant people say it's in their blood, otherwise, why? Frieda created for herself the only acceptable choice that she believed her family would approve. Her brother joined the business out of gratitude--for not having to attempt to be a doctor. But he couldn't handle his parents' relentlessness. Frieda grew up in restaurants in the City. She wanted no part of Wassergold Enterprises. But on the other hand, her rare free time in school was spent learning to cook for herself. She didn't want to eat out in restaurants. It was easier than she thought, realizing that being around kitchens was essential to her culinary learning. She volunteered to help the cooks on board the E.A.C.H.S. No help to her figure, she thought, but then there was no reason to eat like a bird. Frieda wasn't in her best photographic condition, and hadn't been for a few years. But she had given it some thought as the E.A.C.H.S. approached Zanzibar City.

She kept in touch with Birdy Wire. Sometimes she wondered if more by happenstance than anything. Even though he worked for Wassergold Enterprises, he could never be part of the family, the employee family yes, but never the inner family.

St. Joseph's Cathedral in Stone Town was where they were to meet. It was late morning, wearing jeans was a poor choice, given the humidity. Thinking about how sticky her legs felt only caused Frieda to perspire more. She at least didn't want to sweat all over Birdy when they embraced. Getting to St. Joseph's early brought her some reprieve. She was able to sit in the pew and cool off, thanks to the cathedral builders. Plus, she was able to freshen up in the lavatory. By the time Birdy stepped inside Frieda felt much better.

He looked good, observed Frieda, really good. She always thought he was handsome. Still skinny. And she remembered well enough never to say he looked like Barack Obama. He hated being told that.

Entering, Birdy shook like his namesake, for the rain started a few minutes ago. Heavy, by watching water fly off him. He was dressed for this part of the world. Loose khakis, linen shirt. He went immediately to Frieda, arms out, and a wide smile. In their embrace she was overwhelmed by the odor of cinnamon, which seemed to leak from Birdy's pores. She loved the smell of cinnamon.

"You look good, girl!"

Not believing him, Frieda echoed, "You look good."

"I look like a skinny soaked, khaki cinnamon stick! Let's sit here for a sec, the rain's comin' down hard."

"You smell like a spice rack." She smiled.

"Just came from Pemba. Nice little farm they got there. I like working with them."

They sat for a few moments in silence. School children were traversing the front of the cathedral, giggling and poking each other--the thick stone walls pinging their giddy voices about the empty spaces. A number of older women came into the cathedral and took their place separately in the pews they always sat in.

"It's more and more comfortable to me--been here three times now," said Birdy in a soft voice.

"I don't think you had a good time when we were here that summer," he added.

Frieda didn't respond. She remembered being sticky, sweaty, and an uncomfortable stranger in an African country--on an island more distinguished to her by Islam than any other attribute. True, the kids they helped teach that summer were Catholic. A few Catholics surrounded by Muslims. And Frieda, being Jewish, teaching at a Catholic school in a heavily Muslim country--that was just too strange. Her other classmates didn't seem bothered by it all. But then, they were all Christian at least, and male. She remembered telling Birdy about her being weirded out by it all. Vanmeter Symthe was also with them. The three were together for six weeks in Zanzibar, mostly on the island of Unguja, where they were now, in Stone Town, the old section of Zanzibar City. Frieda recalled they tried to cheer her up and have a laugh at it all.

Finally, she said, "It wasn't so bad." Unconvincing, thought Birdy.

Frieda began to cool down as Birdy began to dry.

"I checked out the staff on the trip before. A few are still here. Remember Father Cletus and Father Damian? Still here. You remember Brother Jack Davis, Jack "Thrash" Davis?"

"I remember Brother Thrash. Big guy, taught painting. Liked to drink beer with us," remarked Frieda.

"He's in Rome now," said Birdy, restless. He stood up and looked around. As the doors swung open by a local woman, he noticed the rain had stopped.

"Let's bolt before another downpour."

She liked cathedrals, only having been in two, St. Joseph's and St. Patrick's in the City. Gothic, miniaturizing everyone inside. Towering arches bending upward that strain the neck. Immenseness contained in a structure designed and built by man, by design, to awe. St. Joseph's was a humble third cousin, not shy about its lesser stature because it was unaware of any other--only itself. Catholic churches seemed to have a life of their own. The Chapel of the Holy Spirit on campus at Duquesne University has a life, Frieda recalled, although kind of dull.

Outside the humidity still soaked, less so by a breeze through the car-empty, stone streets--being too narrow for even an old Morris mini-minor. At the bottom of the stairs stood a staring, tallish man, ridiculously hirsute, Jesus hair, but blown about. The humidity was doing his hair no favors. Now he flashed an equally ridiculous wide grin up and at Frieda and Birdy, who halted their descent at his sight.

Frieda recognized him. A member of the crew just hired, coming on board in South Africa. She wasn't sure what he did on the E.A.C.H.S., never seeing him during her shift.

He bounded up the steps, his quickness startling, elevating Frieda and Birdy's sudden tenseness.

"Last place on Earth I'd see either of you, much less both of you." He was grinning and sweating. His low West Virginian accent had been tempered by locales not exotic, and not particularly noteworthy, other than being far away from West Virginia.

"Vanmeter, you look like you escaped from some hillbilly commune!" said Birdy grabbing his shoulders.

"You sir, look and smell like a dank cinnamon stick," said Vanmeter, his accent exaggerated.

Vanmeter released Birdy and embraced a shocked Frieda before she could react. So much hair, she thought, her cheek pressed against his prickling hirsuteness, but not unwilling to accept his squeeze, aside from her awareness of her plump self--slightly plump she rationalized, but still plump.

"You knew I was aboard and didn't come to see me?" She was afraid he didn't want to see her because of, well, her not being the stringy, long distance and cross-country runner she once was.

"I would like to say I am blessed with a capital B, but I'm currently on the down low--I do apologize," grinned Vanmeter. Frieda looked at Birdy for translation. He gave a pursed lipped, left shoulder shrug, tilting his head slightly left, as if clearing a minor crick in his neck.

Frieda had forgotten his gesture. She realized she missed seeing it.

"Let's go to my hotel, it has a rooftop bar, plus a view of your hospital ship." Birdy led the way, moving in front of a still grinning Vanmeter. Frieda followed, still in shock.

The three were the odd site through the narrow corridors of Stone Town. The sky was now Africa blue, the air less moist. Overhead, clusters of phone and electrical wires drooped between three and four story buildings, as if burdened by endless abuse. Below on street level, shop owner men sat at their doorways, observing, seemingly indifferent to prospective customers. Thick prayer beads in their knuckle bulging hands. Behind them, exquisitely ornate, were tall and wide heavy wooden doors that betrayed the long Arab influence. Now through the courtyard markets--cloth and rug wares were bright with primary colors--blue, red, yellow. Dr. Bulugu's art gallery attracted Anglo tourists to zebras and lion portraits in bursting colors other than their own.

Atop the hotel, under canopy and welcome shade, the trio settled into their chairs. It was turning out to be a day tourists post endlessly about on their blogs and other such travel websites. The welcoming color of the sky, emerald water, and so on. And looking towards Stone Town one could not help noticing the corrugated roof tops, many rusted red-brown. With enough drinks one could find charming rooftop patterns of the rusted and soon-to-be roofs, as if a yet-to-be discovered artist was arranging the rooftops with intent. Dwarfing all boats in the small harbor was the E.A.C.H.S., remarkably free of visible rust, given its age.

A Sauvignon blanc and two whiskeys--neat, were set on the table. It was the first time all three had been together since graduation from Duquesne. And as was their custom, they sipped their drinks first in silence, none necessarily in any rush to start conversation. And once it started, it became familiar in its pace and rhythm, part of why they enjoyed each other's company.

They raised their glasses to each other.

Birdy eyed Vanmeter, who then put his glass down.

"Okay, I'll start," said Vanmeter. He raised his empty glass and the lonely waiter was quick to take his glass and fetch a refill. It was Frieda's day off--today I'll have a few, she said to herself. The first glass extended her dizziness of having them both here. She thought a second wine would help her to be more at ease in the moment. Not uneasy, thought Frieda, but more reacting to a circumstance she never envisioned to take place again. Well, now it has, she thought, grateful for these kinds of surprises.

With a second whiskey in hand, Vanmeter began.

"I was a fair programmer back in the day, you may recollect. Geek track dude, one name I remember being called." His laugh was that of a man confident in his skin. Vanmeter knew who he was and what he was about. He loved his beard, because how and when he stroked it drew the right proportion of attention. His Jesus hair was now ponytailed back into some sense of control.

"I went to the dark side of the internet, with supreme intent to take the money and run. A lot of naïve, and a fair amount of stupid. I met some fascinating people. Some, very strange. But they're all genuine criminal behavior type people. I am no genuine criminal. I just hacked to get in where there seemed little chance to get in. Got paid for it. Stayed out of touch for a reason. Addicting. I understand my Momma a bit better because of it all. But I'm out of it now. Been there, done that."

Frieda and Birdy were well aware of Vanmeter's love for his Momma.

"Won't tell you how I knew Birdy was here on a spice run," said Vanmeter, and looking at Frieda, said, "Or how I knew you were on that huge boat over there, doing your duty."

"Not too hard to figure out how you knew," blurted Frieda, with wine flushed cheeks.

"You called my parents and they told you everything!" Frieda laughed, hers sardonic, but very tame, her way of inviting a response of counterpunching wit.

They all laughed.

Birdy said, "And you're on the down low because of why?"

Vanmeter sipped whiskey number two. He stroked his beard in ludicrous slow motion.

"Turns out it's rarely the authorities you're hiding from. It's your, quote-unquote, 'associates.' I'm not in desperate trouble, just enough, though. A former associate wants me back in the game, and is very persistent."

"You're outta shape. Never thought I'd see the day," said Birdy.

"That I am sir, that I am," replied Vanmeter, adding, "But that is going to change."

Now Frieda was embarrassed. She was the one not mentioned. Birdy noticed and bolted up from his chair.

"Remember Ben E. King? Supernatural Thing Part I?"

Birdy sang, "Interplanetary, whoa, extraordinary--love!" He could sing.

So could Vanmeter. He sang King Floyd's, "Groove me baby, move me baby, oh sock it to me, mama!"

Vanmeter said, "I'm sorry to tell you Birdy, you look like King Floyd, and no one else."

"Thank you Jesus--beats Barack," said Birdy.

Frieda laughed so hard her bladder begged for relief. The track team's nickname for Vanmeter was Jesus. Birdy had his own nickname, but they liked to whisper,

"Go B.O. go." In their junior year, Vanmeter showed the team pictures of King Floyd. Most got the message. The assholes never did, or really cared to.

"Alright, alright. Tell me what's going on here?" Frieda was tipsy and disoriented. Afterall, being in Zanzibar City, with Birdy and Vanmeter. The last time was over ten years ago.

"Ok, I know why Birdy's here. He's a spice trader these days, and he works for my Dad and Mom. How that all came about is still cloudy to me, but...here you are-- buying...I don't know what you're buying, other than cinnamon."

"Vanilla and nutmeg," said Birdy, thinking he should have started with beer first instead of whiskey. Too early in the day, and no breakfast.

"Ok, cinnamon, vanilla, and nutmeg," repeated Frieda, half way through her second glass of wine.

"And I'm still afraid to ask you what you're up to, Vanmeter," said Frieda.

In mid beard stroke, Vanmeter smiled, now lifting up his chin and looking down his nose at Frieda.

He said, "Doctor Frieda, the less you know the better. It's a chancy deal, might not work out, but I'm committed to it now."

"Well, that was completely un-informing, thank you!" said Frieda, finishing her wine. She was now fully disoriented, but very happy to see them both, and very conscious about her weight. She hoped neither noticed.

Frieda looked at Birdy. "You know what he's up to?"

"Nope, not yet, but he's gonna tell me soon because I'm flyin' outta here tomorrow."

"That's how it is then, is it?" frowned Frieda.

"That's how it is," said Vanmeter, adding, "But how's this, I'll stay in touch much better than the last ten years. How's that?"

"You and Birdy have kept contact all along and didn't tell me?" asked Frieda.

"Nope," said Birdy quickly, continuing, "Maybe three months ago he texted me. But I didn't know when we'd meet up." He glanced at Vanmeter.

"Mr. Clandestine," smirked Birdy.

"Mr. Down Low," chimed in Frieda.

"Mr. Sneaky Sneaky," added Birdy.

Vanmeter said nothing, just grinned and stroked his beard. Just earlier he had summoned the waiter with a glance and a nod.

"I'm starved, I'm ordering lunch," he announced, and ordered fish of the day, with a grand portion of fried calamari as appetizer, for the table. Vanmeter switched to bottled water.

Frieda wasn't in the mood to ponder over a menu and ordered the same. Birdy followed suit.

Vanmeter ate most of the calamari. The fish was pan fried, too much so. No mention of it by any of the three. They all switched to bottled water, Birdy insisting the bottle be opened at the table. The waiter understood, but did nothing to mask his annoyance.

"Your father still play bass around town?" asked Vanmeter.

"Still does, but the late gigs he won't do anymore," said Birdy.

"He wants to be in bed by ten, no later."

"Your mom alright?" said Vanmeter.

"She is, and she still asks about you--and you too, Frieda," said Birdy.

"Frieda's parents are still working all the time. They never stop," added Birdy.

Frieda said, "They work too hard. You can't tell them to slow down or they'll get irritated. They feed off each other, always thinking about the business. Their business is their life, their marriage, how they think about everything. My brother's the opposite."

"They're gonna try and drag you back into it when something happens to them," said Vanmeter.

Frieda ate the remaining portion of her lunch in silence.

"And your mom, how's she doing?" asked Birdy.

"Still at Walgreen's, and she's got yet another new boyfriend. He claims to be sober. Handyman kinda guy, plumbing, lays tile, electrical, some carpentry. Momma says he's good so far."

"Have you met him?" said Birdy.

Vanmeter pushed his plate away, reaching over and picking on the few remaining bits of calamari. "No hurry to. I know the type. Besides, Momma hadn't made it a point for me to meet him."

He added, "I thank the Good Lord for that Walgreen's manager. Hope he never dies. As long as he's around, Momma's got the job."

The breeze stopped. It was now too hot to be outside, even under shade. Frieda felt her blouse sticking to her back. She wanted coffee but that would be too much. She'd never stop perspiring. She tried to pay the entire bill but both men refused to let her. Birdy said the lunch was on him, but Vanmeter would have none of it. They agreed to split the bill between the two of them.

Frieda thanked them both, saying, "Birdy, would you like a tour of the ship?"

"I would."

Once aboard the tour took an hour. Afterwards Frieda was drained, only wanting a shower and a nap. Birdy and Vanmeter left Frieda in her room after agreeing on a time for dinner that evening. Frieda insisted she'd pay, as long as it was a different restaurant than lunch. And, with air conditioning.

Birdy followed Vanmeter through the narrow corridor, up the tight stairs to the main deck.

At the gangplank, Vanmeter said, "I can tell you now or later this evening about my plan."

Vanmeter added, "Med school and all that training has left Frieda a little worn, don't ya think? She's got a little gray hair showing."

Birdy replied, "A little worn, but not bad. But I know she's uptight about gaining some weight. She'd lose some, she'd feel a lot better."

He said, "Tell me tonight. Right now, I need to go make sure my spices are set to travel back Stateside."

Birdy left the ship thinking Frieda still looked good to him, although her narrow chin he was partial to was not as prominent at the moment.

Vanmeter leaned over the rail, saluting Birdy as he turned back to wave. He'd go it alone, thought Vanmeter, but he really preferred he had someone along with him. And Birdy was his man. At least he was his man, if he was the same dude Vanmeter knew back then. Today he hadn't noticed he changed at all. Same Birdy Wire.

Frieda wore a black dress to dinner. She had stopped by Vanmeter's quarters but he wasn't there. Although they had not discussed going together to the restaurant, Frieda assumed they would. Her taxi driver was very familiar with the Emerald Grill. It was less than five minutes from the ship. Even at late dusk, the air was warm and sticky. The trades were still absent. There were people about, but Old Town tonight appeared restrained.

During the short taxi ride she thought about them both. The too careful eye contact she had to deliver to each man, individually, without the other seeing her. Her expressions, her movements. So much calculation. Frieda was out of practice, well, not true, she never had occasion to practice, and her anxiousness was becoming acute. She had to glance at each of them in unison, first Birdy and then Vanmeter, and then switching order. As each of them looked at her during lunch Frieda would get mixed messages, or at least she perceived so. She may never know if she was right, she thought. When would all three of them ever be together again? Lunch was stressful enough.

That both Birdy and Vanmeter worked at some time for her parents now amazed her. Maybe she was making far too much of all this body language hoopla, she thought. They both have much more interesting things to focus on, and very likely other women too. Frieda wanted a pleasant dining outing with two old friends from the college track team. Nothing more. But as she paid the taxi driver and walked into the hotel lobby where the restaurant was located, she knew she was deceiving herself. But she didn't know exactly why. That too, was a deceit she admitted, as she was escorted to the table where Birdy was seated. Vanmeter had yet to arrive.

Birdy got up and took over duties from the maître de, pulling out Frieda's chair. He allowed the maître de to place her napkin on her lap.

"What are you drinking?" Frieda asked.

"Vodka martini, very nice," he said. "You look great by the way."

Frieda smiled, blushing. She thanked him. Birdy looked good too, she thought. He wore a black linen sports coat, an open white shirt, and light grey slacks. She'd never seen him in a sports coat. It fit him well, which surprised her.

"Would you care for something from the bar, madam?" The voice came from behind Frieda. She turned slightly and was caught off guard the man was Caucasian.

"Sauvignon blanc, if you have it by the glass," she replied.

"Certainly madam," said the man as he came into full view. He wore an open collared white shirt, impeccably ironed, and sharp black slacks.

Frieda stared at the man and became shocked. It was Vanmeter, with no beard, and his hair was cut short and combed back. Somewhere along the line both of them stopped dressing as college slackers.

Birdy laughed out loud.

"My God, you, you…unbelievable!" said Frieda, now very much wanting her wine. She stared at Vanmeter as he sat down, the waiter placing wine in front of Frieda, along with a whiskey for Vanmeter.

"You're not looking too bad yourself," said Vanmeter. "The fish here is much better than at lunch. I've been promised," he said, holding up his drink for a toast. They lifted their glasses, each looking at the other as their glasses clinked. Frieda missed them both, and was happy at that moment.

The fish was superb. Frieda had made up her mind not to worry, not to think too much. She surprised herself. They talked throughout dinner, all of them declining dessert. Frieda was thankful the restaurant was air conditioned, and took a chance and ordered coffee. It didn't take much for her to start perspiring. More nervousness than anything else.

Frieda had little to say about all the years in medical school and residency other than it was a grind, wanting to be done with it all far sooner than she could realistically expect. Birdy had no issue talking about his experience in the Pennsylvania Army National Guard. His dad, being prior Army, and after thirty years, still wore a uniform as a Junior ROTC instructor in Percy High School, in Pittsburgh. He talked Birdy into joining the PAARNG.

"I didn't have a plan, much less a solid plan on what I was going to do. My Dad said I ain't living with them anymore--go join the Guard," recounted Birdy.

"Became a medic at first. Thought I might be a nurse. Then I had a chance to fly helicopters, so I became an Apache pilot. Now I work for Frieda's parents, buying spices. I like it. I don't have a boss. Just got to get the spices to NYC," said Birdy. He shrugged, like it was no big deal. Not now it's not, he thought. But when he started it was harsh. New York restaurant people--the one's he met were assholes. Frieda's parents were all business, with more than a hint of assholeness.

"Flying helicopters had to be cool," said Vanmeter.

"Yeah, I love flying helicopters, but I never got out of PA, except for deployments. I wanted out of PA."

"Zanzibar?" said Vanmeter, with a sly grin, stroking his chin, now missing his beard.

"I'm in and out, it's not bad. I got a small place in Brooklyn, it's not bad either," said Birdy. Vanmeter wasn't convinced, and his plan was counting on his perception of Birdy's state of being.

"And no one's on social media!" laughed Vanmeter. His comment turned the mood sour as they remembered-- The Scandal.

"Ok, sorry I brought it up. It appears to be my turn."

Vanmeter noticed the restaurant was never crowded that evening, and only one other table remained occupied. He got on with his story.

"You may recall I did a short stint in NYC working for Frieda's parents in a small restaurant in lower Manhattan. Crash course on how to be a waiter and not get fired."

"Frieda, ever hear of Kule Fat?" asked Vanmeter. She shook her head.

Vanmeter wasted no time. He'd been dying to tell it to Birdy and leave Frieda out of it, not because she wouldn't listen, just the opposite, but he didn't want Frieda anywhere close to any controversy should his plan go awry. Vanmeter missed Frieda.

Kule Fat was a famous chef--in chef circles. A specialist with few equals. He, of course, claimed he had no equals. He brought Chinese culinary traditions to the best white fish and the finest tenderloins, and his vegetable dishes were copied by anyone who wanted to be someone in the best restaurants in the world.

"Kule Fat's a short, fat man--shocking," laughed Vanmeter.

"He noticed me for some reason--I still don't know why. He actually would speak to me, and I was not a kitchen guy. I knew to avoid any confrontation with chefs, especially Kule Fat. But he never said much to anybody as far as I could tell. He did a lot of finger pointing and grunting. His eyes would get large and small, he'd give you a look, with his hands behind his back looking up at you. I mean, he's a short dude."

"He came in one evening. The restaurant was crazy busy. The kitchen master chef was not Kule Fat, but a big scary looking Ukrainian. I was running entrees out to the dining room when the Ukrainian grabbed me. He told me Kule Fat was ill and I was to take him home...now."

Vanmeter had no car in the city. He hailed a cab and he took Kule Fat to his apartment. Kule Fat appeared very weak and let Vanmeter hold his elbow as they made their way up to his apartment. They said nothing to each other. Vanmeter never got further than the grand foyer, with only glimpses of the large high ceiling living room, looking over Fat's head. The apartment was three times the size of Vanmeter's, at least. Upper West Side.

Frieda interrupted him. "I know that name now. I know that name! He was in the papers. The Arness Art Gallery. My parents know the owners! They were selling forgeries. And Kule Fat was accused as being the forger!" Frieda started to perspire.

"Well," said Vanmeter, "I can't say for sure anything about that."

"But..." chimed in Birdy, who admitted to himself Vanmeter's story had him curious.

Frieda said, "I have to go to the bathroom. Wait until I get back. I don't want to miss anything." As she made her way, she handed their waiter her credit card and told him to put the dinner on her tab. Except for them, the restaurant was empty. Waiters were beginning to close up for the evening. While Frieda was absent Vanmeter continued his story to Birdy.

"But...," Vanmeter echoed, "I now know a whole lot more about what it takes to make a damn fine forgery. And it's just not the painting itself, although that goes without saying. But it also is the type of canvas, paint, brushes, frame...the whole thing. And that's what I want to talk to you about."

Vanmeter looked over his shoulder, "Frieda paid the bill. She looks good, doesn't she?"

Birdy nodded. Frieda then sat down, out of breath, afraid she missed something.

"You continued without me?" she said. Any lingering self-consciousness about her body language and overt eye contact, and reading Birdy's eyes and Vanmeter's body language had vanished. Vanmeter's story held them in a spell.

"Thank you very much for dinner," said Birdy. Vanmeter said the same.

"Go on Vanmeter, go on," urged Frieda, smiling in recognition of their gratitude. Vanmeter continued telling about the other man in Kule Fat's foyer. He never gave his name. It seemed one of his jobs was to supply Fat with all the necessary materials for his paintings. Fat called him the Materials Man. He was older. Kule Fat had feigned his illness. The whole purpose was to introduce the Materials Man to Vanmeter. Fat was leaving the country that night.

The manager arrived. The restaurant was closing and they had to leave.

Once outside, Frieda was thankful for the cool breeze, and she stopped perspiring. She demanded they walk back to the ship. Vanmeter finished his story.

Vanmeter accompanied the Materials Man on a tour, what he called the 'Tour of Acquirement.' He had just completed the tour prior to him taking the position on the E.A.C.H.S. Eastern Europe primarily. The Czech Republic, Poland, Slovenia, Slovakia, Hungary, Romania. The Materials Man was from one of those countries, Vanmeter didn't know for sure. Nor did he ask. It was a time where he kept his mouth shut and listened and learned. The dollar went a very long way in those countries. He finally told him his name, which Vanmeter did not share with Frieda or Birdy. He figured it was an alias. The less Vanmeter knew about him the better, he thought.

Frieda said, "Why would this man take you all over Eastern Europe, teach you what to look for, where to acquire such materials, the whole thing? I don't get it."

"Kule Fat asked me if I wanted to do something very, very out of the ordinary. And I tell you he asked me in just that way. He said, 'If you don't know about human nature, this endeavor will teach you a few things.' 'An endeavor,' that's what he called it."

"Full of himself, sounds like," said Birdy, who, until that time had said nothing.

"Yeah, to be sure Birdy, to be sure. But there you have it. Besides, who ain't?" laughed Vanmeter. Birdy smirked.

They reached the disembark ramp of the ship.

"There's more to this story, I know it. I have a hundred questions!" said Frieda. First on her mind was what was going to happen when Birdy left and she and Vanmeter went aboard.

During Vanmeter's telling about all the countries he and the Materials Man were visiting Birdy was thinking the same thoughts as Frieda. Whereas Vanmeter had been thinking about it since the restaurant. He, being in full control of the evening's conversation, had been way ahead of them.

Birdy said, "I leave tomorrow back to the States." Birdy definitely missed Frieda. And Frieda definitely missed Birdy. It showed in their embrace and fleeting kiss.

Birdy gave Vanmeter a man hug, saying, "Keep in touch."

"For sure," said Vanmeter.

Later that night, Birdy's phone buzzed. Vanmeter wanted to meet him early tomorrow. Birdy texted back that 6 am will have to work. Vanmeter said he'd be at Birdy's hotel then.

Frieda had not slept that soundly since she came aboard the E.A.C.H.S. She apologized over and over for the finger nail gouges she placed in Vanmeter's back that night. Vanmeter smiled, stroking his chin. At the time however, he did everything in his control not to shout out. A quality reminder of her, he said afterwards. A most supreme high quality. At one moment she thought she was unsure whether she dug in thinking about Vanmeter or Birdy. And for the time being, Frieda was not fazed by the uncertainty.

****

Hebborn, Myatt, Keating, Tetro, and Beltracchi. For some time, Vanmeter read everything there was to read, watched every documentary and internet news story about these forgers he could find. He found short online courses on painting, concentrating on how paint colors are created, the specific properties of pigments, made out of what elements. All the great forgers have a deep painters knowledge of the times of the masters they copied. Paints, pigments, canvas, brushes, everything. Vanmeter believed he had to know at least as much as the forgers themselves. That's all Vanmeter knew about painting.

And he had to assume Thrash Davis did not have a forgers mind.

Clara had left Vanmeter a phone message. His Momma rarely called, and if she did, she never left a message.

"Vanmeter, my baby, come see me soon, will ya please?"

2

"It could very well be lazy thinking--of descriptions of the valley that are cemented in the minds of those that don't hail from here. But to those that do, most still are never of a mind to leave. That could be said for anywhere, true enough. Maybe because of a top rule of the way things are. That rule is--place is damned most of everything. Even when place can crush a soul, and leave a soul exasperated as to why, why, why. Weakness and failure can always be explained away because of place. In those times, that's your explanation to your soul. And it works. Strength and success could come from anywhere, inside to out. Anyhow, there is much of West Virginia to love."

This is one of the few reflections Clara told her son. He remembered. She was stingy with sharing her reflections, but not her affection. Clara had Vanmeter when she was thirteen years old.

Vanmeter stayed at the best Best Western he could find, about thirty miles from where his Momma lived. That was just close enough. Vanmeter's sense of place was not the same as his Momma's. And his Momma did not chasten him for it. He always rented a shitty little rental car, and dressed as he did when he lived there. Not that he had accumulated any significant wealth since his departure, but what he had saved stacked as tall as a Redwood over the amounts of most everyone here.

Thirty-three hours prior, at six am in Zanzibar, he met Birdy at the Abeid Amani Karume International Airport. With no trade winds, the morning air was sticky warm. The tarmac was waking up. Birdy's spices were ready to fly to New York City.

"One more time now--you are going to Rome to find Brother Davis? You want him to forge paintings for you? You don't know what kind of paintings? Old stuff? New? And--you provide the paint and materials? And you don't know yet who will sell the forgeries?"

Birdy shook his head and produced a smirking grin. He wasn't done giving Vanmeter shit.

"You tried recording all this you told me on your phone and playing it back to yourself? No? Because you know how it will sound, don't you? Not crazy, but stupid crazy."

"And you want me to go with you? Why again? Because I can be helpful? In Rome, with all my Italian homies?"

Birdy knew Vanmeter slept with Frieda last night.

Vanmeter wished he had his beard to stroke. Rarely lost for words or a worthy comeback, Vanmeter couldn't reply. He wanted Birdy to come with him because Birdy Wire was like no one else he knew. And he always liked hanging with Birdy because he was unflappable, and kept his common sense and good nature well up front. But Vanmeter also knew one thing for sure--if he said his Momma was the reason for this high-end adventure, Birdy would go. Because the truth was, his Momma came first--but hopefully Vanmeter would come in close second, not far down the line.

Birdy knew Vanmeter wanted him to go. They were a Starsky and Hutch kind of match. They could do something together now, because later it may not be a realistic proposition. This was their time to do something stupid, but not reckless, wanting-to-die stupid. Just chancy enough some part of it might be pulled off.

"I thought Frieda might be part of why we team up on this little endeavor," said Vanmeter.

"That makes no sense, drunk or sober, whether in Zanzibar or back in the States," said Birdy.

"I want to be in Rome now, because I'm in the zone now--to convince Thrash Davis now," said Vanmeter. But he could not go now. His Momma wanted him back in West Virginia. Still, he was pressing Birdy to see if he would go with him when the time came.

"What does Frieda have to do with your forgery scheme?" pressed Birdy.

"Tell me you don't want her in this whole mix," said Vanmeter.

"Why? How?" said Birdy.

"It's my Momma. I have to go back Stateside--and put Rome on hold for a week--tops," said Vanmeter.

"Your Momma--you serious, or you doing a lame ass job of changing the subject?" said Birdy.

"You and I go back Stateside and do what we have to do. But I am going to find Thrash Davis and make my proposition. I want you there with me all the way. It's chancy, but it's not life threatening chancy. Could be very worthwhile."

"Fool, you know anything about forgery? And Frieda?" Birdy was pissed.

"You see Frieda, you talk to her. You tell her my proposition," said Vanmeter.

"She's on a hospital boat, here, in Africa," snapped Birdy.

"Figure it out," said Vanmeter.

****

"It's my teeth, baby. My mouth hurts so bad."

Clara Smythe--five foot, ten inches on the best days, a solid frame, good figure, a high cheek boned face and skinny chin that most men noticed in quick fashion. She remained a survivor. Quit meth, never liked Mountain Dew, kept a job, maybe a functioning alcoholic--Clara tried hard. It depends on the man she's with. She smoked and quit, countless times. She vapes. Maybe too much. Clara walked fifteen miles a week, started a few years back and has not given it up. She walks to work, regardless. Saves gas and wear and tear on her old Toyota.

Now's she's too skinny. Hurts too much to eat. Her cheeks are sucked in. Clara knew she was deteriorating. She wished she could have seen a dentist growing up. She left her man and called her son. The only time she ever called him about her worries. She needed him now.

****

Birdy worried again about being frozen in time. Ever since he was witness to evil. He called it that. But it seemed half of the world thought little to nothing of it. He became fearful of being frozen in place. Which is why he agreed to be a spice buyer. That and he kept a connection to Frieda. He couldn't stay in Pittsburgh, couldn't stay in the Army National Guard. Applied for helo pilot jobs in Pittsburgh, but nothing came of it. Neither had anything to do with his fear, but they were both within the same neighborhood in his mind, Pittsburgh surely, but so too with the Army. He loved them both, but he feared they were like ice cube trays that are never used, frozen to the bottom of the freezer, freezing him in place.

****

Frieda felt bad she didn't answer Birdy's call. She wanted to talk to him--she wanted to see him. His message was Birdy-cool.

"Hey girl, great to see you. Been too long. Text me when you want to hear about this crazy ass scheme Vanmeter has. He wants me to be his tag-along. He wants you in it, too. Maybe you know already. You know what I'm talkin' about?"

Of course, she was going to text Birdy. She had no intention of not staying in touch with him. She didn't know what Birdy was referring to. She and Vanmeter didn't talk much that night. Even less in the morning. The next day she returned Birdy's text.

"Always great to see you! No idea what you're talking about but I am very curious! Will text you soon to see if you're available to chat!"

After hitting send, Frieda cursed. Too many exclamation points.

3

On this visit, Vanmeter never let his Momma's upsetting appearance show in any aspect of his demeanor. Maybe that was why this time Clara withheld some of her full affection. It had been almost two years, and as his Momma she wanted what she deserved. Too long to be away, thought Vanmeter. Clara was staying with her girlfriend Jess Lee, in a tiny bedroom, in a neglected single wide, angled next to others in an ad hoc herringbone design, in a tired trailer park.

"Kinda a tiny car, ain't it baby? So nice to see you. I missed you so much," said Clara. She stared at her son after kissing him like a lover. She was aware Vanmeter flinched.

"Yes, yes, my ex old man knows where I'm stayin', he knows, but he won't come around. Jess Lee has two shotguns, both sawed off. Men haven't done her right, either."

"I believe it's y'alls choices in men, Momma," said Vanmeter, his twang returning.

"Men--do you think they all think the same way?"

"Is it an all-pervasive stink of desperation?" asked Clara.

"You're a smart woman, Momma. What you really think?"

"Not many women around here completed two years of junior college. I loved English…"

"You're why I went to college," said Vanmeter.

"Not true, you went 'cause you got the scholarship you deserved. Any you didn't quit, you finished. It was such a joy to be there for your graduation."

"Bobby's not mean or violent. He's a quiet drinking man. But he's a day drinker, plus he gets possessive. It's too bad, I mean, I like the guy. But I feel that drain on me livin' with him. And with my teeth hurtin' so bad I'm overwhelmed with being stuck and in constant pain. And I'm scared to death of killin' the pain, which is easy enough to do, you know. But that path leads to a decisive destruction."

Vanmeter asked, "So you're telling me we can go over to your place and talk with Bobby and explain to him you've got to get help with your teeth and you're taking all your things?"

"Not my place. It's his. And I don't have much there really. Nothing that I can't live without. Some jeans, tops, bras and panties, and makeup."

"What about your job at Walgreen's? Your manager thinks you're a great employee, right?"

"He does. Sweet man." Sitting on her old springy bed, Clara had been fidgeting the whole time.

"Can you get a job in another Walgreen's? Like a transfer?"

"Why would I want to do that?" Clara's fidgeting was now a distraction.

"What are you on Momma?"

"Nothing baby, nothing. That's the trouble. I quit, knowing you were coming to see me." Clara's tortured smile meant many things.

Vanmeter sat by his Momma. He told her his plan. He had to ask her to let him finish more times than he expected, but not much more. But he knew in the end he would win her over. They were going to be together for a while. Clara's eyes indicated the weight she should never have to carry had been lightened, just enough.

Vanmeter replaced his shitty little rental with a Ford SUV. The last time Vanmeter was in town he convinced his Momma to store anything of value in a rental storage unit, to see how bad she missed what little she had. If she missed anything she could always stop by and take whatever she missed most and keep it with her. Clara said, "Don't bother to stop." Vanmeter stopped anyway.

In less than a half hour the Ford was loaded with all that Clara wanted to take.

Before leaving for New York City Vanmeter stopped by the Walgreen's where Clara had worked for years. She stayed in the car while Vanmeter had a private conversation with Thompson Ruddgy, the Walgreen's manager, and second cousin to Clara.

She was scared--bad. Being with her son made no dent on her fear. That told her something. But it wasn't because Vanmeter didn't have anything lined up like he told her he had. Like where they were staying, the New York dentist who was going to fix her condition, in Pennsylvania where she could settle and initially work at Walgreen's. Vanmeter had a plan, and that's all. Clara believed what her son told her. Could she succeed in living without pain, without any weight on her, without having any excuse to be rescued--from anything? Being without her constant companions--she had reared them with vigor for too long. They grew to be monsters--her personal collection--her Monsters of Fear.

Vanmeter knew his Momma believed him. He accepted Clara's fear of leaving West Virginia as Fear Number Two. He suspected that fear was far easier to handle than Number One. Driving to New York bought him time he needed to arrange and lock in all the parts of his vision, his plan. Not a scheme, but a grand vision. Frieda's help would be easy. It was Birdy he needed to work on. Not only for getting his parents help in taking care of his Momma, but for getting Brother Thrash Davis to agree to paint. Every piece of his plan was up in the air, but he believed they were still within his grasp to manipulate into proper place. Nothing had crashed and burned. It was too early. All the pieces had just been tossed up, and they floated, unaffected by the gravity of the outlandishness of it all.

Road trips made Clara sleepy. She nodded off soon after leaving Walgreen's. Maybe the pain was giving her a break, thought Vanmeter. The sky was thick with low gray clouds. The windshield wipers were worn. If the cold rain didn't let up Vanmeter would be forced to stop and replace them.

Vanmeter was happy. It was in this time, at this time, dashing off following his wits, in a billow of giddy uncertainty that Vanmeter knew he was in his element. He was immune to the needy intimidations of collectivists of any type or category. He was outside. The dark web, of all places, taught him that. Outside ephemeral ethics, the kind one wears as part of an earnest fashion ensemble as a plea to be noticed by just the right collectivists. Beyond the touch of the appointed judge and jury who reinforce whatever lie that they need to enforce. And definitely beyond those who have assumed to be the appointees of judges and juries. For they all feared uncertainty as a thief of their own empowerment, and especially feared losing the grasp of the fantasy of power. Vanmeter was also happy his Momma didn't have to think of these things.

But Vanmeter could also go inside the crowd anytime and hide in plain sight, just like all those who do. Inside, most played the game as a passive, the objective of course evading judgment, lest a jury decide for them to wear their shame as a neon blinker, a flash warning to all who fear banishment from the tribes they envied. Vanmeter didn't worry about judgement, no tribes sought him out, and he developed a seasoned loathing for them all. His indifference was his war paint, and those who cared about such things let him be, judging Vanmeter not worth the confrontation. That's how the others successfully played, he observed, and mimicking them took little effort, because he didn't give a shit. All this, Vanmeter saw clearly.

4

Birdy was beginning to get comfortable in his job. Frieda's parents gave him enough instruction through a few long-time employees on how to go about being a credible spice trader. They weren't used to hiring those that weren't Jewish. Not rarities, but not too common. Harold and Myra Wassergold were used to living with their friends (all Jewish), those in the neighborhood (most Jewish), and of course the Synagogue. Birdy believed them when they said to take nothing personal from what they say or how they say it. His father was obsessed with not taking anything personal. Not as a black man. Never. It served him very well in the Army.

"You wouldn't be with us if we thought you couldn't contribute to Wassergold Enterprises," said Myra. Her smiles were short and tight, and far too frequent not to be distracting. She looked you in the eye in an uncomfortable way. Even at five feet three, she locked her eyes onto, and into yours. Without blinking. She'd smack your arm if you attempted to look away. Not hard, but enough to know her intent. Then her eyes would soften and her smile lengthen, like a mother temporarily satisfied a teaching moment had been achieved.

The spice import business was a splinter of their Enterprise. The Wassergold's were not afraid to venture into new opportunities. Always with calculation, never in haste or frivolous excitement. The Wassergold's hired Birdy because of his answer to why they were thinking of hiring him.

He said to them, "It isn't because I'm a good friend of your daughter so much as it's my pigment--a dark skinned man you think is better in Africa buying spices."

The Wassergold's looked at each other and relayed their mutual approval using eyebrows and lip curls.

"That I admit, that I admit," mused Harold. Birdy was impressed Harold spoke up so soon. It was Myra who seemed beyond fear. Birdy took note.

"Plus--you look like Obama," added Myra. Her smile was tight, fleeting, and irritating.

Birdy knew that comment was inevitable. He despised the comparison, but he had a clear picture of the reality of the moment. Regarding looking like Obama, he had no firm opinion, he simply despised being compared to anyone, especially someone well known. But he respected their naked honesty.

Harold and Myra's parents immigrated to the United States after World War II.

Frieda spoke to Birdy, relaying what her grandparents repeatedly told her parents, "My parents said they used to talk about Buchenwald--no one now can relate. It is beyond any comprehension. They said now we no longer talk about what you will hopefully never understand. Because we believe, in your life time, you're safe. HaShem, HaShem."

Birdy interpreted their words as a prayer, hopefully answered. Reflection first, before reaction, was implanted in him by his father--through Birdy's observation of his father's habits of personal interaction. By paying attention to Porter Ballentine Wire, Birdy paid attention to the world. And Birdy viewed Mr. and Mrs. Wassergold as fearless and bullet proof. Both traits he did not see in Frieda.

Birdy lived in a rent controlled one-bedroom apartment, comfortable, and partially furnished (old thick European dining table and chairs, coffee and end tables, a giant hutch). The Wassergold's owned the apartment building. A fifteen minute walk to work. In fact, a fifteen minute walk to any place he needed to go.

In the two years working for the Wassergold's he had taken only a few days off, usually making a four-day holiday around one of the big holidays, going home to Pittsburgh to visit his parents. Birdy never asked for a vacation, nor did Mr. and Mrs. Wassergold suggest taking a vacation. Birdy wasn't aware they'd ever taken one, other than going to Florida on weekends, leaving noon Friday and back midmorning on Monday.

Vanmeter's quest to find Brother Thrash Davis in Rome and convince him to forge paintings had kindled a light in Birdy's mind, allowing other thoughts to finally germinate. With regard to Vanmeter's schemes, it was not the first time this happened to Birdy. In college, when Vanmeter was able to find ridiculously cheap tickets online, he would suggest ridiculous weekend ventures--Paris and back, Amsterdam, LA, New Orleans. He was always able to find cheap tickets because he was an up and coming hacker--plugged in, in the small hours of every night. It was love-hate with those trips. Thrilling going--and there was a drinking while racing about experience--but grueling on the return. Birdy had not been on any trip since their post-graduation visits to Hong Kong and Tokyo. Just to Pittsburgh. He didn't count deployments with the Army National Guard. He knew why he stopped traveling, and many other undertakings. No one else knew. Which was exactly the way Birdy wanted it to be. This was an opportunity to maybe kill the kudzu he felt spreading on his mind. Maybe the opportunity. It was that memory; it wouldn't leave him alone. Choke it and kill it for good.

A very curious woman, Mrs. Wassergold asked, "Where you planning to go in Europe?"

"Rome."

"For how long?"

"Leave on a Monday and return the following Monday?" said Birdy, in the form of a question, unsure how long to ask for, or how long it would take to find Brother Thrash Davis. Then a feeling of regret overcame him. He shouldn't have asked for a vacation. Not for a Vanmeter scheme.

"I see--well--let me talk with Mr. Wassergold about this." She flashed her tight smile, fleeting as always. He thanked her and left her office, relieved. She made him nervous for some reason, and Birdy didn't believe he was the nervous type. Maybe just around fearless and bullet proof people, besides his father.

Now Birdy could finally reply to Vanmeter's endless texting, pressing him on when he was going to ask for a vacation. Vanmeter and his mother were scheduled to be in the city tonight. Birdy bought two air mattresses and situated them in his living room. He met Vanmeter's mother only once, at graduation. She seemed overwhelmed by it all. He remembered her brown front teeth were askew, as if they revolted, yet failing to fight their way out of her mouth. Otherwise a pretty woman.

They arrived at Birdy's place just before 11 pm. Exhausted and with no appetite they showered and went to bed, Clara sleeping in Birdy's room, Birdy and Vanmeter on the air mattresses. Little was said, and Vanmeter was grateful. There was a lot to talk about, but he needed sleep. Both of his plans relied heavily on Birdy and his parents. A lot to ask for, and he hoped not too much.

The next day found them all tired, sleeping in unfamiliar surroundings in a city such as New York were Clara and Vanmeter's excuse. With Birdy, it was others staying in his apartment. Having a mother of a friend in his apartment was a stressing dynamic he hadn't anticipated, making Birdy irritable. Just being at work was going to be a highlight of the week. Clara's dental appointment was at 1030, a 20 minute cab ride to Midtown. The dentist referral was compliments of Frieda.

Actually, it was her parents recommendation. Clara was up and dressed, knowing Birdy needed his room to get ready for work. She only drank tea, and Birdy had plenty of tea. He was a coffee man during the week and tea on Sundays. Vanmeter asked to join him walking to work. He told his Momma he'd be back in less than an hour with breakfast.

Outside was agreeably cool. High, thin overcast, with a good chance of some sun. They walked at an athletic pace to Birdy's coffee shop. The side-walks were filling up.

"The first day in Rome may be long, coming in from the red-eye, unless we can locate Brother Davis fast. He'll turn me down flat right away I figure, so we need a couple of days hanging out waiting for him to come around to the idea, which I already know you think is crazy. I know it's crazy. But that's my plan."

Vanmeter stayed quiet while they waited for their coffee. The shop was filled with morning regulars. Birdy didn't want to think about any part of Vanmeter's scheme, how it relied entirely on someone who would actually sell the forgeries, knowing they were forgeries. What kind of person does that? Only one kind of person, he thought. Couldn't be any other kind. He wanted absolutely nothing to do with any of it. He didn't want to think any more about it, and it was already becoming a distraction.

Back on the sidewalk sipping their coffee, they resumed their walk to Birdy's workplace.

"I will not be present when you lay all this out to Brother Davis. And you're gonna tell him I have nothing to do with any of this. You got that?"

Vanmeter nodded. Birdy stopped in the middle of the sidewalk, an obstacle, diverting the flow of people passing by, going around them both, now converging, heading where they needed to go. He stared at Vanmeter.

"I got it Birdy, I got it."

"Damn right you do," said Birdy and he resumed walking.

"I'm there. See you tonight. Should be back by dinner, but if you and your Mom get hungry don't let me stop you. I'll text you when I think I'll get back."

As they walked, Vanmeter shook Birdy's hand and thanked him. Birdy nodded and went inside to work. Vanmeter returned to the apartment with a giant blueberry muffin for his Momma. He wasn't hungry, but she insisted he share the muffin with him.

Vanmeter had spent considerable time while they drove up to New York explaining to his Momma what all-on-four implants were and what was required to get a complete new set of teeth. She was very worried about the cost. And the pain, mostly the pain. Her worry seemed to increase during the morning, and by the time they caught a cab she was not talking at all, just staring out the passenger window. She was not looking at anything in particular, simply staring out.

Vanmeter couldn't read her mind, and didn't want to. Instead he ran through how he was going to connect with Brother Davis, how he was going to present his proposal to him. Clara grabbed his hand and squeezed. Brother Davis left his mind. Vanmeter wasn't too worried about how he would pitch his plan to Davis, the direction he took in their conversation would most probably change anyway, depending on too many factors, most of which Vanmeter would have little control.

Dr. Ira Steinem was an oral maxillofacial surgeon of some renown. His patient waiting area was far too bright for Vanmeter, it felt intentionally impersonal. Dr. Steinem was all business, with just enough of a bedside manner not to be an ass. But Vanmeter thought he could very well be a galactic-sized ass, and so he was on his best behavior. He was equally business like, with just enough display of concern for his Momma so as also not to look like an ass. Clara had never been in any hospital or doctor's office like Dr. Steinem's. She agreed with her son. The place looked polished, like the porcelain teeth he implanted in patients. Far too much white. The longest wait was for the 3D CT scan. The next longest wait was for Dr. Steinem to review the scan results.

Over two hours after they arrived Dr. Steinem called them into his office. He gave Clara her first full dental exam since she was a small girl.

"You qualify as a candidate for all-on-four and I understand you traveled from West Virginia to see me. I can appreciate that. I have scheduled you for this Friday."

"You good with Friday?" He no longer seemed a borderline ass, much less a galactic one, thought Vanmeter. A flash of embarrassment passed through him.

Dr. Steinem recognized Clara was overwhelmed.

"My team will take great care of you and you don't hesitate to ask any question you may have. And if they can't answer them, I will." Clara could only give a slight nod.

In the cab, returning to Birdy's apartment, Clara finally spoke up. She was exhausted from the appointment.

In a quiet voice, she whispered to her son, "I'm worried the pain will drain my will, and I'll end up having a bad wanting for those painkillers that nice man will give me. That's just between us, son, just us."

That evening Birdy didn't return to his apartment until after 8 pm. Clara wasn't hungry and was already in bed. He brought some food from the restaurant. In the afternoon Vanmeter had stopped by a liquor store.

Vanmeter waited, thinking. When Birdy returned, they ate warmed up duck tacos and sipped Bulleit Rye.

"They let me use a big closet as an office—a desk, chair, and laptop computer. It's above their big restaurant. At least it's air conditioned. I'm not in there much. I get the spices through customs and drive them back to a warehouse near La Guardia. I deliver them to the restaurants, and so I get to know the chefs and owners. I've learned a lot. Like I know I'd never want to be in the restaurant business. But supplying restaurants? Different story."

The rye softened Birdy's irritation about the week, even after agreeing to let Vanmeter and Clara stay at his place until the middle of next week. Friday was the big day, and she would need to stay in the city for a few days more for follow on checkups.

"You've convinced me to ask my parents if you and your mom can stay in their garage apartment until your mom gets a job at the closest Walgreens. I remain impressed," said Birdy, now shaking his head and smiling. He brought back his glass from the fridge filled with ice and poured another.

"I know they'll agree. They always liked you, Vanmeter. You never bull shitted my dad, knowing you never could get away with it. He knew that you knew you couldn't get away with it. My mom's a pushover."

"The whole Walgreen's thing--what's that about?" Birdy was feeling no pain.

"Momma's a long-time loyal employee--and I had a talk with her manager--they're cousins--he put the word out to Pittsburgh," said Vanmeter, stretching out the 'ee' in employee. He was letting his West Virginia come out.

"She has to leave. The place is gonna put her in too early a grave. Not her fault.
I had to get her outta there."

"Pittsburgh don't compare to New York City, but it also ain't small town West Virginia either," said Birdy.

"The best hope I got is she starts out with new teeth and someone I know will help her get a new start--in your old neighborhood, or somewhere around there."

"I'm leaving Friday to Pittsburgh. I'll be back Sunday night."

"How much is getting a whole new mouth of teeth setting you back?"

"Everything I've saved. Plus more. Don't know the exact bill. But I'll be starting all over after those chompers are implanted."

"And you think your crazy ass plan forging paintings will bring in some money?"

"Hey, for some reason, I'm the guy with the storage room full of materials to make forgeries. Could never have predicted that. And I am now compelled to follow this through."

"For some reason," said Birdy.

"Yep, for some reason," echoed Vanmeter.

They finished their rye and Birdy was ready for bed. Birdy now had a reason to go along with Vanmeter. He was soon to be broke helping his mom. But Birdy knew that wasn't the reason Vanmeter was doing this forgery thing. Vanmeter would have followed this through if he were the richest man in West Virginia.

Vanmeter was not ready to sleep. He poured them another.

"It was the Czech Republic, and the Materials Man--I just call him MM--had us visiting a village outside of Zlin, a cool named town called Vizovice. Zlin itself looked too planned, the buildings were either square or rectangular. I felt like I was in a city of aluminum framed glassed blocks thirteen stories high, a lot of aluminum. Plus, brick buildings, rectangular, a ton of concrete, and right outside of the city, clusters of reddish brick homes looking like factory replicas. Homogenous. The planners worked way too hard trying to be efficient or something. We stayed in Zlin when I attended the Masters of Rock festival, in Vizovice. World famous as I've come to know. It's held in July. Un-believable guitar players."

"I know MM's name, couldn't help seeing his airline ticket, he didn't try to hide it. But--I won't say his name. It keeps me at a distance. Maybe him too. But I don't know, he never said not to call him by his name, he just never mentioned his name to me. As if not to bother. Although he called me by my name. He'd put a pause between Van and Meter. Van...Meter he would say. A bit dramatic."

"It was there MM introduced me to a hulking Polynesian. Soft high voice. Built like a touring bus. His name's Kale, and MM says he knows art people everywhere in Europe, East and West. Pronounced 'Kah-le'. He's a *mahu*, I've come to find out later."

"No phone numbers, no email addresses, nothing. If I need more help I need to go to Rome and sit outside the Papa Rex on a Tuesday at 5pm. Can you believe they want me in Rome? Unbelievable--that's what I say-- unbelievable."

Vanmeter watched Birdy in silence, waiting for a reaction. The thing about Vanmeter was his stories were not made up. Maybe embellished sometimes, but he couldn't help himself, he was a born storyteller. Birdy drained the last bit of rye in his glass.

"Let me know which Tuesday you plan to be there," said Birdy. He went to the hall closet and pulled down a small suitcase from the top shelf. He asked Vanmeter to check with his Momma so Birdy could get some clothes to pack. He'd be leaving early the next morning. Clara got up from the bed and gave Birdy a kiss on the cheek. She thanked him for letting them stay and making them feel at home. She apologized for not getting out and visiting the city. Birdy knew her worry and pain didn't allow for tourist kinds of activities. He thought the city frightened her. Birdy didn't know what else to say. He had no intention of telling her everything was going to be fine because he had no idea what to expect, other than he believed she wasn't going to sleep much that night.

In fact, none of them slept well that night. Just before going to bed Frieda sent a group text to Vanmeter and Birdy. She was checking in to say hi and jokingly asked when they were planning on coming back over to visit.

"I'll let you answer that question," said Birdy to Vanmeter. Birdy missed Frieda, but he only texted her twice since Zanzibar--replying to her texts. He'd refused to think about her, knowing it would be a persistent distraction that had no upside.

But Vanmeter had been in contact with her. She'd been texting him since they left. The worst form of communication ever invented, thought Vanmeter. Especially with women. You could get yourself into a whirling dervish of a mind twist attempting exegesis of a series of texts. And he loathed emojis. Texting women he was intimate with was as painful as he imagined his Momma's pain. Frieda was trying to shield herself from hurt by texting Vanmeter apologies for their rendezvous. It made no difference what he texted in reply. He sensed she wasn't receiving the words she wanted to read, and Vanmeter could only guess what those words might actually be. Testing him? Probing for signs of--what? If she should actually hope for a sign of a potential for some kind of relationship? He was embarrassed for her.

Vanmeter group texted Freida and Birdy that a Rome trip was being planned and he'd let her know when they would be arriving. Vanmeter had no problem confronting Frieda face to face. Only to stop the texting.

The aftermath of their next encounter was impossible to predict, and Vanmeter was fine with that uncertainty.

On the train to Pittsburgh the next morning Birdy read Vanmeter's reply. Frieda came back with fifty happy faced emojiis, plus a few hundred exclamation points, or so it seemed to Birdy. He had now another reason for going to Rome.

5

Reclined in the chair, nauseous, and squirming to distract herself, Clara waited for Dr. Steinem. She was petrified. His two assistants were moving too quickly about the room for Clara. She let their quick movements affect her already miserable disposition. Dr. Steinem was young, thin and tall (too tall for a dentist he would realize too late in life), with green eyes so magnified by his special glasses that Clara found she felt some relief from her nausea fixating on his face. His voice was distinct, a low resonance, and calming. She then clung to the sound of his voice and stared at his magnified green eyes. She was now in a pain free haze, words sounding blurry like her sight. She felt pressure on occasion inside her mouth, which was clamped open by some mysterious force. She remembered releasing her grip on the chair arms, and she blushed when she thought she passed loud gas. Clara couldn't tell for sure, yet she blushed bright all the same.

Afterwards, in another room, in half sleep, she squinted at the fluorescent ceiling lights. Clara had no idea where she was or why she was so sleepy, why she couldn't move. Vanmeter's face then appeared before her. He beamed a wide smile, pointing to his teeth, and then pointing to Clara. She didn't understand. He produced a hand mirror from somewhere and put it in front of Clara. She was aware enough that when she looked at herself, she looked like absolute hell warmed over.

"Smile Momma," whispered Vanmeter. He whispered again. There clearly was nothing to smile about, she thought, as she became more aware.

"Go 'head, smile!" She couldn't see him because of the damn hand mirror in front of her. She opened her mouth, then wider. She then forced a smile, the last thing she wanted to do. At that moment, she lapsed into shock, confused at what she was seeing. Then she almost fainted. She didn't recognize herself, now convinced she was looking at a photograph of someone else. She looked into the mirror again, and smiled wide. The shock remained, as she cried hard. No one in the room could console her.

6

"Will he be fine with it? I don't know, I don't see why not. It's not the first. You bring in someone that needs to be brought in, brought to somewhere. It's not like they're boozy, druggy, gang banger types. You managed to stay clear of them, at least you've convinced me. Maybe you're father too. Maybe." Birdy's mother Arlene, smiled.

Arlene Wire was lean and tall, and, as with most all women her age, beauty left her, but as with only some, many hints remained. She tried to retire but the hospital begged her to stay on. She only worked three days a week, six hours a day, often during the graveyard shift. She was currently mentor to the new nurses on the oncology ward, previously the neo-natal ward. That was her true calling-the tiny precious babies clinging to life. They didn't pay her near what she deserved. That was Porter Wire's rub with the job. You should at least be offered what you truly deserved to be paid. Whether you accepted that pay was another matter. But the employer should always be prepared to pay what was deserved.

Now Porter Ballentine Wire was a man that, if those who knew him knew everything about him--what made him tick, what compelled him throughout the day, why he made and makes the decisions he does--those who knew him would find him to be not an ordinary man. He was also tall and lean, a man whose bald head looked good. He observed, "I got symmetry." But Porter B, as he was called, never had any compunction to let everyone know everything about him. What for? Respect? Adulation? Power? He already possessed all of these, in the measure in which they were only necessary, if they were necessary at all.

Porter B could be a very challenging husband, and equally challenging for his children, his wife having at least a choice. And Arlene was a woman who willingly took on the challenge, having been assertive almost fifty years ago, during times almost as disruptive as these present years. She knew a white woman being married to a black man fifty years ago was nothing like today. Nothing like today.

Porter B was out that evening. He played bass with The NFB, (Neighborhood Funk Band), and wasn't due home until 11 pm. As long as the gig ended no later than 10 pm he'd still play, but no later than 10 pm. And no more than twice a month on Friday nights, no weekdays anymore. If the band was to play other nights or past 10 pm then they had to bring in a substitute. But fans of the Neighborhood Funk Band would get to the bar early because they loved watching Porter B slapping the bass and grooving and moving like nobody's business. When Porter B came home, he'd have two beers, he never drank during the gig, and sit in the living room and unwind--listening to Charley Pride. He loved country music. Charley heard him play bass many years ago and tried to recruit him for his touring band. But Porter B declined. They still kept in touch and Porter B takes Arlene to see him if he is performing in the area. Having moved way too many times serving thirty years in the Army had its effect on him. The only time he traveled was on their annual vacation, in the summer, usually a month long stay somewhere. Arlene planned every trip. She'd find a place to rent and they would use that place as their base of operations, exploring out and about, on their schedule. This is how Porter B referred to it.

Arlene had gone to bed. Birdy heard his father driving into the garage. He came out to help unload his father's amp and bass, and his equipment bag.

"Good gig?" asked Birdy.

"Just right." Porter B gave his son a tight embrace.

"Back in the day you used to dislike immensely helping load and unload."

"Because Mom made me set my alarm to help you unload, back when you'd come home at 3 am."

"Those days a long gone, man, long gone." Porter B snuck into the bedroom, gave Arlene a peck on the cheek, and took a long shower. Birdy cracked a beer and waited for him in the living room. He was unsure how his father would react to Vanmeter's Momma living in the back apartment. Birdy wanted to tell him about Vanmeter's ridiculous plan to find Brother Davis in Rome and paint forgeries. But that was not going to happen. He couldn't tell his mother because she never kept anything from his father. But then, neither ever asked about anything other than what Birdy was doing at the time. They didn't seem to have a need to know. That's how Birdy thought his father would describe it, if it ever came up. Never did.

Porter B came from the kitchen with a cold beer. He was in his maroon silk robe, worn-white cotton pajamas, and old-style, slip-on, polished house shoes. From bass player in a funk band to Mr. Recline for the Evening-- that's how Porter B described himself in the late evening hours.

"You remember Vanmeter's Momma from graduation?"

"Felt sorry for her. She was out of her element," said Porter B.

Birdy told the story about Clara's current situation and Vanmeter's intervention. Porter B listened until his first beer was finished, excused himself and went to get his second. He came back with a beer for Birdy, went to the turntable, and played Charley Pride in low volume. Birdy never got country music. Birdy never listened to music on his own much anymore, and his father thought that was a shame. Music was necessary for life; Porter B knew that to be true. He couldn't imagine living without listening to music. But Arlene was the same as Birdy. She never would have listened to music on her own. But married to Porter B, she had little choice. It was also clearly not a burden.

Birdy reminded his father Clara was only thirteen years older than Vanmeter. Porter B had lost count of how many girls got pregnant at the high school over the years where he was the Chief Sergeant Major of the Junior ROTC program. Most of those girls never gave birth to their babies.

"She have drug problems. Or drinking?"

"She did in the past," said Birdy.

"My experience tells me they have those problems the rest of their lives," said Porter B, finishing his beer. He missed Birdy being around. He missed his daughter too. Birdy's older sister Patti was in California, teaching at a small college. But Patti never came home to visit anymore. The divide, she thought, was too wide. Porter B couldn't see the divide. That was the major problem Patti told him. It didn't matter if the divide was of Patti's own making, said Arlene. Arlene told her husband that the only way Patti would come visit is if they believed how Patti saw the world. Because Patti believed she knew exactly how the world was made up. The complete and total injustice tightly woven into society. You have to feel the anger of the injustice of it all. But Arlene and Porter B couldn't see it or feel it, and therefore couldn't be angered by it. This made Patti more furious, to the point where she cut herself off from her parents, and Birdy too.

Porter B said she lived in the flurry of fury.

"I'm putting a poetic spin on a damn shame, a damn sad situation," said Porter B.

"We'll let Clara stay a while," he decided. Porter B knew she wouldn't stay in Pittsburgh long. She may only be thirteen years older than her son, but she was too old to transition to a city, even a small city like Pittsburgh. But maybe he's wrong, he thought. Rarely, but maybe.

Porter B asked about Vanmeter, how was he doing, what was he up to these days. He asked about Frieda, too. Birdy told him Vanmeter was still a dreamer and a schemer, but a great dude who'd stop and help out a friend anytime. Frieda was doing what she was born to do, help people in a way that mattered. And taking care of those young people who had monstrous growths on their face and body, she was using her skill as a surgeon to bring them as close to normal as she could.

"Let Clara know what we expect of her. You know what to say."

"Will do," said Birdy. In silence, they finished their beers and went to bed.

7

Frieda arrived in J.F.K. from North Africa. The E.A.C.H.S was in Djibouti for a scheduled maintenance stop. The medical crew had been given almost a month off. She took a taxi into the city and surprised her parents. They were in their respective offices, her mother on speaker phone with one of their restaurant managers. It was a booming conversation, the only kind of conversation her mother engaged in. She refused to wear hearing aids. Frieda passed by her mother's office so as to not be seen and knocked on the closed office door of her father. He was startled, dozing in front of his computer monitor, overcome by the monotony of six hundred and fifty lines of inventory.

"Frieda!" he yelled and whipped out of his swivel chair and embraced her.

"Your mother know you're here?" Frieda shook her head.

"You hungry? You just come in from Africa? Where again? Djibouti, or somewhere? You must be hungry. How long's that flight? You must be hungry," said Harold, out of shape and out of breath. He says, "Exercise was for people who thought they could live long enough until the big corporations figured a way to let them live forever. Imagine the profits." He used to say exercise was for young people. Now it's old people too. "Who'd want to do such a foolish thing?" He never was a big eater, or a big drinker. Besides, he lived in the city. Walk, walk, walk.

He grabbed her arm and marched her into her mother's office.

"Frieda!" yelled Myra, telling whoever was on the phone, "We'll continue this later."

Myra said, "Djibouti?" Just how hot can that African place be? I couldn't bear to be that hot. I can't take the city's August heat, or July or June--and don't talk to me about Florida before November."

"You must be hungry! Or maybe you're too exhausted to be hungry? Which is it?" said Myra, hugging her daughter, kissing both cheeks again and again. They agreed to go out for dinner that evening, and have Frieda go home, take a long shower and relax. Myra went back to her office and got back on the phone. Harold followed Frieda downstairs and out to the street, kissed her again, and let her go. She had already dropped off her luggage at home. It was a pleasant day and she wanted to walk. Her feet were still puffy from the eighteen-hour flight. Business class helped some.

Fast walking, Frieda reflected on the other worldliness of Djibouti compared to the city. The Afar women, their arresting facial features. She imagined Afar women on New York streets, in their manner of dress. Afar clans mixing with Uptown, Midtown, Soho clans. She had no idea if they would even desire to assimilate. Why would they? Would they migrate out of Africa--in numbers as staggering as those from India and Asia? And El Salvador, Honduras, and Guatemala?

She liked Zanzibar City and Djibouti--like young American travelers do--the immediate excitement of stark visual differences compared to their familiar places, of strange dress of people, envisioning daily life here, hustling to see everything they could in two days, maybe three. The imaginary comfort of daily living with limited choices, as opposed to our overwhelming choices in the U.S. Of almost everything.

She was helping these people after all, and in doing so she met the patient's parents, brothers and sisters, grandmothers, and aunts. Frieda was invited into their homes for celebration. Dancing, singing, and drinking of hot tea, with too much sugar. She wanted to wear a Yankees baseball cap but instead wrapped a white scarf with black paisley print around her head. While there she was asked twice about her last name. Fearing they hated Jews, both times she said she was Catholic, one time shy of St. Peter, she thought.

She conveyed excitement describing her visit to Our Lady of the Good Shepherd Cathedral. She didn't mention it looked like a towering, ornate half pipe, from an 80's science fiction movie featuring rad skate boarders, affixed with a giant stark white cross on top. The families would smile, politely. Frieda wanted to tell them about the Church of the Good Shepard in Beverly Hills she visited twice, but knew she'd get nothing more than polite smiles in return, with perhaps some later evening private conversation about how strange she was. That was fine with Frieda. She was excited about being the strange one. The attention she might receive dampened her loneliness.

Her Beverly Hills girlfriend Frieda visited the second time got excited telling her stories of Central and South America, how she'd be perfectly content to live in a dirt floor house in Guatemala--she spent two nights in such a house and felt free.

Frieda was very tempted to subject her friend to The Obvious Question.

"Free from what, exactly?" Frieda knew she'd get a rambling explanation why her girlfriend felt the way she did living in a dirt floor Guatemalan two room house, with no indoor plumbing and bare bulb lighting from a used, noisy gas powered generator. She felt she must be convincing to her Guatemalan acquaintances, convincing them their life was wonderful. Because she felt wonderful being there. She felt it was a duty to feel wonderful in a dirt floor house. And behold, she felt wonderful.

Frieda resisted the temptation to ask.

Frieda was intent on losing weight. She wanted to run again. The cramped exercise room aboard the E.A.C.H.S. was filled with sweat soaked, rusty and creaky treadmills and bike machines. She tried getting into exercise regimes she could do in her room, designed for the happening, busy people. She found none to her liking. She was busy, not happening. She believed her weight was a needling factor in her knees hurting. She had three weeks. Then she was off to Rome to rejoin with Vanmeter and Birdy. Both had sent her texts. Birdy said it was going to be a Vanmeter show, pure seat of the pants, with a healthy mix of high life storytelling, mostly bullshit, but maybe not.

Vanmeter's text read--"I'm confident I don't know what I'm doing, but I'm doing it anyway. For Momma, myself. It may be that the stars align and it works like a dream. And the downside shouldn't be anything I can't handle."

Vanmeter was that man you follow into an experience you'd never conceive of yourself, whom you let convince you it's most likely to work out fine. For everyone.   And if not, the downside was recognizing truth that peeks through illusion--that is, what actually happens in life.

That's what Birdy told Frieda.

She'd never been on a Vanmeter trip. Who was she to say otherwise? This was her best excuse in years to lose weight, and she was not going to waste the opportunity.

8

Vanmeter was not convinced all was well with his Momma. Clara texted him otherwise. Birdy texted she was doing fine. Living in Birdy's parent's apartment above the garage. Taking the fifteen minute bus ride to Walgreen's. The bus stop only two blocks away from Birdy's home. Clara getting along with Porter B and Arlene. Clara loved her new teeth. As did everyone. It was too good to be true. Vanmeter now had a ten thousand dollar debt he sort of planned on. Vanmeter had a visceral reaction to debt that affected his judgement. There shall be no debts--ever.

Vanmeter squirmed in his middle seat, on both sides were snoring fat women-both perturbed the middle seat was occupied. The passenger in front of him cranked his seat full aft. For the first time he thought of claustrophobia. Did he have it? He wanted to erupt. He was unable to conjure up any pleasant thoughts. He stayed drunk thanks to a gay, flirting flight attendant who discretely passed Vanmeter six mini bottles of vodka, a cup of ice, and a cup of sliced limes while taking away his meager dinner tray. A magician, thought Vanmeter, stroking his regrown beard. Two triples and watching a moronic American young adult movie about a hyperactive robotic super dog succeeded in helping Vanmeter falling asleep forty-five minutes prior to landing. He awoke as the cabin lights illuminated, at first unable to reorient himself to his surroundings, then upon doing so wishing that he snored an order of magnitude louder than the two women on either side of him--plus the one in front. By their stares deplaning he either succeeded--or passed serious, foul gas. Either or both possibilities pleased him immensely.

Her goal was twenty-five. Upon boarding, Frieda had lost thirteen and a half pounds. The half-pound mattered because she only now had to lose eleven and half pounds more. It seemed so much closer to ten pounds, which in itself seemed most definitely achievable. Her business class seat was the full recline type, and she had finished arranging her seat nest to her satisfaction--headphones, book, glasses, toiletry bag, pillow and blanket just so. Her overpriced sandals were tucked in the foot crevice. The sparkling wine was welcome. Frieda had never been to Rome. The E.A.C.H.S. was ready to leave Djibouti. Frieda sent word she might be delayed in returning-- family matters to attend to. After her second sparkling wine, that is how she characterized her renewed relationship to Vanmeter and Birdy--family matters. She was buzzing, pleased with the characterization.

With no intention, Birdy was aboard the same flight as Frieda, also in business class out of JFK. She was early to board and up front--he, late to board and in the last row. As a spice trader, business class was now standard. The Wassergold's were generous in that regard. Birdy too built his nest. His bourbon was just right. He was not concerned with how Clara was doing in Pittsburgh, he had the gift of trusting his parents who convinced him she was doing well--to Porter B's most welcome surprise.

But this trust was also what was concerning him. He told them of Vanmeter's scheme. They grilled Birdy as to his exact role. He had no answer despite their persistence, all but proving to them and Birdy it was 100 proof recklessness, and according to Porter B, because of its obvious, heavy ruinous scent about it all.

"Malodorous," he called it.

"Like stripper's glitter sticking to you on a sweaty night, that scent won't come off easy. You gotta live with what happens after." Arlene didn't care for the comparison, but she agreed with her husband. But she was also intrigued by the whole forgery scheme. Maybe she had spent too much time in one place, in safety and comfort beside a man who was clearly not ordinary. Was she bored? She asked herself that question the next morning. She felt terrible for thinking this way. But only for a moment, because she could drop a thought in the same time a thought could dash into her mind.

Birdy noticed Frieda as she got up to use the bathroom, just before the aircraft doors closing. He stood up when the bathroom door opened. He gave a slight wave. From twenty feet away Birdy could see Frieda blush as she smiled.

Frieda's glitter, he'd welcome. Although she wore a black dress, he swore she'd lost weight.

In the middle of the flight, with everyone trying to sleep, Birdy and Frieda stood in the front galley, talking for a few hours. Birdy convinced her to let Vanmeter tell her his reason for going to Rome, after all, it was his scheme. It was their first opportunity to fill in the details of each other's family happenings, and details of the last ten years. The ride was without major turbulence. A friendly flight attendant served them bourbon at least twice. Birdy suggested they try to get a few hours sleep--no telling what Vanmeter had in mind upon their arrival.

Definitely lost weight, observed Birdy.

9

This May, Rome was hot and humid--Florida in August hot and humid. Sticky, no breeze, one instinctively searches for shade or air conditioning. Drinking hot anything was a bad idea, and Rome is stingy with ice. Regardless, Vanmeter was an all-day coffee drinker. Caffe Fredo worked, but Caffe Ghiacciato was Vanmeter's choice. In Rome he had to settle for sugar in his caffe. The first barista looked at him like he was an idiot when asking for no sugar. That did the trick. He did not want to shave his beard, but it was damn hot and humid. He'd give it 24 hours and decide then.

He arrived a day earlier than Birdy and Frieda. He selected their apartment in Aurelio, in between Vatican City and the Duquesne Italian campus. He knew the area because he spent a semester here. He was on the injured list for outdoor track season his junior year. A torqued right knee that was stubborn in healing. Otherwise he wouldn't have been permitted to spend a semester abroad. He could speak bar and restaurant Italian. He got by everywhere else. It was enough.

The furnished apartment was modern and small. Two bedroom, one bathroom. But it had air conditioning, and that was worth the price. Vanmeter gambled it would be hot in May. As a bonus, the building had an elevator. The apartment was too cute by half, but the place looked as it did in the photos. An additional bonus. Frieda would take one room and Vanmeter gave Birdy the other. He'd sleep on the pullout sofa.

He took a long cold shower, cleaned up the bathroom, dressed and took a taxi to the campus. He'd been rehearsing in his mind what he would say to Brother Thrash Davis since dropping off his Momma at Birdy's parents' house. Which was the reason he couldn't sleep the past few days. No matter how he laid out his proposal to himself he couldn't get past the ridiculousness of the idea--or how he could make some money without coming off as a greedy asshole. They knew Brother Davis from his track days. He was an excellent discus and shotput coach-his specialties. But he was also a good jump coach, and as a high jumper, Vanmeter would seek his advice on occasion. Brother Davis was the hip Brother, and very popular. He'd stop by the bar and drink two beers with the seniors. Only two. Why he chose to be a Brother, Vanmeter never asked. And Davis never volunteered. Vanmeter entertained the idea of coming all this way to seek out his advice on joining the religious. But he was convinced Davis would see through him and once that occurred, he predicted Davis wouldn't listen to anything else he had to say.

That's why he needed Birdy and Frieda with him. They liked him too. It had been ten years, but Vanmeter knew Davis would remember them. If not for the track team, then for the online scandal they were involved in. Vanmeter sometimes joked to himself he still believed in God because they were all exonerated at the end of the investigation. But the investigation was a living nightmare. It focused Vanmeter's unfocused perspective on life. He knew it changed Birdy and Frieda too. The fact that they remained friends afterwards was a second small miracle, and Vanmeter chocked that up as another reason God existed. Vanmeter hoped the scandal wouldn't be why Davis remembered them, but he was prepared to talk about that too.

The Duquesne campus was housed with The Sisters of the Holy Family of Nazareth--within the Nature Reserve Acquafredda. A few large classrooms, small library and living facilities, a stylish red bricked chapel.

Isolated, considering it's in Rome, seven miles west of Vatican City. Like the other students, Vanmeter disliked the remote locale. He took a taxi to the campus and asked the driver to wait ten minutes, paying him ten Euros extra. He went into the administration office and introduced himself as a Duquesne grad and a Rome campus alum, giving the secretary his name and cell phone number on a piece of paper, telling her he knew Brother Davis from the Pittsburgh campus and would she give him his number. He will be here tomorrow, she said.

As his taxi driver left, Vanmeter gave a quick scan of the campus, noting nothing had changed, how small it seemed, how innocuous it felt. The driver dropped him off at a grocery store within easy walking distance of the apartment. The driver asked if he should wait. Vanmeter was tempted but his finances were tight. He thanked the driver and gave him his best 'arrivederci.' Ciao was too easy, but more appropriate. Vanmeter thought of these things. In the grocery store he purchased bread, cheese, prosciutto, three bottles of Montepulciano, a six pack of Moretti La Rossa, and olives. He'd let Birdy or Frieda buy the whiskey. By the time he returned to the apartment he was drenched in sweat. He showered again, full cold, guzzled a bottle of beer, and fell asleep in his briefs, on the sofa, under the air conditioner on full blast.

His phone buzzed, waking Vanmeter up. It was near 1130 am and he was famished. The apartment was cold, just how he preferred it.

It was Birdy.

He and Frieda were on the same flight and would be at the apartment in an hour or so, depending on customs and traffic. Vanmeter got up and put on pants and shirt--after some time in front of the mirror, his unkempt hair now less so. He decided to keep his beard. He went out for a quick bite to eat. But at the restaurant he decided otherwise and ordered a small carafe of house red. It had cooled down some outside and he was energized from the nap. He walked in and throughout the unremarkable neighborhood. Few residents were out mid-day. Vanmeter thought it would only help him concentrate on what he was going to say to Brother Davis. Otherwise he'd people watch.

Returning to the apartment he received another text. Brother Davis remembered him, asking if meeting at 4 pm tomorrow at the campus would work. Maybe a beer after a quick campus tour? He looked forward to hooking up. Vanmeter texted he'd be there with Birdy Wire and Frieda Wassergold. Brother Davis texted multiple 'thumbs up' emojiis along with a handful of exclamation points. With hesitation, Vanmeter returned the thumbs up emoji.

Back at the apartment, sipping a beer, and after reading the latest news from the U.S., he changed his mind on what he was going to say to Thrash Davis. The news was more improbable than he could ever guess, but it was now his best angle, he thought, still knowing full well he had no idea what he was doing.

10

Frieda loved the apartment. Birdy took issue with taking the second bedroom but Vanmeter would have none of it. Vanmeter insisted they shower and nap--who knew how long the night would go? Vanmeter noticed Frieda's weight loss.

She knew they both knew, and she was pleased.

After showering, Birdy couldn't take a nap, but Frieda crashed hard. Vanmeter and Birdy took a walk to the liquor store. It was less hot and humid, still, they took their time.

"Momma's no kidding doing alright?"

"My folks say so," said Birdy.

"Amazing," said Vanmeter, trying to keep his pace slow to avoid sweating. That's in essence what Porter B said, but Birdy kept that to himself.

"I'm in the hole ten grand for Momma's chompers."

"Those are some amazing teeth," said Birdy. Birdy knew Vanmeter hated debt, to the point of distraction, to the point of making high risk decisions.

"When do you plan to tell Frieda about what you're gonna ask Brother Davis to do?"

"When we get back, after she has a glass of wine. She can stay in the apartment if she chooses. But I'm going to see Brother Davis."

"How long are we in Rome? Frieda wants to go full tourist," said Birdy.

"What about you? Ever been here?" asked Vanmeter, holding open the liquor store door. The conditioned air flowed strong in the whiskey section, and Vanmeter thanked God for the small things.

"Nah," said Birdy, also welcoming the air conditioning. While he was perusing the whiskey and scotch, Vanmeter asked about the best Italian whiskey that wasn't too expensive. The African émigré came from behind the counter and pointed to one bottle. Neither Vanmeter nor Birdy recognized the name. The liquor man insisted it was the best for the price. Birdy placed two bottles on the counter, along with another six pack of Moretti. The liquor man asked where they were from.

"New York," said Birdy.

"Ah, New York. Da best!" said the liquor man.

Back at the apartment, Frieda was sitting on the sofa, wearing a bright summer dress and the pricey sandals. She popped up when they entered.

Birdy placed the whiskey and six pack in the refrigerator. Vanmeter poured a glass of wine for Frieda. Birdy held up a beer in front of Vanmeter. He nodded.

Handing the glass of wine to Frieda, Vanmeter said, "I think you'll have some time to visit places. The apartment's rented for a week."

"But--why am I really here with you two?" asked Frieda. She was happy.

Vanmeter gave her his phone. She read the first few paragraphs of the article.

"It says no one knows where he is--and that he's an art forger. OK..."

"He left me a key to a storage room filled with art materials, paints, brushes, other stuff he used. I don't know why. He wants me to find another painter to use all that stuff. It's worth something for sure. And I have to pay for Momma's chompers."

"Okay, why are we in Rome?"

Birdy chimed in, "Remember Brother Thrash Davis?"

"Yeah, from the track team. The shotput and discus coach. Nice guy. And, what about him?"

"He's supposed to be a first-rate painter. Came from an artist family. Taught painting too. He's here, on the Rome campus," said Vanmeter.

"I didn't know any of that," said Frieda, finishing her wine. She was officially fascinated.

"He's the only painter I know. Maybe he knows someone who's interested in all that stuff in the storage locker."

"Knows a forger?" Frieda looked at Birdy. It was the, 'Is this a Vanmeter scheme?' look. Birdy nodded. Birdy looked at Vanmeter. Vanmeter ignored Birdy. Vanmeter figured they'd been talking since departing New York, which was fine by him. They were both here now. He stroked his beard, and then summoned a taxi driver.

"Taxi's ten minutes out."

"You coming with us?" There was no doubt in Vanmeter's mind.

"What do you think he's going to say? Coming all the way to Rome and dropping this on him?"

"I think anyone with a nickname Thrash can handle all kinds of things," said Vanmeter. Frieda was ready for another glass of wine. But she held off.

11

Brother Davis gave them a twenty minute tour of the Rome campus. Same as it was when he was here, thought Vanmeter, except for different color beige paint, but same dull green carpet. The dorm rooms seemed smaller than he remembered.

Thrash Davis was a very large man, huge hands, thick legs, but not near as heavy as they all remembered him. He kept his blonde, wire brush hair closely cropped. As Vanmeter listened to Brother Davis give the tour, which he had obviously done many times, he noticed Davis's eye for detail in his descriptions. No doubt served him well as a coach, and obviously as a painter, Vanmeter thought. Back then he was a garrulous man, larger than life, animated, with energy to burn. That's how Vanmeter recalled him. But seeing him now, he seemed different, quieter, moving with spartan efficiency, as if saving his energy for some higher purpose. He appeared to interleave being in the moment with them and out of the moment somewhere else.

Birdy noticed a difference too, but wasn't as familiar with Davis as Vanmeter. Frieda remembered him well-- friendly, encouraging to the other athletes--those that were not shot putters and discus throwers. He was a hard-ass to them. She thought he was the same as back then.

Davis was grateful to see them--that they remembered him. He didn't remember them being as close as they seem to be now, but that was satisfying unto itself.

"You drink beer?" Thrash surprised Frieda with the question.

"With these two?" she said. She liked beer, but she really liked the fact she was close to losing the entire twenty-five pounds.

Davis announced, "Give me five minutes to change and I'll take you to my bar.
There's not many close by, but I found one."

"I'll get a taxi," said Vanmeter.

"Good luck out this way," replied Davis. "Bus leaves in ten minutes across the street. Drops us right in front of Bar Tutta la Vita. Fifteen minutes, give or take. I'd take you all on my motorcycle, but..."

They all rode in silence, each staring out the window. The four of them on a bus with only six other passengers aboard--Birdy next to Frieda, Vanmeter and Brother Davis behind them, sitting across from one another, with no one seated next to them. The day remained sunny and hot. Not much traffic out here, thought Birdy. He was thinking about what Vanmeter told Frieda at the apartment, about finding a buyer for all that junk in storage, rather than what he told Birdy. Birdy knew it would all come spilling out, and then some. He also knew Vanmeter hadn't told him everything. Birdy knew Vanmeter didn't have it worked out yet. Not even close. And maybe because of this he was starting to get interested in Vanmeter's scheme--would it succeed? How slim is the chance? Of course, the only certainty at the moment was it all depended on Brother Davis.

Frieda could not recall having felt this at peace with herself. It bothered her initially--why she could not figure out why. Then she told herself to stop trying to figure it out. It worked. She mused, when does that ever work? She was able to blank her mind for a few minutes. Delightful, she thought, to take a pause in self-lecturing. Even more delightful if she could stop self-lecturing. Stop, she then said to herself. Stop.

For Jack Davis, his thoughts were--these three are a pleasant distraction from his three current distractions. In no particular order they were Pico Natambe, Honoraria Duse, and his mother, Vera, who died a year ago the day before. Weak hearts ran in her side of the family. Plus, his time in Rome was coming to an end, no more extensions, as Davis was being assigned back at Duquesne in Pittsburgh.

Pico was the most talented painter he ever come across, and Pico had in his mind an unwavering commitment to helping his family back in Ghana. Pico challenged Brother Davis to see who could replicate a painting chosen randomly from painters Davis had exposed him to while under his tutelage in Ghana. Out of a Yankees baseball cap Davis chose Edward Hopper's 'Sunday'. Not a particularly difficult painting to replicate. Afterwards, the copies were given to Honoraria Duse, a close friend of Davis's who owned a small art gallery in Rome. Davis thought the idea childish, for the whole thing reminded him of his boyhood training, replicating paintings his Mother Vera would choose for him. From pencil sketches to chalk-water colors to oils, Vera chose what Davis would copy next. She never seemed to be fully interested in what Davis wanted to paint--being a respected painter herself, as well as teacher--only what she was interested in having him paint. She tutored him until he left for college. She was the one who gave him his nickname, an embarrassing fact at the time, but over time he grew into it, and later in college took pride in being called Thrash. Forbidden to play football, Jack's high school football coach was despondent in his failure to convince Vera otherwise. At least she permitted him to try out for shotput and discuss--the football coach was also the track and field coach. Davis excelled in both, and soon it became his habit, after releasing the shot and discus, to leap high, flailing both arms and legs in the air, encouraging the flung object to continue moving down field. Davis's vertical leap from stand still was impressive, and after his mother finally came to a track meet to see him compete and witnessed his high flailing, she confronted him.

"And just what is all that thrashing about afterwards? You should see yourself Jack," she said, well within earshot of many of his track teammates. He wasn't aware he was thrashing, just adding encouragement to the object he'd flung. His nickname stuck immediately.

"You're an above average painter, Jack--and on occasion, a very above average one," critiqued Vera. She was that kind of mother. Thrash thought she may have been proud to know that Honoraria judged both his and Pico's replica of 'Sunday' to be extraordinary, and she would not say which version was the better. Pico was very pleased. A testament to Thrash's painting and tutoring skills, perhaps Vera might say. But Thrash doubted it. He wished Honoraria was with them this afternoon, now smiling as the Bar Tutta la Vita came into view.

Vanmeter spent his bus time going over what he was going to say to Thrash, and while doing so, not embarrass Frieda or put Birdy in an uncomfortable bind. As they got off the bus and entered the bar, Vanmeter had decided. Or, he could start off the conversation and completely change tack--he was ready for whatever was to come.

12

It was surprisingly cool sitting outside, under a trellis thick with a thriving vine with scented, flat white flowers, covering most of the patio. No breeze this late afternoon. An old thigh-high stone wall separated the patio from the sidewalk, which was not nearly as busy as the street. The chairs were rickety and Thrash always picked one that looked the strongest before sitting down. This afternoon he asked Frieda to swap chairs so he wouldn't be drinking on his butt. There were five small outside tables, and Thrash received a head nod from the waiter to slide two tables together. Frieda ordered the house red and the rest ordered beer.

"Cin cin," said Thrash. They all repeated like school children. Vanmeter started right away--telling the story how he, Birdy and Frieda came to be in Zanzibar City. Birdy jumped in, as if on cue, telling about being a spice buyer, with Frieda interjecting about being aboard the E.A.C.H.S., and how they remembered Thrash had served in Zanzibar for a time, and went to the Cathedral to find him. Another round was ordered. Looking at his friends, Vanmeter thought affectionately, that went well. They seemed to have captured Thrash's attention. Then he remembered Thrash had a two beer rule back at Duquesne.

Vanmeter was anxious to get things rolling.

"But how did you end up in Zanzibar City?" asked Thrash, to Vanmeter.

"Aboard the E.A.C.H.S. as their IT and electronic technician guy," said Vanmeter.

Looking at Frieda, Thrash said, "And you didn't know he was aboard?"

"You should have seen his beard. I had no idea it was him. Rarely saw him anyway. He was stashed away wherever they stash the computer guys."

"Quite impressed--traveling to the other end of the world to reunite," said Thrash, sipping from his second beer.

"Now let me tell you about Kule Fat, maybe you've heard of him," said Vanmeter.

"Nope, never have," replied Thrash. Vanmeter unfolded a damp copy of an article about Fat's disappearance shortly before the D.A.'s office announced their investigation into an art forgery scheme. Thrash skimmed the article.

"He's apparently well above average, and prolific, according to this," said Thrash, returning the article to Vanmeter. Apprehension stilled Frieda and Birdy; their drinks remaining on the wobbly table.

"I met him while he was still a chef, working in a restaurant owned by Frieda's parents. After about a month Fat asked me to get him a taxi to his apartment. Once there, he invited me in. I met this other man. Sounds weird, and it is, but not that kind of weird."

As Vanmeter was unfolding the entire story Thrash caught the waiter's attention and ordered a third round. When Vanmeter finally mentioned the storage room, he took out an old smart phone from his back pocket and gave it to Thrash, telling him to look at the photos of the contents of the storage room. Thrash took out a cheap pair of foldable reading glasses and looked closely at the photos. Frieda and Birdy started drinking again, but remained silent, staring at Vanmeter, who only raised his eyebrows once to them. Vanmeter talked about the paints, the brushes, the old wooden frames of various sizes, the parchment and paper and canvas from other paintings. The storage room was filled with these materials.

"Alright...fascinating," said Thrash, handing Vanmeter back his old smart phone.

"You're the only painter I know," said Vanmeter, stuffing the phone in his back pocket.

"And you three thought it would be fun to go to Rome, find me, and show me these?" Thrash's tone was ambiguous at best. His body language offered no other clues as to what he'd say next.

Frieda jumped in. "Well, I certainly thought it would be fun to go to Rome--never being here before. I didn't know Kule Fat personally, but knew he was a sought after chef that my parents were proud to have working for them."

Birdy followed. "Back in the day I'd go with Vanmeter on across the world road trips, forty-eight hours, maybe seventy-two. They were non-stop, go-go-go, shoot from the hip. I was exhausted when I got back."

"Is this one of these trips?" asked Thrash.

"Well, now that you mention it, maybe--but no go-go-go," said Birdy, adding, "And I have no idea about what this storage room full of art shit is all about."

Sipping his third beer, Thrash could see there was something about Frieda being here that definitely interested Birdy.

Thrash carefully pushed his chair back from the tables. He needed room to tell his story.

"The first temptation was my lovely mother. She was my only art teacher and she made me copy paintings until I went to college. Did she encourage me to be a forger? Not directly. I never saw most of those paintings again. She had taken them and told me she was storing them in a safe location. She died last year."

Thrash spared them from feeling obligated to say something about his mother's passing by continuing.

"The second temptation was by Pico Natambe, a very talented young man--from Ghana. I met him while on mission there. He's so good I arranged for him to study in the States. He studied with my mother, not coincidentally. Not long ago he caught me in a weak moment, challenging me to copy a painting he chose, and he did the same. He wanted to know who was the better copier. Pico took the competition seriously, more so than I imagined at the time."

"The third temptation was from a friend here in Rome. What does she do, you might ask? Runs a small art gallery. I've gotten to know a few art people since living here. Well--she was the 'judge' if you will, of our little copying contest. Who won, you might also ask? She gave us 200 Euros and told us a very interested customer bought the copy. Which one? We don't know. I refused to take a dime. I didn't ask Pico if he took the money. She told us she destroyed the other copy."

"We're both very, very good--she told us," said Thrash.

While Thrash paused to sip his beer Vanmeter jumped in. "And I'm your fourth temptation."

Thrash lifted his beer. "You said it, not I."

"Alright, your turn. Who here needs money?" Thrash only looked at Vanmeter when asking the question.

"Before all this, he was a hacker," said Birdy, grinning, enjoying the moment.

"And now you're looking to get into the forgery business because some perceptive dude named Kule Fat bet you'd take the bait. Because you can't resist this, can you? You get a charge out of all this."

Vanmeter lifted his beer. "You said it, not I."

"And this Kule Fat just gave you the keys to the storage room?"

"Not only that, he paid Vanmeter to go on a long trip throughout East Europe with another shady dude to check out all the places where he gets all that stuff in storage," volunteered Birdy, now thoroughly enjoying the moment.

"I thought you didn't know shit about the storage room," said Thrash.

"I don't know shit about what's in there, just what I told you," said Birdy.

Vanmeter was aloof to Birdy's color commentary. The conversation was sparking thoughts, and his plan was morphing. It was better than he imagined it might be. This was going somewhere. And it started to feel familiar to him. Birdy may or may not be witting, but he was helping. You can't get angry with Birdy. He's that kind of guy.

Frieda sat there, taking it all in. It was a completely different world than being aboard a hospital ship. Of course, hers was a world that might seem to others, as other worldly. But not really to doctors and nurses. Here, now, she felt she was in a thrilling movie. A double thrill--watching the movie, yet part of it too.

"How's the food here?" she asked.

"Simple, but good," said Thrash. He turned to Vanmeter. "You really believe this Kule Fat dude is going to give you all that stuff, pay for you to hop around Europe, and expect nothing from you? Some kind of a forger's altruistic code? To a stranger, a non-forger?"

Vanmeter grinned. He was barely in the conversation now, as he imagined how all this could possibly unfold.

"Crazy, right?" said Vanmeter. Thrash paused. He summoned the waiter and ordered for the table. Frieda understood part of what he ordered. It didn't matter. She was ready to eat anything, diet be damned.

Pointing at Vanmeter, Thrash said, "And you two believe him?" Thrash was irritated, but the reason was not apparent. Frieda and Birdy both shook their heads.

"Next time in the States, I'll take you all to see it," said Vanmeter.

Thrash, as if some urgency overcame him, asked, "Here's what else I want to know. Why is it none of you have your phones out, or checking your phones every once in a while, like everyone else your age and younger?"

With no pause, Vanmeter said, "Maybe they're not afflicted by FOMO, you know, fear of missing out. Frieda shrugged her shoulders. Birdy's eyebrow arched up as he too shrugged. Vanmeter laughed.

"What about you?" asked Thrash, to Vanmeter.

Vanmeter whipped out his old phone with the pictures on it and held it up.

"This device requires a label--like a pack of cigarettes. Harmful to your health. Especially if you believe there's such a myth as your own personal truth, or feel the need for endless distraction, if you feed on anger and find vengeance thrilling, or crave sentimentality, are afraid of being excluded--from anything. Any of those, or any combination of those--this device takes you to a place--now--if you put this thing down and think about it--you'll start to believe there is no meaning to life. And if there's no meaning to life--shazam--back to your phone you go, without thinking. An unhealthy substitute for action, for sure."

"And...where did that come from?" asked Thrash.

"I read a lot. I mean a lot. I also used to build those algorithms you read about that all the big tech companies use." Pointing to his head, Vanmeter said, "Owning what's inside up here is to own your behavior. Ridiculous money, ridiculous. And to own every behavioral impulse you have requires watching you all the time. You know where this leads." Pulling his phone back out of his pocket, he held it up.

"Yeah, I use this thing sparingly. And you don't want me to go off on Google."

Thrash sat back and stared at Vanmeter. He glanced over to Birdy and Frieda, both now smiling. Nobody spoke. After a time, a slow smile appeared on Thrash's face. He excused himself to use the toilet.

While motioning for the check, Vanmeter said, "You two go on. I'll tell Thrash your tired and wanted to get some sleep."

Birdy shook his head. "Let's settle the bill first. If you two want to continue on after, fine by me. Nice rant, by the way."

"I'll take you up on wanting to get some sleep, after saying goodnight to Thrash," said Frieda. She didn't care she ate too much.

At the same time Thrash returned, the waiter left the check. A faux squabble ensued over who was going to pay the bill. Vanmeter collected Euros from Frieda and Birdy and together with his contribution paid the waiter. Thrash thanked them, reminding the three he had money and just because he's a Brother doesn't mean he can't pay his own tab.

"They have bourbon or whiskey here?" asked Vanmeter.

"Jack Daniels. I like to think they keep it for the token Americano. Round's on me."

Vanmeter said a Jack on the rocks would be fine. If no ice, then just pour it in a glass. Frieda and Birdy declined. They said goodbye to Thrash and Vanmeter and left for the apartment.

Thrash and Vanmeter talked over two rounds of Jack. It was an all-of-over-the map kind of conversation. More than an hour later, in their respective bedrooms, Frieda and Birdy were asleep when Vanmeter finally returned.

13

The next day was hot. All sun, no clouds, no breeze. The apartment was cool from the air conditioning and Frieda and Birdy didn't rouse until 7 am. Vanmeter had been up since 6 am, already having two expressos from the tiny café in the ground floor of their building, now on his skinny laptop, completing payment for tickets to the Vatican and Vatican Museum. The night before Thrash had texted a friend who gave private tours throughout the city, but whose specialty was the Vatican. It was Friday, and the Vatican was open in the evening. He was burning through his last two thousand dollars too fast, and was going to need money soon. As he never had any quibble reminding himself, he hated having any debt, at any time, regardless of circumstances. His credit cards were going to be paid off by the end of the month, he swore. Debt payment motivated him more than almost anything. He had once worked almost 40 hours straight writing code to release him from a deal he knew he should have never made in the first place. The customer didn't think he could pull it off and when Vanmeter did, the customer was not pleased. At all. Vanmeter was released from his deal, and advised by his customer not to program for anyone they knew, and they knew almost everyone in the trade. If he had to, Vanmeter knew he could get back into it. His specialty was imitating North Korean hackers, although he was competent imitating the Chinese. He had no shortage of customers, none legit.

Mentioning to Thrash the night before, Vanmeter said his Momma was the key. By taking care of her, he could learn to take care of someone other than himself. He produced a wry smile as he thought about it. He rarely displayed any other. He knew the paradox of his plight.

He knew it very well. Vanmeter was trying to grow more of a conscience, or at least be more serious about life's meaning. Augustine of Hippo would smile the same smile, he thought.

Thrash was meandering through a crisis of vocation--not to leave the Brotherhood, but to become a priest.

The night before, Thrash said, "I've found the one truth. Live only within the holy sphere of Christ. Live for just the sake of God. That requires emptying oneself. Of everything. You have enough Catholic education from Duquesne to know what I'm talking about."

Vanmeter recalled giving him his full attention.

"And it's an absolute bitch to pull off," said Thrash.

"What is?" asked Vanmeter.

"Emptying oneself of everything."

"Does it have to be everything, no shit?" said Vanmeter.

"Everything, no shit." That's how Vanmeter remembered the conversation. During his confession about growing a conscience, Thrash said nothing. But he was paying close attention, Vanmeter knew.

Vanmeter thought Thrash's current vocation, with his flexibility to serve abroad (Duquesne had another satellite campus in Dublin), and back in Pittsburgh, to paint, mentor, teach...Vanmeter thought that was a clear win in life. To be a priest? Would that, in fact, change everything, no shit?

Confessing while drinking with strangers is easy. The chances of meeting again are as low as the chances of changing one's way in life. Vanmeter and Thrash knew each other only through track and field, as athlete and coach, and a decade ago.

They weren't complete strangers, but mostly so.

Vanmeter's other obsession, besides debt, was to win against the odds of life--not against sickness or cancer, those circumstances out of your control, but circumstances within a partial ownership of control. To change your will and change your being. As Vanmeter routinely said, "I read a lot. I mean, a lot."

Walking back from Bar Tutta la Vita to the apartment the previous night, thinking many things with many extended variations, Vanmeter now came to believe his best chance for finding a willing painter was not Thrash, but Pico Natambe. He was slated to meet Honoraria Duse, Thrash's art gallery friend, somewhere along the Vatican tour the next evening. She knew Pico's current whereabouts, more or less, according to Thrash.

The previous evening, Birdy and Frieda's conversation was over a bottle of wine Vanmeter provided. This morning, both had been awake well before 7 am, in their respective rooms, both thinking about what they said to each other the night before, recalling things they said that maybe they shouldn't have, but neither finding any good reason why they shouldn't have said them, other than embarrassment of small revelations. Birdy thought he stopped short of explicitly telling Frieda the two wounds of his being, one deep, and harrowing, and the other one, new, shallow, and stubborn. One he expected to never heal, the other of trespassing sentiment, and by its nature, questionable. But as he lay awake, he thought maybe he said more than he meant to. Just before they went to their rooms, he was engaging in vague word play while trying not to be the annoying coy dude. That morning, he settled on a believable reality; the wine loosened his tongue last night, and limited his memory in the morning. But, he acknowledged, he very much welcomed the trespass.

They had kissed, after all.

That was Frieda's first thought in the morning, amongst the many, many other thoughts pinging her conscience. She told Birdy she wanted to get married, have children, and raise a family. Giving up her practice if necessary, although she put far too many years into getting to where she was now. You study, train, study, train, and years later you are announced as a doctor. She was an excellent surgeon, she knew, like Thrash knew he was an excellent painter.

Birdy sat, sipped his wine, and listened, like a good man should, thought Frieda. All that was fine in her mind, she recalled in the morning. What was cloudy was how she attempted to describe her parents' thoughts towards marrying someone who is not Jewish. And the unmentionable, their thoughts on Birdy. She knew she never brought up in their conversation that her parents sometimes used the Yiddish word in her presence, and there was never any reason to talk about a black man in relation to their family. But Frieda was uncertain of what Birdy was thinking. She had no idea what a black man thinks about these things, but she knew they did think about them. And perhaps think about them every waking moment. She made the assumption that was what Birdy did, think about them every waking moment. In the shower, rinsing her muddled thoughts, she remembered Birdy's mother, Arlene. Could she be like Arlene?

Thrash didn't sleep much that night. He liked all three of them. Vanmeter was a guy he felt he understood well. He liked him, yet he didn't want to like him. The thought they were too much alike produced a dismissive laugh, alone in his small room, and single bed.

He reflected once again whether he could empty himself, of everything, and remain empty, waiting to be filled by the Holy Spirit. As dawn came, Thrash knew being a priest would no more empty himself than being what he was now. Being a priest would not cause an emptying, but he knew that living like a priest was the best path towards a total poverty of spirit. How could anyone else achieve such a state?

And what about painting? Did he have to empty himself of recreating beauty, no matter its actual absence of divinity, in order to only remain within the sphere of Christ? Inspiration by divinity does not necessarily infuse divinity into painting. does it?

He told himself he needed to reread Jacques Maritain, and he remembered a quote, "Let us not go faster than God, it is our emptiness and our thirst that He needs, not our plenitude."

Does painting make him full, or complete? Thrash thought so, and as such, he had been out of sorts for some time.

Vanmeter thought it made no sense whatsoever, and was surprised Thrash was attempting to make a false choice. Clearly, it's a false choice, Vanmeter thought, but said nothing to Thrash at the time. Who knows all the thoughts of a man contemplating such a radical and severe calling--how one thinks about how to find God and doing everything in accordance to God's will?

And the abnormality of celibacy? In today's times? A seeming bigger problem now since the Catholic Church was a twelve-car Interstate pileup these days. After the wreckage is cleared, the dead are buried, and the lookers-on drift away, what next?

Vanmeter thought, maybe you can find God in art, because art reflects the artist's response to beauty, or some such thing. But maybe it's the other way around? That morning, Vanmeter could not exactly recall which thoughts were his and which were Thrash's. It poured out of Thrash like a water from a busted main, under unsteady pavement, whose cracks finally gave way. But Thrash seemed tormented, thought Vanmeter. It was as if a deadline was approaching and a decision must be made. Must? Should? Vanmeter didn't pretend to know, but he was decided on seeking out Pico rather than press Thrash any further. He was pressing himself enough.

14

It is a mistake if anyone believes you can escape the crowds by touring the Vatican in the evening. Not anymore. It is clear that segments of civilization are doing very well, for the crowds appeared to be all established middle class, at least the non-Asian tourists, which for some reason Birdy thought they would be wealthy types. Of his economical equivalent, he noticed not many. He was Catholic and the Vatican fascinated him. The Vatican museum more so. There was no chance they could see everything that evening, so their tour guide, Honoraria Duse, chose particular paintings, sculptures, and tapestries that in her highly opinionated mind everyone must see. She was an excellent guide, admitted Birdy, and as he watched Vanmeter watch Ms. Duse, he thought Vanmeter believed the same.

After meeting her, Vanmeter's confidence received a lift because as the tour went on, he came to believe he may actually offload the storage room of art materials and make some money. Finding buyers--he needed to find buyers. Far outside his sphere of influence and contacts, until tonight, he thought. Even better was when Thrash told him in confidence that he had mentioned the art storage room to Honoraria. Above and beyond, thought Vanmeter. Therefore, he reasoned, she had contacts with those who would pass forgeries on to either patrons of the art, or other dealers.

These thoughts led to Vanmeter's reassessment of Thrash.

Frieda was enthralled. She ignored wedging between tight clusters of visitors being led by their respective guides, all shuffling while looking at everything they possibly could, as if their minds included photographic capacity, capturing glimpses in order to be recalled at their leisure sometime afterwards. How so not true. Sometimes interesting persons in the crowd were direct competition for her attention rather than another priceless painting of the Madonna that Ms. Duse spoke so knowledgably about.

It may have been Ms. Duse's lower register voice that blended in with the voices all about them. Straining to hear the history and significance of the painting Frieda looked elsewhere, and she discovered couples, friends, strangers aside strangers, all with the same look about them. Their expressions, their clothes, their real motivations for being there.

She didn't want to be like them. Twice Birdy had to grab her hand in order not to get separated from Vanmeter, Thrash, and Ms. Duse.

During their conversations at dinner afterwards, there was unanimous consent amongst the three first-timers that St. Peter's Basilica was the primo experience, regardless of crowds, and to revisit they all agreed would be their reason to return to Rome. And only to visit the Basilica at night. And climbing to the dome. And gazing across the city at night on the walkway outside the dome. Frieda's giddy excitement along with Honoraria's amiable nature fueled the table conversation as soon as the first glass of wine was consumed. Honoraria was tiny, bone thin, and exceptionally pretty. She tanned well. Initially Vanmeter guessed she was in her forties, but now that they were at table, he guessed she might be in her early fifties. Frieda loved her dress, and thinking it must be obvious to anyone--she reminded her of Audrey Hepburn. She could wear anything and look fabulous, she thought. In Rome, no less. Older than Thrash by some years, thought Frieda.

Honoraria and Thrash seemed very comfortable together, with just the right amount of attention paid to each other. Since, in Frieda's mind, there was no such thing as a man and woman being merely very good friends, her imagination drifted into speculation about them. Frieda then thought, if she was speculating about them, certainly at least Honoraria was doing the very same about the three of them.

Vanmeter was patient. It was during the second bottle of wine when he asked Honoraria how she got into the art business.

"Oh, I can honestly say art found me. It was the first job I got when I arrived in Rome. I was on the street, looking at paintings in a small gallery window, and outside popped a man full of life, who clearly loved to eat, and asked me what I found so appealing. Without hesitation, I told him I was fascinated by the chiaroscuro in painting. I only knew the term from taking a film class. He grabbed my hand and start shaking it as if I was a long-lost niece. I felt that way at least. I started working there the next day. He was a widower, his son had died many years ago. I felt sorry for him. His whole life was now paintings, and he taught me everything. Michael Baglione."

Vanmeter heard a panoply of accents--did he hear Italian, English, French, Spanish, and American? Because at times she used pronunciations from all of them. He didn't recall her speaking this way during the tour. Now he found it distracting, but he was willing to ignore the fact it was borderline annoying. After Frieda and Honoraria excused themselves to visit the ladies room, Thrash told Vanmeter and Birdy that Honoraria's father was an American naval officer, a Captain, and her mother was from Naples.

"When Signore Baglione died, Honoraria was left with the gallery. She made it profitable, very profitable. Baglione would have been very proud of her."

Thrash too, appeared very proud of Honoraria.

"Let me answer the questions in your heads. She's had suitors, but she told me she never married. The other question you have--we are friends. She thinks I'm a very good painter. She pesters me to focus on originals."

"And Pico?" asked Vanmeter.

"She likes Pico, she wants him to be successful. Pico wants to be a superstar."

After Birdy summarized his background to Honoraria during dinner, he sat back and observed. He enjoyed the interaction between Frieda and Honoraria, who were getting along very well. Later, he started thinking. What's next--after this little fantasy trip to Rome? Vanmeter made no mention of his Momma. Birdy wondered about her too, and how his parents were doing with her living in the garage apartment. But soon his thoughts came back to Frieda. When would he see her again? What were her serious plans after her commitment on the E.A.C.H.S.? Did he have any sway as to her returning to New York?

But the evening's most consequential impact to his overall feeling (although Birdy disliked the word 'happy', there was no acceptable definition) was Vanmeter telling him to pursue Frieda. This private announcement came during the tour of the Vatican museum, when Vanmeter and Birdy ended up being side by side, bumping their way through the crowds, on to the next painting Honoraria was taking them.

As the tour finished, Thrash could see the three were excited by Honoraria's invitation to go to her gallery for a night cap. It was a fifteen minute walk from the restaurant. The madcap traffic and horns could not distract from the pleasant temperature and cloudless night sky. All of it synchronized into an experience of a memory demanding to be lasting. Now Birdy and Frieda were walking arm in arm, as was Thrash and Honoraria. They were the sight, a former shot putter with the tiny art gallery owner--him tilting towards her, her arm up, perpendicular to the street. Vanmeter absorbed it all happily. He had no problem with the word 'happy.' It was his Momma's favorite word.

15

"Natambe Pepper is what my father calls it. It is a special place near our house, full of vines that always fruit. Crazy!"

White pepper. No one knows for certain who planted the pepper vines, but when Pico's father purchased the small cocoa farm, he was pleased with their presence.

Pico never stopped talking to Birdy after he picked him up at the Accra airport. They rode in the Natambe family's orange Datsun 720 pickup, the exterior looked well taken care of, although the orange paint had the fade of the forty-year vehicle it was--the air conditioning had long been inoperable. Who knows when the odometer ceased to count the miles or how many times the front bucket seat had been upholstered--now in cloth plaid the Scottish would have dis-owned. But the engine ran smooth. Secured by burdened bungy cords, Birdy's luggage bounced about in the back.

Pico was as tall as Thrash although seventy-five pounds lighter, spoke the Queen's English, and looked like a model. He wore wired earbuds, with the right bud dangling down in front of his shoulder. His enthusiasm was near over the top, his eyes alive, as if on amphetamines, thought Birdy. But he drove like an old man going to the gas station, and according to Pico, a two-hour drive was ahead of them, near Lake Volta, on the southern shoreline.

Once on the highway, the traffic became sparse soon after leaving the Accra airport. Birdy spoke up only after Pico finally caught his breath--talking non-stop for a half hour about his love of painting, his love of the States, hip-hop and soul music (although he was very proud of local pop music too), and how he loved Thrash's mother tutoring him. Birdy thought Pico loved everything.

Birdy got to the point.

"I understand you want to become a citizen? Then join the Pennsylvania Army National Guard. I'll help, I used to be a Guardsman. You can stay at my parents place until you get situated. Fast track you to citizenship. And my friend Vanmeter will take you to the storage room with all the painting materials and shit--that's between you all."

"I'm excited about the prospect, very excited!"

"Now, if your father has two hundred pounds of the white pepper you claim he has I'll pay him fair price, but I need help with customs and export rules and whatnot. I know nothing about Ghana, although I hear Idris Elba is from here."

Birdy thought Pico's eyes could not get any brighter, but he was wrong.

"Woooo-woooo! Idris, woooo!" This was accompanied by arms pumping up and down, the Datsun now being controlled by Pico's long skinny legs clamping around the steering wheel. Birdy now wasn't so sure what he had gotten himself into by letting Vanmeter talk him to going Ghana, and less sure Pico was an Army National Guard type. That was Thrash's idea, which surprised Birdy that Thrash knew anything about the National Guard.

"No worries about export procedures. We export cocoa."

"Cool."

"Yes, very cool," smiled Pico, speeding up and noticing Birdy beginning to nod off, his head leaning on the door, now being buffeted slightly by the hot, wet wind from the rolled down window.

In his sleepy state, Birdy wondered if Pico had ever witnessed what he had, and if so, did it stay with him in the same way it did with himself. Birdy asked himself that question with every person he met. Vanmeter, Frieda, everyone. It was compulsory. Maybe that was how he was supposed to remember it, as if his conscious made it compulsory to ask himself the question every time he met a new person, or someone he already knew. Maybe that was a reason for not being as outgoing as he ought. Not wanting to ask the question anymore, knowing he could never forget. He didn't want to ask himself the question anymore, but there was no stopping himself, just as there would be no stopping himself judging a woman attractive or not, or any judgement based on any observation of anything. The only ones he thought might have witnessed what he did was his mother. And Frieda. Everyone else he guessed never had the tragic misfortune. Fortunate for them.

Birdy peeked over at Pico and noticed him placing his right ear bud back in his ear. He was bouncing to hip-hop, mouthing the words, beating out the beat on the steering wheel. They appeared to be ten years difference in age. Pico seemed born to succeed in the States, perhaps anywhere. Looks, spoke English with a non-American accent, talented painter, an intensity of curiosity and corresponding excitement to today's happenings. Birdy now wondered what Thrash's mother was like, and the things she said to Pico while advancing his painting skills. Did she have an effect on him? Did Thrash? Who did?

Birdy compared himself to Pico. He looked like Barak Obama, college educated, Army veteran, combat medic and helicopter pilot, now in the spice business. But the difference was Pico's intensity. That, Birdy did not think he possessed. Also, Birdy could tell Pico had the persistent quality of confidence, no matter the trials. Maybe it was being in the early twenties, the age of where you believe you can walk on water and be invisible at will to anyone, everyone. Birdy concluded Pico wanted it all in life. That was fine by Birdy. He drifted off into a deep sleep.

The first rut in the dirt road bumped Birdy awake. He jolted up, disoriented in place and time. It was no shit Africa hot, he thought, once his bearing was established. Tropical greenness, hilly, humid. Some women in bright color dresses walking with purpose on the side of the road. It was a proper dirt road, more than wide enough for opposite traffic. Sometimes they were on worn asphalt roads. Now they were back on a narrow dirt road, ruttier than before. The Datsun's shocks were new, but Pico and Birdy still bounced to the roof, even with Pico driving like an old man who only ventured out once a week.

"Mr. Birdy, almost there," said Pico, ear buds removed and put away. There didn't seem to be any chance of Pico calling him by just plain Birdy.

Pico's family was lined up outside their house, modest in outward appearance, painted a weathered yellow, but without a doubt sturdy built. His father and mother were both tall and lean, along with three younger skinny brothers, in descending ages almost three years apart. Mrs. Natambe's head wear was the same material as her lava orange dress. The father and sons all wore white long sleeve cotton shirts tucked in khaki shorts, and Adidas tennis shoes. He felt he was in a television travel series, as if what was shown on television was really real, not conjured and molded to fit expectations.

Pico sprang out of the Datsun and led Birdy to meet his family. He was overwhelmed, and felt like he was in a pleasant, but strange dream state. This dream state remained for the length of the overnight visit, only to dissipate as Pico pulled up to the Accra airport the next afternoon. It was nothing like his first visit to Zanzibar, and he couldn't figure out why. Without hesitation,

Birdy judged Mrs. Natambe's handshake to be the firmest, and her eyes blazed like Pico's. The brothers unloaded Birdy's bags and disappeared into the house. First there was to be a quick tour of their three bedroom house (tidy, plain furniture, few decorations, one wall filled with photographs of the family throughout the years). There was the pullout sofa where Birdy was to sleep, the tiny bathroom to wash up, and then to the porch for lunch. Following cheese sandwiches and sweet pickles, Mr. Natambe led Birdy and Pico to their pepper vines, and the sacks of white pepper, ready for shipment. Mr. Natambe spoke eloquent Queen's English, his manners and movement matching his soft tone of voice. Birdy had done some internet research on white pepper and from the looks of Natambe Pepper, it was an easy decision to purchase all they had harvested.

At dinner Birdy felt a welcome breeze, and the younger brothers took turns refilling his glass with cool water. He couldn't get enough. Birdy thought his lightheadedness was because of dehydration. The night was filled with loud insect sounds, the louder the bigger, he thought. He also thought about snakes. The pork was delightful, moist and spiced with turmeric and cinnamon, and the cold salad was the best he'd recalled eating in years, not that he was a salad guy. Mrs. Natambe kept the conversation rolling, and Birdy was surprised Pico was subdued for the entire evening. All the members of the family were deferential to Mrs. Natambe, but Mrs. Natambe paid special attention to Mr. Natambe in particular. They exchanged stories about their families. Birdy mentioned little about his sister. The youngest son had been waiting all dinner long to ask how Birdy got his name. He was disappointed at the answer.

The next morning the Natambe family traveled to Ho to attend Mass at the Sacred Heart Cathedral. In order to get Birdy to the Accra airport on time for his flight the family had to leave at 6 am to make early morning Mass and purchase sundries for the household. The white pepper was to be delivered to the Wassergold's New York warehouse. There was no negotiation. Birdy guaranteed half payment now and the rest on delivery. Mr. Natambe had his sons load the pepper into the Datsun and they took two vehicles to Ho, the other a large four door, hatchback Mitsubishi. Almost the highest level of trust was given to Birdy when he told Mr. Natambe he was also Catholic. They didn't know Black Americans were Catholic.

Now the Natambe's were no exception. To Birdy's frustration, he asked himself the same question he asked every new person he met. He decided none of them had ever witnessed what he had. A blessing never to be taken for granted.

Birdy could not sleep the night before. He was ready to return to New York.

Mass was packed the next morning, not one person under dressed. All the women and girls wore dresses, the men and boys long pants and collared shirts. Mrs. Natambe made sure Birdy knew what to wear. She ironed Birdy's crumpled slacks and shirt along with her husband's and sons Sunday clothes--white shirts and black slacks.

During Mass he became distracted by Pico's insistence on leaving his luggage and peppers unattended in his truck bed. The distraction evaporated once the lively choir opened up full during the entrance hymn. Everyone sang the hymns. Everyone's face glistened with perspiration, and though no one could ignore the heat, there seemed to be no irritation about what was a given. If it wasn't for the temperature and humidity, Birdy would prefer to attend Mass here. It was just too damn hot. He went through two bandanas wiping his face.

After communion Pico nudged Birdy and whispered they'd leave now, because after Mass everyone would want to meet him and he'd miss his plane. Back in the pew, Birdy motioned goodbye to the Natambe family. The younger sons waved. Mr. and Mrs. Natambe both gave formal nods. Pico received more than a few looks from young ladies.

Back in the Datsun, Pico asked Birdy for a sandwich his mother had made them for the airport trip. Birdy wasn't hungry, and was finally cooling off.

While finishing his cheese sandwich, Pico said, "Mrs. Davis made me copy many different originals from the masters, European mainly, a few Russian, some American. In all styles she wanted me to be exposed. She knew the masters as if they were her close relatives. And she made me paint and sketch only on very old parchment and paper. Where she got all the old materials I don't know. She would keep them around for a week or so and then they would disappear. She told me she kept them in a safe place and I could get them when I returned to Ghana. But I told her to keep them. I want to be an original painter, on my own standing. I say this because I know what your friend's storage room must have. The same as what Mrs. Davis had stored away somewhere, maybe my paintings are in that same place."

"Have you seen Thrash's paintings?" Birdy said he had not.

"He is very, very good," said Pico, smiling, "and also a good teacher. Intense, but not like his mother's intensity. Less pressing on you, more on himself."

"And your parents? What do they think about you wanting to go to the States?"

"They say to go and be a painter."

"What about being a U.S. citizen?"

"They say as long as I remain a Ghanaian citizen too. They are unbelievable parents. I am very lucky."

"What about your parents?" asked Pico.

"I'm lucky too," replied Birdy.

His sister thought different. He thought he understood where her anger came from, and could understand why you'd be angry thinking about certain things, but why did you have to always think about them? And make your anger part of who you are? Like a large tattoo impossible to remove? And have to behave and react in only certain ways? He never wanted to be accepted that bad, made no difference who or what. At least not now. Not even back then. In his Army Guard unit, medics were a different breed anyway. Don't want to piss off a medic. His father said that to him. It's not why he became a medic.

None of this he was inclined to share with Pico.

"Your friend wants to show me this storage room full of frames, old canvas, old paints, old varnish--that kind of stuff."

"He said old painting supplies. I haven't been there. I'm not a painter, I don't know," said Birdy. But he knew enough. He didn't want to talk about Vanmeter's schemes. That's between them.

"You only use that stuff if you want to make the painting look old. I learned all about aging techniques from Mrs. Davis. She knew everything about it."

That struck Birdy as odd, but not odd enough to give into temptation to want to talk about painting. What he had no intention of talking about was forgery.

"Thrash knows all about aging techniques. Learned from his mother too," said Pico.

"All that's for you and Thrash and Vanmeter to talk about," said Birdy.

At Accra Airport they confirmed each other's mobile phone numbers and email. Pico assured Birdy he'd take care of the shipping of the peppers to New York. Birdy said to let him know if he wanted to join the Army Guard. Pico would think about it. Birdy couldn't tell if Pico was interested or not. He had an enthusiastic spin on everything, obfuscating intent.

While saying goodbye, Pico asked, "Mr. Birdy, you like being a spice trader? I say this with respect, but a spice trader is not what I'd expect you to be. The cocoa traders I know are not like you at all."

"Oh yeah?" replied Birdy.

Inside the airport, Birdy searched for a place to shower, which he knew was doubtful. He found a lounge that he was eligible for and used the men's room sink to wash up and put on a fresh shirt.

16

Vanmeter was broke. Now back in New York he was staying with Birdy and began waiting tables again for the Wassergold's. He could pay off his loan in almost a year but only if Birdy let him stay rent free.

The storage room of painting materials was a bust. Brother Thrash Davis wasn't interested and Pico had no money to speak of--even if he was interested. Birdy told Vanmeter that Pico was enthusiastic as a matter of habit, but that didn't translate to any commitment Vanmeter could rely upon.

Now Vanmeter made contact with hackers he knew were still active. They advised him to stay away, whether that was because of a threat to his life or they didn't want the competition Vanmeter was unsure. He suspected both.

After a month, Vanmeter knew he couldn't stay much longer with Birdy. Frieda was returning to New York soon, her commitment to the E.A.C.H.S. was coming to an end.

****

Vanmeter's original intent was to stay a few weeks longer in Rome after Birdy and Frieda had departed. Honoraria insisted, and Thrash thought it was a good idea. He crashed on Thrash's sofa, and during the day hung out with Honoraria in her art gallery.

It was the Sunday after Birdy and Frieda left. Vanmeter accompanied Thrash and Honoraria to 730 am Mass at the Sisters of the Holy Family of Nazareth. Afterwards, they went to Honoraria's apartment where she made breakfast; scrambled eggs, sausage, roasted potatoes, and thick toast with jam. Along with squeezed orange juice and coffee. She made the country breakfast for Thrash only on occasion when she knew he was missing the States. Her apartment smelled like an American diner.

Vanmeter recognized Honoraria was not well. He first caught notice in Mass. The way she grasped the edge of furniture to steady herself, her cautious steps as if she was a woman thirty-five years older. Here in her apartment kitchen, he noticed a tinge of gray in the paleness of her skin. However, she was unworried, both her expressions and voice reflected as much. Vanmeter wasn't sure why he hadn't noticed earlier. He gave himself high marks for perception. He suspected she was exerting much effort to mask pain. That alone tires you out, he thought.

"You have a fire inside you for art, yes?" Honoraria's accent now seemed melodious, her voice firm, yet soft. He found her very pleasant to listen to. The reason for the change? At the time, Vanmeter never thought about it. Her eyes were difficult to avoid gazing into. Bright, knowing, entrancing, dying.

"I know nothing about art, only that I like paintings and sketches--the European masters, some impressionists, a little of the modern stuff," said Vanmeter. He sipped his orange juice. Thrash lounged on the red sofa reading the International Tribune, Sunday Edition.

Honoraria had already passed judgment on Vanmeter, as she had always done with anyone interesting and worth getting to know. She believed him when he spoke about his Momma and her problems. She knew he worried about only his mother. Worrying about what you cannot control, even fully knowing you have no control is such a wasteful struggle. She knew this to be true. But he wasn't a man frozen sick in his own worry.

He possessed antidote traits; ambition, confidence, and agreeability. His big plus, she thought, was that he spoke well. He was direct, clear, no hesitation--his slight West Virginian accent was appealing. And he didn't feel the need to talk on and on, and in so doing, repeat himself. He caught your attention, said what he intended to say. If he didn't know, he didn't pretend to know. He was the person she was looking for. It's easy for me now, thought Honoraria, my future is known. It was a luxury she never would have thought about, had she not known.

Thrash went back to the campus. He would meet up with them for dinner. Honoraria took Vanmeter to her gallery. She talked about running a gallery.

"Yes, yes I love paintings. I do, I do. But--it is about clients," she said.

"The ones who must have paintings in their home, or homes. The ones who have money to spend at will. You do not have to think too hard about their motivations. To possess, and to show others what you possess! That is how I make a living. Oh yes, I can still--thank God--look at a painting and be filled with the same excitement I had as a young woman. And--I am also like a miner--searching for that thick vein of gold. To discover a painter who is a thick, stretching vein of gold. Rare find. I must tell you; I am a miner. And you, are a miner."

Vanmeter at first was convinced she was just being polite to a stranger, knowing that she must be feeling very tired. Her frailness. She talked for four hours about the day-to-day life of a gallery owner. Sometimes she stood up and slow paced the gallery, then she sat at her desk, and finally she rested on the blue velvet sofa with a white marble coffee table in front, filled with art books and journals.

Vanmeter followed her and listened, asking questions only when he thought she was hinting for him to ask a question. He did not want to disappoint.

When they returned to her apartment, Honoraria announced she would lie down for a while. She encouraged Vanmeter to visit a few churches. She gave him directions to three close by.

"Afterwards, find a café, sit and have a beer or glass of wine. Watch Romans on a Sunday afternoon. I'll see you at 6 pm. Thrash will have the restaurant selected and we'll go for a short dinner." She gave him a kiss on each cheek and went to her bedroom and closed the door.

Vanmeter wasn't to the first church when he received a text from Birdy. His Momma had not been at the apartment. Birdy's mother went to the Walgreen's where she worked and they told her Clara Smythe hadn't been to work in two days. Birdy's parents entered her apartment and discovered she had packed her things. Her mobile phone was on the tiny kitchen table.

Vanmeter left for the States the next day.

****

"That was too much to ask of your Momma, just too much," said Thompson Ruddgy, Clara Smythe's cousin, and manager of the Walgreen's in West Virginia where Clara worked for many years.

"She's got her old job back. Found her a nice trailer for rent in the best trailer park around. But that place has its fair amount of miscreants and ne're-do-wells.
No escapin' it around here, as you ought to well know. I also know you tried to do the right thing by Clara, which is a darn good thing. But she don't possess the strength to go to some strange city and start all over. Not by herself. That was just too much to ask of Clara."

"Now you're up in New York City workin', and that's all fine an' all, but that's not doin' Clara much good, either. No one wants to see her slippin' back in to her old ways. Not with those brand new teeth you got her.

My, they look really nice. She takes real good care of them. She tells me every day. It's you, and her brand new teeth. Both, her pride and joy, she says."

"She wants desperately to see you but she's ashamed of not makin' it in Pittsburgh. She's doin' alright. She walks to work and I give her a ride home every night afterwards. And she comes over every Sunday for supper. I think she's doin' alright. But we can't be her babysitter. And as much as it pains me to say, she needs to be watched over. She's a smart lady, real smart, but she ain't got the strength, not on her own. And that's my take on the matter of Clara."

In addition to his Momma and some others, Vanmeter realized that Thompson Ruddgy was a man deserving of his daily prayers. He included him in his prayer list from that phone conversation on. The least he could do. The last person Vanmeter would ever pray for was himself. It didn't seem right.

He held the belief his Momma was going to make it in Pittsburgh. He went through his self-critique checklist in his mind. He called it the Illusions Check List. Vanmeter believed he could live a life free of illusions, or, at least the giant ones that sucked you up and never let your feet touch the ground. Being tethered was very important to Vanmeter. It was as clear as anything

17

Frieda's elated surprise was once in a lifetime, as she imagined it would be. But her elation could never quash the acute anxiety anticipating her parents predictable reaction. Frieda had spent far too much time, she knew, imagining the follow-on conversations she would have with her parents, after Birdy asked for their consent to marry her. She knew they were always too busy with their business and social activities to ever sit for a few moments and think of matters that may not accord to their will. Because life was always about bending to their will or, at barest minimum, being intimidated by it. That is how one must live your life. They were a match of matches. Each thinking the same way, complimenting one other in using their respective talents to get their way. They took failure in stride, knowing it was the ingredient to success. But the specific nature of the failure, how to reduce the failure's essence, and then how to use that knowledge, that was the secret sauce. Frieda heard this time and again growing up. Getting married to Birdy was going to be seen as their failure, she thought, and at their age, there may be insufficient time to account for failure of this magnitude.

Birdy insisted he would meet with the Wassergold's by himself, and likewise, Frieda insisted she would tell her parents she would give up her medical practice to continue Wassergold Enterprises. Everyone knew Frieda's brother not only did not want the job, but would ruin the business.

They talked with Birdy's parents first. They were not as approving as Frieda thought they might. Their travails were arguably easier, in that Porter B never knew his father, and his mother died during his first tour in Vietnam. Arlene's parents never got over her getting married to a black man. Only in their dying did she return to her parents, and their approval was withheld even in death. Most likely after death too, said Arlene, remarking that she wouldn't judge them. That was up to God. They were the most reverent of Catholics. The fact Porter B was Catholic didn't puncture their disapproval. Arlene knew her parents believed it was a lie that Porter B was Catholic.

Arlene said all this was a very good reason for her to never give up on their marriage, and thankfully she never had any second thoughts about Porter B. But to make a claim their marriage was easy in the eyes of everyone else would be admitting she was an idiot. But everyone else eventually didn't care enough to make their marriage an affront to whatever their beliefs happened to be. Clearly, they were not unwavering. Somewhere in all this, there was a blessing, said Arlene. Mixed, for sure.

Frieda took what Arlene said very seriously. Birdy had heard it before, nevertheless, took his mother's talk as serious as Frieda did. In this matter, Porter B stood by Arlene, as she did all the talking.

Upon asking the Wassergold's consent to marry Frieda, Myra fired Birdy right then, and pointed to the stairs. Frieda was waiting on the first floor, and watched Birdy descend the stairs slowly. Myra yelled at Frieda to come up at once. She walked up three steps, stopped and grabbed Birdy's arm, whirling him around, and together marched up the stairs and into her mother's office. In this matter, Birdy stood by Frieda in silence, as she did all the talking. At some point in the shouting, Frieda motioned Birdy to leave. He shook his head, but Frieda would not have it. She guided Birdy out of her mother's office, whispering to him. He turned and left, descended the stairs and exited the building.

Those few employees downstairs who heard the eruption swear everything they had ever heard previously from upstairs was a mere volcanic burp compared to that morning's going's on. From then on, the Wassergold eruption leaked into certain societal crevices, the ones empty of old covenants, apparently waiting for something shaming and salacious to fill them up.

Outside, everyone on the sidewalks seemed jazzed. It was a bright cloudless day, and the temperature was perfect for walking. Birdy joined everyone. He wasn't in any mood to give a shit about where he was going.

Frieda's parents paid her half of what she could make as a pediatric surgeon; covering health insurance, rent, and a leased Mercedes SUV. She moved out of her parents apartment and into a comfortable two bedroom in another building her parents owned, different from Birdy's, a short walk between.

Birdy was to keep his job and his apartment.

If she was strong enough, Frieda thought, she would soon sever the arrangement she agreed to with her mother.

"If he's going to stay, the more often Birdy's on the road importing things, the better," said Mrs. Wassergold. She didn't care where he went.

"But you and Dad like Birdy very much." Frieda's plea should never have been uttered. Her parents said nothing, only communicating with Birdy through Frieda, which was Frieda's suggestion. She put her medical practice on hold and showed up to Wassergold Enterprises every morning at 9 am and submitted to learning every facet of the business. Every detail, and every manipulative technique the Wassergold's employed to beat their competitors. They gave her Birdy's little closet of an office. She was now Birdy's boss, which she clearly did not intend. Frieda developed a new found appreciation, although well short of admiration, of her parents relentlessness. They were mad, she fumed. In actuality, ruthless. She felt like an idiot for not realizing sooner. If she did, it wouldn't make much difference in their relationship, she thought. But now, it's different.

Back in Rome, Vanmeter said to her, "One has to choose no more than two worries. Most times worries choose you. You always have a choice to say no. And saying, 'I had no choice', of course is a choice."

He warned, "You appear not concerned about the 'main worry'. Maybe just deal with worry number one."

It was difficult not to be attracted to Vanmeter. He was a natural. Just listen and say the right thing at the right time. Don't get sucked in. Don't be tossing about in someone else's spiral of their own creation, not yours, which is the definition of a loser. She knew that was all well in good, with one exception--Vanmeter's Momma.

To that exception Vanmeter admitted, "Vows and commitments are in a different category."

That's exactly right, she thought to herself. Frieda had no intention of losing contact with Vanmeter.

Only if it meant losing Birdy. But the inescapable worry was that her parents had said the 'forbidden' word regarding marrying Birdy. She vowed to herself she would never lose him.

The Natambe's white pepper arrived less than three weeks after leaving Accra and in less than two weeks Birdy had sold all of it. Why he chose to keep it a secret as to its origins he couldn't exactly say, other than Vanmeter suggested why not--something may come of it. Turns out, there was something very unique about its taste. Birdy learned everything he thought he cared to know about peppercorns from the chefs he sold them to. After the first chef's tutorial, Birdy asked all his other customers to help him know more about peppercorns. They all willingly contributed peppercorn tutorials. One chef was animated because he was convinced these peppers possessed a high level of piperine. He gave a sample of Natambe's peppercorns to a friend in the health supplements business. That friend had another friend do a chemical analysis on the peppercorns and confirmed the chef's suspicions. An unusually high level of piperine. The supplements friend became very excited and begged his chef friend to give him Birdy's cell phone number.

White pepper comes from the same plant as black pepper. Black pepper is picked prior to ripeness and allowed to dry, turning the skin color black. White pepper stays on the vine until well ripe, then picked, and running water removes the skin to reveal the white peppercorn. That was all Birdy really cared to want to know about peppercorn. Black or white pepper didn't do much for Birdy. Didn't take him away to a world outside his own mind. Not like cinnamon.

Soon Birdy was in the health supplements business, one business sector the Wassergold's had no stake in. Birdy was curious about the contents of the soil on Natambe's farm. Did the cocoa possess enhanced cocoa properties?

But wasn't it all about the hype? And hype took a lot of energy to generate profit. Birdy thought Vanmeter seemed much more in tune to this thinking. Birdy wasn't into hype; he knew what he wanted. He wanted to marry and raise a family. It was old fashioned thinking but he didn't care.

He talked with Frieda enough to know she wasn't dependent on some group's way of thinking about current affairs. She belonged to no group as far as Birdy knew, and she had no dependency on social trending of anything. She would forget to bring along her phone.

She didn't mind disagreement. Frieda left the door open to being persuaded, knowing she could kick it shut whenever she chose to. Her door was heavy, and if she was going shut it, it took effort. Frieda didn't mind being wrong. Maybe her medical training instilled this in her, maybe she was born that way. Maybe it was her ruthless parents.

Her upbringing taught her Jesus was not the Son of God. There is no Second Coming, never was a first. Yet she went to Duquesne. Attended Mass. Did not convert to Catholicism. She seemed comfortable in her contradictions. She didn't believe she was self-contradictory.

Frieda resisted being invigorated by anger. It disgusted her, chafed against her being as a clear-eyed surgeon. The conflict between her conscience and the way things are was a clear picture. She despised being attracted to any level of self-righteousness, no matter the cause of arousal. It was masturbatory. A time waste. The definition of a loser.

Birdy thought there was just so much he should know about someone. He knew no one knew what another person was actually feeling, much less so thinking. And he felt he knew enough about Frieda to know that whatever else he discovered; he would never kick the door shut. This was love, he reasoned, and that was more than sufficient.

After Birdy saw Frieda's roomy kitchen, her apartment became the dinner place. Birdy was becoming a good cook. According to Frieda, that's why he got a key.

"Not anywhere near chef standards," she teased, thankful she didn't have to cook. Although she was quite proficient, it was never an interest or a skill Frieda felt she had any obligation to acquire.

She said, "You can't help picking up tips. Some chefs love to show you everything they know in the kitchen. So why not learn from them?

Birdy liked to cook chicken. Steaming vegetables was no problem. Neither desired starch with dinner, and Frieda was appreciative of that. Birdy knew he should eat more fish but wasn't yet inclined to learn how to prepare fish.

Frieda loved the new routine. Come home after exercising, shower, change, and drink a glass of wine while Birdy finished preparation. She talked about work, learning the restaurant trade from an owner's perspective, and complained about her parents peccadillos, and being workaholics.

"You got five minutes of sport bitching--total," reminded Birdy. He watched Frieda twirl the engagement ring he bought her. She wore it every evening and took it off after Birdy left. He never stayed over. Nor did Frieda stay over at Birdy's place.

They told no one else. Only Vanmeter.

"Guts", Vanmeter said, God you have guts." He added them to his prayer list. Put them at the top, just below his Momma. He asked his Momma to pray for them too. Clara had been praying for all three of them for years now.

"We'll have to hire an au pair," said Frieda, while clearing the table one evening. Birdy's expression prompted her to explain what an au pair was. After the explanation, his second expression, the one with one eyebrow raised almost to the ceiling, peeking eyes, and lips pursed as if he sucked half a lemon--made her stop clearing the table. He knew what an au pair was.

"Frieda, you kinda read my mind, because before I leave for Africa, I wanted to talk about--you know--the whole timetable of events here. Now, hiring an au pair is a few events ahead in the timetable, quite a few."

Then Birdy paused, and Frieda let him.

How Birdy proposed to her, specifically, how he started the conversation with Frieda, and her moving reaction to what he told her, prior to asking to marry him, he knew he should always give her as much leeway in any conversation she wanted. He knew he also had to work on his facial expressions. That was gonna require effort, Birdy thought.

At the beginning of the engagement conversation, Birdy first explained to Frieda why his apartment smelled like cinnamon (she never asked). Cinnamon released his thoughts of what he saw that night. He was going out a second time with this girl he really liked. Janelle. He was picking her up after work. She was a nurse assistant. Birdy was early, the clinic was closed, and she told him to wait in a small room next to the procedure room. She was all business.

"Fifteen to twenty minutes and she'd be finished. Just had to wash up and change," said Birdy. Twenty minutes came and went, he recalled. Then he went to look for Janelle.

"I cracked open the procedure room door and witnessed the dismembering of a tiny, tiny baby. They put the pieces in a steel pan. Janelle was assisting a nurse who was assisting an old doctor." Birdy never saw the mother's face. The amount of blood on the nurse, and Janelle, he remembered too well.

"I slid to the floor and puked my guts out--all over myself. Then got up and ran out of the building." He thanked God he never saw the mother's face. But he could not forget the masked faces of the doctor, nurse, and Janelle.

"I left a trail of puke all the way out of the office."

During this time Birdy watched Frieda rock back and forth.

Birdy would have willingly confessed to Frieda for an hour about what he did next and his recurring thoughts about that evening, and all the hours of thinking about what he saw, and what he didn't do. But Frieda did not ask. He wished she would have asked him questions. Frieda was the only person he ever told about that evening.

He asked Frieda if she ever had seen such a thing. She said no, and Birdy believed her. Maybe he'd never know anyone else who'd seen what he had. He didn't want to know anyone else who had.

"Will you marry a man who saw what he saw, and ran away?"

She wiped her eyes, and stood.

Frieda said yes, and emptied her mind, only focusing on putting on the engagement ring Birdy then presented her. Saying to Birdy he was not at fault, and not to shoulder any amount of blame--that wouldn't have made any difference.

Later, when she was alone, she believed four thousand thoughts collided in her mind as Birdy told his story. All the thoughts of her life--she knew they were trivial, but they seemed to self-form into an accretion of trifling thoughts. They are part of self. And they resist being easily disposable.

But from those thoughts blistered a realization-- endure the world, or, live with one foot in, and the rest of her body out.

Yes, she thought, something didn't feel right. Frieda wanted St. Paul's unyielding pursuit, without the zealot streak. And she didn't want to go it alone.

So, in recalling the engagement conversation, Birdy figured if Frieda wanted to talk about an au pair now, before they married and suffered from her parent's condemnation, before getting pregnant and having children, then Frieda had every right to do so. She was entitled to tell him scary, sad, crazy shit, with or without context, or nuance. That was a clear picture in his mind.

19

Thrash didn't mind recounting stories to Honoraria. It was her wish, after all. She lay in bed in her apartment with Thrash sitting beside her on a cold and thick overcast afternoon. Before she drifted off, he told her again about meeting Pico.

"I was assisting in the summer program in Ghana for almost three months as the sports coordinator and art teacher. A great gig. Although, I didn't know jack about soccer. But I did get some kids interested in track. Long distance, sprints, long jump, and triple jump. Some of them were bad attitude cases and you couldn't reach them. I couldn't, at least."

Honoraria thought Thrash had a terrific smile. Not too much teeth.

"Pico Natambe's a natural. He could handle the soccer ball like a world cup pro, an excellent sprinter, and everyone liked him. The girls, especially."

Thought Honoraria, no doubt that was true. She was at the moment comfortable, her pain subsiding.

"But--and without a doubt, the highlight of that summer, was discovering Pico was an artist. He has it. The absolutely wonderful eye, and the skill of the pencil and brush. He swore over and over he learned everything from the internet. Maybe. But you got to have the obsession. And he's obsessed. He had no real art mentor until I met him. He's fearless--can't teach that."

Honoraria's closed eye smile was a hint not to ramble. But she loved a grand story with all the accoutrements, as she liked to say, and a grand story required rambling. When the story started, she would drift off. He assumed she was listening, even if snoring. Drinking wine, telling her stories, that was the least Thrash could do--hospice care was provided by Honoraria's insurance company.

The Filipino ladies are saints, said Honoraria, and she was honored to be their patient, although their Italian was poor, their English was passable.

"Pico's so talented my mother agreed to take him on as a student. That was my best achievement as an art teacher. Passing him on to my mother."

Honoraria pouted. Her eyes remained closed. Grimacing, she shifted to her right side, sliding her thin, white laced blanket up to her sharp chin.

"What is Pico's favorite subject to paint?" she asked with her eyes closed, knowing Thrash would not know the answer.

"Soccer balls as red balloons with mint dental floss as string," replied Thrash. Honoraria's eyes opened wide as she laughed. Every answer to this question was always a surprise.

But no surprise ever topped Thrash leaving the Order and asking her to marry. Three months married and three months more to live. She stopped wishing it was thirty years and thirty more. The symmetry of threes was something Honoraria believed to be just right. But she wasn't sure of the whole picture. Morphine does that. She began to snore.

Before being bedridden, Honoraria introduced Thrash to all of her clients and contacts. It was not nearly as difficult to meet them all in person due to her grave illness. Everyone had stopped by to see her. Thrash had met many of them previously. Whether they would remain clients after Honoraria died was uncertain in Thrash's mind--but not Honoraria. She believed them all to be loyal, even after her death.

Now Thrash had a big notion, and unless something else became more compelling, he was going to follow that notion. That is, after her Rome memorial service that Honoraria planned and paid for already. Thrash was to fly her to Pennsylvania to be buried in the Davis's family plot. Rome only rented burial plots in overcrowded cemeteries, and at the end of the burial lease her remains would be placed in a common burial site. That was unacceptable. And she was adamant about not being cremated. When Thrash mentioned the family burial plot, Honoraria shouted out and clapped in excitement.

"That is that!" she said. The fact Honoraria had never been to Pennsylvania made no impact on her sudden decision.

"It is taken care of," she said.

"Should I see pictures of where I will rest?"

"Do you want to see the place?" replied Thrash.

"I'm not sure," she said.

"I'll have Vanmeter go and take some pictures. If you want to see the place, we'll have the pictures at least."

"Perfecto!" she said.

There was prayer, and there was planning and execution.

Thrash assessed his praying skills to be average, maybe below average, for a Brother. His daily habits were solid, he thought, but from listening to the others describing their prayer life in those irritating sharing sessions, he concluded they were far superior in prayerful contemplation. Communal praying was one thing. Alone with your conscience--that was a bitch--as Birdy would say. Thrash had nothing on St. Augustine's Confessions. That depth of contemplation, he couldn't fathom. He fantasized in his earlier years about enjoying being a monk whose monastery brewed beer. How long would he have lasted there? Far less than he lasted up till now. He didn't feel guilty. He loved Honoraria, believed she was a gift from God. He married a woman he loved. Maybe when grief arrives, so will guilt, he thought.

His deepening sorrow was quieted by planning and executing. It all sounded too military, he thought. But that's what Honoraria insisted upon, and it made sense to him. She would have been a good soldier, he told her. She said that was a romantic thing to say, thinking no one had ever came close to suggesting such an outlandish idea. But it made sense to her.

The steady cool rain lasted through the night, the smell of rain on the city seeped through the slight open windows. Thrash sipped wine, watched his wife sleep, and texted Vanmeter. Within minutes he replied. He had been wanting to communicate with Vanmeter for some time. He was part of the far from clear big notion Thrash wanted to plan and execute.

20

Vanmeter was still staying with Birdy in the city. That was working out because he spent more time at Frieda's apartment, but never overnight.

The back and forth from New York to West Virginia was corrupting the pleasure of road trips. Clara's trailer park was considered above average for the area, and that meant little. Between the two of them they couldn't yet afford to move her into a decent apartment complex. He had only paid a third of what he still owed for her new teeth.

He was in the worst rut of his life. But he thought of his Momma, who knew nothing but being in an endless rut. At least for Vanmeter, this was temporary because he believed he could change circumstances. He'd done it before. But his Momma, she had nothing other than knowing every inch of a Walgreen store. She wanted to teach English--read classics, discuss them, and write essays about them. Neither she nor her son could figure out a way to get to that circumstance. Even if Clara decided teaching wasn't for her, she said that even getting to the circumstance to try was a road she could not see.

Vanmeter received Thrash's text to go to his mother's place and take some pictures of the family burial plot. An hour before entering West Virginia he'd decided to take his Momma with him. It was just outside Pittsburgh. On roads he had never taken.

Something different, for both of them.

Clara was in a foul mood. Rarely had Vanmeter seen her in such a nasty disposition, sober. He couldn't in fact remember a time. She didn't want to talk. No kiss on the cheek. She went into her room, closed the door, leaving

Vanmeter on the couch. He had a small bottle with him, poured two fingers, prepared the couch to sleep on, took a quick shower, stretched out on the couch, and sipped his whiskey. He was still intent on taking her with him to Thrash's place.

In the morning her disposition wasn't much better, although after eating breakfast at a local spot, Clara appeared to improve. She finally said something when she realized Vanmeter was not driving back to the trailer park.

"Going just outside of Pittsburgh to Brother Davis's mother's place. He wants me to check on a few things. The drive will do you good."

"Honey, I tried to like Pittsburgh, I did...try, I mean," said Clara. She didn't seem unopposed to the trip. Vanmeter reminded her who Bother Thrash Davis was.

It was dense gray overcast, although not hanging so low as to be claustrophobic. The dampness and temperature were typical for that time of year. The leaves had not begun to fall, except for a few trees just off the road, as if they were in a hurry to get bare.

Clara found a country station on the radio. She listened and staring out the window. Vanmeter guessed she was in an immediate dry spell after a binge and therefore miserable in being off whatever she had been on. But after all her bouts, she was still in fighting spirit, and Vanmeter was irritated he could only think of distractions at this juncture, distractions for his Momma, until the circumstance presented itself, or Vanmeter was able to conjure one up. He was convinced it was just a matter of time before her spirit weakened again. This caused a dull ache in him, and he had to be conscious of not letting panic seep in.

Clara refused the offer to stop for lunch and as such they arrived at Thrash's place just before noon. It was on multiple acres, the house offset a hundred yards from the road.

Dull red brick, single story--viewing left to right it appeared long, and going around to the left and behind the house they discovered it to be U shaped, the wings half as long as the front, with the garage on the left side. Vanmeter couldn't make out the age of the home, perhaps thirty or forty years old. The front had been mowed recently. The place was well looked after. Vanmeter was unsure of the paint color. Some kind of uninteresting green, with white framed windows with inside white shutters, the louvers tilted down, but not fully closed. Between the U shape was once a garden of some kind, now overgrown, but not grossly so. Somewhere in there was a prominent narrow, long flat rock with a corner broken off, and under the broken corner was to be a tin box containing a key and alarm codes.

Clara remained in the car, and soon after Vanmeter disappeared around the back of the house, she got out and went searching for him, calling his name.

He startled her coming out of the middle of the garden.

"You want to come in?" asked Vanmeter.

"I want to go find the family cemetery," said Clara. He gave her his phone and asked her to take plenty of pictures of the whole site. He pointed to where Thrash texted him--walk on the path ten o'clock from the garden for a hundred yards. Through the trees and into a small clearing.

The overcast drooped lower. The anticipated rain arrived. Misting. Inside, the house did not smell moldy as Vanmeter predicted. He was only interested in finding where Thrash's mother would have kept Thrash and Pico's paintings. Not much dust about and the furnishings were ordinary, nothing stuck out. Supposedly Thrash didn't know where the paintings were. Vanmeter was skeptical about that, and about Thrash's motivations, as if it was any of his business. He found the art studio soon enough. Sprawling, at the end of the wing on the far right, two sides of the room were windowed almost from floor to ceiling. The thick cream colored curtains were drawn shut. He opened the curtains to see views into the garden and to the thick forest of thirty-footers, twenty-five yards away, at the border of the cut grass.

Even in the gray, lonely overcast, it felt as if an artist was still in residence, still painting. Nothing put away, it looked like the room of a busy person, maybe someone who indulged an impulse to hoard. The closet door was easy enough to find, although the key to the lock took some time to locate. Vanmeter sat in the desk chair and his eyes canvassed the room. Where to keep the keys to the closet? The location depended on Thrash's mother's willingness to give up its contents. How much of a secret was it to her? Not much, Vanmeter discovered. The key was under the cushion of the desk chair.

He hadn't a clue as to why he lifted the cushion to check.

Inside the closet was a room as large as her studio, and was organized according to the painters--Mrs. Vera Davis, Jack Davis, and Pico Natambe, and others. It was too easy, thought Vanmeter. Organized in pristine exactitude, the opposite of the studio. The paintings were binned by the artist they were copying. The sections that were not labeled Vanmeter guessed were their originals. Vanmeter didn't look closely at them. They weren't in alphabetical order, and Vanmeter thought they might be organized by country of origin, or period.

He immediately went to find paintings they all three had copied. He found what he was looking for. He picked a small painting, about 18 inches by 24 inches, and leaned the three next to each other. He went back to the studio to find a roll of tape and a marker. Vanmeter marked each piece of tape by their initials, except Mrs. Davis. She labeled her copy "Mrs. D." Unsatisfied with the poor lighting in the closet he brought all three out to the studio and leaned them against the window facing the garden. He already tried the light switch, no power. He pulled the chair from the desk and placed it in front of the paintings. He sat down and studied them. It was a painting of three men in the evening, outside a tavern, under a street light. Gas light most likely, judging by the men's clothing. They were smoking strange long pipes and appeared to be in low conversation. The street light illuminated their faces quite well. They were bearded, older, well to do.

After a few minutes of staring at the paintings Vanmeter started to see differences in each. What eventually stood out was the lighting, or values of shade, as Vanmeter recalled his painting research. He was attracted to how lighting was captured in painting, especially oils. Then he looked at the artist's signature. It was difficult to read. It looked like "L. Witherspoon," but he was unsure. However, he could definitely notice the differences in each signature.

Not having viewed the original, he thought they all looked very good. All appeared to be very old. The idea occurred to him then. He went searching for the laundry room. There he found a stack of old towels in a cabinet above the washer and dryer. Returning to the studio, Vanmeter wrapped each painting in towels and took them to his car and placed them in the trunk. Then he went to find his Momma. The rain had stopped.

Her feet tucked under her, she was sleeping in a severely weathered Adirondack chair, one of two, at the foot of one of the two headstones, in a generous sized plot surrounded by a two foot stone wall, guarded by three Eastern Hemlocks in a triangle spaced twenty five feet apart, easily fifty feet high. The area was filled with hemlocks. Thrash's parents were here, his mother Vera dying not long ago, his father Matthias Robert, ten years earlier.

"Nice place to be laid to rest, guarded by these big old trees," said Clara, her eyes still closed. With effort she untucked her legs and swung them to the ground.

"We can go now, unless you want to see the house," said Vanmeter.

"Anything worth seeing?" she asked, taking Vanmeter's phone out of her jacket pocket.

"Not really," he said, thanking her for taking the pictures. He quickly scanned the photos she'd taken. She had taken a few shots standing back, attempting to get the huge hemlocks in the pictures.

They walked back to the house.

Halfway, Clara stopped, and said, "Did you know your father was half Italian?"

"No idea," said Vanmeter, perplexed why she brought up the subject.

"Yep, half Italian," said Clara. She was now hungry.

Before getting something to eat, Vanmeter made a stop at the Kule Fat's storage room full of painting materials. It was twenty-five minutes out of the way.

Vanmeter's mind had been racing ever since he discovered the paintings in Mrs. D's home.

In Kule Fat's storage room, Vanmeter left the three paintings he'd taken. On the back, right corner of each canvas frame he made tiny marks. One dot for Mrs. D, two dots for Thrash, and three dots for Pico. He then removed the pieces of tape he had placed on the back to identify the painter. As instructed by the Materials Man back when he was given access to the storage room, Vanmeter placed a short thin paint brush on the floor, to the left of the door frame. He took the old towels he wrapped the paintings in with him, stacking the paintings in a large blue plastic tub in the far corner.

Afterwards, Clara was in the mood to eat. Denny's. Vanmeter asked her if she wanted to go in the storage room, but she'd wait in the car. She never asked what her son was taking out of the trunk, or what the storage room was all about.

Clara was having a tough enough time finishing her dinner, thinking about getting high was the priority of her mind. She was poor company, and she didn't tell Vanmeter why. He was smart enough.

What stuck in Vanmeter's head driving back to West Virginia was not how his Momma was doing, but what his father must have been like, and why Clara told him about being half Italian.

The idea, and acting on the impulse. He could feel it-- he was getting out of the rut. He took paintings not belonging to him. Let Fat make the call. Might not be a bust after all.

It was clear that he had to get out and stay out of his rut if his Momma had any chance of escaping hers.

21

A month later, the simultaneity of significant events gave Frieda a feeling of recklessness. Viewed apart, the feeling was not infectious of course, but the impression of recklessness remained. Maybe Frieda thought this way because she was a doctor. She couldn't decide if it was contagious or something less ominous. But ominous wasn't the right description either, she thought. It bothered her that another description failed to come to mind. Regardless of the diagnosis, a picture of what lay ahead was not at all clear.

When Frieda asked Birdy what he thought about the simultaneity he smiled. He couldn't explain it either. But he was untroubled. Maybe partly because he was no longer reliant on the odor of cinnamon to escape his thoughts of the abortion and associated regret. But he didn't tell Frieda this, because he was not yet convinced of his hypothesis as to why. Birdy thought he saw a convergence of some sort. Most things coming together. It was vague but he could feel the intertwining of events. An unrecognizable sort of excitement seeped into his disposition. Birdy didn't want to think too much about it all.

She didn't mention to him that contagious came to mind. She was troubled by her impulsive description. Getting married was definitely not an impulsive decision. Was it a sign of her hidden regret? Did she in fact have regret?

Regarding simultaneity of events, either way, Vanmeter had no regrets. And though the picture ahead was definitely unclear, he aimed to make his own picture, like a painter who painted life as it is to come. This is the first time he ever felt like an artist.

****

Birdy's parents found Cantor Caroline Bloom. Actually, it was Father Desmond who found her. Desmond was just out of seminary, a Pittsburgh local, now serving as associate pastor at Porter B's and Arlene's parish. Cantor Bloom was Father Desmond's close friend in high school. She was never Desmond's girlfriend, but he had a thing for her in those days.

There wasn't a persistent demand in Pittsburgh for interfaith weddings, but Cantor Bloom and Father Desmond thought they may have a future together performing mixed faith marriages. But first they had to marry Frieda and Birdy.

A lot of firsts, thought Porter B. But he knew all about firsts.

Porter B said, "Alright now--rent the hall at our parish, or the synagogue three blocks away, or the VFW hall in between both?" He and Arlene were all in on supporting Birdy and Frieda. Their decision to marry in Pittsburgh was an obvious choice. Whether it was a small consolation to blanket the smoldering humiliation Frieda perceived her parents were experiencing in marrying Birdy, Frieda wasn't so sure.

Frieda announced, over the phone to Porter B, "It will be held in the hall at Duquesne Heights Jewish Center. Cantor Bloom has it reserved."

"I appreciate the offer to talk to my parents Mr. Wire, and you don't have to offer again. I'll let you know if I change my mind." Birdy's father was just shy of insistent, thought Frieda.

From her parents office rolodex Frieda assembled a lengthy list and finished writing out all the invitations her parents would have invited if they had approved of Birdy. Frieda placed them in a box and mailed them to her parents' home. Other than Vanmeter, his momma Clara, Thrash Davis, and Birdy's parents, no other invitations were going out. The Wassergold's were in Florida. They had never been away more than a week, and they refused to say when they'd return, leaving Frieda to run the whole Wassergold operation. It was a test within a test within a test, she thought. After hours, she used their time away to immerse Birdy in full to the business enterprise. Wassergold employees knew they were getting married. Most were indifferent, some were happy for them. Frieda's brother didn't have a clue.

A biting cold had settled in, and the precipitation god couldn't decide if it was to be rain, snow or ice. It was an early December, Friday afternoon wedding. Three older couples, longtime associates of the Wassergold's, also attended. (One could argue if they were friends). Frieda was shocked. She knew them all. How they found out she didn't know. She sent her parents the box of invitations, and none were mailed out. Another big surprise was the attendance of Frieda's brother. He came solo, and out of family obligation to represent, making it known he was not here to give consent.

Birdy disagreed that Thrash Davis attended without Honoraria. She accompanied Thrash from Rome in her casket, to be interred in the Davis family plot the next day. Vanmeter and his Momma got in early two days before, staying in the Birdy's parents apartment above the garage. Vanmeter kept speaking to everyone in Italian, then translating what he said. Birdy and Frieda agreed that too was an irritating surprise.

"This dude in New York has been a fantastic Italian teacher. He works for your parents. Lucky find," said a recharged Vanmeter.

Clara looked healthy for being pale and skinny. The return of cigarette smoke about her was not surprising. She tried vaping, but the experience could not replace a real smoke. She managed to limit herself to five a day. These days, it was just nicotine and caffeine. Vanmeter agreed he'd rather see her smoking cigarettes and drinking coffee than anything else. Although, if the occasion called for drinking Clara now preferred Prosecco.

The Duquesne Heights Jewish Center had a smaller room available, but it was too small to fit everyone. The large hall could accommodate two hundred people easy. Because of the sparse attendance in such a large space, Frieda felt diminished at first. And on such an otherwise joyous occasion sadness was also expected, and it did not disappoint. Frieda missed her parents. Thrash missed Honoraria. But Frieda gave full credit to the enthusiasm Father Desmond and Cantor Bloom brought to the ceremony. They were very excited, and they managed to lift her gloom.

Frieda didn't think about the kitchen being adjacent to the hall--the scents of broiling fine beef tenderloin and baking au gratin potatoes filling the air. The sumptuous waft may have been the reason gloom was finally overcome. So much the better, thought Frieda, as Vanmeter escorted her down the aisle. Her brother wasn't interested in substituting for their father. Vanmeter whispered corny Italian romantic phrases as they walked up to the front. Frieda elbowed him in the ribs to shut up.

No one recalled any glitches before or during the wedding. The dinner was served hot and there was plenty to go around. Afterwards, everyone but the three older couples and Frieda's brother went to the nearby bar where the Neighborhood Funk Band was playing, along with Porter B, who was in rare funk form, as was the band. Birdy and Frieda had never danced together. Clara never had so much fun, and danced with her son. "Well, ooh la la," she shouted out loud, to no one in particular. Thrash danced with Arlene Wire. Father Desmond and Cantor Bloom never left the dance floor, and slipped out after the first set.

Porter B grooved the crowd until after midnight, well past his normal quit time. He wasn't interested in seeing anything other than what he was watching from the stage. He could replay that night every night. That was plenty of clarity for him.

Thrash Davis had spent the night at the Wire's but was up early to drive out to his family home to meet with the Fullman Mortuary representative, Octavia Younst. He let Vanmeter drive, as he spent most of the time on his phone attempting to get full clarification the back hoe dug the hole at the proper location and did not run over his mother's head stone as was previously communicated to him by text. Vanmeter wasn't nearly as hungover as he thought he might be. He sipped his large coffee and concentrated on not slipping off the icy roads. This morning was blustery cold, and ice rain pinged off the car.

Although Arlene and Porter B, along with Clara, tried to convince Thrash they'd attend the burial of Honoraria, Thrash insisted he was very thankful for the offer and it was not necessary. Birdy and Frieda were now on the road, checking out of the Penn Hotel where they had stayed the past three nights. Both were ready to return to New York. They were on a 6 pm flight, but first they were attending Honoraria's burial.

"Everything squared away?" asked Vanmeter, watching Thrash put his phone back in his coat.

"Yeah." Thrash was not hungover. He stuck with club soda after the celebratory champagne toasts.

Thrash turned towards Vanmeter, and said, "Alright here it is---Honoraria wants you to take over her gallery. I promised her I would. I knew when I promised her, I wasn't the type to run an art gallery. I have to believe she knew it too. But I promised anyway."

Vanmeter interrupted.

"You may have heard last night I've been taking Italian lessons. I found this guy in the city I work with. Sort of. I've got a knack for languages."

"My Momma told me recently my father's half Italian. You know Italy has a process to let you become a citizen if you're a descendant of Italians?"

"Let me finish," insisted Vanmeter.

Thrash stopped him. "Honoraria talked to you about the gallery that day. Did she also asked if you were inclined to try to run her gallery?"

"That is what I think she was thinking," said Vanmeter. He stopped talking, watching Thrash put it all together.

"You'd run her gallery?"

"For you, of course. You're the owner now I take it?"

Thrash nodded.

"So, a promise kept then," said Vanmeter. He was beginning to recognize the surroundings. Smoke was coming from the chimney. Lights were on in the house. The hearse was in the driveway. Thrash was going to miss Rome. Knowing how much deepened his sorrow.

****

The simultaneity of significant events...Frieda was the only one amazed by it. As for Vanmeter, this is what he sought after, believing that strands of connection are woven into something real--something you can press against, and come to rely on its resiliency. And in believing there was a reason it was none of anyone's business to know any more than what was before them. Because once you believe it's your business to know more, the world appears to revolve around you, and that was an embarrassing illusion he'd never sign up to. Maybe Birdy and Frieda thought the same.

Frieda wanted to talk to someone about her observation. Birdy reacted as though he needed reminding what was so simultaneously significant. He was still oriented towards being singularly grateful his marriage to Frieda had replaced cinnamon, diminishing his feelings he was a lesser man.

22

After burying Honoraria, and after gathering with Birdy and Frieda for a few glasses of wine and finger sandwiches in the living room, Thrash and Vanmeter found themselves alone with little motivation to talk any further.

Six feet of earth--3500 pounds--the weight of dirt atop a coffin, and it was nothing to the dead. Vanmeter thought that Thrash, already sunken by grief, was having to carry 3500 more pounds. From his nights in front of a computer, Vanmeter knew too many stupid facts. This stupid fact mattered.

"Let me take you to the storage room I told you about. It's not far. Won't take long. I'll drop you back off here and I'll head back to Pittsburgh."

The rain continued. The dreariness was taking its toll on Thrash, thought Vanmeter. Their silence made the short distance trip longer.

Immediately after Vanmeter lifted the storage room door he went to the plastic container where he had placed Mrs. Davis's, Thrash's, and Pico's paintings the last time he was there. As he picked up the container of paintings Vanmeter began telling Thrash about the contents of the storage room, pointing at canvases, boxes of paint, frames, pieces of old wood, brushes, and paper. He pointed to the far right corner suggesting Thrash start his exploration there. As Thrash turned his back and started looking about Vanmeter peeked into the container and found a stuffed envelope and only two paintings. He shoved the envelope in his jacket pocket and checked to see which painting had been taken. He closed the lid and slid the container to a spot where Thrash had already explored.

"My mother would have loved all this," remarked Thrash, his back still to Vanmeter, who wasn't sure Thrash meant to say that out loud.

"Kule Fat's stuff, eh?" said Thrash. Vanmeter nodded.

"He know your mother?"

"No idea," said Thrash. Thrash was finishing his exploration. His initial flash of curiosity had given way back to weariness.

"Pierre Bonnard," said Thrash, softly.

"Who?" replied Vanmeter.

"You asked me in Rome was there one particular painter I liked that my mother also liked. I never answered your question." Vanmeter didn't recall ever asking Thrash that question.

"As a matter of fact, Pico also likes Bonnard's work. Thinking about it, I'm not sure Pico dislikes anyone's paintings."

Vanmeter asked if Thrash wanted to take anything from the storage room.

"Me?" Thrash shook his head no.

"My Mother? Oh yeah, all of it."

"It was Bonnard's use of color later in his career. Fabulous and inspiring. That, and he preferred to paint from memory. I'm very attracted to that technique. So was my mother. You should check out his work. You have a lot of research in front of you to run an art gallery. Your Italian's coming along. That'll help."

As Vanmeter drove back to Thrash's place, he thought again about Thrash's reaction to the not so hidden room in the house where his mother kept all their paintings.

"I appreciate you finding this room," said Thrash, closing and locking the not so hidden room door. He held up the key Vanmeter had given and nodded in thanks.

Regarding Thrash's grief, Vanmeter could only compare to a weight barely bearable. All that was going on inside Thrash's head, thought Vanmeter. But they had a thicker connection now, much more than threads between them, and Vanmeter had every intention of ensuring more threads came about somehow and were woven together and strengthened in time, to be like a glorious castle's great hall tapestry that cannot be shorn. From a business perspective, that is.

Thrash was his new boss and Vanmeter aimed to succeed.

23

Birdy awoke in business class, and as he had fallen hard asleep, it took a while to get his bearings. The first thing he did was grab his plastic water bottle and finish off the remainder. Putting the bottle aside his wedding band caught his eye. He twirled it about his finger. Still strange to wear a ring of any sort. After clearing customs, he picked up a cab to the hotel. Flying in from London gave him the most options getting to Zanzibar City and Birdy preferred a mid-morning arrival to get a lengthy walk about in Stone City, cool off and shower, and take a nap. He welcomed the heat and humidity for about five minutes, enough to forget about the New York winter, but walked on anyway, sweating like in a sauna, getting the funk off him, as his father would say. Tomorrow Birdy would take the short flight to Pemba. It was cooler than Zanzibar City, and he looked forward to driving through the deep green hills to get to the farms.

In Zanzibar City, Birdy stayed awake most of the night. The time change from New York was not helping. He had gone over in his mind what he was going to say and more importantly, not say to brothers Vin and Noro, the two no-nonsense farmers whose separate small farms were adjacent to one another. Both brothers were single, which didn't surprise Birdy so much. They were both small, lean, and of ruddy complexion, who worked sixteen hours a day. Birdy communicated by emails to their younger associate named Joseph who had a mobile phone, and spoke very good English. Maybe the brothers assessed Birdy to be OK after he lay in the cinnamon for a few hours that night on his first trip to Pemba. On that trip Birdy spent the night on the floor of Vin's simple living room. He was attempting to make a good impression. Birdy didn't sleep at all that night either, mostly because Vin snored from his nearby bedroom. A harsh, cacophonous snoring that never abated. Birdy had no intention of spending the night up there again.

After the short flight to Pemba airport the next morning, Birdy rented a Toyota truck and drove to the farms. As he was overcome by the green hills, he rolled down the window to take in the cooler air. It was a clear morning, with small batches of puff clouds meandering over the island.

He took his wedding band off. Not that the brothers were inclined to ask him anything personal in nature, but he wanted to avoid answering any questions about Frieda that Joseph might ask. He was a curious, talkative type, and told Birdy repeatedly last visit how much he admired Barack Obama, and how Birdy looked like Obama.

What Birdy thought about driving up was this; he being Catholic, Frieda being Jewish and white, Vin and Noro, Muslim, and most definitely Joseph, who was most definitely Muslim. Proud to be, and bold, he told Birdy on his first trip. It did not matter to Birdy if he was unreasonable or not in his paranoia. Now that he was married, he became more conscious of uncertainties. And these days his slim attraction to uncertainty had weakened considerably. Birdy wanted to complete the transaction, say nothing about anything, and leave. He still had to go to Ghana to secure an order of white pepper from Pico's family.

Communicating with Joseph over emails, Birdy doubled the previous order, three hundred pounds of cinnamon.

Where the clouds came from, Birdy couldn't guess, and a hard rain anticipated Birdy's arrival. The last few miles to the farms were through sloppy, rutted dirt roads, smearing his white rental brown. The brothers and

Joseph were waiting on the tiny front porch of Vin's small house.

Exiting his rental and stepping into an ankle deep puddle of deep brown water was never a good sign, thought Birdy, and his pricey chukkas flooded to his ankles. It was much cooler in the hills than the Pemba airport.

"You seem to have brought rain," announced Joseph from the porch. Rain beat on the porch roof, necessitating elevated voices. Vin moved forward and shook Birdy's hand first, and then Birdy moved to Noro, and Joseph last. Birdy sat down on the short section of the L-shaped porch bench and Joseph, Vin, and Noro sat on the long section. On a circular table was a teapot and cups. Joseph poured for everyone. Birdy drank it quickly. Far too much sugar, he thought.

"You are not on Facebook?" asked Joseph. Birdy shook his head.

"Not on any social media?" Birdy said no.

"I know--you use a fake name!" pressed Joseph.

"No," replied Birdy.

"Why not?" asked Joseph, leaning forward towards Birdy.

"You're on Facebook, I take it?" said Birdy.

"Of course!" said Joseph, adding, "And I searched for you and couldn't find anything! How strange."

"And Vin and Noro, they are on Facebook, too?" said Birdy. Joseph straightened up.

"They don't have internet. Or a mobile phone. They're missing so much I tell them but they are not interested."

"But you are American, and all Americans are on Facebook," declared Joseph, "except you." Birdy struggled to ignore the accusatory tone. It was what was behind Joseph's tone that raised questions. He was close to Birdy's age, he guessed, educated, and at least ten years younger than Vin, the older of the two brothers.

Joseph was their cousin, according to Joseph. Birdy swore to himself he never met a short, assertive dude who didn't remind him of a boss wanna-be. Joseph was that dude.

"Your President now--don't you find it unbelievable he is President? After President Obama? Your country seems to be in conflict, yes? I read about it all the time, every day."

Vin and Noro appeared uncomfortable. Now, Birdy's thoughts turned to his sister. He felt he was in one of her conversations that started out innocuous for a second, but which only served as a misdirect that switched to a rant on whatever raised her ire at the moment. With his sister, there was never a scarcity of anger. He told her once he never needed to draw upon anger as a source for any motivation. His sister snapped back, lecturing him that was because he was repressing the fact of his oppression. Simply put, Birdy was in denial, his sister lectured. Her living on the West coast was fine with Birdy. He sometimes imagined her as an angry warrior clown with a rainbowed colored circus afro.

Joseph did not appear he was going to become angry, but he was restless, and the source of his restlessness may well be the same as that of his sister. Maybe, maybe not. It didn't matter, thought Birdy. Joseph was an asshole.

Birdy was in no mood to talk about why he wasn't on social media, and never in a mood to talk politics. Politics bored him as much as it bored Frieda, thank God.

Birdy stood up.

"About the cinnamon, the same payment arrangement as before? May I see the cinnamon please?" That was all Vin and Noro needed to hear. They arose quickly, saying something quietly between themselves. Joseph too stood up, and put out his arm, halting the brothers.

"The price is not a settled matter," said Joseph. This announcement was not surprising to Birdy. From the email communications prior to his arrival and up and until now, he felt less confident about this transaction. It was all in Joseph's tone. Vin and Noro stood by in silence.

"You are not Muslim. Are you Christian?" asked Joseph.

The source of his cocksureness? It was muted last trip, but not anymore. Birdy speculated, then he imagined him too in a circus afro, clown-frolicking about with his sister. Vin and Noro were not displaying the same attitude. Joseph's motivation? Birdy further speculated. Birdy knew his offer was generous.

"Why is the price not a settled manner?" asked Birdy.

"We are an online trading company now, and we have had other offers that exceed yours." Birdy moved past Joseph and now faced Vin and Noro. Birdy told them the price he offered to Joseph. Vin nodded. Noro followed Vin. Joseph turned and stated the new offer. It was outrageous. But Joseph's continuing attempt to throw Birdy off-balance was not reflected in Birdy's demeanor. Vanmeter came to mind, and thinking of him kept Birdy calm. He knew what damage Vanmeter could do to their online business prospects, which in turn would affect any business they conducted. At least, that's what Birdy imagined. It was this thought that Birdy held (along with Joseph in a rainbow circus afro) as he finished up with Joseph. He imagined Vanmeter's internet intervention destroying them all, and Vin and Noro taking their vengeance not against Birdy, but Joseph.

To Vin and Noro, Birdy said, "My offer is very good. I leave Zanzibar City tomorrow. Call me. If not, I will find another cinnamon supplier."

He shook Vin and Noro's hand, ignoring Joseph. Birdy hadn't noticed the rain had stopped. The sun amped the humidity. Sitting and sweating in his rental, his back towards the porch where they stood watching, Birdy unlaced his chukkas, poured out the water that had not soaked through, took off his socks and wrung them out, placing his shoes and socks on the passenger seat floor. If they called and accepted his original offer, Birdy would honor the agreement. But any future transactions would only occur without Joseph in the mix, should there be any.

Before texting Frieda, he convinced himself she would approve his visiting Vanmeter in Rome--after business in Ghana with Pico's parents.

24

Without Pico along, the drive to his parent's farm seem to take twice as long. Maybe it was the gloomy cloud cover. Birdy liked Pico, and Pico had placed his trust in Birdy. Birdy thought Pico might trust everyone. As he approached the highway turn off, Birdy began to recall his first visit here, meeting Pico's parents and brothers, and Mass at the cathedral. It was a pleasant visit, and he hoped for another this trip.

Frieda texted back to have a good time with Vanmeter in Rome--and not to stay too long because she had a matter to discuss with him, but not over the phone. Nothing urgent, texted Frieda. Nothing to worry about. Birdy wasn't sure he knew Frieda well enough yet to accurately interpret, 'matters to discuss but not over the phone and nothing to worry about.' She could have said nothing other than 'have a good trip.' Birdy speculated, and debated whether he should be worried.

Later she texted, "Take a lot of pictures!"

This visit, the Natambe sons were not outside lined up waiting for Birdy. He didn't see either truck on the side of house. Birdy got out of his rental and stretched. Puddle free, he observed, looking down at his chukkas, now dried but clearly not in the same condition as before Pemba. Birdy did not like wearing dirty shoes, especially in public. And tennis shoes were not appropriate. The skies threatened rain. But the clouds were moving fast.

"Not going to rain just yet, but you should get inside," said Mrs. Natambe, from the porch. Mrs. Natambe said nothing while watching Birdy take off his chukkas and placing them outside the front door. The house appeared empty. She said everyone was working.

"I'm pleased to say we have almost two hundred pounds of pepper for you," said Mrs. Natambe, smiling, and motioning Birdy to sit at the dining table as she poured cold tea. She pushed a small plate of cut-up sandwiches towards Birdy. He thanked her and sipped tea in between bites of sandwich. She watched him eat. She appeared comfortable in the silence, which made Birdy comfortable.

"I wired the full payment to your bank last night," said Birdy, finishing the last sandwich and emptying his glass of tea. He declined the offer for a refill. Mrs. Natambe thanked him.

"On your advice, Pico is wanting to join the Army in Pennsylvania--I think that is the place. The Guard, or something, I'm not sure what that means," she said.

"Each state has an Army National Guard. I was in the National Guard. And my father too," said Birdy.

"He's very excited to fly a helicopter," she said, clearly missing Pico, and worried.

"You will watch over him?"

"I will. And he's staying with Thrash Davis now that he has returned from Rome. It's a big house, plenty of room for both of them to paint."

"We send Pico money, not very much, every month," she said.

"I don't believe Pico would make a good priest," Mrs. Natambe mused aloud, adding, "All the women like him."

"Thrash Davis is Mr. Davis now, he left the Order," said Birdy. Mrs. Natambe didn't know, and Birdy figured she didn't know Thrash was married briefly to Honoraria, and she died. Mrs. Natambe stood up, taking Birdy's empty plate and glass to the kitchen. Birdy stood up and thanked her again for the sandwiches and tea. She smiled. The inside quiet was punctuated by the clinking of the plate and glass in the sink.

When Mrs. Natambe returned, Birdy asked if she or her husband knew of any cinnamon growers in the area. She didn't think so.

"I'll ask my husband tonight," she said, and said nothing as Birdy made his way outside, and put on his chukkas. He thanked her one more time for the hospitality. She kissed him on the cheek.

"Pico," she said softly.

"I will," promised Birdy. Mrs. Natambe waved once and went inside. A mile past the Natambe farm Birdy remembered he'd had forgotten to take any pictures.

He'll take pictures in Rome, he thought, although, we already have lots of pictures of Rome. He drove the rest of the way back to the airport in pouring rain.

Birdy knew Thrash would never counsel Pico towards the religious life. But now that Pico wanted to join the Army National Guard the burden of looking after Pico fell to Birdy. He had arranged the visit to the recruiter, a woman Birdy knew from his time in the Guard. There was a reason she was a recruiter. And there was, of course, Porter B.

Pico stayed in the garage apartment that weekend of the recruiter visit. He listened to every word Porter B said about life in the Army.

Pico joined Birdy and his mother to listen to Porter B's band. He was very impressed. He said these experiences were his new inspiration to paint. He was going to be painting eight hours a day, he said. He had never painted musicians before.

The rain slowed Birdy's return, and yet the storm was the reason his flight to Rome was delayed. Otherwise Birdy would have to spend the night and take a morning flight. He wasn't so much anxious to get to Rome as he was ready to leave Africa.

25

Vanmeter's text read, "I'm at the gallery."

Birdy gave the taxi driver the new address. Traffic was reasonable in Rome at 11 pm.

"Buonasera," said Vanmeter holding the door open as Birdy lugged his two suitcases in from the cab. It was raining steady.

"Come é stato il tuo volo?" asked Vanmeter.

"Fine. If you asked me how was my trip," said Birdy, wiping the rain off his jacket.

"Your flight," said Vanmeter.

"You always work this late?" Birdy reached out and gave Vanmeter a quick hug. A half full bottle of whiskey and two glasses were on the desk.

"Cleaning up. Honoraria promised this local guy she'd have a showing for him. I made good on the promise tonight."

"Any buyers?" asked Birdy, thanking Vanmeter for the whiskey. They clinked glasses.

Vanmeter shrugged.

"A couple bought two small paintings. I mean the size of a five-by-eight kinda small. They were friends of the guy. Very shy, looked more geekish than an artist. Didn't cost me too much though. Only went through a case of wine, a block of cheese, and two boxes of crackers. Good way to practice Italian. I still suck, though. I may have made fifteen Euros."

"And...Momma went missing again. Her cousin I told you about--he can't find her."

"And...Kule Fat stopped by last night with the Materials Man."

All this news, told just as a matter of facts. Standard Vanmeter, thought Birdy.

"They stopped by here?" asked Birdy, motioning Vanmeter to add to his empty glass. Vanmeter nodded.

"Thrash emptied the storage room Kule Fat put me in charge of and it's now all at his house. Paid me three grand for the stuff."

Vanmeter didn't say that he used some to pay down his debt. He also didn't mention the Materials Man was leaving envelopes of cash and taking the copies Thrash was leaving in the storage shed. The same copies that Thrash, his mother, and Pico made that were stored in the not-so-hidden closet in the Davis house. His debt was down to five grand--very manageable now---but he only had two weeks to pay the rest, on his determined time schedule. Living on cheese, crackers, and cheap wine sounded like a lame country song, and it was a song Vanmeter was tired of hearing.

Thrash repeated what Vanmeter had done with the first set of paintings. He marked them the same as Vanmeter, placing them in the storage room. But instead of just one set, Thrash left four sets of paintings. Thrash didn't tell Pico anything, and, by which pictures were taken, and which remained, he didn't need to. Vanmeter would be interested, though. Thrash was relieved none of his were selected.

He wasn't interested in being a forger. Like any painter, he copied to learn. He bought the materials in the storage room because he knew Vanmeter was tight on money. But the storage room brought back memories of his mother's own, similar collection of supplies. He never thought about replicating old paintings as a youth, believing it was part of learning to be a painter.

It was a curiosity that Thrash thought about for a short time, but not long after, he let the curiosity wane, as he did with his enthrallment of his mother after he left home. Whether she was or wasn't didn't make any difference to him.

Vanmeter wasn't at all enamored with the forgery business. If he was going to hustle paintings, he'd only hustle originals. Not counting Fat, he now knew two painters, but had yet to see one of their originals. That he had not seen the works of Thrash and Pico didn't worry Vanmeter. He'd sell their paintings, he knew it.

They drove back to Honoraria's apartment, where Vanmeter now resided.

Birdy asked, "What does the K. Fat dude want?"

"He's definitely taking a risk being seen. He's wanted back in the States. He didn't seem to care. Looked relaxed, lost a lot of weight," said Vanmeter.

"What did he want?" asked Birdy, now unsure he was that interested to know one way or the other.

"To congratulate me for getting into the art business so quickly, and that he'd be in touch," said Vanmeter. This much was true. But Fat said more, and what else Fat said was what had been keeping Vanmeter up at night. Thinking about what's next in his own plan, and maybe no longer on his own schedule--but on Fat's.

All Birdy could manage was a silent nod. He was exhausted. He didn't quite believe Vanmeter, but he was aware enough to know what Vanmeter was going to ask of him.

At the apartment, Vanmeter said, "Help me find Momma, and get her on a plane to Rome." Vanmeter went to his bedroom and came back with Clara's passport.

"No way I'd leave it with her. From now on, no-shit, I'm the only one responsible for her well-being. But I've got to stay here to square away a big arrangement."

"I know where's she's at. And where's she's at is not a good place for a black man to be about."

"So--you really mean you want Frieda to find your Momma," mumbled Birdy, as he started drifting off to sleep on the sofa.

"Afraid so," said Vanmeter. Vanmeter poured another whiskey, went to his room, and sat on the bed. Of the many thoughts bouncing around in his mind, one question was why Thrash really bought all the materials in the storage room.

26

Thrash Davis was living off his trust, and he refused Pico's offer to pay him two hundred dollars a month he got from his parents, not including painting supplies.

It took a while to settle into a routine. Pico's nervous energy was discharged as much through painting as by running and the cross-fit exercises he got off the internet. The house was not close to much, and Pico wasn't ready to drive around on his own, even though he had an International driver's license. Thrash had given up regular exercise for some time now. He stayed at home and painted.

Everything Thrash and Pico did was on their own. They made an agreement to text each other first before entering their respective areas. Neither watched television, not that there was much other than what could be picked up by an old dish antenna still clinging to the roof. Pico listened to music on his earphones, Thrash played vinyl albums. He looked forward to flipping the album over almost as much as listening. His smart phone was nearby and he had accumulated hours of music on it, but he preferred to choose an album from the house collection, dust it off, place it on the turnstile, and select play.

Pico only painted in natural light, so used to his home in Ghana. In Pennsylvania, the ever present overcast never sombered his work. Whereas Thrash used whatever light was available.

Later, when Vanmeter finally saw their works, he made a perceptive observation of their paintings done while living at the Pennsylvania house. He spent more time than he admitted to himself trying to guess what went through Thrash and Pico's minds during that time.

He was less distracted about being right about what was going through their heads than creating a compelling storyline that he would tell to prospective buyers.

Thrash introduced a number of well-regarded art critics to Vanmeter, and he read much of their critiques. He watched all of John Berger's early 70's BBC shows on art, and read some of his essays. It took no time at all to convince Vanmeter he was not a John Berger fan. Marxist bullshit versus making some money.

****

"I accepted their third counter offer. Higher than what I should have paid. I like Vin and Noro. Hard working dudes. Everyone loves their cinnamon. It's the jackass younger cousin Joseph. He's got a high and mighty thing going on. He just needs to tamp it all down, man, tamp it down."

Frieda listened to Birdy while reading over documents at the dining table. She asked about Vanmeter.

"I think he's exactly where he wants to be. Out of his element, picking it up as he goes along, trusting his instincts. If it weren't for Clara, he'd be kicking it into high gear--I know it. And Clara, oh by the way, has gone missing again. Vanmeter's asked me to find her and get her to Rome."

"Got your full attention now, don't I?" smiled Birdy.

"You're going back to Rome--with Clara?"

"Vanmeter says where Clara is now is no place for a black man, and he wants you to go find her," said Birdy, pouring another cup of coffee and sitting down opposite Frieda.

Frieda scoffed.

Birdy said playfully, "C'mon now, you got some free time now that you're going back into practice. You know, before you sign those papers and start being a doctor again."

"I start on Monday," said Frieda.

"Four days, plenty of time," said Birdy.

"Find her, wherever she is, get her to Rome and be back by Sunday? Ridiculous," said Frieda. She was warming up to the idea but giving nothing away to Birdy.

"I'm going with you, no matter what Vanmeter says."

"Why? You don't think I can do it myself?" shot back Frieda.

"Oh, you can run the whole world baby, I know you can," said Birdy, getting up to put his cup in the sink.

"This is our week to get pregnant. You forget?" said Frieda.

"Hotel sex is molto benne," said Birdy, bending over and kissing Frieda.

"Your parent's garage apartment is not a hotel room."

Birdy never seriously considered Frieda going alone. The timing was perfect to also pick up Pico and take him to the Penn National Guard weekend orientation which started on Friday.

He went to the couch. Frieda joined him. He mused, everything's always on a timeline. He thought about being outside of time. Was there such a thing? He wasn't moving back into his old closet for an office that Frieda left now that she was going back into practice. He didn't want to work out of the house. He'd find a spot in the warehouse.

Maybe if he lived out of time while her parents stayed in time, then it might all work out. He wasn't sure about the spice trade business. Other than wanting to be married to Frieda, he wasn't sure what he wanted. He didn't want to talk to Frieda about it. Anyway, she'd shy away from the subject. He knew what his father would say.

He had never asked Vanmeter for advice on work. He'd laugh at the idea of being boxed into a 'profession.' The only box Vanmeter would accept is one with the walls flattened, like cardboard, with no chance of reforming. Birdy knew he was from the never-had-much and got-nothing-to-lose school. Vanmeter had the smarts and perception to wing it. He knew it, and it thrilled him. You inherit that, you don't decide to be that way, thought Birdy.

The idea of being a stay at home father made Birdy queasy. To be that meant manhood had pissed out of him, onto the street, down the gutter and in to the sewer and on to a treatment plant. He imagined his manhood as some kind of liquid property swirling about in the sedimentation tanks. Getting the first treatment, the second, the sludge treatment, and back out into the water supply, and from there who knows where. No longer any semblance of manhood, that's for certain.

Birdy had no intention of losing his manhood, as he positioned Frieda to get her pregnant now, on the couch.

****

The next morning Birdy and Frieda flew to Pittsburgh, rented a sedan, and drove to meet Clara's cousin Thompson Ruddgy at his Walgreen's. It was twelve degrees outside, not a cloud around. The air was filled with undetectable water droplets-now crystallized, adding sparkling, tiny glitter to the morning blue sky. Birdy noticed and mentioned it to Frieda, who was listening to a public radio news program. North Korea and Iran provocations, Russia too, and England flummoxed at the moment on how to exit the European Union. Globalism and Nationalism, the climate. The propensity of shoving everyone into some category in order to be vilified or venerated--that attraction to a power built on some brittle foundation of dubious quality that took the form of shame and then shouted it out--in order to silence. Dubious, all of it.

Frieda said she never paid too much attention. In med school and residency, she studied, worked, ate, and exercised when she felt she had 30 minutes to spare. She didn't remember sleeping. While stationed on the E.A.C.H.S. she worked most of the time, and the few hours of free time she slept. Sometimes she ran on the treadmill and listened to medical podcasts. Sleep came first.

"It's overwhelming thinking about everything going on. You can get swept up in it all. It's beginning to become scary," said Frieda. She stared out her window, eyes not focused on anything in particular, unaware of anything within her periphery.

"Um, hm," said Birdy. He wasn't planning on saying anything about what she was listening to. He'd much rather listen to jazz, sometimes classical music. Much of the time Birdy had nothing on while driving. Frieda listening to radio news programs--this was something recent, thought Birdy.

Frieda turned to look at Birdy, "Don't you think it's getting scary? All of it."

Birdy took a while to answer. He reached over and held Frieda's hand, giving it a squeeze.

"Any scarier than five years ago, ten years ago, twenty? Maybe five years ago," he said.

"The status quo is being looked at hard, and those who prefer whatever status quo they live in get upset when their status quo gets knocked. And then there's those who demand you gotta live in the status quo they prefer, otherwise you're wrong, and when you're wrong, you're highlighted, and not in a good way."

"But, hey, you're cool under pressure, you have to look at the facts presented to you, and then you make a decision, right? You don't go into surgery any other way, right?"

"Umm," said Frieda.

"You don't listen to the radio and television people to get your facts before going into surgery, right? They aren't the experts you turn to, am I right?"

"Don't be ridiculous, is what you'd say to that, right Frieda?" She didn't answer.

"Well, I'm not convinced I'm getting many facts from the radio and television people, just what they want me to hear. So, what they say doesn't scare me. Now, I think it's a fact they say a lot of things in only the way they want to present them and attempt to pass them off as facts--that irritates more than it scares me. So, I don't listen to them. And if I care enough about something for whatever reason, I'll go and do some research on it. No need to rush to conclusions on most of what's out there. The TV peoples urgencies aren't mine. And that goes for every politician, too. And just because they're all excited doesn't mean I'm excited."

"Now you baby, you get me excited," said Birdy.

"All this worry about everything isn't about having a baby, is it?"

"I don't know," she said. Frieda changed the channel and found a country station. A drunk in my beer song, sung by a woman. They laughed. When the song ended, Frieda reached over and turned off the radio.

****

Frieda and Birdy stopped first to visit Clara's cousin. He was in his small, worn office in Walgreen's.

"I promised my wife I wouldn't get wrapped up in Clara's mess anymore. But I want to help her, and I don't know how much more I should get involved," said Thompson.

"Her girlfriend's an enabler, and where her girlfriend is, that's where Clara will be. She moves to different apartments for a short time, but never far away. Here, I made a list. One of these five places is where they'll be. Her girlfriend's name is Vicky Cooper. She drives a blue Ford pick-up, beat all to hell. Clara has a white Corolla, thanks to Vanmeter."

Viewing the list, Birdy said, "Vanmeter thinks it's not safe for me to reach out to Clara."

Thompson asked, "Is it true Vanmeter's in Italy? What in the Lord's name in heaven is he doing in Italy?"

Thompson looked at his watch. "Vanmeter's got a point. You lookin' for a white girl around that area won't go over too well." He told them he had to get back out on the floor.

Now in the car, Frieda said, "How are we going to get Clara to come with us? What if she's so impaired we can't get her out of the apartment? What are we going to tell her when she asks why Vanmeter's not here?"

"Like Vanmeter said, we get her on the phone. He said leave the rest to him. He just needs to get her on the phone," said Birdy.

"I'll call Vanmeter once we locate the apartment. And we'll get her on the phone."

Birdy wasn't seeing what the worry was. It was late afternoon on a Wednesday. Birdy's parents knew to expect them this evening. They were not happy about the plan. Porter B insisted he come along. Birdy said no. For whatever reason, Porter B backed off.

"Vanmeter needs to be here, not in Rome, to take care of his problem," said Porter B.

"Yeah, he should be, but he's not, and we agreed to help," replied Birdy over the phone.

"And Frieda, did she agree too, or did you agree for her?" Porter B was worked up. Frieda could hear him. She grabbed the phone from Birdy and said, "I agreed for myself, thank you." Birdy told his father he'd check in later.

Frieda drove with Birdy navigating. Fifteen minutes later they arrived at the first apartment complex, a series of worn-down duplexes clumped together. Distinguishing between abandoned and operable cars in the parking spaces was almost impossible, although the flat tires helped. It was too cold to hang out outside, which gave Frieda a small measure of security. She made one pass through all the connected parking lots and did not see either the blue pickup or white Corolla.

Ten minutes later they were in the parking lot of a two-story apartment complex. Rough, thought Birdy. Again, no pickup or Corolla.

Birdy and Frieda said nothing.

The third stop was twenty minutes away, another series of duplexes next to an abandoned trailer park. The worst looking of the three, by far.

"Blue pick-up, to the right," said Birdy, looking for the Corolla, which he could not find. Birdy texted Vanmeter he found Vicky's pickup but his Momma's car was not there.

"Find a place to park and wait. She'll show up," texted Vanmeter.

"How long?" texted Birdy.

"Until twilight," answered Vanmeter. Birdy told Frieda what Vanmeter said.

"Birdy..." Frieda was now frightened and angry.

"Half hour and we'll leave."

There was no good place to wait. The duplexes were at least a mile from a small, shopping center, and two miles from a grocery store. Frieda elected to wait in the grocery store parking lot.

Ten minutes later Birdy spotted a white Corolla parking up close to the entrance. Out of the car came

Clara, walking very slow into the store. Twilight was fading.

Birdy texted Vanmeter the details of their location. Ten minutes passed. He got out of the car. As he closed the door, Clara came out with three full plastic bags of goods. Birdy motioned for Frieda to move to the passenger side.

"As Clara gets out, I'll drop you right by. Call Vanmeter now and get his ass on the phone. Hope she's in good enough shape to pack and go."

"And what if she's not willing to go?" said Frieda.

"Then we are done and back to Pittsburgh."

Clara's difficultly recognizing Frieda did not dissuade her motivation to follow through on the plan. She followed Clara into the duplex in front of where the blue pickup was parked. Frieda shut the door.

Birdy thought of the times he waited in Iraq, waiting through dangerous circumstances and uncertain outcomes. The tension builds and seems to bloat you, he recalled. Weighs you down, slows you down. Maybe that's why time seemed to slow down too.

The banging on his window caused Birdy to flail his arms up and a wave of shook surged through him. Again, the baton banged on his window. Now a flash light blinded him, and he attempted to block the beam with his hand.

"Get out the car--now," roared the sheriff deputy. With precision slowness, Birdy unlatched his seat belt, letting it rewind into the housing, turned off the ignition, and reached for the door handle. The deputy opened the door.

"Out of the car, please." He was bundled up in at least two coats and he wore a black watchman's cap to his eyes, with a small badge in front--in place of his sheriff hat. It was still twelve degrees outside.

The deputy pointed the flashlight into the car and he peered inside.

"You'd better be Birdy Wire," he said.

Still in shock, Birdy looked up and uttered, "Yep." He was wearing too thin a coat, and was now too cold to be anything other than in shock.

The towering deputy pulled off his thick leather glove and said, "Big-Bill Becker, I'm a friend of one each Vanmeter Smythe. Let's get in my car. I'm a pussy in cold weather."

Once inside, Big-Bill Becker sat for a few moments to warm up. Birdy continued to shake.

"Here's what we're gonna do. Your bride is with Clara, is that right?" Birdy nodded.

"I'm gonna go get them both, put 'em in my car and you're gonna follow me."

"We'll drive a bit, and I'll stop and you can take them wherever you need to."

"Got it," said Birdy.

"Good. The only reason nobody's beat the shit outta you is on account it's twelve fucking degrees outside."

"I'll remember the number twelve then--as good luck," said Birdy, the shock lessening, the adrenaline still pumping. The deputy laughed.

Clara slept in the backseat all the way to Birdy's parents' house.

"She didn't say much to Vanmeter on the phone. He did all the talking," whispered Frieda, not knowing what Vanmeter said to his Momma. Clara packed a small old suitcase, and brought along a huge tote back, stuffed with makeup, moisturizers, and lipstick--her entire collection she'd purchased at Walgreen's over the years with her employee discount. She reeked of cigarettes.

"We don't have to take her back to New York," said Frieda.

"You sure?" said Birdy.

"Clara promised Vanmeter she'd get on the plane at Pittsburgh," said Frieda, adding, "We have to get her on that plane. Then our job is done."

Birdy's phone buzzed. Frieda read Vanmeter's text.

"I'm in New York, staying at a hotel at JFK. I'll take Momma to Rome tomorrow evening. Thank you, thank you, thank you." The only reason Birdy didn't call Vanmeter right then was because he didn't want to wake up Clara.

Back at Birdy's parents' house, Birdy and Clara went to the garage apartment, where Birdy lay on the sofa that night. He had no intention of letting Clara slip away. Frieda slept in Birdy's old room in the main house. She'd never slept in the room before. She kept the night stand lamp on and looked at everything on the shelves and posted on the walls. It was the story of Birdy's life from when he was a boy, including his Army decorations and memorabilia. After a long while, she turned off the lamp. She felt like a stranger in his room. No one really knows anyone, she thought, never as well as you think you do.

Frieda didn't waken until well after Birdy and Clara departed for the airport. She was surprised she dreamt of Vanmeter instead--in Birdy's old room, with all of his life around her. Outside, snow fell, but it was too warm to accumulate.

Clara was silent almost the entire trip. Birdy stopped trying to make conversation about how much she was going to enjoy Rome. She stared out the window, clutching her tote bag, in bad need of a cigarette. He mentioned Big Bill Becker.

"Always was a pain in the ass. Big guy, but a little pain in the ass, really. Not a bad kid. Always got along with Vanmeter. But then, Vanmeter gets along with everybody," said Clara.

"You can grab a smoke before we get into the terminal," said Birdy.

"I'm good," she said. Nah, thought Birdy, she wasn't good.

Birdy watched Clara pass through security and walk towards her gate, which was beyond his line of sight. He stayed in the airport until her plane departed, going back to the check-in to smooth talk the agent into confirming for him Clara was on the flight.

Driving back to his parent's house, he texted Frieda to see if she still wanted to go with him to visit Thrash and pick up Pico to bring him to the Penn Army Guard Orientation weekend. She texted back saying she wanted to go. The snow stopped falling and the sky gray gloom began to lighten some. By the time they reached Thrash's house, muted afternoon sunlight appeared.

27

Birdy and Frieda's visit to Thrash's place was short. Pico had a small bag packed and was ready to go. But neither Thrash nor Pico were ready to show their paintings to anyone. They hadn't shown each other their paintings either, agreeing that in one more month they'd invite each other to their respective studios for a tour.

Frieda found that odd.

The house looked as she expected a house to look with two bachelors. The place wasn't untidy, the kitchen sink and counters were clear of dishes. But the overall feel was that of needing a thorough sweeping and vacuuming. They kept the house cold, maybe they opened windows to clear out the smell of paints and thinners, she thought. If so, they were unsuccessful.

Thrash put on more weight and Pico looked the same, thought Birdy. Thrash wasn't so much sullen as he was contemplative, with an obvious hint of melancholy.

Pico was very excited to see them. His nervous energy never seemed to dissipate. He very much wanted to show them his paintings, but his agreement with Thrash stood.

Birdy was particularly disappointed not to see their work. Unless it gave them another way to motivate themselves in order to stimulate their creativity, or some such excuse, thought Birdy. Yeah, it was some artist bull shit like that, he was sure.

"Next month, promise," said Thrash, handing both Frieda and Birdy fresh brewed coffee.

"Live on this stuff," said Thrash, lifting his coffee cup up.

"I'll check my messages more often, too," laughed Thrash.

They drank their coffee in silence. It was a shared sensed they all wanted to get on with the tasks of the day.

Thrash gave Pico a bear hug, followed by Birdy, and then Frieda. She wondered how long Thrash had been wearing the red checked flannel shirt.

"You'd look so much younger if you shaved," teased Frieda. Thrash got a kick out that comment.

"And lost my gut, too," he said. Frieda smiled, and nodded.

In the car, Pico, said, "I'm sorry I couldn't let you see my work. There's one in particular I want you to see."

Driving back to Pittsburgh Birdy's phone buzzed. It was Thrash saying it was good to see them both. Then Vanmeter texted. He and Clara were on the plane to Rome.

Birdy filled Pico in on what to expect this weekend during the orientation.

"It's really an interview to decide if you are someone they want to work with for a career. More like interviewing to get into a family. And that you're not some lazy, blame the other guy kind of dude. Many of them stick around the Guard for at least twenty years. It's not like active duty, where you rotate to a different base every few years. You're with each other for the duration, for better or worse. Unless you quit of course, or go to another Guard unit in some other state. Yeah, it's more like an interview to be in a new family. Think of it that way."

"Why did you quit?" said Pico.

In the driveway, Birdy shut off the car and turned around to Pico.

"It wasn't because I didn't like who I worked with. They were almost all good dudes. The women, too. I left because I thought I wanted to do something completely different."

"But isn't that why being part time is so you can do something else?"

"You know how long my dad was in the Guard?" said Birdy.

Pico didn't understand. Frieda did.

28

Frieda did not join Birdy and his parents for noon Mass on Sunday. During the homily, Birdy's phone buzzed in his pocket. It buzzed again. And soon after, a third time. He did not take his phone out, but he was unable to concentrate during the rest of Mass.

He now thought about dropping Pico off at the orientation, catching up and introducing him to the older guys and gals he knew that were still in the Guard. He missed the Guard, but he never allowed himself to dwell on it too much. He knew he shouldn't have let the fact that his father was an institution at the Guard sway him to quit, knowing he couldn't be his father. No one in the Guard ever said anything about his father being the bad ass that he was. Birdy more than held his own--the guys in the unit told him. But he left anyway. The consequence of that decision was that Birdy was never going to quit anything again. So far so good, thought Birdy.

Porter B drove them home and Birdy finally checked his phone. His friend, the hot recruiter, had been leaving him messages to call her.

The phone rang once when Gwen answered. It was a very brief call.

"OK, I'll call you back in a few", Birdy said.

Porter B looked at him through the rear-view mirror.

"Pico was killed early this morning. Vehicle accident during maneuvers."

Turning to look at her son, Arlene whispered, "His mother, his poor mother."

"Dropping you off at the house Arlene--going to base with Birdy."

Out of the car but leaning back in, Arlene said to Birdy, "I know I'd rather have my husband tell me the news rather than anyone else." Birdy nodded and Arlene closed the door. It was almost an hour drive. Porter B avoided the fierce temptation to revert to Sergeant Major mode and take charge of every detail. Instead he drove with what appeared to be little sense of urgency.

"Anybody else injured, or worse?" Porter B finally asked, checking for signs of shock on Birdy's face.

"Driver's in bad shape, two others in back are banged up. Not sure how bad," said Birdy, now calling back Gwen to let her know he was on his way.

Dropped Pico off on Friday and he's dead on Sunday morning. Birdy made a promise to Pico's mother. You can never keep that kind of promise. Birdy knew that, but he promised anyway. He fought back nausea--his legs began shaking.

Memories returned fast to both Porter B and Birdy. Of the times they had to handle immediate, and then later affairs of the dead. There was a five-hour time difference between Pittsburgh and Ghana. How many times a minute in this world is that phone call made? Birdy did not want to make the middle-of-the-night call.

He started to go through a checklist out loud, actions he needed to take care of, in a particular order. His father listened and on occasion affirmed with a "Yep, that's right."

Frieda just sent a text asking if she could be of any assistance. Birdy texted back, "I'll let you know."

Driving past the base gate guard, memories poured into Porter B. It was a drill weekend, troops were everywhere. Blackhawk helicopters filled the flight line, main rotor blades in a whir, pilots and crew chiefs on headphones completing checklists, preparing for a multi-ship launch. As much as Birdy missed the action, and he did miss it, he turned his eyes away from the airfield.

Birdy was barely aware he was now out of the vehicle and walking with his father towards the clinic. His mind was stuck in the shock of hearing of Pico's death, yet his body was in motion. His inability to synch his mind to what he was actually doing caused disorientation. Something had to give, either his mind needed to get unstuck or he had to stop, and move no further. Now, he and his father were inside the morgue. Birdy became dizzy.

"Broke his neck when the vehicle rolled. Barely any other bruises on him," the morgue attendant said. On the table, Pico looked as if asleep. This was not where Birdy needed to stop. He bent over, placing his hands on his knees, as if he completed a long run, barely recovering from the final sprint. Porter B nodded to the attendant and he covered Pico.

Birdy's friend Gwen arrived, and Birdy let her lead him out to the empty clinic lobby. She sat with Birdy. No one spoke. After a half hour, Birdy took out his phone, realizing that in addition to Pico's, the only other phone number Birdy had was Pico's mother.

Birdy recalled what his own mother told him not three hours ago.

He got up, walked outside the clinic, now watching two Blackhawks lift off. He followed them until they were specks on the gray horizon. He left a message on Mrs. Natambe's phone. He did not say it was urgent, only that he would like to talk with her and Mr. Natambe. As Birdy hung up the phone, he watched Porter B returning from visiting the commanding officer. Birdy had been unaware his father was absent.

Porter B leaned out his window and motioned Birdy to get inside. They drove slowly past the flight line on the way out of the base. Birdy watched the flight line action this time. He was synched up again. The drive back home seemed to take twice as long as it should.

An hour later it was Mr. Natambe who called back. After a short conversation, Mr. Natambe thanked Birdy for offering to escort Pico's body back to Ghana. Looking at Porter B's eyes through the rear-view mirror, Birdy insisted to Mr. Natambe that no money was needed to be transferred as the National Guard was taking care of the arrangements. Porter B nodded his head. Mr. Natambe said he'd call back in a few hours and let Birdy know his decision whether to bring Pico back himself. That was Mr. Natambe's inclination, he admitted, but he needed to confer with Mrs. Natambe.

Birdy came around later in the afternoon, but as evening came, he grew quiet again, and after dinner returned to the apartment by himself. Frieda walked with him out of the house, insisting softly she accompany him. He relented. Frieda went back to the house to gather her belongings.

That night they talked until very late. Frieda was sure she failed to assuage Birdy's guilt, even though he insisted she did.

29

Early the next morning Birdy and Frieda drove to Thrash's place. Telling him in person was the only option. Thrash bounced outside of the house, greeting them with a wide smile, a fresh shaved face, proudly showing off a different flannel shirt. Birdy waited until they were in kitchen to tell Thrash the news of Pico. Thrash sat down immediately, slumping over the kitchen table.

For a time, silence and the fresh smell of strong coffee also occupied the kitchen. Frieda wondered when there'd ever be a good time for her to say what she had to say. Now Birdy poured three cups of coffee, placing Thrash's cup in front of him. His head lifted as he grabbed the cup handle.

After taking a sip, Thrash said quietly, "It's time, then."

Thrash stood up and led Birdy and Frieda to the room where Pico painted. On each wall was a horizontal strip of photos, from waist high up to about the elbow of an outstretched arm held above the head. Pictures of his family, all together, individual, just his parents, just his brothers. Other walls had photos in no particular order of subject; of their farm, the house, the faded orange Datsun pickup truck, clear sky days, cloudy sky afternoons, sunrise and sunsets. Pico had pictures of when he was in Rome. Churches, crowds on the streets on bright days, days when it poured rain. Also, were pictures of huge puddles in pothole streets, with reflections of the city in the puddles. One reflection held a pack of runty street dogs. Photos of frail, bare trees on winter sidewalks. A single file of ten nuns in habits and walking in order of height, in a narrow cross walk, across a wide thorough fare.   On the floor were numerous small stacks of 8x10 copies of photos that either didn't make the cut, or were waiting to be taped up.

On the big desk were dozens of sketches. One easel had a dozen watercolor paintings stacked one behind the other. Along the floor, below the photos and leaning against the wall, were his oil paintings.

"Last month we visited Andrew Wyeth's museum in Chadds Ford," said Thrash, not wanting to touch anything, even more hesitant to closely inspect any of Pico's work.

Frieda went to another easel covered by a canvas. She looked at Thrash, and he motioned her to lift the canvas. On the easel was a nude. Thrash, stunned, quickly moved in front of the painting.

Thrash peered at the painting.

"Wow," said Frieda, dumbfounded, recognizing it was Honoraria. She was standing in a bare room next to a window, peaking through drawn curtains on a sunny day.

Birdy and Frieda drew together, watching Thrash inspect the painting. Thrash laughed. His outburst startled them.

"He snuck into my studio!" exclaimed Thrash. Frieda and Birdy remained silent in their confusion.

"Come with me!" bellowed Thrash, and he rushed out of the room. He stopped at the door and demanded, "Come on!"

Opening the door to his studio, Thrash seized a painting hung on a wall and raced out of the room. It was the same painting of Honoraria they had seen in Pico's studio.

Returning to Pico's studio, Thrash slid a third empty easel next to Pico's Honoraria, and placed his Honoraria nude. He stood in front of them both. Birdy and Frieda moved off to the side, and found themselves watching Thrash more than looking at the two paintings.

Birdy found both paintings unsettling. Frieda thought they were beautiful. She had a difficult time distinguishing between the two.

"Hah!" shouted Thrash, bending over, inspecting the bottom corner of Pico's Honoraria through his glasses he had on a cord around his neck.

Thrash whipped off his glasses, turned around and said, "He signed his own name! Ha Ha!"

"Ballsy!" Thrash was completely beguiled by it all. He dashed around now, looking closely at all of Pico's paintings. Silence filled the room once again, and Birdy motioned Frieda to let Thrash be alone. She followed Birdy out of Pico's studio and back into Thrash's studio.

It was filled with sketches of Honoraria, not all nudes, but many. Frieda recognized that these all were done over the course of her last months. They depicted her severe weight loss, hair loss, her body collapsing upon itself, her face changing color, its shape narrowing and hollowing, her beauty fleeing. But in all the paintings, Honoraria was smiling. Her expression depicted a weary sense of lightness, never morose, not even close. The backgrounds of the paintings were explosions of bright color, as if to place the stark realism of Honoraria dying within a dream world. That's what it seemed to Birdy. Neither had seen any paintings like these. Frieda was then drawn to the sketches of Honoraria. Her residence memories of the dying in the oncology ward were back in full.

Standing in his studio doorway, Thrash watched Frieda and Birdy. Tears streamed his face. Frieda turned and looked at Thrash. She rushed to him, and hugged him.

"Beautiful. They are beautiful," she whispered.

"Pico--that man was a painter. Magnificent," said Thrash.

"You're a magnificent painter," said Frieda in a bold manner, shaking Thrash gently. The realization of Thrash now being completely alone struck Frieda right then.

"Let me show you why Pico is so damned good," said Thrash, releasing himself from her embrace. He motioned them to follow him back to Pico's studio.

Time slowed. Thrash was now conscious of the act of each leg motioning forwards. His heightened response to death's aftershock, of viewing beauty apart from death, of sadness within himself, and of thinking the Natambe's, surged his heart. But as he approached Pico's paintings it was their beauty in his vision, competing with his mind's vision of the absence of not only Pico, but of Honoraria, that caused his heart to pump wildly.

For almost fifteen minutes Thrash described Pico's paintings, with a vision of Honoraria in his mind.

Brilliant colors, the fantastic capture of light--these were what Frieda last remembered. She woke up on the floor, Birdy holding her head, Thrash dashing to the kitchen to fetch a glass of water.

"I'm starving," she said weakly.

"Probably because I'm pregnant."

30

When Mr. Natambe finally called back it was Thrash who convinced him not to travel to the U.S. and that he and Birdy would escort Pico's body back to Ghana. Only after Mrs. Natambe gave full consent did Mr. Natambe agree.

A week later, taking off from JFK, Thrash fidgeted in his economy class seat, trying to get situated, trying to sleep. Pico's coffin was below in the storage hold, and Birdy sat motionless, thinking about the hours he spent on Pemba lying on the ground looking at the trillion stars, immersed in the dense aroma of drying cinnamon. Lying in the cinnamon, before thinking about black and green mambas, Birdy recalled feeling as if released, outside his own skin. It was the same feeling he had now as they lifted off the runway.

But he knew it was Frieda's pregnancy that separated Birdy from his malaise--like a shedding of skin. He also wondered if praying for permanency from it, now that he could identify it, would help.

"Never believe praying never helps," his mother said. "If you arrive there, you're not in a good place, and you need to recognize that and pray all the time. Pray all the time, that's what I do. Stay out of that place."

At altitude, Birdy stared out the window, cupping his hands around his face, straining to see as many stars as he could, on a clear, moonless night.

Birdy thought about visiting Vin and Noro unannounced. Maybe Joseph wouldn't be there and he could barter with just the brothers. Birdy was again thinking being a spice trader might not work out. He thought of Frieda, and what it must feel like to be pregnant.

Frieda told him no matter what he thought about pregnancy, his thoughts couldn't come close to actualizing what being pregnant is. "Even I don't know yet what being pregnant actually is. You cannot know."

"But, the Y chromosome...", she said, "That difference between us is knowable, and absolute!" She laughed. It was her way of telling Birdy the reason for differences in any perspective they had. She would say, "It's due to the 'Y', and that's why." Frieda didn't say it very often, and when she did her tone was light, because she was very cautious about being a lecturer. She swore she'd never be like her mother.

Frieda's mother would say, "It's our very nature to tell men what should and should not be. Otherwise, who's to tell them, really? Who do they really listen to, if they decide to listen? The woman!"

That was not Frieda, she swore to herself, but she admitted her mother got most things right, most of the time. Maybe that's because she's a woman, maybe not, Frieda thought. But that is certainly what her mother taught her to believe.

Her father would say to Frieda, "I listen to your mother. I have to. I have no choice. You should too. You should have to, too, I mean." But he'd wink while saying it.

Birdy woke up. Thrash was not in his seat. He sensed they were descending. He then realized where he was, and why he was going to Ghana. He thought of Pico below in the cargo hold. It hit Birdy, then. Mr. and Mrs. Natambe, what could they be thinking? He became queasy at the thought of them pouring out their anger onto him. Blaming him. Accusing him of their son's death. Screaming, tears streaming, all because of him.

Thrash plopped back in the seat. "Starting the descent, thank the good Lord," he said, looking at Birdy. "You

OK?" Birdy just nodded, and reached for his water, draining the bottle.

"This is your second time. Taking the dead home--I mean," said Birdy.

"A habit I much prefer to shed," said Thrash, squirming about while buckling his seat belt.

"You never had to escort your guys back from Afghanistan or Iraq?" Birdy shook his head.

The airline held their luggage while they waited for Pico's coffin to be unloaded. (Thrash kept the carrying case with Pico's paintings with him)

"Hello Brother Davis," said Mr. Natambe, who came up from behind. They embraced.

"Mr. Wire," said Mr. Natambe to Birdy, shaking his hand. It was a genuinely neutral greeting. No put-ons. The best Birdy could hope for at this time was to be given the benefit of the doubt. Thrash and Birdy turned around to see the entire Natambe family. Father and sons wore black suits, a white shirt, and a black tie. Mrs. Natambe looked regal in her mourning dress. She hugged Thrash. Not hesitating, she turned and embraced Birdy, and his knees buckled for an instant as relief came over him.

The Natambe's brought both pick-up trucks to fit everyone. The mortuary in Accra city the Natambe's contracted took care of all the repatriation details. Thrash and Birdy accompanied Mr. Natambe, and Mrs. Natambe drove her sons in the other pickup to the mortuary where a viewing was to be conducted for the family.

Thrash and Birdy remained outside the viewing room while the family gathered around the open casket. After some time, the family emerged. Mrs. Natambe invited them to early dinner at a local restaurant. They knew the owners very well. The surviving sons never said a word.

Before dinner was served Thrash presented the portfolio case to Pico's parents.

"You don't need me to tell you again how talented Pico was as a painter," said Thrash, presenting them with the case of Pico's work.

"But I do want you to tell us again Brother Davis--and thank you," said Mrs. Natambe. Thrash knew the weight on him from Honoraria's death was also on Mrs. Natambe. It was her collapsed shoulders, and she appeared to labor keeping her head high. She was otherwise a hold-your-head-high woman. Thrash bowed his head towards Mrs. Natambe. He had much more to say, and did not disappoint.

"And...his love for his family...well, when you view his work, you'll see," said Thrash. Mrs. Natambe thanked them as she placed the artwork case next to her, her left hand remaining on the case.

Thrash told them about him leaving the order to marry Honoraria. He described Honoraria with a passioned urgency, her loss still deeply affecting him. He told the Natambe's about her excitement when she saw some of Pico's paintings. Thrash went on to talk about her gallery in Rome, now being run by Vanmeter, Birdy's best friend.

"I'm sure there will be many here in Ghana that will find his work excellent," said Thrash, getting nervous now that he thought the Natambe's may think he was up to something.

"I'm just saying--if Honoraria was still alive, she would use all her persuasion to convince Pico to let her showcase his work. And she was very persuasive, that I can promise you." Again, silence at the table.

Then Mrs. Natambe lifted her head high, her shoulders unfolded, and said, "Thank you Brother Davis. I know you wanted the best for Pico. You...and your mother too, may she rest in peace. I am very sorry for the loss of your wife, whom I'm sure was a wonderful woman for you to have left the order."

Birdy believed Mrs. Natambe, although there was a slight, yet perceptible edge to her words. He wasn't sure what she was thinking.

Thrash caught it, too. Leaving the order to get married. That's what he believed to be the source of her edginess. Of course, her oldest son is dead now, he thought to himself. It could be one thing, or everything.

She said nothing to Birdy regarding the circumstances of Pico's death. Birdy's relief could be felt by everyone at the table.

After a succinct good-bye from Mrs. Natambe, Mr. Natambe drove Thrash and Birdy to the airport while Mrs. Natambe drove her sons home. Mr. Natambe mentioned he didn't know when he could deliver the next crop of white pepper, but he'd let Birdy know soonest. Birdy thanked him, again sharing with Mr. Natambe the high compliments he received back in New York regarding the superb taste of his white pepper.

Knowing Pico wasn't to be buried until next week, Thrash and Birdy had booked the redeye flight that evening to Rome. They found an airport bar, and from there, drank their way to Italy.

Thrash wanted to talk about painting. "I have some of Pico's work still at the house--while he studied under my mother. I kept the painting he did of Honoraria. I just had to keep...for a while at least."

"I'm gonna copy him. I have to," said Thrash. He babbled on about trying to convince the Natambes to allow Vanmeter to present Pico's work at the gallery.

"I feel I owe it to Honoraria, and Pico, too," said Thrash.

"What about your paintings? Gonna let Vanmeter show your stuff, too?"

Thrash grinned. He finally got somewhat comfortable, closed his eyes and slept, still grinning. Birdy poked him now and then when his snoring started. Then Birdy fell asleep. Nearby passengers were unsure if their loud drunk talk was more preferable to their drunk snoring.

31

"I accept the challenge of getting Pico's parents to let me have a show for him," said Vanmeter, not withholding his excitement. He was thin, his beard returned, (well-trimmed this time around), and according to Thrash, Vanmeter's Italian seemed to be further improving.

"I'll handle it for now," said Thrash.

The three drank coffee in the apartment while they huddled around Thrash's laptop as he showed Vanmeter photos of Pico's paintings and sketches. Vanmeter was impressed, anxious to see them all and get copies of the photos at least. All the discussion about Pico's paintings was making Thrash very impatient to return and paint. He had to get Pico's work out of his system.

"Ok, now show me some photos of your paintings," said Vanmeter. "Birdy said your Honoraria collection is amazing. I want to be amazed."

Thrash smiled. "Not yet." Vanmeter kept at him, but Thrash did not budge.

"Look, if I'm gonna make it as an art dealer, I'm gonna need art to sell. Right now, I've got little left in the gallery, thanks to all of Honoraria's friends who bought most of the paintings, feeling sorry for me. I know of two artists, one alive and one now dead way before his prime. You are the painters I need."

"I assume you want me to succeed, for Honoraria, of course."

Thrash nodded. "Yeah, and for you too. You'll get to show them."

****

Vanmeter's Momma had already left for work. She was now taking the bus to the Duquesne campus where she worked in the kitchen, and as a dorm room cleaner when students hired her.

Before she started working, Vanmeter had to ensure she was sober. Two distressing weeks later, he was satisfied she could present herself well at the campus. Her remaining vices were caffeine and nicotine. The agreement was Clara would only quit smoking when she was ready. Vanmeter offered no argument.

"With a cig and a coffee, you fit right in here in Rome,' he said, not pleased in the least she couldn't quit smoking.

Clara shot back, "Not pleasant for me either--son. It's a gigantic city where everyone is going a hundred miles an hour. And they talk even faster. Can't speak Italian. Don't know a soul. Work in a kitchen. Clean dorm rooms and toilets. I mean, c'mon Vanmeter, this ain't no dream vacation. And, you're a lousy cook."

The two weeks were the most unpleasant he had ever spent with anyone, even himself. He would not let her out of his sight. She came with him to the gallery every day. They sounded like brother and sister yelling at each other--obnoxious teenagers. They screamed about stupid stuff. At least most of the fighting was in the gallery, after business hours. But not all the time. One fight in the apartment got the next-door neighbors riled up. They banged on the front door until Vanmeter and Clara finally quit yelling. But that time was over now.

He warned, "I'll learn to cook." Clara appeared unconvinced, but that put-on was for show, just between them. By the end of two weeks, she began to tolerate her new, strange routine. Barely. She hated foreign, and still hated having to speak Italian only for one hour a day with Vanmeter. My God, that boy has a dogged way about him, she thought, knowing that was his strength.

Clear enough, but my God she wanted to kick his ass up and down the streets of the damn city for it. Rome didn't seem like a holy city to Clara.

She softened a bit. "I never knew any nuns back home. Weren't any around, as you know. These nuns here are just fine. I believe they have tolerated me well, and haven't tried to convert me just yet." Clara smiled when she said that. Her teeth were still free of cigarette and coffee stains, to her complete amazement, musing, "Maybe it's a miracle. Everyone likes my smile."

"Then don't let the people down and take care of those chompers," said Vanmeter.

"One more month and they'll start paying me." She reminded Vanmeter she was still on kind of a probation period. It was Thrash who got her the job. No matter what, the campus administration loved Thrash. And Vanmeter was beginning to make an impression on the teachers and administration, too.

His Momma accompanied Vanmeter to Mass every Sunday at the campus chapel. She didn't think about Catholics one way or the other. Maybe that they were a bit strange. But she couldn't say much, with all her experience in her small church with the rattlers and moccasins. Christianity is just strange, she thought. Trying to make sense of all the suffering--that she understood was a human need. But did it make sense to try to make sense of it? She didn't think so.

She still remembered her fiery West Virginia preacher shouting, "The only way to heaven is through the Cross! Christ suffered, and we will suffer, through the cross, through the cross!"

But to suffer on purpose? Wasn't there enough suffering by accident or bad luck to go around for everyone, just because of the nature of things, little and big?

As utterly strange as she firmly believed the calling was, she did like the nuns. They were Godly women, she admitted, but she felt sorry for them. To be a nun seemed like suffering on purpose, and that made no sense.

Clara had more time to think about things than she ever did. The strangeness of everything around her began to dissipate once she realized that in this time-- going from the apartment to the campus, working until 4 pm and catching the bus back to the apartment, showering, then walking to the gallery to check on Vanmeter, together walking back to the apartment, buying dinner groceries first, cooking, cleaning up, watching some Italian TV, and going to bed--the strangeness of Rome began to slip away, just as dreams do when you awake. But, Clara knew, the strangeness was gone only because Vanmeter was here too. Without him--well--she never liked to think about him not being here.

Clara knew she kept him from finding a woman, and that was starting to trouble her. Maybe she should look for a man. But her tendency to gravitate to men no woman should be with was occupying her thoughts as of late. She had to rethink men altogether, she thought, watching them on the streets and on the bus. She wondered, an older man, a widower? Someone who wasn't a jackass. Someone who spent a moment or two thinking about somebody else besides themselves.

She didn't know where to start.

****

They all went to Thrash's favorite bar, and drank beer all afternoon. They talked excitedly about Birdy being a father, Thrash painting, and congratulating Vanmeter for helping his Momma regain her sense of self, even if it had to be across the Atlantic. The strangeness of meeting in Rome was also bandied about. Beers flowed. They shrugged, laughed, and had another beer. At this time, their individual thoughts were on all they'd been through separately, and together, were colored with a feeling of gratefulness.

Thrash was staying overnight at the Rome campus and returning to Pennsylvania tomorrow. Birdy would stay with Vanmeter, also returning tomorrow, on a different flight than Thrash.

That night, Vanmeter sensed Birdy was losing interest in being a trader. But he couldn't see him as a stay at home dad, either. That notion was strange, and everything seemed just beyond explicable these days.

He encouraged Birdy to return to Zanzibar to establish a contract with just Vin and Noro. He seemed to be waiting for Vanmeter to give him the nudge. Birdy agreed. He changed his plans, didn't announce the visit, intending to talk with only the brothers, and avoid Joseph altogether.

He was going back to Frieda from there.

32

The news was not unexpected, in fact, Frieda had been expecting to hear what was told her. She had more patients than she should. The demand was high. But to tell them all she could no longer be their doctor, that made her angry, which of course reinforced the mandate not to perform surgeries due to her elevated blood pressure, and risk of premature delivery.

"You can still be their doctor," said Birdy. He was careful on the subject, but he wasn't backing down. Frieda continued to be in no mood to listen, preferring to stew in frustration.

"You have no idea, so it's best to keep quiet," shot back Frieda. There was no comfortable position on their sofa. Her water weight gain made her feel like a hippo, she said, and maybe she would feel better floating around in a river.

Birdy had been back from Zanzibar for two weeks. Frieda's attitude hadn't changed since his return. She had zero interest in any part of Birdy and Thrash's trip. Wasn't interested in the latest about Vanmeter and his Momma. That surprised Birdy the most.

New York was warming up. The sun was bright the whole week, not a cloud about. Women responded by shedding coats and wearing short skirts. Men wore t-shirts in reaction to the warm week, rare, as they knew it would last only so long, before cold, blustery, and rainy days took over for a while longer. Birdy's mood was elevated by the sunny days. Frieda could care less if the sun shone. She never asked about Birdy securing a contract just with Vin and Noro, without Joseph in the mix. The latest shipment of cinnamon was impressive. Nor did she ask about the Natambe's deciding to stick with Birdy as their importer of white pepper. Mr. Natambe even went so far as to recommend to his friends that Birdy be their importer. Frieda's father was actually saying hello to him in the morning, and 'good evening' as he walked down the stairs to go home. Frieda's mother offered only an occasional head nod, grudgingly given. On her face was not a smile, just her lips stretched across her face, for a moment, then gone. Birdy was staying longer hours at work. Mr. Wassergold couldn't blame him.

"Frieda said some terrible things to us last time she visited," he reminded Birdy. Birdy remembered. She was on a tear, and she didn't leave him out either.

What precipitated her funk slide, Birdy later found out, was when her senior partner at their practice, a dear friend of her parents, pulled Frieda aside.

"You're not returning until your attitude improves. I built this practice and you will not be the one who brings it down."

Dr. Mandel lectured Frieda that if she thought she was the only woman in all of civilization who was miserable while pregnant, that's what he characterized it, then human kind would have gone the way of the dodo bird some time ago. This did not sit well with Frieda. If she was in reach of scalpel, Dr. Mandel's balls would now be adorning the top of his head.

All the while, Birdy was learning to become the best cook he could be. He was not going to be that guy who could not serve whatever entrée his miserably pregnant wife demanded.

Their sofa was where she spent most of the day, flicking between cable news shows, and getting herself worked up over Beltway politics. Lathered up TV personalities chattering about the existential crisis's of our time, even competing with climate change. She never watched TV until now.

Frieda began texting Birdy's sister in Berkley. Frieda didn't know his sister, and got her number from Birdy's mother. It was a conversation with Arlene Wire about her daughter that Frieda never forgot. She felt terrible as Arlene described her own daughter's change. Arlene didn't know what happened. She attended Berkley, and after her first semester, she never returned home to Pittsburgh. On that last visit, her daughter gathered them in the living room.

Arlene said, "Patti gave us an ultimatum, either actively support me and what I believe in, and renounce what I don't, or I will never come back."

The Wires were shocked. Renounce Christianity? Renounce the United States? Renounce the traditional family? They refused. The daughter, anticipating their response, went to her room, grabbed her packed bags and walked out, demanding no one talk to her or follow her. Porter B followed her out of the house. She screamed one continuous scream until the Uber driver mercifully arrived early.

Once a month Arlene and Porter B left a phone message, asking how she was, and that they love her. Patti never returned the calls.

It was at this time that Frieda thought to reach out to their daughter. It was an impulse that grew into a temptation.

Before Birdy had closed the apartment door, Frieda said, "You know, your sister is very smart. She keeps up with politics, I mean right up to the latest news event. She's very insightful. You should speak with her more often."

"My sister's a true believer. There's nobody who can change her mind. Above all, any man."

"Maybe she has every reason to not trust men. Maybe something happened to her," said Frieda, now getting off the sofa and following Birdy to the kitchen. He grabbed the bottle of bourbon from the cupboard and poured himself two fingers worth.

"Hungry?" he asked.

"No."

"When did you last eat?" Birdy had stopped mentioning to Frieda she was too thin. "I don't remember," she replied, just short of being curt. He went and sat down on the opposite side of the sofa where Frieda had been laying all day.

Standing in front of Birdy, Frieda said, "You know, your sister has got me thinking about all kinds of things. I feel like I've been living in a bubble when I listen to her."

After deciding it was a noble attempt to reconcile Birdy's sister with her family, Frieda gave little further thought as to why she reached out to Birdy's sister.

"What have you been missing?" Birdy didn't want to ignore Frieda, but he also had no desire to continue the discussion, especially when his sister was involved. "Everything!" Frieda plopped down on the sofa. But she was not really preoccupied by the cable news people. They were a distraction to what she had been contemplating of late. It was what Birdy's sister had said about her pregnancy. It was Birdy's sister who said, "It's morally wrong to bring another human being into the world until we get the right people to change every aspect of this shameful country."

Over the span of a few phone calls and furious flurry of texts, Birdy's sister convinced Frieda to rethink her entire life--being married, starting and raising a family. But she had already done that. Frieda thought about the freedom and flexibility to fully aspire to the top of her profession. Of what is of value in her life, and what is not of value to her.

Birdy's sister went on to say, "Think about your life, your career, what's important to you, yes. But more important, what's important for the future of us all. That's your responsibility. It's not a sacrifice at all, you are contributing in a very real way to the future of us all, the future of this world."

Frieda had already thought about what responsibility did she have, to whom, and why. Whether she was acquiescing to Birdy, a man.

She thought about it before, and again now--when is it too late to change your mind? Depends on what's at stake, of course. Besides myself, whom else do I have to answer to? Why do I owe anyone else an answer? To Birdy? Because he was traumatized by being a fleeting witness to a partial birth abortion? Certainly not. To Birdy? Because he is the father?

Frieda was not sleeping well, and Birdy's sister made her think about it all, again. She was determined to have a conversation with her obstetrician on her next checkup.

Now Birdy was not going to question Frieda about what she and his sister texted or talked about. But he knew that his sister's hatred of him had not dimmed. His sister lumped him into the category of men in general. He was 'one of them', she told him repeatedly before she ceased all contact. Her anger was always close at hand, begging like a dog to be stroked at any potential opportunity. Where did the anger come from? Was it a traumatic relationship or encounter? When did she begin to feed her anger? What was she expecting to grow? Not knowing any answers to the whys, Birdy was convinced of the result. His sister became poisoned, and spread poison.

Birdy wasn't sure if Frieda was starting to become angry. He finished his bourbon, returned to the kitchen and took out two pre-made meals from the refrigerator, set the oven to bake at 375 degrees, and poured himself another.

"I'm not hungry," said Frieda, now watching TV with mute on, and captions on.

Birdy ignored Frieda, heated both meals, set the table, and returned to the sofa. The TV personalities were still lathered up, and still chattering about the mounting existential crisis's of the times.

When time to eat, Frieda remained on the sofa watching TV. Birdy noticed she didn't seem to be interested one way or the other what the TV people said. She was staring at the TV, not watching it. He finished his meal, put Frieda's dinner in a left-over container, returning it to the refrigerator, fully recognizing the absurdity of his actions.

He asked Frieda what else she would like. She said she didn't want anything. He sat on the sofa and watched the cable news program on mute, and read the captions.

"When's your next checkup?"

Still staring at the TV, Frieda replied, "Two days."

"I'd like to go with you on this visit," he said.

Frieda turned her head and snarled, "Why? What's so special about my next visit?" He nodded his head and said nothing. Her glare didn't seem as if she meant it, he thought, and silence was critical.

But he couldn't help himself.

"I love you," he said, leaning closer to Frieda. She turned her shoulder, and returned to staring at the TV.

"Yeah, I know. Thanks for the offer, but I'll go alone to my next checkup."

33

Clara told Vanmeter she was uncertain if her prayers had any influence. Vanmeter insisted otherwise.

"Yeah? How so?" pressed Clara, curious, but mainly pinging Vanmeter to see what he'd say next. They were getting along as of late. Clara was now earning under the table wages working at the campus. She was talking with the nuns more, as they seemed to have a curious interest in her.

"The fact is, Frieda is doing much better now, according to Birdy. She's even going back to work part time at the practice. Not performing surgeries, but seeing patients again."

"That may be a fact, but it's not a fact that prayer helped," said Clara, not necessarily pressing Vanmeter on his proclamation, but pressing on the fact that he tended to make proclamations, not based at all on facts.

Vanmeter shrugged.

A month ago, Frieda's last check-up had gotten her obstetrician worked up. Frieda's blood pressure was too high, she was too thin, the baby was too lethargic, and Frieda was not talking calmly about why an abortion may be the best thing for humanity. Her doctor cut her off in mid-rant and called the desk to start admission procedures. Soon Frieda was sedated and located to her own room. Her doctor called Birdy and advised him to come to the hospital. He came straight away.

"Have you two discussed abortion? If so, why am I hearing about it for the first time today?" Frieda's obstetrician was very worked up. She was past sixty, thought Birdy. She reminded him of the older flight attendants, still working after 35 years plus, and senior to secure only the choice overseas routes. They were tough old gals. Most still took care of the passengers, as if they were their own kids, and grandkids. Dr. Ravens was still interested in her patients. Birdy read that doctors were horrible patients. He asked Frieda later if that were true, and she ignored the question.

Dr. Ravens watched Birdy begin to pale. He collapsed in the waiting room seat, looking as if he'd been notified his condition was terminal. She left him alone for five minutes. She too needed the time to regroup. Upon her return Birdy received a lecture on the responsibility of the father during pregnancy. She was forceful but not harsh, although she was clearly out of sorts, as Birdy's mother would say, not so much at Birdy, but as to the very thought of contemplating abortion, after trying so hard to get pregnant. It was the first time any patient of hers had ever appeared to change her mind about giving birth. Dr. Ravens was as stunned as Birdy, although she knew she shouldn't be. She had three children of her own. She wasn't in her profession to facilitate choices, but to contribute to birth.

The only thing he could say to Dr. Ravens was that he strongly believed Frieda needed to get back to work, in some capacity. He never mentioned his sister.

While Frieda was in the hospital Birdy got her a new phone number. His anger towards his sister surfaced upon his thought of her, but he prevented it from rising to the level to drown his concern for Frieda and their baby. He had worked hard before to never think of his sister, and soon, he again never thought of her. It was not a matter of forgiveness. It was a matter of self-protection from a contagion of hatred. Birdy was at ease in letting God judge him for his act of self-protection.

Dr. Ravens demanded Frieda remain in the hospital under observation for three days. Birdy visited every evening, after Dr. Ravens made her last round. In 32 hours, Frieda had an appetite again, even finding the bad hospital food palatable. She never asked for her phone. She stopped watching TV mid-morning on the second day, spending her time reading medical literature she asked Birdy to bring. Her parents visited every morning. They knew nothing of Frieda's disposition prior to admittance, just the doctor's concern for the baby.

At work, during this time, Frieda's mother began saying 'good morning' to Birdy. He replied, and smiled. Mrs. Wassergold had not yet managed to do the same. Mr. Wassergold, on the other hand, would stop by and talk to Birdy about spices, always asking about how he was doing.

On third day, Frieda came home, restless to get back to work--never speaking of the incident, as if she excised it from reality. That was fine with Birdy, who had no stomach to ever talk about it again. It had become clear in his mind what his priorities were, and as these priorities became a guide for him, he found himself thankful for the outcome of the affair. But he harbored a persistent, low worry in general about his wife. He wasn't sure the old Frieda had fully returned.

Frieda and her mother now talked on the phone almost every day, usually when both were at work. Before, it was every other week. Mr. Wassergold would stop by Birdy and Frieda's apartment on some weekends, with little prior notice. He never stayed long, maybe five minutes, but long enough to hug his daughter and shake Birdy's hand and ask about their plans for the rest of the day.

"You call him MM, the name of a chocolate coated, colored peanut for God's sake?" Clara was letting her Appalachian twang fly. She always had the ability to dial up or down her accent, depending on who she was talking to. Vanmeter the same way, although he learned to almost completely hide his. But not when talking with his Momma. They reverted back to the years when she was barely eighteen, raising a rambunctious five year old, mostly by herself.

"I never knew his real name, at first. I had to give him a name, didn't I? -- and I did," answered Vanmeter. Clara pretended she was on his case. She was feeling pretty well, and she didn't mind thinking so.

"MM, the Materials Man, the very same guy who gave me the key to the storage room full of painting stuff," said Vanmeter.

"The same man you galivanted over Eastern Europe with, or so you claim," scoffed Clara.

"Yep, that guy."

"It remains abundantly clear to me why you don't tell me most things about your goin's on. Because I think you know full well that I'm doubtful--to say the very least."

Vanmeter's shrug was his signal he knew nothing else should be said, no matter what. What he told her might could be the way it is, as a matter of fact, but then it didn't matter what she thought about it, being true or otherwise. Whether or not she believed him, Vanmeter always told her the truth--when he decided to tell Clara anything. He was fine with the way it was between them.

It was MM who stopped by the gallery while Vanmeter had stepped out for a coffee. It was MM who enchanted Clara in less than ten minutes, giving him permission to unload a small van's worth of crated paintings to the back of the gallery.

By the time Vanmeter returned, MM was gone. Clara blushed hard as she described him. It stopped Vanmeter from getting worked up about his unannounced visit.

He most definitely matched the description his Momma gave, from his trimmed mustache and thick salt and pepper hair, cut like a movie star, down to the stylish, zip up the side brown boots he wore all the time Vanmeter had been with him. Always in a bespoke blue suit, crisp white shirt, and no tie. "He's not real tall, though" she said.

"Said he has your number. Said he'd be in touch," said Clara.

Vanmeter shot back, "And what else?" Vanmeter knew there was a 'what else'.

"I'm going out," announced Clara, going into the back room, grabbing her light coat from the corner pedestal.

"Told me to tell you to check out the paintings today. His employer wants your opinion," said Clara. Her 'as a matter of fact' tone and her lightness in step leaving the gallery re-calibrated Vanmeter's thoughts at the moment.

"Get his real name then, if you're so interested," Vanmeter said aloud to himself after the front door closed, smiling as he watched his Momma walk away. He locked the door and hustled to the back room.

MM brought along two men to deliver thirteen crates of various sizes. With care, Vanmeter crowbarred open two crates he chose at random. Each painting was meticulously protected in layers--covered in a dark, thick plastic bag, bound by foam insulation boards and cardboard, and wrapped by what seemed to be an outrageous amount of high-end packing tape. While unpacking, he had plenty of time to imagine the contents, but making some money was his primary thought. That would be molto bene, seriously molto bene, he thought.

He then decided to unwrap all the paintings but not remove the last covers, instead he'd wait to remove them at the same time, with the paintings facing away from him. He turned them all around. After doing so, he left the back room and went to his desk, pulled out the bottle of bourbon, poured four fingers worth, returning to the paintings--eyes closed.

Vanmeter had no originals left in the gallery. Instead, he carried quality prints of classic paintings Rome tourists might be tempted to buy. He was relying on monthly contributions from Thrash to pay the bills. Thrash was still in conversations with Pico's parents to permit Vanmeter to showcase Pico's work. Given his death, it wasn't a subject to push too hard. Although Mr. and Mrs. Natambe seemed willing to give Vanmeter the opportunity, there was no timeline for a decision, and Vanmeter's frustration level ticked up a few notches. He knew he could sell Pico's work, because he believed in his gut Pico's work would sell.

And Thrash? Birdy had told him about his paintings--Vanmeter had yet to see any of them. The collection was a definite crap shoot, Vanmeter concluded, but that crap shoot was deemed high stakes by his own account, and therefore energized him more than Pico's paintings.

What was clear in the flash of a moment was none of it was making sense. For the moment.

Thirteen paintings leaned against the wall. Vanmeter took his first sip of bourbon, thinking of the first time he met Kule Fat. Still wanted in the U.S. to stand trial for a list of charges, but no longer in the news. Vanmeter thought about what that meant, or implied.

After Vanmeter's second sip, he opened his eyes.

Within seconds of viewing all the paintings, disappointment overcame him. He found himself wrestling in his mind what he could realistically expect to get for them. Also within seconds he was able to see the theme of the collection, as he assessed the monetized potential of each by itself, and together as a collection. Vanmeter knelt to the floor--looking for a signature. Sliding by each painting, he located Kule Fat's logo-ized version of K and F together, the same as his chef logo.

Vanmeter stood up and slid a metal chair over, sitting down by each painting. He was two fingers into his four finger pour. He ignored the screech of the chair sliding across the concrete floor as he maneuvered in front of each of Kule Fat's works.

Halfway through the paintings disappointment gave way to a creeping realization--something he saw in Fat's work. Were they really nothing like Pico's or Thrash's paintings? Was there similarity? Not overt, not copying. They seemed all to be realist painters, Vanmeter thought. But there was a twist.

Then Vanmeter lifted the chair and sat about fifteen feet from all the paintings. As he finished his bourbon, his Momma snuck in the back room. Clara waited a while before telling about her little adventure, watching her son stand up and confront each painting again, as if demanding an answer from each one.

"You are not gonna believe this, but I swear to you MM's name is Michel--fancy name for Michael I reckon-- Michel Maritain. Sounds French, but I have no earthly idea what his accent is, which don't sound French to me. Probably a fake name. That man can charm, let me tell you."

His Momma not saying anything about the paintings confirmed to Vanmeter his immediate challenge. Kule Fat was bringing the pressure. Vanmeter had every intention to deliver. Now he had two collections that were crap shoots, one in front of him, and Thrash's, yet to be delivered. A conversation with Kule Fat was in order.

"I'm going back to the apartment, unless you need somethin", said Clara. He was too preoccupied, she thought. She had yet to get all excited about paintings. The nuns encouraged her to visit the Vatican Museum. She told them she would, but she wasn't in much of a hurry. Clara had high confidence in her son about most things, but getting into the business of selling paintings was something she never gave a thought. Why would she? Walking back to the apartment she almost started worrying about him, but Michel had made an impression. Just a ten minute chat over a cup of expresso and a cigarette. She allowed herself to have certain thoughts again. The sun was out. She didn't mind the gusts sending her hair in all sorts of directions. Free, that's what Clara thought, she felt free. But she wasn't going to spoil her mood by thinking about what she was free of.

Vanmeter poured a sip of bourbon as he turned on his laptop. Opening the folders of photos of Pico's paintings, Vanmeter sat in front of Fat's work, studying Pico's paintings, comparing them. Now he wasn't sure. He always had the discipline not to fall into the well of his own digging, the well that held the water of wishful thinking. Not this time, either, he told himself. He turned off the laptop and put it back on his desk, next to his empty glass. After locking up, he walked.

The wind's bluster was blunting an otherwise nice walk, he thought. Instead of going right, back to the apartment, he went left. As he continued, he realized he'd never gone left after leaving the gallery. The realization soon softened him up a bit, and he thought about Thrash Davis. There was something about all of their paintings. Some connection, something. He wanted first to talk to Thrash.

Urban hawks. Red-tailed hawks, specifically, were on Frieda's mind. Little Bernard, precious boy, would not stop talking about them on his visits. His scoliosis was borderline operable. There were known risks. A long, painful recuperation period. Likelihood of a better life of course, depended. His parents worried. He was ready for the operation. Frieda envied his fearlessness.

Bernard wanted to know all the details of Frieda's pregnancy. He had no brothers and sisters. Loved babies. Wanted to hug them, all of them. Bernard had the vocabulary of a freshman college student, at age seven. Red-tailed hawks and babies were what Bernard talked about.

Later, Frieda imagined being a red-tailed hawk, maybe the one that perched on Bernard's window during a furious snowstorm last winter, unable to get back to the nest. But, as Bernard told the story, as soon as the snow stopped falling sideways, the hawk took off. And its instincts were sound. Very soon the snow storm backed off, and within a half hour the front had passed.

But what's a day in the life of a New York City hawk, and the observations Frieda, as a hawk, would make in her business of feeding herself and family? What would she see? She knew nothing of hawks, red-tailed or otherwise. What would she notice? What would make fixed impressions on her?

There was another patient, while aboard the E.A.C.H.S., who moved Frieda more than the others. They all moved her, but most could not speak English or would not talk with her during the course of their stay. Even after surgery, when it was clear their lives were changed, their growths removed, their appearances close to the kids their age, they said little. But not Asha, she spoke English and was as fearless as Bernard. Asha and Bernard would hit it off straightaway. She was not a pretty girl to begin with. The orange sized growth between her left eye and ear marked her as grotesque. But she refused to stay at home, refused to be hidden away. It was as if the legendary boxer Mohammed Ali had possessed Asha--she was a big fan. She had guts and swagger for a tiny girl. She quoted Ali when she was in pain, when she was bullied.

"Ali says, impossible is not a fact. It's an opinion. It's a dare. And that's what I say."

"I believe in you," she told Frieda, moments before going under for the nine hour surgery. What child tells her surgeon that, wondered Frieda?

When the time came to remove the bandages, Asha stood at the mirror, next to her mother, and Frieda. Asha inspected her face closely, lightly touching her pronounced scar. The swelling was almost gone.

"You might not need to look pretty to be beautiful, but it helps," said Asha. She extended her hand towards Frieda.

"Thank you," said Asha. Frieda bent down and kissed her fresh scar, and whispered, "You are beautiful." Asha's mother erupted in tears.

Bernard was undaunted when his parents decided not to go ahead with the surgery.

"I'm waiting until you have your baby, and then you can do my operation," Bernard told Frieda.

Frieda extended her hand to Bernard. They shook hands.

"Deal," winked Frieda. She never saw Bernard again.

As a red-tailed hawk high above, looking across and back through the years, Frieda viewed a clear picture of what she had now. She didn't want to know the future. It was not hers to have. She had plenty already, she thought. Plus, she had the names for their baby, whether a daughter or son.

36

Harold Wassergold hustled downstairs from his office and caught up with Birdy as he was leaving for the day. Myra was on the phone, as usual, working her passive aggressive magic of intimidation and flattery on a seasoned supplier.

While walking, he said to Birdy, "Look, I'm just trying to live my life out in crazy times and attitudes that disturb me almost as much as those days back in Germany. Not quite, but almost. I could see the sixties happening, a lot of us could. It was little surprise. The seventies on--until now, you know, I was working to build the business. I didn't look up and out much for a long time. We stayed local, very local. I include Florida as local, you know."

Harold caught his breath, wanting Birdy to slow his walk, but not wanting to tell him outright. Birdy didn't think about his pace. His pace was his pace. Thank God for the red light, thought Harold.

"Believe me when I tell you, I'm not sure whether to die as a retiree or not. That seems to me to be giving up. I don't follow sports, don't read for pleasure. Gambling bores me. Music is nice but, I'm not a fanatic. Travel? To where? I like to work, build a business. Myra, the same. I'm lucky. Then one day, I'll die. I want to die first but that's very selfish. I should die last, and honor the memories. But that also means I have to live in crazy times. I get tired of living in crazy times. But I tell you this, I'm not letting crazy times win out."

Birdy thought of his father after listening to Mr. Wassergold. Now Birdy learned that Mr. Wassergold would too say something, just like Porter B, but not actually reveal now that something he either wanted to say, or might say later--or, not say at all.

"How's Frieda?" asked Mr. Wassergold. He clasped Birdy's elbow for a brief moment, startling Birdy.

He whispered, "Has the old Frieda returned yet?"

Birdy stopped and stared at Mr. Wassergold, now stepping back to move closer to the department store window to avoid the fast-moving crowds on the sidewalk.

Mr. Wassergold caught his breath. Thoughts rushed his mind. Crazy times, thought Harold, looking at the mannequins behind the looming glass pane. He couldn't distinguish them from young men or women, not by their looks or what they wore. Until lectured recently by his wife, he still thought queer was queer. But not so. So many classifications now, and all of them really from within a tiny percentage of everyone. But that wasn't supposed to be the point. He shrugged. None of his business. He felt lucky he had a daughter that was going to have a baby. Harold was looking forward to focusing on his daughter, her baby, and Birdy too. He liked Birdy. He didn't have to be distracted by all the other goings on in the world. He could stick to his business with Myra, and his first grandbaby. He thought he'd never have a grandbaby the way things go now. Such prosperity we have now! Just little things to worry about, but blowing them up into ten feet tall boogey men. No such thing as a boogey woman? He had thoughts otherwise.

Birdy could see Mr. Wassergold was not staring at him but just slightly passed him. Birdy waited until Mr. Wassergold's eyes returned to Birdy. It wasn't too long, but the pause was long enough.

Birdy finally replied, "You noticed too?"

About Frieda, or the mannequins? Mr. Wassergold said this to himself, turning away from the mannequins staring at him, smiling now because he recognized a bar he used to frequent years ago when he was a regular drinker. Now, not so much. Lost interest in drinking too, he thought to himself. He used to love to drink. He tucked his arm into Birdy's and led him to the corner. They crossed the street in silence, as life around them blared. Inside was busy and blaring too, and they found a high table opposite the long bar, halfway down.

"Ever been here?" asked Mr. Wassergold.

Birdy shook his head. Unlike his father, bars never became a habit for him.

"I was a regular here when Giuliani was mayor. He was a great mayor."

"I'm having a Manhattan...you?" asked Mr. Wassergold.

"Rye, neat. Bulleit," said Birdy. Harold went up to the bartender and ordered for them both. Harold turned around and surveyed the old bar as if looking to buy the place. Much fancier now than back then he thought, and the clientele more Birdy's age. He asked the bartender about Jonathon, the main bartender back when Harold used to frequent the place. The bartender said he had been working there for going on six years and never heard of a Jonathon. Harold nodded. Jonathon was older than Harold, a survivor of the camps. Harold knew, but he doubted anybody else did. He settled the tab, grabbed the drinks and placed Birdy's rye in front of him.

"To your baby. Wishing good health--for everyone," toasted Mr. Wassergold.

"Now, you were about to say something about Frieda," said Harold Wassergold, settling into his stool. His lower back would remind him later of stool sitting at his age.

"She's back at work, that's good, and talking with Mrs. Wassergold more often, it seems. I assume that's good too." Harold nodded and then angled his head quickly sideways, as his eyes glanced towards the ceiling. Birdy took that to mean exactly what Mr. Wassergold wanted his expression to mean.

"Hard to say about Mrs. Wassergold. Unless she comes out and says it, she can fool you that she's thinking one way, and it's another," remarked Harold. The Manhattan was as tasty as he remembered it being. He might want to have one now and again. But all his old bar mates were either dead or no longer out and about.

Birdy wasn't sure what Mr. Wassergold was after, or whether he knew about Frieda talking about an abortion. He wasn't saying anything to anybody about that.

"She misses surgery, but she's not down about it. I think she's adjusting to working in an office that's not aboard ship. I do think she missed working on that hospital ship. From listening to her, she loved it."

Harold nodded his head. "She wrote letters then. Old fashioned these days. But we loved getting them. We were worried. She kept telling us not to. She loved being on that boat."

"You don't have to worry about me, Mr. Wassergold. I love Frieda and I'm gonna be a solid father. Solid," said Birdy, lifting his glass towards Harold.

Harold nodded. "You've done well getting our little spice import business going. Didn't know what would happen, didn't know much about that business. But the chefs want those peppers and cinnamon."

"Frieda has started talking again about interviewing an au pair. We'll need one if I stay working. To afford an au pair the business needs to grow."

Birdy was coming to expect Mr. Wassergold's nod. Or maybe it was less expectation and more of a want.

"Father's stay at home these days more and more. I read that," said Mr. Wassergold. His delivery was like that of a TV person rote reading a teleprompter.

"Yeah," said Birdy, not getting the nod his was hoping for.

"Got any names picked out for the baby?" asked Mr. Wassergold, almost half way through his glass. Birdy noticed the Manhattan wasn't lasting long, and felt compelled to match Mr. Wassergold's pace.

"We haven't talked about that much. We'll make two lists since we both agreed not to know whether it's a boy or girl until that time."

The bar was full, the din rising. Birdy then matched Mr. Wassergold's slowed sipping pace, as Harold realized he was too quick.

They sat in silence for a time. Mr. Wassergold finished his Manhattan, and struggled to stand from the high table. His angry back was talking to him.

"Well, I'm very excited for you both--and Mrs. Wassergold is too, you know."

Birdy nodded, shook Harold's hand and thanked him for the drink. They walked out of the bar together and down the rest of the block in silence. Engulfed in the sidewalk crowd, they said nothing more to each other. At the corner, Mr. Wassergold grabbed Birdy's elbow. Birdy nodded. After Harold let go, Birdy turned the corner and walked home.

Birdy never did answer his question about Frieda, thought Harold. He crossed the street, ignoring the mannequins he stared at earlier.

Or maybe, Birdy did.

"I can tell you; he's not going to be doing much more in our business. The spice adventure was just an idea that came to me," said Frieda's mother. Myra called Frieda after three-thirty, knowing she did not have patients for the rest of the day.

"What's he going to do for a living?" pressed Mrs. Wassergold. This conversation was an extension of the last two Frieda had with her mother. More like Groundhog's Day than an extension, Frieda thought.

Frieda interrupted, "I know the seeds you're planting in my mind, Mother."

In the beginning when her mother started calling on a regular basis, the conversations were such that Birdy's name never needed mentioning. Frieda enjoyed those conversations, not because Birdy wasn't in them, but because it was like talking with a mother that she always wanted but never had. They talked about other things.

Frieda was not only angry that she never suspected her mother would then shift the conversation to Birdy, but angry at the things she suggested, and even angrier, because what her mother suggested was no surprise at all--not from her.

"No, it is not one mistake, now two," monotoned Frieda, parroting her mother's refrain.

"Zero mistakes, Mother, zero."

"And, it's you who must get over it. You." Frieda decided she was only texting her mother from now on. Her mother hated texting.

"And...his name's Birdy. Goodbye Mother," declared Frieda.

As Frieda hung up, Myra winced, pinching her eyebrows together with thumb and middle finger. After a while, she yelled out, "Such a preposterous name."

No one was around. Harold was out with Birdy. Myra knew, because she watched Harold chase down the stairs just after Birdy left work. She slumped back in her chair, pinching her eyebrows together.

We don't have friends anymore, she thought. They're all gone. Why is that? Never mind. But if we did, what would they say? I know what they would say, she thought. But we'd never hear it from them. But we would know what they were saying. We would know.

And they would be right.

"I know you haven't said anything. I really haven't given you the chance."

It had been a long time since Frieda and Vanmeter talked. She texted him for a good time to call. She was calling to check in on him after he moved his Momma into hospice.

"You've told all this to Birdy?" asked a stunned Vanmeter. It was the first time in the thirty-minute conversation that he said anything--other than saying to Frieda, "Momma was doing as expected, I guess."

"You mean me ranting about an abortion to protect the planet? Birdy knows all about that from my OB GYN. We haven't talked about it since. No need."

Her humiliation was bearable because of Birdy, for reasons she felt wasn't her right to question. Vanmeter tucked that away for another time--when he and Birdy would get together.

Not long ago, Thrash had texted Vanmeter informing him Mr. and Mrs. Natambe agreed to have Vanmeter represent Pico's work, also permitting Birdy to escort Pico's paintings to Rome. This was after Birdy stopped by Pemba to inspect a new shipment of cinnamon. Vanmeter was waiting for Thrash to reply back. He wanted to talk again about representing the Honoraria Collection. Vanmeter had a fine plan, and Clara thought so too.

"And what led you to believe two weeks before your son's birth that he was going to need major surgery right away?" He liked the name Bernard. There was no reason, she told Vanmeter. There was a reason, and it was conjured out of the air in response to wanting to have a feeling of foreboding. Foreboding gave her a strange sense of comfort for a short time, for reasons she could not explain. Vanmeter sensed Frieda wanted him to ask the 'why' and 'what were you thinking' questions. But he did not.

"Now the surgery fantasy, I didn't tell Birdy about. I was afraid what he might think. Like, just who in the hell did he marry?"

"And Bernard, he's fine, right?"

"Oh God, yes." Vanmeter now had plenty of pictures of Bernard. Vanmeter listened to the story of why Frieda chose Bernard for a boy and Asha for a girl.

"And your au pair, she's working out too?"

"Yes, yes. She's Austrian. Hannah. She's twenty, speaks German, French, and Italian. Not too pretty." Vanmeter wasn't touching that remark.

Frieda told him she liked her job, and she was studying up to prepare to return to surgery. She told him she was saddened over the decision not to operate on the other Bernard. His parents sought other opinions, and she hasn't seen Bernard since.

"Alright. You seem to be doing fine Frieda. Your parents are good, you and Birdy are good."

Frieda's sigh was audible. "We are, I am, and yes, we are" she said.

"So, you're not crazy, then."

She laughed. He was not going to ask if any other thoughts were going through her mind. But he suspected she was one who had certain thoughts stand up now and then, and were difficult to kill off and bury.

Frieda used him as her confessor, without a doubt, thought Vanmeter. How Catholic of her. He was used to it. Others had too. His Momma had often enough, especially these days.

Frieda finally remembered Clara was in hospice and expressed her sorrow. Vanmeter recited all the medical details regarding ovarian cancer he was told by the doctor. Frieda asked no follow-up questions. She thought of the expense.

Clara agreed to become a Catholic, not quite getting all the requisites accomplished. Duquesne had taken her on as an employee with benefits, and Kule Fat's no interest loan, arranged by Michel Maritain, was paying for the remainder.

"Smokin' didn't get me, my woman parts did," Clara said, one long night.

He decided against telling Frieda about Michel Maritain, aka MM, the Materials Man, who visited Clara daily. A relationship Vanmeter had no burning interest to understand. Mysteries were a good thing.

Vanmeter definitely was not going to mention Lia, the woman born in California but lived in Italy since she was ten. Nor her current occupation. Maybe a story for Birdy.

"You live in Rome. Still so strange. I miss you," Frieda told him.

"You lived on a ship off the African coast. Miss you too. I'll be back Stateside in a short while, I imagine. And I'll see you and cute little baby Bernard then."

Frieda hung up thinking Vanmeter must really be relieved to never have pursued her.

Vanmeter poured a single finger of bourbon. Before taking a sip, he received a text from the MM, who was at the hospital. After reading the text he stared at his glass, and put it down on the desk. There would be plenty of time to drink afterwards. He grabbed his jacket, locked up the galleria, and began a quick walk down the street, searching for a cab.

While still searching for a cab, Vanmeter slowed his walk. He began to recite aloud the exchange between he and his Momma every time before he left her bed side.

"Anythin' else to tell me?"

"I've said evethin' I could ever think of, Momma."

"Me too."

"We've said plenty to each other."
"We have. We're lucky, we are."
"Yes, we are."
"I love you."
"I love you too, Momma."

"Clara had more friends than she'd ever expected at the end of her life. She told me many times when I was much younger she was to die alone, and that she had started preparing early. It bothered me that I never knew what she meant by that. It wasn't something I'd care to think about further."

"To save her life the best I could, I had to put her on a plane and fly her to Rome, of all places. We're from nowhere-ville West Virginia. And it came to be the right decision, because of you all, your generosity, kindness, and compassion."

"And she became a Catholic, no less. Never would I have predicted that."

"Everyone here today, I thank you for coming. My Momma, Clara, I know is very happy."

The first out of the chapel was Kule Fat, who sat for the entire service in the far back pew, alone. Michel Maritain sat with Birdy and Vanmeter up front. The nuns, teachers, students, and administrative types clustered together on the left side. Soon the nuns left to set up the refreshments in the cafeteria.

Addressing Vanmeter, Michel Maritain said, "I will miss Clara very much, and I will pray for her soul every day." He bowed, and left.

Birdy and Vanmeter were still cloudy from last night.

Pico's paintings were now in the gallery, and the night before, while opening the crates, they finished off a bottle of exceptional Kentucky bourbon, compliments of Michel Maritain. Plus, a half case of Menabrea Bionda. They walked about and sat about, viewing both Fat's and Pico's paintings, all of them on the floor, leaning against every available wall space.

Looking around and waving, Vanmeter said, "What do I know about all these? They're interesting paintings, sure. I like Pico's use of color. His action. Fat's stuff is very different. Would I hang one of them in my apartment? Maybe you need an eye of a rich person to really see. What do they see?"

"I know what they see."

"They want to possess, in order to impress," said Birdy, proud of his Mohammad Ali rhyme.

"That's mo' definitely, exactly, correct," said Vanmeter.

Again and again, they drank to Vanmeter's Momma. Birdy showed pictures of Bernard. He was still in shock he had a son.

"That baby boy Bernard is way too cute," admired Vanmeter.

Birdy was preoccupied with Frieda's mental strength, and occasionally about Pico. He didn't know Pico, didn't blame himself for his death, but--he wondered why he didn't. That brought no sympathy from Vanmeter.

Vanmeter capped off his minor tirade by saying, "Stick to worrying about the living. And snap out of whatever stupefaction reverie you happen to be in, and get to it being a father." Birdy shrugged, then nodded vigorously, and slipped off the chair onto the floor.

"Stupefa--wha?" mumbled Birdy.

Vanmeter's phone buzzed in his back pocket. It stopped. Buzzed again. He looked at the phone. It was Thrash's number.

He answered the call.

Vanmeter threw his phone against the wall and it broke apart, scattering about the floor.

"When does it end?" he screamed. He pointed to Birdy and said, "Don't answer that."

Birdy sat on the floor, too drunk to know if Vanmeter meant the phone, or the question.

Thrash was found in his studio by the neighbor who looked after the property. He died painting. "Not sure yet how," the neighbor said, "awaiting the autopsy." Vanmeter wondered if the painting killed him.

40

Michel Maritain was back in the empty gallery, sitting in front of Vanmeter, who was behind his desk, finishing up notes on a legal pad.

"Amongst others, impatience is also a Fat trademark. These present times, it's dominant," said Michel Maritain, who did not share Fat's impatience. From what little Vanmeter knew of him, MM seemed to have actual disdain for impatience.

Vanmeter's phone buzzed in his back pocket. He motioned to Michel with his hand, and withdrew his phone. Birdy was boarding the plane back to New York.

"I didn't recognize him at the memorial, but I knew it was Fat. How much weight did he lose? Fifty pounds? And who knew he had hair?"

"Closer to seventy-five," said MM.

"He always prefers distance," said MM.

"Kinda challenging as a chef," said Vanmeter. MM's small smile wasn't necessary, thought Vanmeter. Getting to the point was. Vanmeter's flight back to the States left that evening. Vanmeter had formed three possibilities as to why MM was back, sooner than later. It was one of them, Vanmeter knew, or a hybrid of two, or all of them. He decided to talk first.

"I leave tonight. I'm going to Pennsylvania, settling Thrash's estate, packing up his Honoraria Collection at minimum, and returning to Rome. This place is too small. I'm going to have to rent another place to present Thrash's, Pico's, and Fat's paintings.

"I'm going to get hold of every contact Honoraria left me. She knew a lot of art types, and they know the money types."

"I need a lawyer to help me with this list of things," said Vanmeter, ripping the top sheet from the legal pad, the sheet Vanmeter filled with everything he could think of that needed to be considered--lawyer-wise and everything otherwise.

"It's not complete. I don't pretend to know things I don't know. I'm going to make sure Mr. and Mrs. Natambe get every Euro their son's paintings and prints fetch, and everything else that has to do with Pico. Fat gets what he gets. It's his art. Maybe he'd consider paying off my hospital debt as commission. And I'm getting everything that Thrash's work fetches. They're now my paintings."

Vanmeter was in the zone. There was no other place to be.

"Fat appreciates the idea of presenting his work with the other two. Resources, Fat has. A lawyer, Fat has. Contacts, Fat also has," said MM.

"I've got a price in mind for each painting of Fat's and Pico's. No idea if I'm even close," said Vanmeter, tearing out the next two pages of pricing and handing them to MM. On the back of every painting Vanmeter placed a piece of tape--F1, F2, and so on, and wrote an asking price. He did the same with Pico's paintings.

MM's smile was not helpful. He folded all three pages in half, and then half again, and slipped them inside his suit jacket.

"Fat is impatient with the timing of the showing. He wants it soon. I know it cannot be as soon as he desires," said MM.

"I ask you to be quick, as quick as you see fit, but be quick. Fat will support. I will secure a venue. The lawyer is involved. She is always involved."

"I am curious about what you call the Honoraria Collection. Any details you care to share?" said MM, rising from the chair.

"How about letting it be a surprise," said Vanmeter. Even during the whirlwind eight days he spent with MM in Eastern Europe, Vanmeter never got to know him. They sat in separate rows on the airplane over and back Stateside. MM only ate dinner, leaving Vanmeter to eat breakfast by himself, and skip lunch. None of which bothered Vanmeter. What bothered Vanmeter then was why MM was taking him on the trip. An interview, Vanmeter finally concluded. If the trip with MM was intended as anticipation of showing Fat's originals, that made kind of sense. Fat picked him for some reason, and discovered Vanmeter was out of options at the time. And now? Vanmeter only had one option, and he had no choice but to pursue it. But the option was given to him by Thrash, not Fat.

"Fat believes an event has happened that will soon spread. This belief has expanded his impatience. I'm in the habit of believing Fat," said MM.

"Thrash is my priority at the moment, Fat is not," declared Vanmeter. A meeting of the eyes took place in an instant. Vanmeter was confident his message had been received.

Changing tack, Vanmeter asked, "You and Fat...?"

"Short story, but never told," said MM. He bowed and left.

Vanmeter called Lia and invited her to dinner. There was a restaurant she'd been wanting to take him.

41

It was now odd to Birdy why Frieda had not mentioned the apartment being too small. Then again, it was odd that both he and Frieda never thought too much about the apartment being too small. And, what could it be that caused them both to not see what was now obvious? He thought for sure Mrs. Wassergold must have pointed this out to Frieda. Many, many times, he imagined.

These thoughts played over and over again in Birdy's mind, like a recorded drum loop--from boarding the plane in Rome until arriving by taxi to their apartment. During this time, the drum loop became more elaborate. Leveling off was when the notion of teleworking was added to the loop. Added almost simultaneously was where else to live besides the City. In the taxi, the most distracting sound within the incessant loop of beating thoughts entered--being a stay at home father with Bernard. This thought was a piercing, non-stop bang to the high-hat, and it was way too loud in the mix.

Keying the front door lock, Birdy imagined Frieda meeting him with a kiss. That would put his looping thoughts on a welcome pause. But baby boy Bernard was screaming now, and Frieda's voice began to louden and turn shrill. He heard the au pair apologizing, "Es tut mir leid, es tut mir leid--Nee, nee, nee!" Birdy's deep breath while opening the door was preposterously insufficient preparation for the homecoming.

Only Bernard remained quiet after Birdy entered, although Frieda and the au pair stopped yelling for a moment, startled by Birdy's entrance. Frieda slid Birdy's luggage with her foot away from the door and handed Bernard to Birdy. The au pair was already packed.

Frieda re-opened the door and the au pair picked up her two suitcases, adjusted her bulging back pack, and rushed out.

Noting the coincidence of his earlier thoughts, Birdy's looping thoughts ceased. He wasn't a born smart-ass, but immediately a remark formed in his mind. It took everything he had to keep his mouth shut. Bernard pawed at Birdy's nose and drooled on his coat sleeve. No sooner than Birdy's mind cleared, a picture entered. Not a single picture that captured it all, but a picture that he knew would direct him to another picture, and then another.

Staring all night at Pico and Fat's paintings, and listening to Vanmeter's drunk interpretation of what they were viewing--that experience was as exceptional in Birdy's life as the other four exceptional experiences Birdy counted up in his mind. But without Vanmeter's attempt to expound on what they were viewing and the impacts the paintings may or may not have had, that night would not have meant much else, he concluded. It was Vanmeter, not because he knew what the hell he was talking about, but because he was not afraid to broadcast his single 3X5 card of knowledge of art while staring at the paintings that he was starting to realize were remarkable. Paintings are important, thought Birdy, and at the moment he didn't care why. Those paintings--the sum of that night--he was trying to grasp the impact. And Clara's service the next day, that too.

Birdy was thinking different.

"In the microwave--Bernard's night time bottle. It's probably cool enough to feed him," said Frieda, and she collapsed on the sofa. She smiled, and waved-- maybe to Birdy, or maybe to Bernard. Standing in the kitchen, his coat still on, Birdy fed Bernard. Frieda waved a second time.

Later, Frieda, pulling up the covers, said, "Clara's in the urn, and now Vanmeter's coming back to bury Thrash?" Bernard was asleep.

After unpacking his bags, Birdy showered. He sat on his side of the bed. Frieda had given an executive summary of the au pair's departure. Of course, the apartment was too small, thought Birdy. But there was more to it, Frieda said, not elaborating further. Birdy was fine not knowing any other details. He possessed a clear picture of near time. Vanmeter told him to read the Roman Stoics, promising him to Seneca along when he returned Stateside.

Birdy turned to face Frieda. "Vanmeter has a woman--sort of. Lia. You'll have to wait to have Vanmeter tell the story. He told me, "It's a doomed relationship likely to keep goin' on--and most likely for the worse."

"Then I have to go with you and Bernard to Pennsylvania to bury Thrash," said Frieda.

42

Vanmeter was briefly disappointed in himself for failing to fully assess the impact of Thrash's death, unexpected or not. Half the Duquesne Rome campus were expected, along with many from the main Pittsburgh campus. Plus, Thrash's Rome friends. And Honoraria's friends...

Birdy's parents sent out hotel recommendations for all the out of towners. The main campus found accommodations for the Rome campus. Vanmeter, along with Birdy, took care of everything else.

Thrash--all his sorrow, thought Vanmeter, still in disbelief. His estate was transferred to Mr. Vanmeter Symthe within three weeks after his death. That was double the time Vanmeter needed to prepare for Thrash's funeral.

Thrash gave Vanmeter everything he had because Thrash had a clear picture of him, and what Thrash saw, he respected. Rescued Clara. Took care of her until she died. Had nothing. Agreed to run the galleria, without a clue. It appeared to Thrash Vanmeter never gave it a second thought, and he was right. Headlong into uncertainty, that was a natural inclination. Thrash wanted to somehow paint all that. Some things you can't paint. So, he gave Vanmeter everything.

MM was Stateside too, stopping by Thrash's home, visiting with Vanmeter, impressing upon him Fat's intent to have the gallery showing a week after Thrash's burial.

Although the timing was very compressed, he thought he had a clear picture. Fat had paid the remainder of Clara's hospital bill, but Vanmeter was more determined than grateful--he wanted to make sure the debt was paid off in full. Always paying off debts, he thought. He and Fat were going to have a conversation, and not through MM.

Beyond Fat, the calm about Vanmeter was due to his profound gratefulness to Thrash. He shifted away from thinking about Fat's paintings and viewed Thrash's gift as a mystery not in need of solving, for certain mysteries can be a powerful reminder of the traits that he must retain. Problem was, the most important traits were exceedingly difficult to retain. With no warning they depart, one by one, most times at the same time, pouring out like sweat from the furious heat of a scorcher of a day. Followed soon after with falsely accusing the scorching sun of blinding. It's not the sun. It's the spreading dark spot in the eye, the expansion of temptation. Vanmeter reasoned the purpose of mysteries were for reminding, and reminding was a powerful motivator to shrink the temptation, and in so doing, shrink the dark spots in his eye to mere motes, for there were a few motes. And maybe, with only a few motes, he could see his way to capturing the most important of traits.

Frieda and Bernard were back in Pittsburgh, in the Ballantine's' living room with Birdy's mother, and Birdy followed Porter B to the basement.

"Time to talk about Buffer," declared Porter B.

The basement was Porter B's rehearsal space, large enough for a four-piece band. He had a basic drum kit and electric piano set up, along with his practice bass amp and two other guitar amps. Four mikes, two floor monitors, all routed to his mixing board next to where he stood during rehearsal.

On each side of the basement false walls hid two rooms, built to survive fire and tornadoes. The room on the west side of the house had an escape tunnel that ran to the separate garage--above was the apartment where

Clara stayed for a short time. Porter B had a small armory in the escape tunnel. The east side, behind the drum kit, was the hunker down room. Both rooms were outfitted with everything needed to for three adults to survive for thirty days--from dried, and canned food to medical supplies, including portable oxygen cannisters, and built-in generators for each of the rooms. The basement bathroom contained a toilet, sink and shower.

Porter B showed Birdy each room. Then he led Birdy down the lighted escape tunnel, surfacing in a walk-in closet inside the garage.

Returning to the basement, Porter B said, "There're different parts of Buffer. All this? This is a couple parts of Buffer. I think you know what I mean," said Porter B.

Birdy had no idea.

"And there's also the most important part of Buffer. You need Buffer for your soul. So, while I may be able to protect me and your mother for a little while, when the daily crazy and stupid shit levels go way up and then turns dangerous, I may not be able to protect us. And you know crazy and stupid shit never goes away, and many times gets dangerous. That's why you need Buffer for your soul. Now, we know that even Catholics are not immune to crazy and stupid shit, but in my mind, they are the only tribe that offers us the best soul Buffer."

"Your sister believes herself and her tribe's power to be her Buffer. That power she believes she and her tribe possesses only exists if other people pay attention and acquiesce to saying what they are scolded to say and behave in such a way, and that way only. Ignore them and they're powerless--that kind of Buffer, like their power, is an illusion."

"I think you know what I mean," said Porter B. Birdy stood there, in awe.

Porter B lifted up and spread out both arms. "So, it's in this context, that I think you're on the right track about wanting to buy Brother Davis's place from Vanmeter. That place is not his speed, anyway. That boy's a chaser. Chasing this, chasing that. Now he's an art dealer. His Momma's gone now, and he's going to chase some more."

"Plus, you gotta get out of New York City."

"It's Frieda's idea," said Birdy.

Porter B gave his son a skeptical look. Birdy nodded it was true.

"Hmm," mumbled Porter B, half unconvinced, but wanting to be convinced.

"I'm going to go up hold Bernard for a while," said Porter B.

"Thanks," said Birdy, in stunned bewilderment, following his father up the stairs. Porter B flipped his right hand back, palm up. Birdy slapped it.

"And, you got to pray for your sister. Every day, every day," said Porter B reaching the top of the stairs. He turned to face Birdy a few steps below, holding his right hand out, palm up. Birdy eyed him, and again slapped it.

Thrash's funeral was held the next day at the Duquesne Chapel of the Holy Spirit. Almost one hundred in attendance. Thrash's friend, Father Chris William, presided. Father Chris asked Vanmeter to say some words but he declined. His excuse was it would be confusing for everyone.

Vanmeter imagined saying, "Hello, my name's Vanmeter Smythe, and I was a friend of Jack Davis, better known to most as Thrash. I'm up here today because...insert a lengthy, confusing story explaining why I'm involved with any part of this."

No.

The funeral was fine, Vanmeter thought, although more formal than Thrash would have preferred, he guessed. Of the almost one hundred, about half drove out to Thrash's family house afterwards. His ashes were being interred next to his parents and Honoraria. Of those fifty, almost half didn't know until today that Thrash had gotten married. But he was fairly certain most knew Thrash was a painter.

Vanmeter had at least met the crowd from Rome, and knew only a few brothers from the main campus. They were there when he attended Duquesne.

Vanmeter employed a catering service Kule Fat recommended. The setup was in the back, behind the house. Tents, tables and chairs, food, beer, and wine. It was as odd as Vanmeter predicted the afternoon would go. Thanking everyone personally for attending, as Thrash's representative, was odd. There were no aunts and uncles. There was no short explanation why Vanmeter was where he found himself to be. Well, there was one. Vanmeter Symthe was a charity case. And if Lia was with him, here? Smart decision staying in Rome. Lia, thank you, he thought.

Although Frieda was disappointed.

Only the lawyer, Birdy, his parents, and Frieda, knew the full details. But he felt as if everyone present knew. Fat and MM suspected, for sure. All of the property and everything in the house went to Vanmeter. Thrash's own inheritance, savings, and investments, too. Managed very carefully and living modestly, Vanmeter would not have to work another day. He thought of Lia, and smiled outright. Now he might qualify as high-end, he thought, but Lia wasn't going to know anything.

It was not only the day to remember Thrash Davis, it was a day Vanmeter knew rumors could start, take hold, and eventually spread if anyone here viewed the Honoraria Collection today. He knew what the impact should be. The same as they were on him.

Thrash's paintings were already shipped to Rome. Packaging paintings. That's what Vanmeter had been doing, in between meetings with the lawyer. Renting a van to transport them to the airport. The expedited shipping and customs clearance services costs were outrageous, giving Vanmeter pause as to whether he should include the Honoraria Collection with Fat's and Pico's work. However, that was the agreement he made with himself. Vanmeter wanted to launch every firework in the salvo at once. Launch all three artists, and with any luck, some brilliant, bursting sparks will fly--and the deep pockets? Excite them.

In addition, Vanmeter went through every room, closet, crevice, and nook. And the attic. Paintings were stored everywhere. Sketches, drawings, false starts. Most were Thrash's mother's paintings and sketches, although some Vanmeter couldn't identify the artist. Students? He discovered some of Kule Fat paintings. Those were unmistakable. As were Vera Davis's. Clearly, she had a thing for A. Wyeth, thought Vanmeter, and with no evidence to point to, he was convinced they knew each other.

Vera Davis appeared to be a technical painter. If he could see it, then a skilled eye would have no trouble. He hadn't had time to view her work thoroughly, but he had a baseless hunch she might not have been gifted with the spark of originality. But Vanmeter knew nothing of her. Thrash never spoke about her. Maybe the caretaker neighbor would know something. Maybe Fat! The idea of talking about Vera Davis excited Vanmeter.

Fat was using the name Xi Deng, according to MM. He managed to keep to himself during Thrash's wake, Vanmeter noticed. He made his move towards Fat as two car loads of locals departed.

"You're a different man from the Kule Fat I met," Vanmeter said.

"I am a different man," Fat replied. It was the first time Vanmeter recognized Fat's New York accent. Thinking back, he swore Fat had the accent of a Chinese. Fat was sipping Sauvignon Blanc.

Vanmeter wasted no time. "I know you're gonna leave soon. Here's a check for Clara's hospital bill. Thank you. It's in Michel's name. I know I'm going to owe you for the showing next week. Michel told me he's taking care of all of it. I'm gonna pay you back as soon as I know that cost."

"You loathe debt," said Fat, accepting the check.

"That I do, sir," said Vanmeter.

"Give me twenty more minutes of your time. I want to show some paintings in the house."

"Mine, or Vera Davis's?" said Fat, in no apparent hurry to doing anything.

Entering the side kitchen door, Fat paused, inspecting the kitchen layout, a habit that would never leave him. The kitchen was a very special place. Sacred.

"Both," said Vanmeter, recognizing Fat wasn't behind him. He returned to the kitchen to find Fat. Vanmeter thought he read the top chefs had supernatural olfactories. Attempting to detect lingering odors of dinners past? Or other memories?

Fat announced, "I've always wanted to return here." So, mused Vanmeter, Mrs. Vera Davis was memorable.

"If I may, allow me to lead on," requested Fat. Vanmeter swept his arm in front of himself, and Fat took the lead.

"I won't be returning," Fat said. Vanmeter was unsure Fat was talking to him. The last room Fat entered was the main studio, having spent some time in the living room perusing, with short stops in all the bedrooms.

"A back room. A large closet actually," said Fat, in a soft voice. Fat went inside the back room where Vanmeter discovered the paintings. He located his paintings, pulling each out and giving them a quick scan.

"Immature work," he said, glancing up to catch Vanmeter's eye to detect agreement. Vanmeter didn't give him the opportunity, bending down to grab his paintings.

"Keep them here. It's where they belong," said Fat, as he moved to Vera Davis's paintings. He took his time going through her work.

Vanmeter was uninterested watching someone he barely knew going down memory lane. Their mystery, that is, the relationship between Kule Fat and Vera Davis was no longer compelling, Vanmeter realized.

"What do you think of her work?" Fat was studying a small landscape painting of hers.

"Critiquing the teacher?" Fat replied, adding, "I still can't bring myself to do so."

"She paints with a technical skill that's very impressive to me. That's my take," said Vanmeter.

Fat remained silent for a while.

"But...something's missing," Fat whispered. Vanmeter nodded in silence. Fat then nodded in reply.

Returning to the main studio they found MM walking about, inspecting like a detective.

Vanmeter said, "You two going to tell me why you picked me in the first place? Giving me a key to the storage room filled with painting stuff. The blur of a trip around Eastern Europe."

It hit Vanmeter then. The storage room! Fat only took Mrs. Davis's copies!

MM deferred to Fat, who in turn, deferred to MM. Vanmeter took turns staring at both of them.

"Hunch," said Fat.

"A hunch?" scoffed Vanmeter, looking now at MM. He nodded.

"Whose hunch?"

"My hunch," said Fat. "I'm guided by my hunches. I follow them. And here we are."

"You too, are guided by hunches. And here you are," said Fat. Vanmeter, unsatisfied with the hunch story, said nothing further.

"You also are a planner, as are we," added Fat.

"Now then, let me tell you the plan in Rome," said Fat, sitting down on the chair nearest the main easel, inviting the other two to sit. Vanmeter and MM took seats next to each other at the small table filled with drawings and sketches.

After briefing the Rome plan, Vanmeter left Fat and MM in the studio to attend to the others. Most had left, except a few of Honoraria's friends, Frieda, Birdy and Bernard. Bernard was well past nap and feeding time. Soon everyone had departed, including Fat and MM.

Vanmeter was exhausted. Fat's plan was less of a plan and more of a flow of events. He handed Vanmeter a script to follow for the gallery opening.

It was straightforward, thought Vanmeter, collapsing on the bed in the master bedroom. 'Fat gets what he wants, I get what I want,' he said aloud, before dozing off. Up until then, he slept on the couch downstairs. He was still a reluctant guest in a strange house. There was too much space, but not enough room to breathe.

It made little sense to him.

43

The sale of Thrash's house and property to Birdy and Frieda was already starting, the day Vanmeter was returning to Rome. The back and forth between them was entirely pleasant, although uncomfortable for Vanmeter, not because of haggling over price and closing details, but because he wasn't sure Birdy and Frieda weren't rushing into the sale. Vanmeter was in no hurry, but he also had no interest in living there. The suddenness of events didn't bother Vanmeter, it was an attractive component of uncertainty.

Birdy and Frieda were not going to be there for the galleria showcase. But Birdy's parents accepted the invitation. Alena Wire was excited about an impromptu visit to Rome. She had never been, and rushed to build an itinerary. Porter B left everything to his wife. He wanted to be of some use in support of Vanmeter's big event.

Porter B called Vanmeter while he waited for his flight to Rome.

"Hello, Mr. Wire. Ever been to an art gallery showcase event? It'll be my first," said Vanmeter.

"Yes, I have. I've had two gigs in my life at art openings, or whatever. Lots of champagne sippin' types, as I recall. Lot of pretty, skinny women trying to get attention. Lot of cats thinking they're somebody. Not my kind of crowd. It was like you see in a movie--seemed all cliché."

"Luckily too, I was married at the time," laughed Porter B. He told Vanmeter they were coming in two days before, and he was a volunteer for anything Vanmeter needed to get done, including the shit jobs.

"Thank you, sir," said Vanmeter, adding, "But there is no way you're going to do anything but hang out, sip champagne, and eat. It may get boring fast. I look forward to seeing you both."

"Will we like the paintings?" asked Porter B.

"That sir, is unknown," said Vanmeter, grabbing his carry-on and walking to the gate.

"Pico's paintings, I mean," said Porter B.

"Understand, Mr. Wire, I understand," said Vanmeter.

"No hint then, eh, Vanmeter?"

"No sir."

"Alright. See you soon, son," said Porter B.

"Look forward to it, sir."

This week was set in motion. Most of the showcase details were handled by MM and Italian friends of Honoraria and Thrash. Vanmeter's own tasks were clear in his mind.

Nine hours flying to Rome--too much time to think. He knew the paintings would sell, not which ones, and not how many. He had no idea when they would begin to sell. Then what? He'd receive a commission for Pico's paintings. Fat's? Vanmeter expected nothing from Fat. Vanmeter could now afford to pay all the associated costs for the event. He owed Fat nothing. The Honoraria Collection? Vanmeter was now unsure he wanted to sell them. His Momma kept coming to his mind whenever he thought about those paintings. What Thrash transferred to the canvas while observing Honoraria until her death, Vanmeter had attempted to capture while observing his Momma dying. She refused to be photographed. Vanmeter took pictures when Clara was unaware. It was the Honoraria Collection that led Vanmeter to photograph his Momma whenever he could. It was not difficult to take pictures of her without her knowledge. It was the only time Vanmeter ever used his phone to take pictures. It was the only time he ever kept his phone in front of him instead of his back pocket.

Vanmeter had distractions, like everyone, but he loathed the mobile phone. It was a product designed to waste time. No, thought Vanmeter, it was a tracking device that could take pictures and make phone calls. It wasn't a portal into other worlds, it was a hole where contemplation tripped and fell in, where distraction climbed out and swallowed you, and lurid and mindless temptations hung out under dim lit lights, whistling to your eyes for attention.

Vanmeter didn't know how many pictures he took. He didn't know if they were good photos or bad. One day he'd look them over. And that day was not clear in his mind.

He had too much time to think. He couldn't sleep, no movies interested him, he had no book to read, and no music was petitioning him to listen. It was too easy to get drunk, and he was in no spirit to go the easy route.

He stared out his little window, looking into the black of night. There was no moon, but the stars he could see--and the billions he couldn't reminded him that he never looked to them for answers. He never wondered at the immenseness of the universe in relation to the infinitesimal fact of himself. And the last thing he ever wanted was to believe the stars had anything to do with anything. Other than the sun, stars had nothing to offer.

Suddenly, two options were before him, once again. The other times he evaded thinking about them because he considered both options absurd. It wasn't either or. There could be other options. But Vanmeter had no clear picture of other options. He had already dissected the two options before. Nothing new to reveal. Absurd as they were, however, they were options.

No clear picture meant uncertainty. He smiled to himself, and fell asleep.

It was as if the bright orange cloth covering the inside front window and glass doors of the Galleria de Honoraria was made even more orange by some photonic effect, suggesting mysterious happenings were taking place inside. This is what greeted a groggy Vanmeter mid-day after arriving from JFK. He dropped off his luggage at the apartment, showered, changed clothes, and made it to the gallery, stopping by his regular café to get an Americano Grande. The persistent drizzle was getting old. He thought of Birdy's parents, arriving in a few days. The grey clouds were low, but moving steady. When finally clear, it was going to be sticky if the winds didn't keep up, thought Vanmeter. Which reminded him to remember to crank the air conditioning down low in the galleria the morning of the opening.

Unlocking the front door, Vanmeter entered. It was just past 4 pm. The galleria was quiet, except for the traffic noise. All the lights were on, overhead and track lighting. Must be the lights, then, thought Vanmeter. The walls were freshly painted and bare, but against the left and right walls were a line of paintings in crates. Leaning against the front window was a four-foot picture poster of Kule Fat standing legs apart, arms behind his back-- taken when he was fat, and head shaved--as people knew him as the big-deal chef in New York, and as people knew him as a wanted man for art forgery. His expression clearly suggested the ambiguity of Mona Lisa's eyes and smile. Ever the copier. Vanmeter wondered how many photographs it took to capture that expression.

Behind Fat's picture were two other pictures, two feet by four feet high. Vanmeter pulled the first one out. The upper half was a photograph of Pico Natambe, compliments of his parents. Below his biography, including date of birth and death. Pico's wide grin showed off his brilliant white teeth. A-list movie star looks, admitted Vanmeter. Tall, lean, wearing skinny black slacks and a rolled up white shirt, with a pair of aviator sunglasses swinging in his right hand.

Behind Pico's poster was a photograph of Thrash Davis, arm in arm with Honoraria Duse, the photo given to Vanmeter by a close friend of Honoraria's. A bear of a man, his beard failing to hide his handsome features. Honoraria was a tiny woman next to Thrash; very attractive, in a white summer dress. Thrash wore jeans and an untucked chambray shirt, sleeves crowded up above his elbow, as if advertising all he wanted was to just wear a t-shirt. Below the picture was Thrash's biography, and date of birth and death. Adjacent to the picture posters were three collapsed easels, awaiting unfolding, standing, and picture placement.

Vanmeter noticed the sheen of the fresh buffed concrete floor and walked to the left wall to get to the back room. The bathroom was immaculate. A floor to ceiling curtain runner was installed with black velvet curtains enclosing the left two thirds of the back room. There was a bar station set up. Next to it a long table. Behind the curtain new ceiling lighting had been installed. The walls, also freshly painted, were bare. The alley way door was open slightly, and smoke drifted in.

Vanmeter peeked outside and found Michel Maritain leaning against the wall, finishing a cigarette.

"Fat have a thing for electric orange?" asked Vanmeter, staying inside to avoid the rain.

"My idea," said MM, extinguishing his cigarette on the sole of his right shoe, and placing the butt in the butt-can next to the door. He produced a small bottle of hand sanitizer gel and cleaned his hands. Then he came inside.

"Here, behind the curtains?" asked Vanmeter.

"Brother Davis's paintings. The Honoraria Collection, as you call them," said MM.

"When do they arrive?"

"I pick them up tomorrow. I'd like to borrow a van," said Vanmeter. MM nodded.

"Fat's paintings will be on the right wall. Pico's on the left wall. Fat chooses which of his paintings are displayed, and in which order. He arranged the crates of Pico's paintings in the order he believes should be displayed, but leaves the decision up to you," said MM.

"What if I disagree which of Pico's paintings should be shown?" said Vanmeter.

"Fat believes you will agree with him," said MM.

"And Thrash's paintings are only in the back room?" said Vanmeter, his tone feigning frustration, but he knew it to be an excellent idea. So much for renting a bigger space, he thought.

"Yes," said MM.

"Fat has to have the serious jitters," smiled Vanmeter, finishing his coffee, needing another.

"About getting apprehended?" said MM, in a mock puzzlement.

"About his public debut of originals," said Vanmeter. MM's expression seemed to convey he never thought about that.

"His paintings--what do you think?" asked Vanmeter.

"I wager it won't matter what we think," smiled MM.

That evening Mr. and Mrs. Wire were coming to dinner at Vanmeter's apartment, along with Lia. Vanmeter was making pan roasted chicken with rosemary, garlic, white wine, and risotto with asparagus. He had made it many times before, not only because he and his mother Clara enjoyed the meal, but it allowed Vanmeter to gain proficiency in preparation. It was a busy day made busier by his commitment to prepare dinner. Tomorrow evening was the galleria showcase event.

Vanmeter's pickup of the Honoraria Collection was uneventful, and worth every Euro to streamline the process, thanks to Honoraria's friends, Isa and Paula, both divorced with well-off settlements from their ex-husbands. School friends of Honoraria who never lost touch. They knew everyone and let you know they knew everyone. Initially Vanmeter was treated like the complete outsider he was. That soon gave way once they discovered Vanmeter applied for citizenship, and more important, his attention and care paid to Clara, who knew Isa and Paula because they smoked cigarettes together in the alley behind the galleria. Clara told Vanmeter they had no children, were bored, flirted about, and were busybodies like nobody's business.

Isa and Paula also knew of Lia's line of work and thought that was tragically exciting. Lia never hesitated to make small talk with them, but that was all. "Honoraria marrying Jack 'Thrash' Davis was more exciting to them than their marriage and divorce put together," said Isa, Paula nodding in agreement. Their attention to Honoraria in her last months of life was near devout, and they were devasted by her death, as well as Thrash's, having flown to the States for his funeral. For now, Isa and Paula were part of Vanmeter's life, while only at the galleria. Outside the galleria, no interactions took place. They also never visited separately. It would not be long, thought Vanmeter, before they would stop visiting. That inevitability was just part of the greater inevitability, thought Vanmeter, and he welcomed its accelerating pace.

The Honoraria Collection was now here, although Vanmeter decided to wait until the next day to display them. After inspecting the contents, he left them in the crates, leaning against the back-room wall, with the black velvet curtain drawn. He parked the borrowed van in his designated parking spot at the apartment, leaving the keys under the floor mat. One of MM's men would pick it up. After taking a shower, he prepared the kitchen, and then texted the Wires, confirming dinner at 5 pm. He dozed off on the sofa until awakened by Lia's doorbell ring.

She presented him with a fresh cut chicken from the butchers, two bundles of tall stalks of asparagus, fresh parsley, rosemary, and Arborio rice. Although she liked Vanmeter's short cropped beard, she preferred not to kiss his cheeks. And Vanmeter, in keeping his distance from Lia, preferred only to kiss hers. Why she still accepted his invitations to dinner continued to surprise Vanmeter. She was arresting, in looks, in poise, and what she wore. Of course, she was, Vanmeter repeated to himself every time they were together. Of course, she was. In his phone contacts, unaware to Lia, he listed her as SHE, Signora High-End.

Vanmeter called her out the first time they had dinner together.

"Your research was flawed, I, most definitely, am not high-end. And your ability to see into the immediate future needs some work, because I don't see any of my immediate plans making me high-end. So, I am not on that kind of list," he told her, well after dinner, walking Lia back to her apartment. That night's temperature was unpleasant--too hot to walk, even in the late evening.

Lia laughed almost all the way back to her apartment.

"I have no funny clients at the moment. I rarely ever do. Only one I can recall, now," she said.

"Old and fat and rich," Vanmeter shot back.

"Too true," she laughed. Hard not to like a woman who laughs at me calling her out for being a high-end prostitute, he thought.

"Not an uncommon story, really," she told him. She was a model for years, never quite making it to the top money jobs. She slept with a banker after a show, and he paid her five hundred Euros, thinking she was a prostitute.

"I cried and cried. I went and stayed with my mother, telling her."

"You know what she told me? The same thing happened to her. She became pregnant, had me, even though her friends told her to get an abortion."

"What do you say to that--I ask you?" Lia convinced Vanmeter of the seriousness of her question, and he remembered, no amount of built-up skepticism prepared him for the rest of the evening's conversation.

It was their respective relationships with their own mother's that particularly impressed Lia. Lia had met Clara, only in the hospital, and then in hospice. Vanmeter had never met Lia's mother, the Countess Bocetti.

Placing the groceries on the kitchen countertop, Vanmeter went and hugged Lia.

"And how was coffee this morning with the good Countess?" smiled Vanmeter.

"She says hello, and is excited to come to the galleria showing tomorrow--oh, and to meet you, too" said Lia, now tending to the asparagus, while Vanmeter prepared the chicken.

"She knows I'm from West Virginia, speak Eye-talian with a twang, and I ain't high-end?" grinned Vanmeter-- receiving a firm elbow in the ribs as a reply.

"Oh, and I'm thinking about being a Catholic brother?" That question was replied with an eye-popping, dead panned, silence--followed by a fit of hysterics.

It would be inaccurate to say Lia was still a prostitute. And how long she was a prostitute Vanmeter refused to address. It was accurate to say, Vanmeter thought, that Lia's start at being a mistress to a banker at the same time he met her was quite a coincidence--and on that subject Vanmeter refused to inquire further. Any further inquiring about choosing high-end prostitution and life as a mistress were in the out-of-bounds category. It would be too damn easy to conclude motivations; with full recognition there was pretzel reasoning going on, full time.

There was no thinking about anyone else so long as his Momma was still with him. But, his commitment to Clara was complete, she told him more than once, in her last days.

It was only tonight, the evening before the galleria showcase, with Lia in the kitchen helping him prepare dinner for the first time, that Vanmeter had some space in his mind to think. And what she didn't say about all her thoughts, Vanmeter didn't say about all his. Contemplating entering the postulancy was starting to compete with what he considered to be the complete absurdity of having a relationship with Lia.

What Lia didn't know but guessed was confirmed through Isa and Paula, ever the gossipers, usually right about their own theories, ever congratulating themselves on their keen insights. Yes, Thrash Davis bequeathed everything to Vanmeter.

What Lia didn't know was Vanmeter took the Thrash bestowment as affirmation of his talents, pointing his thoughts to be ever more mindful of compassion and humility, the two traits Vanmeter sought, and only obtained for a fleeting moment, like the warmth of sunrays on your face between slivers of snow drenched winter clouds. The warmth, most welcome, now here-- and gone. But the memories trap the experience, and bend the mind, on a bitter cold day, into waiting for such an occasion to happen again.

Whereas Vanmeter was indeed a chaser, it was within his motivation to chase that Vanmeter sought to become compassionate, to capture it, and in turn humility would grow. Compassion was the rare fertilizer of the soul...and that's why his seeking the postulancy was a serious proposition.

But wait...This was all but a fantasy, a transcendent temptation to wrap himself in an illusion of achieving sanctity. Vanmeter was a fierce rejector of illusions--but--he desired this fantasy to remain below the surface of the skin of his day-to-day, his life, his chase. Better there, pulsing in the epidermal layer?

Whereas Lia took Vanmeter's inquiry into the postulancy seriously, because she believed it to be a test for her, the test to discover whether she possessed the will to commit to Vanmeter. This test thrilled her like nothing ever in her life.

The apartment entrance buzzer sounded off. Porter B and Alena Wire had arrived.

The dinner was excellent, Arlene announced shortly after eating. After dinner, in the kitchen, Porter B had a few seconds alone with Vanmeter. He motioned his head towards Lia, smiling, raising his right eye brow.

"Way too early to tell, Mr. Wire, way too early to tell," replied Vanmeter, now pondering the great inevitability.

It was light and pleasant talk all around during dinner, and the Wires left near 8 pm. Lia helped clean up, leaving shortly after.

"One night, I'll stay."

Vanmeter said nothing, but kissed her lips.

45

Vanmeter slept well, so well, he went for a run at 630 am, going through his to-do list in his mind. He never worried about what he did not control or was not in charge of. Events were going to flow as the day advanced. Picking up the pieces, if any, was part of the events of the day. Michel Maritain was taking care of Fat's interests, and those interests were well calculated, thought Vanmeter.

The rain stopped, and the day was going to be warm. The streets were filling with cars and delivery trucks. Back at the apartment, before cooling down, Vanmeter did pushups and sit-ups. These days he was grateful he possessed the metabolism of a high schooler.

He taxied to the galleria, bringing along the black suit he was going to wear that evening. The taxi first stopped at his café, and he had to wait in line for his Americano- -while the taxi idled, double parked. At the Galleria de Honoraria Vanmeter noticed the electric orange covering was replaced by white. The pictures of Kule Fat, Pico, and Thrash were not yet in the windows.

Vanmeter was alone in the galleria. He went and cranked the air conditioner lower. He hung up is suit in the back room and pulled open the curtains and set about removing the Honoraria Collection from their crates. He dragged a chair to the middle of the viewing area. He returned to the paintings and arranged them in order of Honoraria's physical decline, or what Vanmeter thought was the order.

Honoraria posed for all of the paintings. In three of them she stood with a fashioned walking stick of her height. In these three standing paintings Honoraria (always in summer dresses) was gradually shrinking below the tip of her walking stick (a very light wood, perhaps ash).

Other paintings Honoraria sat in a modern high back wooden chair made of dark thick wood. One had her sitting on the edge of her bed in a full bright blue night gown, her arms locked in place on the mattress, supporting herself, looking at her feet.

Every painting but two she wore a neatly wound white turban. The final painting Honoraria lay on her bed, on top of the covers, in a full length white night gown, smiling with her eyes closed, and hands behind her head, as if outside on a grass lawn, soaking up the sun. On the back of the painting Thrash had written 'morphine smile'. Vanmeter placed this one first on the wall, then began hanging paintings in no particular order, changing his mind on attempting to order them in any way. These were realist paintings. Every painting had different wall paper design in the room. But the room appeared to be the same room in all the paintings. Honoraria being particularly fond of attention-grabbing wall paper. Lighting was either from a single table lamp or from daylight through a tall, double-hung, curtain-free window.

Vanmeter sat on the chair and viewed the paintings. He thought of the photos he took of Clara, but he had no intention of viewing them any time soon.

He decided then he wasn't ready to let go of the Honoraria Collection. He finished his Americano.

Seeing the Honoraria paintings again left him contemplating whether any significance was attached to anything he tried to accomplish. Any significance relating to what, exactly? Thoughts of memorable significance always point to meaning. He bolted through life in search of meaning. Now it felt like his brakes were on, only inching along, and appearing in front of him now a life-sized maze, made of stone. Immediately it was claustrophobic, because the maze corridors narrowed as he inched along. A new fear--of getting stuck--and unable to free himself from the tightening walls forced himself to step back out of the maze, only to stand at the threshold and wonder. But at the same time, the Honoraria Collection was tempting Vanmeter to re-enter the maze and continue. Apart from this distracting, dizzying feeling, the day was beginning as he thought it would, as he wanted it to.

Being alone for a while cleared his head, and the maze of stone crumbled, but not forgotten, for the mounds of stone were before him. To Vanmeter, the great inevitability had arrived. Details were not yet available. He left to get another Americano. Walking, Vanmeter felt his calves were tight from the morning run. He wasn't sure if he was imagining the lightness in the moods of passersby, including the normally business-like barista, already balding in his twenties. Vanmeter was perspiring from the warm morning walk, but didn't care. The café was crowded, the line no shorter than earlier, giving Vanmeter time to people watch. Italians are people watch worthy, thought Vanmeter. Behind him he heard two young men speaking Russian, recalling a rare day drinking session in a nearby bar with a former Russian submariner, now in the oil business. His English was excellent. His Italian girlfriend was ten years younger and bored out of her mind listening to the Russian brag about his Navy. Decent guy, thought Vanmeter, probably lonely. What he was doing in Rome Vanmeter had no idea.

Back at the galleria, Vanmeter thanked himself for turning the air conditioner down lower. He rinsed his face in the bathroom and sat down at his desk, now pushed off to the right, near the entrance. He leaned the chair back against the wall and surveyed the room. Neither Fat's or Pico's paintings were up yet. He said his prayers he promised he would say, every day. The list of who to pray for had grown. Other than for Mary to pray for them and God to watch over them, what else could he pray for? Any specifics seemed unseemly.

He got up from his desk and went to the back room, slipping behind the closed curtains. Vanmeter stood back to view the entire Honoraria Collection once again, this time imaging what was going through Thrash's mind while painting Honoraria. Every dab of the brush into paint, every movement of the brush on canvas. Thrash was a realist painter, but what was really real in these paintings?

He looked for the suffering within the elevated beauty of each pose.

Suffering can only be acknowledged full on, but that is the easy part, he thought. The difficulty was to not give into temptation. Suffering is a tempter, tempting one to be angry, despairing, abandoning faith, and tempting one towards a false mercy. The false mercy of expedient death--disguised as death with dignity, as if not choosing expedient death was non-dignified. A false god. And endurance in suffering was not for the weak. It can never be confronted, only consented to. Consenting to suffering is the most we can ever muster in defense. You could argue that even consenting is an illusion, but one that can be forgiven. Consent is an attempt to project power over that which you are powerless. Enduring suffering is possible, through the act of resisting temptation to abandon faith for the expedient delivery from it.

Vanmeter wondered, did Thrash think any of these thoughts while painting his dying Honoraria? Was Thrash thinking about faith while painting his wife?

Get to know a life-long sufferer. One who suffers not of their own decision, and one who does. What's the difference between them? Better yet, what are the similarities? Vanmeter tried to recall where he read that.

Is it only when near death, when nothing within a human's grasp can affect anything? Only when God receives back that which He gave will a clear picture appear, and even then, only to the capacity in which can be received--which has to be enough?

There was suffering in Thrash's paintings, Vanmeter thought. But that was not the point of these paintings. It was also not mere remembrance.

Vanmeter recalled what Clara said to him. "You know when you go to the theater, and there's someone up in the rafters controlling the lights down on the actors on stage? Well, I think God is behind the lights, and He shines a spotlight of grace, mercy, forgiveness, hope--whatever's necessary. And it's our choice to stay in the spotlight, or be stupid and move out of it. But the widest beam of all spotlights is Love. You can't move outta that spotlight. You can ignore Him, you can deny Him, but you can't move outta that spotlight."

"The creaky, old snake-handlin' preacher said that one Sunday evening, right after you were born. Now those words are very hard to forget--thankfully impossible to."

Vanmeter was going to have to keep the Honoraria Collection for a while. Until he could figure out more of what they revealed.

"It's Mother, not 'Momma', not anymore," Vanmeter said aloud, to an empty galleria. Taking out his phone, he finally looked at the pictures he took of his Mother.

He sat down and wept. And the maze before him earlier, a maze he had never encountered before, dissolved away completely. Through his tears, Vanmeter now had a clear picture of the world. He leaned back and dozed off.

He awoke when he heard MM and Fat coming through the alley way door. Vanmeter jumped up and opened the curtain, briefly startling the men, and invited them to view the Honoraria Collection. He left them alone, went to the main room, and began to place Pico's paintings on the wall. He left Fat's paintings alone.

Now Vanmeter positioned his chair to view Pico's paintings. They all were bright, enthusiastic, full of movement. Sinuous soccer players jousting, bustling sweaty shoppers in a hot outdoor market, church goers giddy--pouring out of Mass, the NFB in full funk pulse, dancers in tilted thrill at an outdoor concert. The paintings looked to Vanmeter to be more realist, but also impressionist in and around the action, as if to further vitalize action.

But what did he really know about paintings, he thought? He knew little, was minimally exposed to some styles, had no formal art education--but like anyone else who didn't know much about painting, particular works caught his eye. The reasons vary, maybe, but they still caught his eye. Vanmeter felt Pico's work would get people excited. Dying while young was going to be an influencer, he thought. The same for Thrash. That's just the way it was.

The more Vanmeter thought about it, the more surprised Fat was willing to present his original work in the same gallery as Pico. The differences in their work was striking. Fat's paintings were of an uninteresting timbre and mood, including subject and objects.

Then Fat and MM entered the main room. After pausing to quickly view Pico's work, Fat nodded towards Vanmeter, and both men set about placing Fat's paintings on the wall. There was no hesitation which painting was going where. They worked in near silence, occasionally murmuring to each other. Twenty minutes later they were done, and MM began removing the storage crates. Fat stood back and looked at his work. Vanmeter got up and helped MM with the crates.

While placing the crates in the van parked in the alley, Vanmeter asked MM, "What did Fat think about Thrash Davis's paintings?"

"He has said nothing," said MM, shoving the crates forward, next to the back of the seats.

"You were back there almost a half an hour, indicating to me, Fat should have something to say about them," said Vanmeter, MM noticing an edge in his remark.

"They are amazing," Vanmeter declared.

MM climbed out of the van, stretched his lower back, and said, "Remarkable." He reached for his silver engraved cigarette case and selecting one, bounced it off the top of the case and lit it. MM looked at his watch as he noticed another van enter the alley way. He walked around his van and started it up, pulling forward to allow the larger incoming van to park next to the alley door. Caterers.

He knew when the smoking started--the evening's dramatic intrusion was the excuse. The smokers stayed inside for some reason. As if the ingrained habit of going outside to smoke was flicked off the shoulder, like a speck of unsightly dandruff discovered by a detective eye. Or, more probably, no one wanted to miss out on whatever happenings might happen. Vanmeter gave them two minutes before announcing to extinguish their cigarettes in a metal waste basket next to his desk. Dutifully, everyone took their last deep puffs before circling around the waste basket, tossing their butts. There were only ten or fifteen smokers, but enough to produce a comic sight.

Lia and Countess Bocetti were the last to leave, and Vanmeter was grateful they both attended. Both looked stunning. The Countess's charm was top shelf, he told Lia. She seemed delighted by the description. Even now, he was delighted she was delighted--although he never trusted someone with top shelf charm. They're hiding something about themselves they don't want you to know. But, in order to know them well, you should know. Then after, you may not want to know them anymore.

Vanmeter opened the gallery at 5 pm, and by 6 pm fifty or so people filled the place. MM had three guards posted, one next to Fat's, and one next to Pico's paintings. The biggest guard was stationed with the Honoraria Collection. Vanmeter didn't find anything to read into that choice.

Porter B and Alena Wire showed up first, and left by 6 pm. Wise, recalled Vanmeter. Immediately, Vanmeter escorted them to the back room to view the Honoraria

Collection. He left them alone and went back to the main room.

Via four fetching waitresses, champagne delivery was non-stop. Vanmeter avoided the champagne but had difficulty not being ensnared by a very enthusiastic and giddy Paula and Isa. It was the Countess who intervened near 7 pm, giving Vanmeter breathing room to wander about.

Vanmeter had no idea who most of the attendees were. There were older-fifties, sixties, maybe seventies. More women than men, but not by much. European predominantly. Besides Italian, he recognized French, Spanish, and German being spoken. A young couple talking in Russian? And four Chinese men, in their fifties.

Vanmeter handed out his card to everyone in attendance, keeping a stack of fifty on his desk. If someone was interested, they could contact him by email printed on the card. GalleriadeHonoraria.com.

He let the Rome contingent help him spread the word about Pico.

Kule Fat's work was the main draw. Fat's contacts were here, no doubt. The four Chinese men, Vanmeter assumed, for sure. No one asked him about Fat's paintings, or his relationship with Fat. Nothing. Michel Maritain, on the other hand, was engaging with quite a few who gathered around Fat's paintings. Fine by me, thought Vanmeter.

"Tell me about Pico Natambe," a skinny handsome woman asked--looking early forties, tanned. A smoker. Vanmeter guessed French, maybe Swiss. Porter B and Alena also happened to be talking with Vanmeter, giving him the opportunity to step up, clear his voice and tighten the crowd viewing Pico's work.

Vanmeter enjoyed talking about what he knew about Pico. Any further details, other than his good friend recommending Pico's family to agree to let Vanmeter represent him were unavailable. He simply had no other information, other than Pico dying in a vehicle accident in Pennsylvania.

Afterwards, Porter B shook Vanmeter's hand, telling him, "Well done." Alena gave him a mother's hug, and they left, passing Kule Fat, now entering the gallery.

All Vanmeter said to Fat was, "Welcome," and Vanmeter turned around and went back into the crowd, surprised Fat showed up.

At some point Paula and Isa waved for Vanmeter's attention, dragging him to the back room to talk to their newly met acquaintances about the Honoraria Collection. He grabbed his first and only champagne off the newly filled tray being carried into the main room by an exceptionally tall waitress. Behind the curtains were at least fifteen people that Paula and Isa corralled. Maybe they were interested, maybe they were getting drunk and didn't care, thought Vanmeter. It mattered little to him; he had already decided they were not for sale.

With the galleria empty, Vanmeter sipped his bourbon, feet on the desk, recalling his little speech, of which he was proud. Lia and the Countess were amongst those listening. It was time to turn it on, Vanmeter remembered, and he did not fail to disappoint himself. When he was done the Countess gave him a wink and a thumb's up. Almost too American, thought Vanmeter.

He now recalled the 'intrusion'. They announced themselves by high pitched, short bursts from long whistles on a cord around their necks. Brittle sounding, like cheap plastic whistles handed out by county fair hustlers, Vanmeter remembered. He excused himself and returned to the main room.

Numerous strangers in the parting crowd pointed to Vanmeter. In the middle of the main room was a middle-aged man in an older style brown suit, accompanied by two uniformed men with shiny chrome whistles--small black automatic weapons slung to their sides.

Vanmeter remembered scanning the crowd for Kule Fat, while approaching the policemen. He was still there.

Vanmeter liked to think he lived in a world where unrelated happenings and people jumble-mix to create a whirlpool of circumstances. He thought of Honararia's description of being a miner--to pan downstream--a prospector sifting for opportunities--picking out the most intriguing, and holding it up to the sun for scrutiny, determining the likelihood of reality. For Vanmeter, it was clearly not an illusion. The observation of the circumstances he found himself in was verification. An illusion would pervade if he did not sift for opportunities and decide which opportunity to pursue. Hacking was a chosen opportunity, although harmful consequences of circumstances led him to abandon that trade. Then there was the Kule Fat introduction, and the storage locker full of art stuff. That was an opportunity, although Vanmeter was less sure he pursued it, or it pursued him.

Fat's presence that evening was not an illusion, nor were the presence of police.

Everyone parted further, in silence. Vanmeter walked up and introduced himself. The man in the suit shook his hand.

"Inspector DiFronzo," he said, extending his arm towards the door, and motioning for Vanmeter to lead the way. The uniformed police stayed inside, and began to search the gallery.

Outside, a few of the side walk curious stopped and stared from across the street. Their police car was parked in front, with no lights on. While holding the galleria door open for the Inspector, Vanmeter thought of the electric orange cloth that MM had covering the window, taken down after only a day.

The Inspector spoke decent English, telling Vanmeter he was from the Art Crimes Section. He asked how Vanmeter knew Kule Fat, how he came to showcase his paintings, and if he knew where Fat was at the moment.

Vanmeter told him he met Fat in New York at the restaurant.

"What did you think about him?" he asked.

"Odd, and he's got the wrong guy," answered Vanmeter.

Inspector DiFronzo was a thin man as tall as Vanmeter, full head of hair, small black mustache. He was in no hurry, and Vanmeter remembered he seemed to be enjoying himself.

Vanmeter said he only dealt with Michel Maritain, and DiFronzo took note.

"How do you know those paintings inside are Kule Fat's?" asked DiFronzo.

Vanmeter said, "Michel Maritain brought them in, asking me to include his paintings in tonight's showcase. Why would I not want to show them? You've done your research Inspector, I'm sure. You know I'm just starting out, taking over from the late Honoraria Duse."

Then Vanmeter said, "I would like to rejoin the guests inside."

Outside, piecing together a theory, occupied his time. This is all a show, Vanmeter thought, staged by Fat.

Maybe there were reporters inside.

DiFronzo lit a cigarette, saying nothing. Vanmeter thought again about the electric orange covering.

As he casually finished his cigarette, the two uniformed police officers exited the gallery, telling the Inspector there was no sign of Kule Fat.

The Inspector extinguished his cigarette on the side walk. He said, "You should know, there may be some complications in selling Kule Fat's paintings, if they are Kule Fat's paintings."

He smiled, turned, got in the back seat, and drove off with the two uniformed policemen.

Before he left the galleria, Vanmeter pulled his chair to the middle of the main room, viewing Fat's paintings, now recalling his surprise re-entering the gallery to yelling and applause, now wondering how many guests were in on the 'intrusion'.

Wondering if he was in someone else's illusion. He wasn't interested, other than getting them to put out their cigarettes.

Vanmeter thought, Fat had no part in getting him to Rome, in becoming the owner of Galleria de Honoraria, no part in Pico's paintings, and no part in acquiring Thrash's paintings.

Vanmeter now expected Fat's paintings to be removed by Michel Maritain and his crew later that night, after he left.

Done with Fat, Vanmeter turned his chair around and faced Pico's work.

While talking about Pico, Vanmeter recalled introducing Birdy's parents to Countess Bocetti. But he could not remember how Porter B and the Countess got into a conversation about Charley Pride. But her glowing enthusiasm convinced Vanmeter, and maybe Porter B, that the Countess was Charley Pride's biggest fan in Italy. According to her, they were the same age, which Vanmeter found incredulous. Vanmeter wondered, what world does an Italian Countess inhabit? Were the worlds the same or different if she was an imposter rather than the real deal? Regardless, certainly there was an illusion or two involved.

Vanmeter loved Pico's work, and so did Arlena Wire. Porter B? Vanmeter wasn't so sure. Lia and the Countess claimed they loved his work, too.

Now Vanmeter's thoughts moved to the large work of Pico's he did not display. The one Vanmeter found in

Thrash's studio, hidden away. He was sure that Thrash had painted it, attempting to imitate Pico. The painting was dazzling, thought Vanmeter, and it will be the only painting of Pico's he would possess. A dazzling forgery. It will stay hidden, he thought, until... He had no idea how long it would stay hidden. It shouldn't stay under cover, he told himself, but he was uncertain as to when to display it.

Vanmeter got up, moved his chair back to his desk, further dimmed the lights, sat down, pouring himself a finger's worth. The sidewalks were empty, only an occasional car and scooter hurrying by. The older going home, the younger going clubbing. It was a night for both.

He drained his bourbon, set the alarm, and left by the back door. Exiting the alley, he noticed he had the sidewalk to himself. As he started down the street, his phone buzzed in his back pocket. It was going to bend and break one day, he thought, but that's the only pocket he wanted the phone to be.

"Checkin' in to see how the gig went down." It was Birdy on speaker mode, with baby Bernard yapping gibberish in the background.

Vanmeter gave him the highlights, including the police visit, also including his theory Fat set it all up for spectacle.

Frieda spoke up, "What's next?" Neither seemed too surprised by Vanmeter's evening, and Vanmeter knew there was a point to be taken in their muted reaction. He was constructing a theory as he talked.

"Hang out for a bit. You all in New York?" Vanmeter asked.

"Pennsylvania," she answered.

"You sure you're going to hang out?" said Birdy, jumping back in the conversation.

"As opposed to?" said Vanmeter.

"My dad called earlier and told me you're escorting an Italian countess back to the States to go hear Charley Pride--who's on tour and will be in Pittsburgh next week," laughed Birdy.

"We're now going too, with Porter B and Arlena," chimed in Frieda.

"And baby Bernard?" asked Vanmeter.

"Haven't figured that out yet," said Frieda.

"How 'bout I watch Bernard and you all go?" Vanmeter's suggestion was less tongue and cheek than maybe Frieda and Birdy believed.

"I want to meet Lia--bring her too," said Frieda.

"Talked to my dad about this house. Got some plans," said Birdy.

Frieda made a remark Vanmeter couldn't quite make out, but the sarcasm he did catch.

"I'll have to hear about them sometime," said Vanmeter. Then goodbyes and love you's were said all around. Vanmeter pocketed his phone.

Vanmeter swore it was cooler earlier in the evening when he was talking with the Inspector. His thoughts switched back to where he was now--walking alone on a clear night. Maybe tonight gets in the newspapers, he thought. That would make sense, if his theory on Fat's scheme was right. But it didn't much matter to him now. He was keeping the Honoraria Collection, no matter what. Fat's paintings were up to Fat.

Vanmeter imagined Maritain's men approaching the gallery now.

And Pico's work? Vanmeter was going to get the Natambe's every Euro he could.

He wondered how many people have even bothered to try to have a clear picture of the world. Maybe they're afraid to, maybe can't afford to. Now, he fully appreciated painters have a picture--they paint pictures, either seeing a clear picture, or attempting to. But then again, they also are vulnerable to illusion, like everyone else.

Was it the picture they see, or the picture they want to see? Maybe it's the only picture they can see.

Birdy and Frieda? What is their clear picture? They were on his prayer list, as a family.

Ten thirty pm. Vanmeter stood on the side walk, breathing in the warm, dry Rome air, which was preferable to the stagnant cigarette smoke still lingering in the gallery. Before departing home, he walked back to look at Kule Fat's large picture in the window, and Pico's and Thrash's pictures on the doors. He wasn't sure how long to keep them up.

Traffic was down to a trickle.

As Vanmeter walked, he became energized, and hot, taking of his jacket and tossing it over his shoulder. He laughed at his fantasy of being the lead in a movie, cameras catching him in full stroll down an empty Rome street. It was a different laugh when thinking about himself being a family man. Who would he marry? Lia? And it was yet a different laugh when thinking about the meeting he had tomorrow at the Rome campus to discuss the postulancy.

Uncertainty, seen through Vanmeter's monocle, did not present a clear picture of the world, but a world where illusion hid amongst the layers of the day-to-day. However, through Vanmeter's uncertainty monocle, he could detect and vanquish illusion. It was recognizing and confronting illusion that focused how best to live. But he knew he remained vulnerable as everyone else, for his other eye had no such succor.

Entering the apartment, Vanmeter found Lia curled up on the sofa, TV on with no sound, reading a book Vanmeter had been wanting to read.

Made in the USA
Monee, IL
05 May 2024

58009886R00144